Taxation of Specialised Occupations and Professions

Taxation of Specialised Occupations and Professions

Brian Laventure
MA (Oxon), FCA
Grant Thornton 🦉

The Institute of Chartered Accountants
in England and Wales
Chartered Accountants Hall, Moorgate Place
London EC2P 2BJ

First edition 1980
Second edition 1984
Third edition 1992

ISBN 1 85355 2305

British Library Cataloguing-in-Publication Data.

A catalogue record for this book is available from the British Library.

Typeset by Type Study, Scarborough.
Printed by T.J. Press (Padstow) Ltd, Cornwall

Contents

	Page
Preface	xv

1. Introduction
What is a profession?	1
Vocation	2
Profession carried on wholly abroad	2
Overseas partnerships	3
The 25% deduction	3
The 100% deduction	4
Carrying on business in the UK	4
Effect of change of residence	
(1) Income tax	5
(2) Capital gains tax	6
Employments	7
Basis of assessment	7
The conventional and earnings bases	8
Work in progress valuation	9
Conventional basis	10
Mergers	11
Adjustments for past years – earnings and cash basis	12
Changes of accounting date	12
Professional employments	13
Trusteeships	13
Payments for tax under Cases I and II of Schedule D	13
Expenses	13
Post-cessation expenses	15
Companies and professions	15
Service companies	17
Overseas work and companies	17
Interest	18

2. Writers, sculptors, painters
Copyright	19
Gifts of copyright	20

Contents

Income or capital   21
Categories of authors for tax purposes   21
Post-cessation receipts   23
Losses   23
Effect of changes of residence   23
Income spending provisions   24
Public lending rate   26
Painters and sculptors   26
Disposal of works of art subject to CGT and IHT   26
Taxation of awards   27
Pension arrangements   29

3. **Entertainers**
One profession – basis of assessment   31
Overseas work   32
Withholding of foreign tax at source   32
Foreign entertainers visiting the UK   33
'Slavery' contracts and service companies   34
Entertainers and anti-avoidance legislation   36
Capital sums received by entertainers   36
Capital allowances   37
Employment or a profession   37
Freelance workers in the film and allied industries   39
Investigation of income of entertainers by the Inland
    Revenue   41
Loans   42
Tax returns   42
Expenses   43
Subsistence and travelling expenses abroad   44
Travel expenses in the UK   44
Subsistence expenses in the UK   46
Clothing   45
Medical expenses   46
Other expenses   46
Groups' tax treatment   46
'Angels'   47
Pensions and retirement   47
Musicians – sale of instruments   48
TR 796: Taxation of theatrical performers/artists   48

4. **Stockbrokers and market makers**
Rules of the Stock Exchange   59
Incorporation   59
Golden handcuffs   60
Period of accounts   60

'Bear and bull excesses'   60
Returns   62
Dividend income and profits and losses on sales of securities   63
Borrowing and lending securities   65
Market maker's position on purchase of own shares by
    company   65
Interest received   65
Interest paid   65
Unclaimed dividends   66
Stock Exchange attachés and clerks   66
Expenses of members of the Stock Exchange   66
Capital gains returns   67
Anti-avoidance provisions   67
Special forms of investment   69

5. Lloyd's underwriters
General   73
Sources of income and gains   73
Underwriting account   74
Earned and unearned income   76
The closing year   76
Losses   76
Stop-loss policies   78
Interest paid   78
Capital gains – general   78
Capital gains tax position on retirement or death   80
Inheritance tax   80
The special reserve fund   81
Dates of payment of income tax and capital gains tax   82
Run-off syndicates   83
Loss claims   83
Wife's earned income election   83
Retirement annuity and personal pension premiums   84
Subscriptions and other expenses   84
Foreign taxes paid and double taxation relief   86
Non-resident Names   87
Accrued income scheme   87
Reinsurance to close   88
Index-linked US bonds   88
Premium trust funds: stock lending   91
Independent taxation from 6 April 1990   92

6. Temporary visitors to the UK
Employees   93
Residence position   93

Contents

Place of performance of duties   94
Domicile   94
The payer of the income   94
Corresponding payments relief   97
Retirement annuity premiums   98
Foreign emoluments – 1984–85 and later years   98
Travel expenses   99
Requirements of employee and employer   100
The North Sea   101
Returns by North Sea employers   102
Clark *v*. Oceanic Contractors Inc   102
Expenses   104
The Norwegian sector of the North Sea   105
Visiting professors or teachers   105
Visitors for education   106
All visitors – investment income and capital gains   106
Capital gains   107
Visitors and IHT   107
Visitors – departure from the UK   108

7. **Clergymen**
General principles of taxation   111
Types of income that are taxable   112
Exemptions   113
Expenses   117
Second residences   122
Benefits-in-kind   122
Income of contemplative religious communities and their
     members   123
Evangelists   124

8. **Members of the diplomatic service and other Crown servants working abroad**
Place of performance of duties   127
Exempt allowances   127
Other income and capital gains   128
Personal allowances   129
UK residents   130
Life assurance premiums   131
Officials employed by the European Community in Brussels   131

9. **Doctors and dentists**
Doctors   135
Consultants   135
Expenses of consultants   135

Agreement between DSS and Inland Revenue on certain
   expenses   136
Practice accounts   138
General practice   139
Detailed points on GP's accounts – BMA standardised
   practice accounts   140
Model form of income and expenditure account for use by
   general practitioners   141
Aide-mémoire – expenses   143
Further matters on GPs' affairs   146
Superannuation deductions   150
Dentists   151
General case law relating to doctors and dentists   152

10. Practising barristers, barristers' clerks and judges
Cash basis   153
Post-cessation receipts   153
'Fees earned' basis   154
Change of basis   154
Inducement receipts   154
Expenses – travel   155
Expenses – cost of chambers   155
Expenses – court apparel   155
Expenses – patent fee   155
Expenses – books   156
Barristers' clerks   156
Judges   157

11. Members of Parliament
General taxation position   159
Additional costs allowance   159
Car allowance   159
Other travel (by taxi, train or air)   160
Office costs allowance (OCA)   161
Other incidental expenses   161
Pension and retirement arrangements   162
Other income   162
Members of the European Parliament   162
Members of the House of Lords   164

12. Merchant navy and aircraft personnel
General principles   165
Non-resident seafarers   165
Foreign seamen   166
UK residents – 12½% (formerly 25%) or 100% deduction   166

Contents

12½% (formerly 25%) deduction 167
100% deduction 169
Examples – (prior to 1988/89) 170
Definitions 171
Administration 171
Flat rate expenses deduction 171
Seaman's PAYE 171
Aircrew 172
Residence position 172
12½% or 100% deduction 173
Expenses of aircrew 174
Free travel etc. 174

13. **Members of the UK armed forces**
Place of performance of duties 177
Residence position 177
Extra cost of living abroad 177
Travel facilities 178
Exemptions in respect of allowances 178
Hotel expenses 178
Annual subscriptions to a headquarters mess central fund 179
Uniform allowances 179
Gratuities 179
PAYE and the armed forces 180
The reserve and auxiliary forces 180
Pensions 181
War widows' pension 181
Employment after leaving services 182
Capital gains tax and residences 182
Holders of Victoria Cross, etc. 182
Life assurance premiums 182
Death on active service 183

14. **Publicans holding tied houses, hoteliers and guest-house proprietors**
Publicans – basis of assessment 185
Termination payments 185
Expenses 186
Hotels – own consumption adjustments 188
Hotels – date on which trading commences 189
Capital expenditure 189
Plant and machinery 190
Furnished lettings – allowances for wear and tear 192
Hotel building allowances 192
Dilapidations 193

Residences 193
Guest-houses and roll-over relief 194
Income from furnished holiday lettings 194
PAYE 195

15. Credit traders, pawnbrokers, moneylenders, hire purchase transactions
General 197
Credit traders 197
Provisions 197
Valuation of debts 198
Hire purchase business 198
Check traders 199
Computation of profits 200
Pawnbrokers 200
Moneylenders 201

16. Persons in receipt of foreign pensions
Remittance basis 203
Pensions paid by Crown Agents 203
Pensions paid to victims of Nazi persecution 204
Double tax agreements 204
Foreign invalidity benefits 204
Foreign war pensions 204

17. Sportsmen and women
Basis of liability 205
Visiting sportsmen 205
Concentration of earnings and use of cessation rules 205
Service company documentation 206
100% deduction 206
Foreign companies 207
Withholding taxes 207
Expenses 207
General principles of liability of various receipts 208
Footballers' benefit matches 210
Amateur sportsmen 210
Signing-on fees 211
Payments for winning 212
Jockeys 213
Pension schemes 213

18. Persons in receipt of gratuities
General 215
Tips 215

Contents

	Retirement gratuities	215
	PAYE in tips	215
	Other gifts	217
	Prizes	218
	Long-service awards	218
19.	**Insurance agents**	
	Categories of agent	219
	Exclusive agents	219
	Other agents	220
	Casual insurance commission	220
20.	**Trawlermen, river and sea pilots**	
	Introduction	225
	Employed or self-employed?	225
	Retirement age	226
	Special clothing	226
	Capital allowances	227
	Partnerships	228
	Grants	230
	River and sea pilots	230
21.	**Private schools, higher education institutions, teachers, etc.**	
	Definition of a charity	231
	Public schools	231
	Effect of charitable status	231
	Investment income	233
	Covenants	233
	Retrospective covenants	234
	Payment of school fees in the case of separated parents	235
	Capital allowances	238
	Academics, teachers, etc.	239
22.	**Inventors and persons holding patent rights**	
	Expenses – general	249
	The law of patents	249
	Income tax position on expenses	250
	Treatment of receipts	250
	Incorporation of business	251
	Capital allowances	253
	Royalties	253
	Deduction of tax	256
	Foreign patents	256
	Earned income	256
	Spreading provisions	256

Know-how 256
Trade marks and designs 257
Case III and trade marks 258
Capital or income 258
Fees and expenses 259

23. Subcontractors
Tax deduction scheme 261
Main features of the scheme 261
Exemption certificates 262
Vouchers 266
Deduction of tax 266
Payer's position 267
Expenses 268

24. Local councillors and members of Government boards
Reimbursed expenses 271
Attendance allowances 271
Office or profession 271

25. Farmers (including market gardeners) and owners of commercial woodlands
One trade 273
Losses 274
Stocks 276
Herd basis 276
Averaging 278
Capital allowances 279
Agricultural buildings allowances 280
Revenue receipts and payments 281
Partnerships and joint ventures 285
Capital gains tax 287
'One estate' election 291
Quotas 292
Commercial woodlands 294

Table of Tax Statutes 297
Table of Statutory Instruments 302
Table of Cases 303
List of Revenue publications 311

Index 312

xiii

Preface

Since the second edition of *Taxation of Specialised Occupations and Professions*, UK taxation has undergone substantial changes, particularly in terms of lowering the top rates of income tax and rebasing of assets at 31 March 1982 for capital gains tax purposes.

There has also been much tax legislation, case law and practice affecting the specialised occupations covered in the book. Some of the law is now comprised in detailed regulations.

I hope the book answers some of the myriad questions that arise for professional advisors dealing with the greatly increased number of self-employed people that there are today, as compared with 1984.

By including all the published Statements of Practice and concessions where relevant as well as precedents from all sorts of sources, I have tried to cover the official interpretation of the law by the Inland Revenue. This is not to say, however, that their interpretation should not be challenged where there is an argument for so doing.

The law and practice is as stated up to May 1992. As well as expanding the existing content, a new chapter has been added on Farmers.

I would like to thank the very many people inside and outside Grant Thornton who have supplied information for the book. In particular, as always I would like to thank Philip Hardman for passing on so much valuable information to me for inclusion. I would also like to thank my wife for her technical help and forbearance in allowing the third edition, to my secretary for her unfailing cheerfulness and for her help in its preparation, to Ben Melling for his work on the typescript, and to Peter Maw for his contribution and help along with James Rouse in the Herculean task of reading over the final proofs.

Brian Laventure
Grant Thornton
Portsmouth
July 1992

Chapter 1
Introduction

What is a profession?

1 Most of the chapters of this book are concerned with the taxation position of persons carrying on professions or vocations as opposed to trades, or employments. What constitutes a profession is not defined in the Taxes Acts but in CIR *v.* Maxse (12TC41) Scutton L J said: ". . . it seems to me as at present advised that a 'profession' in the present use of language involves the idea of an occupation requiring either purely intellectual skill, or of any manual skill controlled, as in painting and sculpture or surgery, by the intellectual skill of the operator . . .".

Most of the cases which turned on whether a person was carrying on a profession were concerned with excess profits duty and excess profits tax as there were exemptions from these taxes in respect of the carrying on of a profession if the profits were dependent wholly or mainly on personal qualifications, and the word 'profession' did not broadly include activities connected with the making of contracts of a commercial nature. Now for the purpose of assessment, professions are subject to the same basic rules as trades and are included with trades in the general charging section of Schedule D (s.18(1)(a)(ii) and (iii) ICTA 1988). However, whilst the same person can carry on more than one trade, anyone who is practising a profession in whatever capacity is exercising one continuing profession subject to tax under Case II of Schedule D unless any activity is an employment. Thus, in Seldon *v.* Croom-Johnson (16 TC 740) it was held that a barrister who had taken silk was still carrying on the same profession. This is important, as discussed later in this chapter, when a person carrying on a profession changes his or her country of residence.

A profession can still be liable to tax even if it is associated with elements of illegality such as the oldest profession, prostitution. In the recent case of CIR *v.* Aken (1990 STC 497) the taxpayer appealed against Case I assessments raised on her because prostitution was not trading. Whether or not assessments could have been raised under Case II, the court held that as a general principle a trade did not cease to be such for the purposes of the Taxes Acts because it was illegal. Consequently the same principle would no doubt apply to a profession or vocation.

The distinction which is relevant from a taxation viewpoint is between a freelance professional activity liable to tax under Case II of Schedule D and a professional employment liable to tax under the rules of Schedule E. This distinction is referred to in paragraph 14 and in the chapters dealing with Entertainers, Members of the Medical profession and Members of Government Boards.

Vocation

2   The word 'vocation' has a very wide general meaning and is similar to a calling. It means the way in which a person passes his life (Partridge *v.* Mallandaine 2 TC 179). It has been held that a bookmaker, a jockey and land agent are engaged in vocations. However, the winnings of a golf professional on bets on his own matches were held not to be earnings of a vocation (Down *v.* Compston 21 TC 60). Also a person whose sole means of livelihood was betting on horses from his house was held not to be carrying on a vocation, and was thus not liable to tax on his betting winnings (Graham *v.* Green 9 TC 309).

If a person is exercising a vocation, again now it has no special treatment for tax purposes.

The main point for the purposes of taxation is whether it is a vocation carried on with a view to profit, or a calling where no profit seeking motive is present, as is claimed by some evangelists (see the chapter on persons carrying on religious vocations).

3   The main divergence between trades and professions occurs in the practical application of these rules of assessment because of the differing ways accounts of persons carrying on professions are drawn up as opposed to persons carrying on trades. The Taxes Acts and Case Law have had to recognise these accounting distinctions, so that in certain areas there is specific legislation to cover a point – for instance, the recognition of the 'cash basis' or other forms of 'conventional basis' of drawing up accounts in the post cessation receipts legislation, which is most usually met in professional accounts (s.104 ICTA 1988).

In addition, it has been felt necessary for clarification to include professions and vocations specifically in provisions relating to the liability to capital gains tax of non-residents carrying on business in the UK through a branch or agency (s.10(5) TCGA 1992).

Profession carried on wholly abroad

4   Where trade or profession is carried on partly abroad, it is still assessed under Cases I and II.

Where a trade or profession is carried on wholly abroad, it constitutes a foreign possession and is assessed in accordance with the rules of Case V of Schedule D (Colquhoun *v.* Brooks 2 TC 490). A trade will only be treated as carried on wholly abroad if no element of control or supervision as well as no other business activity takes place in the UK (Ogilvie *v*. Kitton 5 TC 338). In the case of a person resident in the UK who carries on a profession not in partnership, this is clearly practically impossible to achieve.

Overseas partnerships

5   A share of partnership profits of an individual resident in the UK is assessed under Case V where the partnership is managed and controlled abroad in so far as the profits relate to activities carried out abroad (s.112 ICTA 1988). In so far as there are UK-based activities, these will be assessable under Cases I and II of Schedule D under the normal rules relating to non-residents trading in the UK, subject to the protection of any Double Tax Agreement. Therefore, unlike a person carrying on a trade or profession on his or her own, a partnership can give rise to income assessable in the hands of a UK resident partner under Cases I or II and Case V of Schedule D provided it can be shown that management and control are exercised from abroad. This will usually entail having a number of partners who are not resident in the UK, the same tests as to where management and control are located applying as for companies. Therefore a UK resident individual who has the opportunity of professional earnings arising abroad may be able to receive them as Case V income by entering into such an overseas partnership with non-resident individuals or possibly a non-resident company. The point is discussed in the next chapter in connection with entertainers.

The only advantage since the abolition of the 25% deduction in receiving Case V income of this nature as against Case II income is now if the individual is not domiciled in the UK, in which case the Case V income is only liable to UK income tax on a remittance basis.

The 25% deduction

6   The 25% (reduced to 12½%) deduction applied in respect of Case V income and income assessable under Cases I and II, as well as income from professional employments for work carried out abroad, provided there were a minimum number of qualifying days spent abroad. This legislation was repealed in the 1984 Finance Act and is, therefore, not discussed in this book in detail.

7   The Finance Act 1984 phased out the foreign earnings 25% deduction, reducing it to 12½% for 1984/85 and abolishing it altogether for 1985/86. The 100% deduction remained. This phasing out applied to income from employments, income assessable under Cases I and II, and income derived from a trade or profession carried on wholly abroad including income from an overseas partnership of a partner resident in the UK.

The changes affected in particular seamen and aircrew, entertainers and sportsmen.

3

The 100% deduction

8 The 100% deduction only applies to employments. It is described in detail in the chapter on seamen and aircrew.

It is designed to give relief from income tax for employments carried out wholly or partly abroad where, however, the period of employment does not include a complete fiscal year so that the person is still resident and ordinarily resident in the UK.

It has been decided that a qualifying day means one where the employee is out of the UK at midnight (Hoye *v.* Forsdyke 1981 STC 711). Also, emoluments related to a leave period will qualify for the deduction but for the leave period to be part of a qualifying period of absence from the UK it cannot be spent in the UK (Robins *v.* Durkin 1988 STC 588).

The advantage of qualifying for a 100% deduction rather than being non-resident used to be that personal allowances were available against income remaining liable to UK tax. However, non-residents who are *inter alia* Commonwealth citizens now qualify (under s.278 ICTA 1988) for unrestricted personal allowances so that this advantage no longer applies. In addition, residents of most countries with whom the UK has concluded double tax agreements also qualify for personal allowances in full.

If the 100% deduction is likely to be relevant for any income, it may be possible for a UK company to receive the income and pay it out as remuneration to the person concerned. in that case, he should not receive it as a director of the company, as part of it will relate to UK duties to which the 100% deduction would not apply (para 2(2) of sch.12 ICTA 1988). It would be preferable for his wife and a professional director to act as directors of such a service company in order to overcome this problem.

Carrying on business in the UK

9 Generally, an individual who is not resident in the UK will only be liable to UK income tax on any profits derived from trading activities within the UK. There is extensive Case Law on the subject which, broadly speaking, has indicated that a person will be treated as trading in the UK if he negotiates and makes contracts in the UK (Grainger & Sons *v.* Gough 3TC 462). This principle was reaffirmed at a recent Hong Kong case where the law is the same (CIR *v.* Hang Seng Bank Ltd 1990 STC 733 PC).

10 The position with regard to the carrying on of a profession is rather more obscure. The circumstances in which a visitor to this country will or will not become resident here for tax purposes are dealt with in Chapter 6. Strictly, however, anyone performing a professional service or engagement in the UK, is exercising his profession in the UK and thus liable to income tax under Case II of Schedule D. In many cases the point will not arise where there is a double tax agreement protecting visitors performing independent professional services, who stay for less than six months and have no fixed base in the UK, from liability to UK tax. However, where agreements give such exemption for professions, it is often the case that there is an exclusion for public entertainers, musicians and athletes from their personal activities, as in the case of the Double Tax Treaty with France.

In certain agreements, exemption is equally excluded for the remuneration of such entertainers and athletes as employees even where they are employed by a company having no permanent establishment in the country in which the performance is given. Thus the Double Tax Treaty with the USA taxes entertainers however they receive their income. It specifically allows the country in which musicians, athletes and entertainers perform, to tax them except where gross earnings are small (less than $15,000 or its sterling equivalent per annum). The absence of a fixed base, and the length of stay are not relevant. If the income of the musician, athlete or entertainer is paid to a related person or company, even if not resident in the country where the musician performs, the income will still be taxed.

To counter non-payment of tax strictly due provisions have been introduced to enable tax to be withheld at source on income paid to entertainers and sportsmen visiting the UK or persons connected with them in respect of any activity of the entertainer and sportsman within the UK (s.557 ICTA 1988 and Income Tax (Entertainers and Sportsmen) Regulations 1987). The detailed operation of these provisions is discussed in the relevant chapters but it is clear that the law envisages any professional activity carried out in the UK as potentially liable to tax here.

11   It is probably true to say that in practice the likelihood of being assessed on any professional earnings arising in the UK will be increased where someone has been resident in the UK at some time. If he ceases to be resident here, but continues to carry on his profession here as well as abroad, and cannot rely on the protection of a double tax agreement, the Inland Revenue would doubtless attempt to assess him on the UK income.

There are, in this connection, powers to assess any agent for the individual concerned under s.78 TMA 1970 if the agent regularly receives the money on the individual's behalf. Returns are also required for agents under s.12 TMA 1970, of payments made *inter alia* to non-residents.

Effect of change of residence

(1) Income tax

12   If a person exercising a profession becomes resident here, it does not necessarily follow that the commencement rules of assessment will operate (Kneen *v.* Martin 19 TC 33). Similarly, when he ceases to be resident, the cessation rules may not apply, unlike the position with a company (s.337 ICTA 1988). It is a question of fact when a source of income first arises. Thus an actor will not change his profession by coming to live in the UK. The same point can apply where the same trade continues to be carried on by a person who

5

becomes resident in the UK and the trade was partly carried on in the UK before the period of residence began so that the trade has been assessed before under Sch D. Case I (Fry *v.* Burma Corporation Ltd 15 TC 113).

Care needs to be taken therefore that continuity of the previous year basis of assessment does not give rise to excessive UK tax liabilities.

(2) Capital gains tax

13 Problems can also arise in relation to capital gains tax on a change of residence in respect of an asset used in a profession, for instance a property or goodwill.

If a person disposes of, say, professional goodwill whilst resident or ordinarily resident in the UK, he will be liable to capital gains tax. If he disposes of the asset having left the UK but not before he has ceased to carry on the profession in the UK, for instance, goodwill sold with a professional practice, he is still liable to capital gains tax. If he disposes of it in a year of assessment in which he has been resident or ordinarily resident in the UK, but after his departure, the normal Extra Statutory Concession deeming the periods before and after departure to be separate years of assessment is not applied for disposals on or after 6 April 1989 (Extra Statutory Concession D2 as revised).

If a disposal takes place in a year of non-residence, s.10 TCGA 1992 may be in point. This renders non-residents liable to UK capital gains tax on disposals of UK sites assets used for the purposes of a trade carried on in this country through a branch or agency. There will not normally be any exemption from liability under Double Tax Treaty arrangements.

There are equally now anti-avoidance provisions to tax any capital gain of a non-resident in respect of such an asset at the time it ceases to be used for the purposes of the trade, profession or vocation carried on in the UK, or when it is transferred abroad (s.25 TCGA 1992). An example might be the goodwill of an architectural practice transferred to an off-shore location. Thus, if the profession carried on by a non-resident in the UK ceases, and after the year of cessation property formerly used for the profession is sold, there will now be a liability to UK tax on the basis of the market value at the date of cessation of the profession. It was previously possible for non-residents to avoid such a liability by selling in a year of assessment after the profession ceased to be carried on in the UK. It still seems, however, to be possible for a person carrying on a profession to separate the profession from, say, the property in which it is carried on while still resident here, for instance by incorporating the business using the relief afforded by s.165 TCGA 1992 for assets transferred to the company, and then in a year after he has ceased to be resident to sell the property free of capital gains tax.

There are now similar restrictions on roll-over relief where a non-resident reinvests in assets which are not chargeable assets, for example where a non-resident carrying on a profession here sells a UK asset used for that profession and reinvests in an overseas asset. Roll-over relief will not be available in such situations.

Employments

14 It should be noted that professional activities can be carried on within the ambit of an employment. This distinction is discussed in greater detail in connection with entertainers and doctors. In connection with professions and the demarcation between Schedule D and Schedule E, it is reported (*Tax Journal* 26 September 1991) that Specialeyes plc won an appeal before a Special Commissioner on the question of whether locum ophthalmic opticians were employees or self-employed. The Special Commissioner decided that "the agreed terms (on which the locums dealt with Specialeyes) reflected the parties' belief that the locums were independent contractors carrying on their own business". It is understood the Inland Revenue have decided not to appeal the case. It is possible the victory could have far reaching effects in other professions where self-employed staff are used on a freelance basis. The main advantages of being assessed under Sch. D rather than Sch. E are the rules for assessing profits, the deferment of the actual payment of tax and the greater opportunity for the claiming of expenses against profits.

Basis of assessment

15 It is outside the scope of this book to examine these advantages in detail. Where appropriate, they will be referred to in the context of the specific profession concerned. The rules of assessment for the opening years under Case I and II of Schedule D are:

First Year: Profits of the actual period.
Second Year: Profits of the first twelve months.
Third Year: Profits of the twelve months accounts ending in the preceding year of assessment or, if no such accounts have been made up, the profits of the first twelve months.

The second and third years' profits may be revised to actual on a claim by the taxpayer (s.62 ICTA 1988).

Where profits have to be apportioned between two years of assessment, they are apportioned on a time basis by reference to months and fractions of months (s.72(2) ICTA 1988).

If the profits of the first period of a new trade or profession are at a lower level than is anticipated in the future, it is probable that the selection of an accounting date falling early in the fiscal year (say 30 April) will result in an outright saving of tax payable, particularly in the third year of assessment, and in some cash flow advantages in later years.

Where there is a change in a partnership and no election is made for the continuation basis, the new partnership is assessed on an actual basis for the first four years of assessment (s.61(4) ICTA 1988). It is, therefore, necessary to be extremely careful before forfeiting the previous year basis of assessment on a change of partners.

Partnerships are commonly used in carrying on a profession. There is, however, the complication for tax purposes of establishing whether, when a partnership is formed from an amalgamation of two professional businesses, or an existing partnership splits into two or more successor businesses, there is the possibility of making a continuation election at all. Essentially such an election is only possible where the business is continuing and is being carried on by at least one person who is the same before and after the change. What constitutes continuation of a business or succession to a business is sometimes very difficult to determine, for instance where a new solicitors' practice is established from the merger of two existing practices.

The Inland Revenue have set out their views in a Statement of Practice (SP9/86) on partnership mergers and demergers. Basically on a merger, it will usually be possible for each old partnership to elect for continuation basis but on a demerger this facility is unlikely because there can normally be no succession to part of a trade or professional business. It should be noted that the new four year rule referred to above does not apply to an individual sole trader taking another person or persons into a new partnership, or to the reverse situation where a partnership reverts to a sole trade. In these circumstances the normal commencement rules will apply in the absence of a continuation election.

16   Sometimes, where a person is in an employment and also starts up a professional activity, for instance a teacher writing for publication, the Inland Revenue press for the freelance professional earnings to be assessed under Case VI of Schedule D until it is established they are sufficiently regular and sustained to constitute the carrying on of a profession.

This approach should be resisted where possible as it means that the period of low profit will be assessed on an actual basis and if there is a loss, it will only be available to carry forward against future Case VI income.

The conventional and earnings bases

17   Whether or not debtors and work-in-progress are brought into the accounts in the case of a particular profession, and the basis of valuation of any work-in-progress which is brought in, may depend upon the law, the requirements of any overseeing professional body or the nature or custom of the particular profession concerned. For example, barristers do not have to take account of outstanding fees because they cannot sue for them, whilst work-in-progress would not be brought into account in any profession where there is no significant employed workforce and thus no direct costs which ought to be carried forward for recovery against specific fees.

Work in progress valuation

18 A tax case has highlighted the difficulties the Inland Revenue have in displacing valuations of work-in-progress for tax purposes where the valuation is in accordance with the rules and practices governing the particular profession, even where this results in substantial payments on account in excess of cost, because partner's time is not a cost, being carried forward. In the case of professions where the work relates to long-term contracts, such as surveyors and architects, material amounts of tax may thus be deferred on the interim profit element although the partnership has the use of the money.

19 In Symons *v.* Weeks, (1983 STC 195) accounts of a firm of architects had been produced for 1966/67 to 1975/76 and during this period, substantial progress payments had been received which were not wholly accounted for as fees. Following accepted accountancy practice for architects, work done on long-term contracts had been valued on a work in progress formula resulting in £2.9 million of the total £5.1 million progress payments being excluded from fees earned and being included in accumulated work-in-progress. In so far as this was in excess of the cost of the work-in-progress, no tax was payable on this 'unrealised profit'. The Inland Revenue put forward two arguments to tax this profit: they argued that the progress payments should have been brought into the profit and loss account as and when they fell due as the contracts were divisible. Alternatively, they claimed that as the accounts were only submitted during 1978–79, they should reflect the position as it was known at that time rather than when they were drawn up.

The Special Commissioners found against the Inland Revenue on both counts and Walton J in the High Court confirmed their findings. On the first point in Sun Assurance Office *v.* Clark, it had been decided that there was no rule of law as to when receipts should be brought into account and the matter, therefore, turned on whether the prevailing system of accounting, in this case not in contravention of any RIBA rules, corresponded with the correct principles of commercial accountancy. The Inland Revenue's argument was, therefore, rejected as they had produced no evidence to the contrary. So far as the second point is concerned, the accounts could not be changed with hindsight. "It could not be right that the Inland Revenue should be entitled to treat the accounts as still open for as long as it might take to ascertain whether subsequent events proved or disproved the accuracy of estimated items in them". The accounts had been accepted in the light of information available at the time when the accounts were approved by the partners, and information which subsequently became known, should be left out of account.

20 This case and the principles emerging from it suggest that the Inland Revenue will be forced to accept, where work on long-term contracts is not divisible, that profits made by professional men on interim bills on account are not taxable until the work is completed particularly where it is reasonable to provide for future expenditure on the contract. Thus in this situation, the earnings basis is preferable to the cash basis in deferring tax liabilities.

Sometimes it is necessary to change the basis of valuing work-in-progress to arrive at a more accurate estimate of the costs of unbilled work. It used to be thought that it was possible to secure a tax-free uplift in the opening work-in-progress where, say, more costs were brought into the calculation of work-in-progress. There was an argument that to achieve consistency, work-in-progress should be valued on the same basis at the start as at the close of the year, applying the principles in Ahmedabad New Cotton Mills Co Limited *v.* IT Comr (Bombay) (46 TLR 68 (PC) and 8 ATC 575). However, the Inland Revenue have said this is not correct, quoting the case of Pearce *v.* Woodall Duckham Limited in a Statement of Practice on the valuation of stocks and long-term contracts (51 TC 271 and SP 3/90). In their view this case decided that where there is a change in the basis of valuation from one valid basis to another, there should be no adjustment to the opening work-in-progress. It is arguable that the Woodall Duckham case only applies to long term contracts, for instance of architects and building contractors. It should be noted, however, the post cessation receipts legislation only applies where there is a wholesale change from the cash basis to the earnings basis to catch what would otherwise drop out of assessment.

Conventional basis

21   Unless debtors and work-in-progress are taken into account in computing profits (the earnings basis) the profits are said to be computed on a 'conventional basis' (s.103(2) ICTA 1988).

Whatever the customs of the profession, the Inland Revenue will allow a person to adopt a conventional basis, subject to two conditions:

(1) The taxpayer must undertake to submit bills regularly and at frequent intervals. The intervals may be chosen by the taxpayer but they should be specified in the undertaking (*Accountancy*, January 1970, p. 84).
(2) A conventional basis cannot be used in the first three accounting years of a profession. If there is a change of partners, the three-year period will recommence unless there is an election for the continuation basis to apply. An exception is made to this rule for barristers in respect of fees not received and persons engaged in a literary or artistic profession do not have to bring in a figure for work-in-progress.

The conventional bases most often met with are:

(a) Cash Basis – no account taken of debtors/creditors or work-in-progress.
(b) Bills Rendered Basis – no account taken of work-in-progress.

22   Since the assessment for taxation purposes is on the profits or gains computed for the basis period, consistency must be applied as between the beginning and the end of the year so that if debtors and/or work-in-progress are left out of account at the end of the period, the comparable items at the beginning of the period must also be excluded (CIR *v.* Morrison 17 TC 325). If a change is made from the earnings basis to a conventional basis, certain items will have to be taken into account in computing the profits for tax purposes of both periods of account. If the change is to a cash basis, all trading/professional receipts in the cash basis period will have to be brought wholly into account, notwithstanding that the profits of the final earnings basis period will have reflected the same items to the extent of the debtors and work-in-progress at the end of that period. If the change is to a bills rendered basis, the double taxation will be confined to the work-in-progress at the end of the last earnings basis period.

23 On a change from a conventional basis to an earnings basis, the accounts for the year of change would be drawn up with an opening debit for work-in-progress on the principle laid down in Ahmedabad New Cotton Mills Co Ltd *v.* I.T. Comr. (Bombay). The post cessation receipts legislation imposes a charge under Sch. D Case VI on an amount equal to the opening debit (s.104(4) and (5) ICTA 1988). If the change is from the cash basis to the earnings basis, the trade debtors (less trade creditors) outstanding at the end of the final cash basis period of account will also be taxable under the post cessation receipts legislation. Thus, if a change is made to the earnings basis, the result will be that for one or more years there will be assessed not only a normal year's measure of profit under Sch. D Case I or II but also Sch. D Case VI income under the post-cessation receipts legislation.

It is sometimes possible to avoid some of the effects of double taxation of debtors and work-in-progress on a change of basis where there is an amalgamation of professional practices, and, say, one practice has to change its basis to conform with the accounting policies of the other. Thus, if the combined practice is to go on to the cash basis, the new partnership can purchase the debtors and work-in-progress, if any, of the old partnerships on an earnings basis and this would appear to eliminate double taxation of such debtors and work in progress where a continuation election is made. Similarly, if the old practice is on a cash basis and switches to an earnings basis as part of a combined new practice, a purchase of debtors and work-in-progress means such items are not assessed on a current year basis under Case VI as opening debits in the new partnership but will form part of the normal Case II income assessed on a previous year basis where a continuation basis election is made.

Mergers

24 Where, upon a merger of firms, one of them has to change the basis of its accounting to conform to that of the other, and there is additional liability under the post cessation receipts legislation in s.104(4) ICTA 1988, in respect of debtors and work-in-progress, top slicing relief was available under an Extra-Statutory Concession (ESC A18). This concession was withdrawn when the top rate of income tax was reduced to 40%.

Adjustments for past years – earnings and cash basis

25 It has happened that persons carrying on professions have received substantial awards of back pay. Adjustment of past years is only strictly possible by relating back the receipt for tax purposes where the right to the extra remuneration was acknowledged in that prior year by the payer, but the amount has not been quantified until a year later and the earnings basis applies. This has happened to opticians who have received backpayments from the Department of Health and Social Security covering the period from 1978 to 1982. If the earnings basis applies, they should all be spread back for tax purposes. If the cash basis applies, they should all be assessed in the year of receipt. However, by concession in this case, it is understood the Inland Revenue allowed the arrears to be spread back.

On the other hand what looks like 'back pay' might not be such. For example, pharmacists are in a different position. The pharmacist's contract provides for the total amount to be paid by the National Health Service to pharmacists to be negotiated on a national basis. Any 'notional overpayment or underpayment' in a previous year is then taken into account and rectified when determining the cost of the National Health Service pharmaceutical services to be provided in a subsequent year. The NHS does not have a vested right to recover a particular amount for any previous overpayment from a pharmacist whilst equally a pharmacist does not have such a right to any further remuneration from the NHS for a previous underpayment. Therefore, when the NHS recover overpayments or make further payments for underpayments, they do it only to pharmacists still trading in that year and by reference to their current levels of NHS trading. In consequence, there can be no relating back of these adjustments which fall in the year of receipt.

Changes of accounting date

26 It is possible to change the accounting date and draw up accounts to the new date. Provided this new date is thereafter continually adhered to, it will be effective for taxation purposes. As such accounts will not be for a period of one year, the Inland Revenue have the power to determine the period on the basis of which the assessment for the following year will be made (s.60(4) ICTA 1988). Unless the date to which accounts are being made up is changed regularly, they would normally exercise this power by taking the period of twelve months to the new accounting date.

27 Consequent on such a change, adjustments may be made to the previous year's assessment to average out profits by reference to the profits of the whole of the period affected by the change. The tests that are applied by the Inland Revenue have been published (leaflet IR 26). The likely effects of a change should be calculated as accurately as possible before a decision is implemented.

Professional employments

28 A professional activity which is an office or employment will fall within the ambit of Schedule E (Mitchell and Edon *v.* Ross 40 TC 11). In certain cases, where a person is exercising his profession in the course of being a director of a company, the Inland Revenue will allow by concession the directors' fees paid for such professional services to be included in a Schedule D assessment on a partnership where the partner brings those fees into the partnership. This happens most commonly with solicitors and accountants (ESCA 37). Otherwise the demarcation is strictly observed between sources of professional income liable under Case II of Schedule D and those where an office is held or where there is a master and servant relationship which falls within Schedule E. In the case of income falling within Schedule E, the basis of assessment is now the emoluments received in the year of assessment.

Trusteeships

29 A professional person, such as a solicitor, who is a trustee and is authorised under the trust deed to charge for his services, has to bring sums so received into his Case II computation for tax purposes (Jones *v.* Wright 13 TC 221). This situation, however, should be distinguished from an annual payment given as remuneration to a trustee as such, and not in a professional capacity, which was held to be within Case III (Baxendale *v.* Murphy 9 TC 76).

Payment of tax under Cases I and II of Schedule D

30 In addition to the greater flexibility inherent in the basis period rules of assessment, income tax on income assessable under Schedule D Cases I and II is payable by equal instalments on 1 January in the relevant year of assessment and 1 July following the year of assessment provided an assessment has been raised in time. If the assessment is not raised until later than 1 June following the end of the year of assessment, it is all due at the end of a period of thirty days from the date of issue of the assessment (s.5(2) and (3) ICTA 1988). This represents a considerable cash flow advantage as compared with the PAYE system which operates in respect of income liable to tax under Schedule E.

Expenses

31 Expenses allowable in arriving at Schedule D Case I and II profits are expenses of a revenue nature which in addition do not fall foul of any specific prohibition, the main one of which is that they must not fall to be disallowed as "not being money wholly and exclusively laid out or expended for the purpose of the trade or profession" (s.74(a) ICTA 1988). It should be noted that it is

13

specifically provided that the same rules apply to trades and professions assessable under Case V of Schedule D as those applicable to Cases I and II of Schedule D where the overseas trade or profession is carried on by an individual ordinarily resident and domiciled in the UK (s.65(3) ICTA 1988).

Two recent tax cases have illustrated the limits of this rule in relation to a profession. In the case of MacKinlay *v.* Arthur Young McClelland Moores & Co (1989 STC 898) removal expenses of a partner borne by the firm where the accountancy firm had asked the partner to move to another office were disallowed as being a personal expense of the partner nothwithstanding the move was designed to benefit the firm. Thus, there was a dual purpose to the expenditure.

In Watkis *v.* Ashford Sparkes and Harward (1985 STC 451) the expenses of partners' working lunches were disallowed on the duality of purpose test, whilst expenses of a partners' conference were allowed on the basis that the hotel expenses were indivisible.

32 This prohibition has been the subject of many tax cases and should be contrasted with the comparable rule allowing expenses under Schedule E where the requirement is that the expenditure should be incurred wholly, exclusively and *necessarily in* the performance of the duties of the office or employment (s.198(1) ICTA 1988).

33 Many cases have emphasised that the rule applicable to Schedule E expenses must be construed narrowly so as to exclude, for instance, expenses peculiar to the situation of the particular employee and only to allow those applicable to each and every holder of the office or employment. In addition, the expenses must be incurred in the course of the employment so that, for example, the cost of attending an educational course, if it is not a condition of service, is unlikely to be allowed as a Schedule E expense (Humbles *v.* Brooks 40 TC 500). By contrast, provided the subject matter were relevant to the trade or profession so that the primary purpose of the expense is to further the commercial interests of the trade or profession, it will be allowed even if there is some incidental personal benefit (Bentleys, Stokes & Lowless *v.* Beeson 33 TC 491). On the other hand, if the private benefit is more than merely incidental to the business purpose, there is a duality of purpose and the expenses would not be incurred wholly and exclusively for the profession. This does not mean that expenditure cannot be apportioned to extract a business element from a total, for instance where household expenses are higher than they would otherwise have been because of a person's business. In that situation part of the total telephone charges have been incurred wholly and exclusively for the purposes of the business.

An interesting recent decision was that in Smith *v.* Abbott and related appeals (1991 STC 661) where journalists employed by Associated Newspapers Limited successfully claimed the costs of newspapers and periodicals. It was found that reading newspapers and periodicals was a necessary part of the duties of their employment and not merely required to qualify them or maintain their qualifications to do their duties.

Post-cessation expenses

34 In the case of partnerships which elect for continuation basis, there should be no problem about the allowance of bad debts and such items as damages for professional negligence. Equally, if the continuing partners pick up the liability of a retired partner in respect of such things as payments under guarantees, where the 'wholly and exclusively' test is satisfied and it can be shown to benefit the continuing professional practice, the payments should be allowable as the case of Bolton *v.* Halpern and Woolf, which followed the principles in the earlier case of McCash *v.* Hunter (1981 STC 14), showed.

However, there is a very real difficulty in the case of expenses and losses incurred after a cessation. Such expenses can only be set against post-cessation receipts. If there are no such receipts, then there can be no allowance for debts which subsequent to cessation prove to be bad, or claims for negligence which arise after cessation. Obviously, it is necessary to delay drawing up final accounts for as long as possible so that the appropriate provisions can be made. Where this is not practicable, the problem remains and is presently still the subject of representations by the CCAB.

Companies and professions

35 An interesting question is whether a company can carry on a profession. If a profession can be carried on only by a person or persons holding the requisite professional qualifications (as in the case of solicitors, accountants and doctors), it cannot be carried on by a company (CIR *v.* Peter McIntyre Ltd 12 TC 1006). But, as that case shows, a company can carry on a professional business, and thus it is thought can, in the case of most professions, be used to hire out the individual's professional services. Is such a professional business a trade where the same business carried on by an individual would be the exercise of a profession? The point is not academic. Although the charge to corporation tax extends to all income, certain corporation tax provisions, principally those relating to losses, refer only to trades, and a trade for corporation tax purposes includes a vocation but not a profession (s.6(4)(b) ICTA 1988). Therefore if a company can carry on a profession, any loss relief is apparently concessional, although it is inconceivable the Inland Revenue would take this point. Because of high rates of income tax, in the past many individuals carrying on professions have formed companies to deal with some or all of their professional activities. Thus an actor might form a company to exploit all his earnings or only his earnings abroad. However, corporation tax at 33% and capital gains tax on the remaining 67% now produce little more than a cash flow advantage over an individual's top rate of 40% on any income. Therefore, the advantage of a company now is that it will suffer lower rates of tax on retained earnings than the top rate of income tax. The abolition of apportionment of the non-trading income of a close company has to some extent simplified the position on whether a company is worth forming for all or part of an individual's activities.

Generally, where earnings are very high, a company can still be a useful vehicle for retaining earnings. Bearing in mind the case of a person carrying on a profession, there is often an element of goodwill. On incorporation of all or part of the business, a capital gain will arise on the transfer of the right to future income or goodwill to the company. There are two methods of incorporation which avoid this charge. Firstly, it is possible to utilise the relief available under s.162 TCGA 1992, where all the assets of the business except cash have to be transferred to the company. To the extent that the assets are transferred in exchange for shares in the company, any chargeable gains will then be rolled over into these shares. By concession, any trade liabilities taken over are not treated as cash consideration paid by the company for this purpose.

Alternatively, it may be possible to utilise the hold-over relief available under s.165 TCGA 1992. This does not require all of the assets to be transferred to the company and is particularly suitable for the incorporation of part of the business (for instance, its overseas activities). The company will take on a reduced base value for any chargeable assets acquired.

36 Additionally, a company can employ a person's spouse as a director and thus there is a greater facility for paying more earned income to a wife than would be the case if she were merely employed as a secretary. The payment, however, should not manifestly exceed the commercial rate for the duties performed, otherwise the excess would be disallowed to the company (Copeman *v.* William Flood & Sons Ltd 24 TC 53).

37 Companies can in addition have shareholders liable at a lower rate of tax than the individual. For instance, shares in the company could be issued to trustees of an accumulation and maintenance settlement in favour of the individual's children. If dividends are paid by the company, and accumulated in the settlement they will suffer tax at 35%. If the small companies' rate of 25% applies (as will usually be the case), there will be the same corporation tax payable whether profits are retained or distributed.

If the settlement is made by the child's grandparents, income can be paid out for the child's maintenance and be treated as the child's income for tax purposes. A repayment claim can then be made in respect of any personal allowances of the child. With the abolition of child allowances for 1979–80, and later years (except for certain limited categories of children), and provided there is no reintroduction of aggregation of children's income, this form of settlement will be a very attractive way of paying school fees. It should be noted that income paid out for the child from a settlement by the parent would be aggregated with the parent's income and would therefore be ineffective.

38 Trading companies can in addition often still provide better pension arrangements for their directors than those which can be provided under the retirement annuity and personal pension provisions for individual with non-pensionable earnings. This arises from the fact that whereas there is an upper limit (s.663 ICTA 1988) on allowable contributions by an individual, no such limit operates in respect of a company's contributions to fund a director's or employee's pension, provided the ultimate pension does not exceed two thirds of final earnings from the company, normally now at least twenty years' service has been given, and the pensions cap is not exceeded.

Service companies

39 Sometimes part of an individual's activities are transferred to a company, or a service company is set up to provide services and charges a fee based on its costs plus a percentage of profit. The service charge must be based on the cost of services provided in the relevant period (Stephenson *v*. Payne, Stone, Fraser & Co 44 TC 507) and must not be excessive. Otherwise it will fall to be disallowed in the individual's trading profit computation as not satisfying the 'wholly and exclusively' test. What is reasonable is what an outside concern would charge to provide the same services.

There is also an increasing tendency for persons who would otherwise receive employment income subject to PAYE from a variety of sources, for instance where they hold directorships of several companies, to form their own personal service company which contracts with the relevant employer for the services of the individual. Provided the arrangements are properly entered into, the fees paid to the service company should not be subject to PAYE, which will only be levied on what is paid out to the director of the personal service company by way of remuneration. There is thus the advantage of flexibility in being able to enter into individually tailored pension arrangements, the ability to retain earnings, and to have the spouse as a director of the personal service company.

Overseas work and companies

40 Because the rules for Schedule E employments, but not for Schedule D trades and professions, allow the possibility of a 100% deduction for earnings attributed to work overseas, it may be advantageous to form a company to employ the individual to carry out overseas work which would otherwise be part of his trading or professional activities fully liable to UK tax.

41 Companies cannot be used to convert income into capital gains on a short term basis. Where the company is formed to exploit the earning capacity of an individual and it accrues income at a lower rate of tax than that which would have been suffered by the individual, and the shares are then realised for a capital sum which represents no more than those earnings, the capital sum is likely to be taxed as income under Case VI of Schedule D (s.775 ICTA 1988). Specific reference is made to this provision in more detail where appropriate.

42 In considering any scheme for minimising UK tax on overseas income in the hands of an individual ordinarily resident in the UK, it is also important to consider whether there is any likelihood that the Inland Revenue will be able to set aside the arrangements and tax the income as the individual's own income under the very wide-ranging anti-avoidance provisions concerning transfers of income abroad in s.739 ICTA 1988. For this reason many arrangements for such individuals will make use of a UK resident company so that the section cannot apply.

Interest

43 Numerous attempts have been made to claim interest and other investment income as earned income as being immediately derived from the carrying on of the profession (s.833(4) ICTA 1988). In the case of both estate agents (Aplin *v*. White 49 TC 93) and solicitors (Northend *v*. White and Leonard and Corbin Greener 1975 STC 317), this claim has failed. A limited exception is mentioned in the chapter on stockbrokers. This now is relevant for enabling the income to be used for retirement annuity and personal pension purposes as being relevant earnings.

Chapter 2
Writers, sculptors, painters

Copyright

44 In order to appreciate the taxation position of artists and writers, it is necessary to consider the nature of copyright and the methods of exploiting it.
45 Copyright is a form of property which confers protection from unlawful reproduction or performance of artistic works. The copyright owner alone has a right to exploit or to grant to others the right to exploit the work in the various ways open to him. The copyright exists for 50 years after the death of the author. Copyright covers literary works, dramatic and musical works, artistic works (paintings, sculptures, drawings, engravings and photographs), films and records. So far as British copyright is concerned, the Copyright, Designs and Patents Act 1988, and for works created prior to commencement of the 1988 Act the Copyright Act 1956, permit the various rights reproduction or publishing not only to be licensed but also to be assigned separately from each other. It is thus possible for the owner to exploit copyright broadly in one of three ways:

(1) To assign it in respect of all or any one or more of the rights in it (for instance, for a period of time within the life of the copyright or in relation to any one or more of the territories covered by it) in consideration of a lump sum.

(2) To grant in consideration of a lump sum a licence or an interest in the copyright, that is, the copyright is retained but permission is granted to do certain things that would otherwise infringe the copyright, for instance, to reproduce a book in paperback form.

(3) To receive royalties for the use of the copyright by someone else.

46 Only sums received under (3) will be income in the hands of a person who is not a professional author. A professional author, for whom copyright is part of his or her circulating capital, will be taxed under Case II of Schedule D on anything received for the exploitation of copyright (Glasson *v*. Rougier 26 TC 86, and Billam *v*. Griffith 23 TC 757).
47 What constitutes a copyright 'royalty' has been the subject of numerous tax cases. As was said in the leading case of Withers *v*. Nethersole (28 TC 501) if a sum is arrived at by reference to the number of times something is used or

19

reproduced, it is likely to be a royalty as opposed to a payment for the acquisition of the property itself or any of the rights attaching to it. Because Miss Nethersole had given up her profession many years previously and made a partial assignment of her copyright as opposed to a licence to use it, this was "a sale of property by a person who is not engaged in the trade or profession of dealing in such property, and the proceeds of such a sale is . . . untaxable capital". Reference may also be made to CIR *v.* Longmans Green (17 TC 272) and Beare *v.* Carter (23 TC 353).

Gifts of copyright

48 Copyright is important for another reason. Professional authors liable under Case II of Schedule D on their income are invariably assessed on a cash basis. As well as providing flexibility on time receipts and thus income, it means that no account is taken of stock and work-in-progress in their accounts. Thus it was decided in the case of Mason *v.* Innes (44 TC 326) that it is possible to give away copyright without attracting the sort of charge that would apply to an ordinary trader giving away stock under the principle established in Sharkey *v.* Wernher (36 TC 275). This means effectively that any such gift, although now potentially attracting IHT, would not give rise to income tax.

49 It could also attract relief from CGT under the provisions holding-over gains on gifts of business assets in the case of a professional author (s.165 TCGA 1992). Therefore, if the copyright is given away before it has proven value or it is assigned in works still in preparation as is possible under the Copyright Acts, this provides a useful means of spreading income around a family at no cost in terms of IHT if it is a PET and with no CGT. A copyright may, for instance, be settled on accumulation and maintenance trusts for the benefit of the author's children. However, it should be borne in mind that once the right to royalties is assigned by the author, the royalties become annual payments taxable usually under Case III of Schedule D on the recipient under s.18(3) ICTA 1988 and, therefore, should be paid under deduction of tax under s.348 and s.349 ICTA 1988 (Hume *v.* Asquith 45 TC 251).

50 In one case, Lawrence and others *v.* CIR, royalties accruing to a charitable trust from the works of T. E. Lawrence were assessable under Case VI although they were still regarded as annual payments (23 TC 333). If the assigned royalties derive from a foreign publisher under a foreign contract, they will be assessable under Case V. Therefore, the author should not assign royalties on their own to a company, otherwise he is converting earned income into investment income of an investment company which could be regarded as a close investment-holding company (s.13A ICTA 1988).

The small companies rate would not be available to such a company. The Inland Revenue could also deny repayment of the tax credit attaching to any dividend paid by the company selectively to shareholders who are not liable to tax (such as minor children), or dividends utilising special classes of shares or waivers by other shareholders (s.231(3A) ICTA 1988).

Income or capital

51   It is important to establish for tax purposes whether a sum of money received in connection with a work of art is income or capital, and if it is income, the correct taxation treatment of that income for the purposes of allowing expenses.

Categories of authors for tax purposes

52   Authors and other producers of works of art fall into three broad categories for tax purposes:

(1) Those who have not produced any work before and have not produced any subsequent work, at least on a regular and organised basis, such as politicians writing their memoirs. They are clearly not carrying on a profession. Any manifestly income payments they receive, such as royalties, are in practice assessed under Case VI of Schedule D on the receipts basis and were treated as earned income for investment income surcharge purposes. It may be possible to spread these sums for assessment purposes (s.534 ICTA 1988).

There can sometimes be a problem about the allowance of certain expenses against any such income, as in strictness many of the expenses such as the cost of materials, travelling and research, may be incurred on preparatory work or in producing an income earning asset and thus be either capital expenditure or incurred in a year before income first arises. The special relief for pre-trading expenditure under which it is deemed to be incurred on the first day of trading is extended to professions and vocations but not casual income assessable under Case VI. In practice, it is usually found that the Inland Revenue are prepared to allow more than the current revenue expenses incurred in the fiscal year in which the first payment is received. However, to avoid having to rely on concessions, as much as possible of any expenditure should be deferred until the fiscal year in which income first arises or alternatively an advance payment of royalties should be negotiated to cover such expenses.

Any lump sum received for an outright sale of the copyright or associated rights will be capital (Beare v. Carter 23 TC 353) and fall within the CGT provisions but, of course, any revenue expenditure would not then be allowable in arriving at any such CGT liability. The sum will be capital on the principles expounded in the case of Trustees of Earl Haig v. CIR (22 TC 725) under which lump sums received for exploitation of a person's personal property, protected by copyright which involve alienation of some of the rights attaching to the property, are capital sums where the person is not a professional author.

21

In that case, materials from the diaries of Earl Haig were incorporated in a book written by an outside author with the profits of the work being shared between the author and the estate. It was held this constituted a sale of a valuable part of the property itself. The trustees were in fact free to make such other use of the diaries as they could so that there was no outright assignment of the publishing rights in them but the reasoning in the case was that little further use could be made by the trustees of the diaries so that effectively their capital asset had been destroyed.

Not all lump sums received by someone who is not a professional writer are capital, and what is being paid for has to be carefully analysed to see if there is a disposal outright of intellectual property. The recent case of Alloway *v.* Phillips (1979 STC 452) is an interesting illustration of this. In the case, the wife of one of the Great Train Robbers sold her story to a national newspaper. She was assessed under Case VI on the sum she received. The Court upheld the assessment apparently because nothing akin to the disposal of copyright was involved but she made a profit of an income nature out of the contract with the newspaper to provide her story. The fact that she was not resident at the time did not protect her from liability as the contract was with a British newspaper and therefore the source of the profit was property in the UK under s.18(1)(a)(iii) ICTA 1988. A professional author who is not resident and carries on writing wholly abroad, should not similarly be caught for the reasons mentioned below.

This decision followed two earlier cases where there was in essence a performance of services rather than a sale of copyright by someone who was not a professional author. Thus in Hobbs *v.* Hussey (24 TC 153) a series of newspaper articles gave rise to profits assessable under Case VI although they were the only literary activity of the cricketer on the basis that although there was an implicit sale of copyright involved, it was a case essentially of a performance of services. Similarly in the case of Housden *v.* Marshall (38 TC 233) the taxpayer provided information for articles ghosted by a journalist and was assessed under Case VI.

(2) Those who exploit their artistic talents on a casual basis. Their earnings of an income nature (fees, commissions, royalties, etc.) will be assessed under Case VI also, but there is usually sufficient recurrence of income to cover expenses which are more likely not to be preparatory expenses if the income is recurring and is thus treated as deriving from one continuing source and there is not merely one work or project under consideration. Any deficiency in this instance would be carried forward against future Case VI income.

Any sums for the sale of the property in the work will remain capital on the same basis as in (1).

(3) The professional author, etc., who is taxed on all his receipts as income liable under Case II of Schedule D including lump sum receipts from the sale of copyright or royalties (MacKenzie *v.* Arnold 33 TC 363; Household

v. Grimshaw 34 TC 966; Howson *v.* Monsell 31 TC 529). Equally, advance royalties receivable, unless they are returnable and are in the nature of a loan, are assessable when received (Taylor *v.* Dawson 22 TC 189).

It was established from the cases of Purchase *v.* Stainer's Executors (33 TC 367) and Carson *v.* Cheyney's Executors (38 TC 240) that in whatever form earnings reached an author, they were either taxable as professional income under Case II or not liable to income tax at all. This meant that anything received after cessation of the profession escaped income tax liability altogether until the post cessation receipts legislation was enacted.

Post-cessation receipts

53   Anything earned before cessation will now be caught either by s.103 or s.104 ICTA 1988. Section 103 will catch anything due to the author by the time of cessation but not received until afterwards and s.104 will catch any professional earnings receivable after cessation. It should be noted that ss.103 and 104 do not apply to lump sums received after death by the personal representatives of an author as consideration for the assignment by them of the copyright (s.103(3)(b) and s.104(1) ICTA 1988). Such sums will be liable to capital gains tax subject to a deduction for any opening value brought into the author's estate for IHT purposes.

Losses

54   The advantage of being classed as a professional author is that any loss incurred will be available to offset against other income of the same or following year under s.380 ICTA 1988 (or carried back under s.381 ICTA 1988 if incurred in the first four years) or against capital gains under s.72 FA 1991 as opposed to being a Case VI loss which is only available against Case VI income. The Inland Revenue will therefore generally resist any attempt to claim Case II treatment in the case of someone who has another main source of earned income until it is shown there is a profit seeking motive and the work is sufficiently sustained and combined with systematic attempts to market the completed works as to indicate a profession is being carried on. Care should be taken not to be too zealous in seeking such Case II treatment in case the losses that are claimed for set off become in future years substantial profits. Whilst the person who is assessed under Case VI on any income has an opportunity to realise a capital gain on the sale of any copyright, the professional author has no such opportunity.

Effect of changes of residence

55   Whether a person is a professional author or assessable under Case VI and liable to capital gains tax, there is still the opportunity of receiving substantial sums free of UK tax if the person ceases to be resident and ordinarily resident in the UK. If a person not carrying on a profession ceases to be resident and ordinarily resident in the UK before signing a contract to sell the copyright, he or she will be exempt from CGT on the sale proceeds. A professional author does not cease to carry on a profession by going to reside abroad but merely carries on the same profession in a different country (Davies *v.* Braithwaite 18 TC 198 and Fry *v.* Burma Corporation Ltd 15 TC 113). Thus, if he can defer receiving substantial sums of income until the year before he ceases to be resident and provided he continues to carry on his profession abroad, in his final year of residence he will be assessed on the previous year's earnings and the high earnings should escape UK tax.

The same principle should apply if the author spends one year completely outside the UK taking his family with him having received high income in the previous year and continuing his writing abroad following the principles established in the Dave Clark case (Reed *v.* Clark 1985 STC 323).

56 However, he should ensure that he does not retain any fixed base in the UK from which he continues to write and publish such work in the UK, as even if he were regarded as a resident of another country under the relevant double tax treaty, such treaties do not normally exempt from tax professional earnings of a non-resident if they derive from activities carried on from a fixed base in that country. Such income would in most cases continue to be liable to UK tax as Case II income.

57 He should not suffer UK tax at source on copyright royalties as, following the decisions in Jarvis *v.* Curtis Brown Ltd and Carson *v.* Cheyney's Executors (14 TC 744 and 38 TC 240) these are part of his professional receipts and not income from property. Therefore s.536 ICTA 1988, which provides for deduction of tax at source from royalties paid to a person whose usual place of abode is outside the UK, should not be applicable as the royalties will have lost their identity as royalties and become part of the continuing professional receipts of the author who is carrying on his profession abroad rather than be derived from the copyright as an independent asset. For his own protection, the payer would be advised to obtain the Inland Revenue's confirmation before making such payments without deduction of tax. This interpretation of the law was confirmed in a Parliamentary answer (*Hansard* Vol. 791 Col. 31).

Income spreading provisions

58 Where a receipt ranks as income of an artist, sculptor or writer, it is dealt with more generously than that of other professions where also income can arise unequally as between one year and another.

59 A contract for royalties is between the author and the publisher, not the reading public, and in the case of an established writer the contract with the publisher can often provide in any event for advances on account of royalties and the royalties themselves can equally be paid by the publisher at intervals to suit the situation of the recipient. Thus, where a person produces a new book and the commercial success of each book is assured, the combination of assessment on the cash basis and a flexible form of continuing contract with the publisher will ensure that concentration of income is avoided.

60 However, the position is different in the case of the author who receives a disproportionately large sum for one work or whose income is irregular because he or she writes more intermittently. To ensure that income may be spread in such circumstances, a measure of relief is provided under s.534 ICTA 1988. This provides, on a claim being made by the author, for a spread-back of a receipt from the disposal of copyright in whole or in part in a particular work by reference to the time taken to complete the work up to a maximum of three years so that one half or one third of the receipt is deemed to have been received a year or two years before the actual time of the receipt. This deemed receipt is brought into the accounts for the purposes of computing the Case II position of that year. The relief is given to an author of a literary, dramatic, musical or artistic work and therefore a company formed to exploit an author's literary work cannot claim, as authorship can only be attributed to an individual or individuals.

61 The relief also applies to royalties except where they are receivable more than two years after the first publication of the work (s.534(4)(b) ICTA 1988). In the case of royalties the relief would only be appropriate where an amount on account of or in satisfaction of royalties is received in one sum. This relief is thus given to someone who is not a professional author in receipt of royalties which are bunched together.

62 The provision generally is only operative where an amount is received in respect of one identifiable work rather than a series of separate novels etc., for which payment is received on completion of the last one (s.534(7) ICTA 1988).

63 In order to cover the different situation of the professional author who may be past the peak of earning capacity, s.535 provides that, where such a person sells for a lump sum residual copyrights in his works which have been before the public for not less than 10 years, spreading may be claimed. In the ordinary way such a receipt would be brought into the profits for a single year and even if it came in as a post cessation receipt after discontinuation of the profession, it would still attract liability in a single year subject to any relief by reference to the author's age under s.109 ICTA 1988. To avoid this situation, where the copyright in such works is assigned or an interest in the copyright is granted for a period of more than two years but less than six years, a claim may be made for the receipt to be spread forward from the date of receipt by dividing it by the number of years for which it is granted and deeming it to be received in equal instalments over the period. Where the period for which it is assigned or granted is six years or more, the receipt is similarly spread forward over a maximum of six years.

If, exceptionally, the author is not treated as carrying on a profession but is assessed on such sums under Case VI, or where the sums would be treated as post cessation receipts assessable under Case VI, any deductible expenses are allowed exclusively against the amount to be spread (s.535(8) ICTA 1988).

As this relief is limited to cases where the first occasion on which the work or reproduction of it is published, performed or exhibited, is not less than 10 years before assignment, etc, it is important to ensure that the author waits for the expiry of this period before entering into the contract to receive such a sum.

64 There are special provisions where the author dies or where the profession is permanently discontinued otherwise than on death before the date of the last instalment is deemed to have been received (s.535(4) to (7) ICTA 1988). As the effect of permanent discontinuance is either to treat the remaining assessable instalments as falling due on the date of the last instalment before discontinuance or, by election, to treat all the assessable instalments as arising evenly over the period from the receipt of the sum to discontinuance, it is advisable where possible to avoid a discontinuance, for instance by the author continuing to carry on his profession even if in a very limited way until maximum advantage is taken of spreading forward.

Public lending rate

65 The provisions relating to copyright royalties comprising returns by payers, post cessation receipts, spreading reliefs and deduction of tax where the owner is resident abroad will now apply to cover payments of royalties made to authors in respect of the borrowings of their books from public libraries (s.537 ICTA 1988).

Painters and sculptors

66 S.538 ICTA 1988 provides a companion relief to s.534 for those who dispose of their works outside the copyright field or work on a commission or fee basis such as painters or sculptors where the copyright would normally belong to the person commissioning the work. The only difference is that the relief is available even if the actual work sold took less than 12 months to create, provided it is one of a number of works of art for an exhibition which took more than 12 months to complete.

Disposals of works of art subject to CGT and IHT

67 It is worth noting in conclusion that, in the case of the disposal of a chattel, such as a tangible work of art, or books, papers and documents other than by a professional artist or author, CGT will be payable only where the proceeds exceed £6,000 (s.262 TCGA 1992). There are also exemptions from IHT (s.30 IHTA 1984) and CGT (s.258 TCGA 1992) for gifts of works of art which are held to be of national importance and provided certain conditions are met. Since, on the basis of the case of Mason *v*. Innes (44 TC 326) a charge to income tax cannot arise on the gift of a work of art, these exemptions also from CGT and IHT may, where the professional artist donates a work to a museum or gallery, make the gift free of all taxation.

68 However, it should be noted that the Capital Taxes Office generally resist the granting of Business Relief on personal copyrights on the basis they are not part of a 'business' but stem from a vocation which does not have a sufficiently commercial motivation behind it. This is now of course particularly relevant when 100% relief from inheritance tax may be at stake.

Taxation of awards

69   The following should be considered.

(1) General principles

It appears that the Inland Revenue have changed policy towards taxation of artists and authors in receipt of *ex gratia* payments from the Arts Council and other patrons. This doubtless reflects a considerable increase in the size of these awards since the previous arrangement was concluded whereby the Inland Revenue did not seek to tax such awards provided that they were unsolicited and provided that the award did not represent payment for work to be carried out by the recipient. Apparently, the Inland Revenue are no longer prepared to provide a blanket agreement, and will look at each award on its merits. On this basis, the fact that the payments are entirely gratuitous would not prevent their forming part of the taxable receipts of the donee's profession or vocation. Cases such as Smart *v.* Lincolnshire Sugar Co Ltd (20 TC 643) could enable the Inland Revenue to sustain an assessment where the awards were intended artificially to supplement the artist's professional receipts. The fact that the Inland Revenue have lost a case before the Special Commissioners where they attempted to tax the winner of the Whitbread Award, the author Andrew Boyle, may not deter them from taxing other awards made by firms to publicise their good names as patrons of the arts. It is understood, however, that the Booker Prize will remain unchallenged, presumably because it is considered to be awarded as a mark of honour to the individual. In particular, unsolicited awards from such bodies as charitable trusts in memory of famous individuals should be claimed as exempt from tax on the basis they are personal awards to an individual and usually not part of any commercial arrangement with the author. Thus it is understood, for instance, that it has been agreed that awards made by the Airey Neave Memorial Trust to authors are not taxable. Similarly the Nobel Prize for literature is not taxable.

(2) Taxation of awards and bursaries made by the Arts Council

The Arts Council and the Inland Revenue have agreed on the tax treatment of awards and bursaries which the Council makes to artists, writers, photographers, musicians and the performing arts. Agreement of the tax treatment of the awards, etc., does not impinge on the rights of appeal against an assessment to tax on any individual receipt of an award or bursary.

Arts Council awards and grants fall into two broad categories. Awards in respect of training schemes, or to enable creative artists to devote time to research and development will be non-taxable. Grants afforded in respect of specific non-training projects will be taxable.

Awards and bursaries made by the Arts Council fail to be treated for tax purposes in the following categories:

Category A *Awards and bursaries chargeable to tax*
(1) Direct or indirect musical, design or choreographic commissions and direct or indirect commissions of sculpture and paintings for public sites.
(2) The Royalty Supplement Guarantee Scheme.
(3) The contract writers' scheme.
(4) Jazz bursaries.
(5) Translators' grants.
(6) Photographic awards and bursaries.
(7) Film and video awards and bursaries.
(8) Performance art awards.
(9) Art publishing grants.
(10) Grants to assist with a specific project or projects (such as the writing of a book) or to meet specific professional expenses such as a contribution towards copying expenses made to a composer, or to an artist's studio expenses.

Category B *Awards and bursaries not chargeable to tax*
(1) Bursaries to trainee directors.
(2) In-service bursaries for theatre directors.
(3) Bursaries for associate directors.
(4) Bursaries to people attending full-time courses in arts administration (the practical training course).
(5) In-service bursaries to theatre designers and bursaries to trainees on the theatre designers' scheme.
(6) In-service bursaries for administrators.
(7) Bursaries for actors and actresses.
(8) Bursaries for technicians and stage managers.
(9) Bursaries made to students attending the City University arts administrative courses.
(10) Awards, known as the Buying Time Awards, made, not to assist with a specific project or professional expenses, but to maintain the recipient to enable him to take time off to develop his personal talents. These at present include the following awards and bursaries, known as the Theatre Writing Bursaries, Awards and Bursaries to composers, Awards and Bursaries to painters, sculptors and print makers, Literature Awards and Bursaries.

It will be open to the Arts Council to make both a grant in A(10) and an award in B(10) to an individual and accordingly in such a case, part only of the sum received by the individual concerned will be treated as taxable. However, it is agreed in relation to these cases that if the expenditure incurred by the individual in connection with the matters covered by the A(10) grant and the B(10) award exceeds the amount of the A(10) grant the excess up to and including the amount of the B(10) award will be regarded as covered by the B(10) award, and to this extent will not be allowable as a deduction in arriving at his taxable profits. The remainder of any of the expenditure will be subject to the normal Schedule D expenses rules.

These arrangements will be followed by the Inland Revenue (whilst the law remains as it is) in cases involving awards both for future assessments and in settlement of appeals now open. The Arts Council will, in making future awards, inform the recipient of the category applicable for tax purposes.

It should be noted that this agreement was published in relation to awards current in September 1979. Further types of award have been instituted since this and reference should be made to the Arts Council for the taxation treatment of any such award.

Pension arrangements

70 There is a special pension scheme for authors and reference should be made to the Writers' Guild Scheme for details of it. In particular, it copes with the problems of uneven earnings and early retirement.

Chapter 3
Entertainers

One profession – basis of assessment

71 An entertainer is assessed to income tax, in accordance with the level and return of his or her activities, in one of the following ways:

(a) if he is carrying on an unpaid vocation, or hobby, and only charges for his expenses, and there is no contract of or for services, he is unlikely to be assessed at all. He is also unlikely to be able to claim any form of loss relief if expenses exceed income;

(b) if, although he makes a more realistic charge than the entertainer in (a) above, he does not make a living from his performance but derives earnings from, say, casual club work, the Inland Revenue are likely to assess him under Sch. D Case VI, in order to avoid any loss claims under s.380 ICTA 1988. Alternatively the Inland Revenue may accept that the entertaining amounts to a Sch. D Case II source but will only allow the carry-forward of losses under s.385 ICTA 1988 against earnings from the same source as it amounts to an uncommercial professional activity (s.384 ICTA 1988):

(c) there may be a specific employment contract, for example a musician's contract with an orchestra. Alternatively, the entertainer may be director of his own service company. In such cases, the entertainer will be assessed under Sch. E in respect of his remuneration from the company;

(d) most full-time professional entertainers are assessed under Sch. D Case II. They are deemed to carry on one profession for tax purposes (see Davies *v*. Braithwaite (1933) 18 TC 198), even if their activities are partly carried on outside the UK in the year in question. But see below regarding entertainers who are working under standard Equity ('Esher') contracts.

This means that, if an actor or singer ceases to be UK-resident, his profession does not cease although he may no longer be within the scope of UK tax. Thus, in Reed *v*. Clark (1985) 58 TC 528, the singer Dave Clark escaped tax on his previous year's earnings by residing in Los Angeles throughout the year 1978/79. As he neither resided in the UK in 1978/79, nor exercised his profession at any time in the UK in that year, there was no head of charge to tax on those earnings (which would otherwise have been assessed in 1978/79) nor was there a discontinuance of his profession in 1977/78.

Overseas work

72 Where there is a material amount of overseas work, but the actor remains resident and ordinarily resident in the UK, it may be advisable to form a company to employ the actor in respect of such work, so that he has, separately from his profession, an employment with the company, the duties of which can be performed abroad. He can then claim the 100% deduction in respect of remuneration from that source, provided that he has performed those duties outside the UK for a qualifying period of at least 365 days (s.193(1) ICTA 1988).

If a non-resident company is used, it is possible that its retained income will, in any event, be caught by s.739 ICTA 1988, unless commercial reasons can be found for its formation abroad, for instance, the involvement of a local manager in the equity of the company. Sometimes an agent will have a company, often based abroad, which specialises in organising the foreign earnings of such people as film and rock stars. To distinguish such an employment, a separate 'slavery' contract should be drawn up between the entertainer and the company, indicating the areas of work for which the company will contract and the relationship between the entertainer and the company in respect of such work. Where a jointly-owned company cannot be used, the accumulated earnings will only escape s.739 if the shares are held in trust for the benefit of the star's family, and he and his wife must be excluded from all benefit under the settlement. In that instance, as established in the *Vestey* case (1979) 54 TC 503, s.739 cannot apply. Instead, the beneficiaries, whilst they are resident in the UK, will be taxed under s.740 ICTA 1988 on any payment to them out of the trust that represents the accumulated earnings. Thus, UK tax can be deferred, or eliminated altogether if the beneficiary ceases to be ordinarily resident here before receiving the payments. However, extreme caution should be exercised and specialist advice sought before such an arrangement is undertaken. The number of cases where an entertainer is likely to be able to circumvent both ss.739 and 740 ICTA 1988 will be very few.

Another way of isolating foreign earnings was used in the case of Newstead *v.* Frost (1980) 53 TC 525. An overseas partnership was formed to receive the US income of the television personality, David Frost. It was held that his share of the profits constituted a separate source of income assessable under Sch. D Case V. Such a separate source would, however, not attract the foreign earnings deduction from 6 April 1986 and is, therefore, no longer tax-effective for those with a UK domicile.

Withholding of foreign tax at source

73 A further complication for entertainers in respect of overseas work is the local tax that may be withheld on payments to them, if they are not resident in the country in question. Where there is a double taxation agreement, this will usually exclude them from any exemption from local tax at source.

In the case of the revised US/UK double taxation agreement, the provisions go further. Payments to UK-resident companies employing an actor may also be subject to such withholding tax. Care needs to be taken, therefore, when arranging entertainers' affairs, to make sure that full credit is allowed for any foreign tax suffered against any UK tax liability. Thus, if tax is withheld on a payment to a UK company, sufficient profits need to be left in charge to UK corporation tax, and not drawn out by way of remuneration, in order to obtain full relief for the withholding tax.

It should be noted that, where UK-resident entertainers are liable to foreign tax on a foreign tour, notification may be made to the UK Inland Revenue, under the relevant double taxation agreement provision on the exchange of information.

Attention is drawn to the 1987 OECD Report *The Taxation of Income Derived from Entertainment, Artistic and Sporting Activities* issued by the Committee on Fiscal Affairs, and obtainable from HMSO.

Foreign entertainers visiting the UK

74   Prior to 1 May 1987, a foreign entertainer coming to the UK was liable to tax under Sch. D Case II or, if employed, under Sch. E Case II, on any income derived from his personal activities as an artist within the UK. Normally a double taxation agreement will not exempt an entertainer from such liability (see Art.17 OECD Model Income Tax Treaty 1977). With effect from 1 May 1987, ss.555 to 558 ICTA 1988, and regulations drawn up thereunder (SI 1987 No.530), changed the rules concerning the calculation of the amount assessable on non-resident entertainers, and introduced a withholding tax scheme.

From 1 May 1987, any person making a payment (to any person) that is connected directly or indirectly with the UK activities of a non-resident entertainer is obliged to deduct UK basic-rate income tax at source. The regulations empower the Inland Revenue to enter into arrangements with payers and artists, whereby a reduced or nil rate of tax may be applied if the Inland Revenue are satisfied that an overpayment of tax would otherwise arise.

Applications to enter into such arrangements must be made, at least 30 days prior to the date of payment, to the Inland Revenue Foreign Entertainers' Unit, at the following address:

5th Floor, City House
140 Edmund Street
Birmingham B3 2JG

A return to connected payments, together with payment of the tax due, must be made by the payer on a quarterly basis. Withholding tax need not be deducted where the total aggregate payments by a payer to any individual payee do not exceed £1,000 in a tax year. A useful Revenue booklet FEU50 deals with many of the practicalities in an easy-to-read fashion.

75 The scheme also applies to 'transfers' ie, benefits-in-kind, facilities provided, loans and transfers of rights.

In such cases, the amount of withholding tax must be calculated by grossing up the cost of providing the 'transfer' at the basic rate of income tax, and applying the appropriate rate of withholding tax to that gross figure.

The definition of 'connected payments' (see **74** above) is widely drawn to include sponsorship advertising and endorsement fees, but excludes payments that are derived from the proceeds of the sales of records. Such payments of royalties including those in respect of compact discs and cassettes are separately liable to withholding tax under the provisions of s.539 ICTA 1988. Payments derived from the sale of video recordings are not excluded from the definition of 'connected payments' so withholding tax appears to be chargeable in respect of such payments.

76 After the end of the tax year in which the relevant activity took place, the artist may make a return of his taxable income and, where applicable, claim repayment of any excess tax withheld. Taxable income is calculated in the same way as under Sch. D Cases I and II, but is assessed on a 'current-year' basis.

77 Income received by certain third parties may also be attributed to and taxed on the entertainer. This treatment applies in the following circumstances:

(a) Where the recipient is directly or indirectly controlled by the entertainer;
(b) Where the recipient is not resident in the UK and will suffer tax at 25% or less in the country where he is resident for tax purposes;
(c) Where the payment is made to a trust, of which, under the UK anti-avoidance legislation, the entertainer himself would be regarded as the settlor;
(d) Where there is an arrangement in force between the recipient and the entertainer, whereby it might be reasonable to suppose that the entertainer may become entitled to an amount not substantially less than the amount of the profit generated by the payment.

This legislation applies to non-resident sportsmen in the same way as it does to non-resident entertainers.

'Slavery' contracts and service companies

78 Very often an entertainer will set up his own service company, to which all his earnings and royalties will accrue. Typically, the entertainer will contract to devote the whole of his working time and professional skill to the interests of the company, and will agree not to work for any other party; he will agree to obey the directions of the company, or any third party to whom his services may be loaned. He will vest all rights in his works in the company, including copyright in products associated with his work such as photographs and the right to use his name, etc., on any products.

However, incorporation is not tax-efficient for each and every entertainer, and in this respect entertainers do not differ from other types of businessman. An entertainer must always give due weight to the commercial benefits or otherwise of incorporation, and these will vary according to the type of entertainer, eg., incorporation is likely to be of more commercial value for a pop star than for a West End actor.

With the lowering of personal rates of tax to a maximum of 40%, incorporation is unlikely to be beneficial in most cases.

The tax considerations are much the same as those for other businesses:

(a) When an individual incorporates his business, his self-employed activities cease. The earnings of some of his years of self-employment will fall out of assessment and some may be subject to an upward revision under s.63 ICTA 1988.

(b) Corporation tax rates are always lower than the higher rate of income tax, but any remuneration drawn from a company will be subject to income tax. However, there is some scope for regulating the flow of remuneration from a company and thereby smoothing out major fluctuations in earnings and, therefore, in tax rates.

(c) As an employee of his own company, an entertainer may benefit from the 100% allowance if abroad for 365 or more qualifying days, but if, as a self-employed individual, he is abroad for a whole tax year, he will not be taxed for that year.

(d) There is no longer any ceiling on employers' national insurance contributions. A self-employed entertainer would only have to meet Class 2 and 4 contributions.

(e) There may be capital gains tax complications on incorporation.

In 1969, legislation, now s.775 ICTA 1988, was introduced to counteract schemes under which entertainers, especially pop stars, attempted to avoid income tax by selling their services to a company in exchange for shares in the company and fixed remuneration. Care needs to be taken on incorporation not to assign valuable copyrights to the company in exchange for shares, otherwise a Sch. D Case VI charge will arise, equal to the value of the copyrights. Instead, the copyrights should be gifted to the company, making use of the Mason *v.* Innes case (1967) 44 TC 326, thereby avoiding income tax on such a gift.

It was at one time thought that the Inland Revenue might try to attack the one-man service company, either on Furniss *v.* Dawson principles, or as a settlement, so that all accumulated earnings would be attributed to the star and taxed on him as income. Some challenges have been made, so, as a safeguard, a genuine commerical structure should be set up, and the earnings should be used where possible to acquire other businesses.

It is essential that no corners are cut and that contracts are actually made with the service company through its sole employee. Where personal contracts are later ratified by the company and where payments due under personal contracts are paid to the company the Inland Revenue could successfully challenge the use of the company. The correct procedure is much easier to follow where there is an agent to negotiate all contracts on behalf of the entertainer.

Entertainers and anti-avoidance legislation

79 Entertainers do not enjoy the reliefs given to writers, sculptors, etc., which enable them to spread their earnings for taxation purposes. Many schemes, therefore, have been devised in an attempt to mitigate the incidence of high rates of income tax on those earnings. These may be of less interest now that the top rate has been reduced to 40%.

In the case of Mills *v*. CIR (1974) 49 TC 367, a company contracted to receive the earnings of Hayley Mills, the actress, from making films for the Walt Disney Studios, and all the shares of the company were settled on trust for Miss Mills until she attained her majority. The income was received by the company, on which it paid tax, and it was then paid to the trust in the form of dividends. It was intended that these dividends should be accumulated free of surtax, and paid out to her as capital on her majority. The Court held that Miss Mills was a settlor of the trust, as well as being the beneficiary, and that, therefore, the income of the trust must be treated as hers.

The lesson to be learned from this case, and from the case of Crossland *v*. Hawkins (1961) 39 TC 493, is that, where shares of a company exploiting an entertainer are held by a settlement, extreme care needs to be taken to ensure that the entertainer cannot be regarded also as a beneficiary under the settlement, as he will always be regarded as the settlor for tax purposes. The result will be to cause any dividends to be assessed on him as his income. It follows that no income must be paid out for the maintenance or education of under-age children of the settlor, as this will simply be treated as part of his income.

In Black Nominees *v*. Nicol (1975) 50 TC 229, a complicated tax avoidance scheme failed in an attempt to convert the future earnings of the actress Julie Christie into a capital sum in her hands, and the sum received was held to be income. The conversion of future earnings into a capital sum is now caught by s.775 ICTA 1988 and any scheme that purports to exploit the earnings capacity of an individual by putting a capital sum at his disposal is also likely to be caught by s.775.

Capital sums received by entertainers

80 An example of a sum that was received by an actor and held not to be income was a payment made by a film company to an actor for entering into a covenant not to act in, produce, or direct any film for any other person for a specified period (Higgs *v*. Olivier (1952) 33 TC 136). However, it would probably be unwise to place much reliance on this case, as the decision does not appear to have general application. The case is not in line with a whole series of other compensation cases that indicate that, where a sum is to compensate for a temporary loss of earnings, rather than to compensate for the complete destruction of the business, it is a revenue receipt. Nor was the decision followed in the case of White *v.* G & M Davies (1979) 52 TC 597, where EC payments to farmers to cease selling milk products were held to be trading income. A payment such as the one to Olivier would probably now be caught by s.313 ICTA 1988. If it were found to be capital, it would now be subject to capital gains tax, by virtue of s.22(1)(c) TCGA 1992, as a payment for refraining from exercising rights.

Unlike a professional author, an actor can, in fact, realise a capital sum if the sum is not directly a return for his own professional work. For instance, in one case, an actor bought the film rights in a novel for £1,700, intending to treat this as an investment to compensate him for loss of earnings. however, he had to sell the film rights to X Productions Ltd because, otherwise, that company would not make the film. The actor starred in the film and received a salary and share of the profits from it. However, the profit on the sale of the film rights was held to be capital because it was not part of an actor's profession to dispose of copyright and, accordingly, he was realising an investment (Shiner *v.* Lindblom (1960) 39 TC 367).

Although such sums would probably escape s.775 ICTA 1988, reference should be made to **95** below for the situation where an entertainer also backs his own show financially.

Capital allowances

81 Musicians may claim capital allowances in respect of their score libraries and musical instruments. Musicians need a substantial library of music, transcriptions, tapes, records and translations. Strictly, the initial cost of building up the library is a matter for capital allowances, although it may be possible to negotiate with the inspector a revenue allowance for replacements on a 'renewals' basis. The problem with claiming capital allowances on instruments is that their market value often appreciates. Many musicians like to keep their instruments when they retire so claims to capital allowances may eventually result in a substantial balancing charge, without any sale proceeds to pay the tax arising. In such circumstances, with his professional income substantially reduced if not nil, the musician may be forced to sell the instrument.

Employment or a profession

82 The decision in Davies *v.* Braithwaite (1933) 18 TC 198 (see **71** above) made it clear that a series of engagements, although each relates to a specific play or film, should not normally constitute a series of employments within Sch. E. However, if a person is contracted to a company for several films, or is a permanent member of a touring company, it may well be more difficult to resist the contention that he is in an employment, on the basis that a master/servant relationship exists, as in the case of the ballet dancer who worked for Sadler's Wells (Fall *v*. Hitchen (1972) 49 TC 433).

The dancer in Fall *v*. Hitchen was engaged under a standard 'Esher' contract, the type of contract approved by Equity. In 1989, the Inland Revenue notified the acting profession that, from 6 April 1990, they intended to assess under Sch. E those earnings from work performed under standard Equity contracts, quoting the decision in Fall *v*. Hitchen as authority for this approach. At the same time, they announced that all existing performers who had been treated as self-employed for the three years ended 5 April 1990 would continue to be assessed under Sch. D if they so wished. Following a meeting in March 1990 with the Inland Revenue, The Institute of Chartered Accountants in England and Wales issued a guidance note (TR796) on 25 June 1990. The note, which is reproduced at the end of this chapter, covers such matters as the changeover from Sch. D to Sch. E, the application of PAYE, travelling and subsistence expenses and expenses whilst touring.

The February 1991 issue of the members' journal of the British Actors Equity Association, reports that the Inland Revenue's Personal Tax Division has now agreed Sch. D status for certain 'speciality' acts. A note has been circulated to tax offices in the following terms:

"Artistes engaged as 'speciality' to perform his/her 'act as known'

(1) Comedians, singers, acrobats, jugglers, magicians, ventriloquists or other speciality acts engaged under Equity contracts to perform 'act as known' (usually in summer seasons, pantomimes or variety shows) can be either employed or self-employed. The Inland Revenue has, however, indicated that, in the following circumstances it would expect, depending on the facts of each case, artistes engaged to perform 'act as known' to be working under a contract for services (self-employed) where pay-as-you-earn is not applicable:

  (i) The artiste performs his/her own routine usually based on material [he/she has] used elsewhere;
  (ii) there is only the minimum of direction over the act by the theatre management;
  (iii) make-up, costumes, props, and musical score (where necessary) are provided by the artiste;
  (iv) payment is made by a global sum per week;
  (v) the artiste is treated for that engagement as self-employed for National Insurance purposes.

(2) Where such artistes are engaged under contracts of employment they may be eligible for 'reserved Schedule D' status."

The February 1991 journal also reported a concession recently given by the Inland Revenue in relation to touring:

"Expenses paid to members working on ITC/Equity Small-Scale Theatre Contracts

'The Revenue has agreed that members with these companies on tours that involve a series of single performances at a different location each day and who 'have responsibilities beyond acting and are involved in, for example, transporting costumes, equipment and scenery from location to location', will not be taxed (if on pay-as-you-earn) on travel expenses and related subsistence.

The Taxation Working Party, formed jointly by Equity, the Theatre Management bodies and the Arts Council, is continuing to press the Revenue on the wider subject of touring and travelling expenses, concerning which it is ruled that these should be taxed if the company has no permanent base theatre from which the tour starts and finishes. Certain companies have been able to obtain dispensations but the ruling as it stands says that, where an employee has no permanent place of work but works at a succession of places, payments in respect of the expenses incurred in travelling between home and any of these places, or between those places, and on accommodation, are taxable.

Peter Finch, assistant secretary of Equity, comments that:

"This is another example of the Inland Revenue misapplying a ruling, that might fit workers engaged on a permanent basis, to those Equity members essentially engaged on a casual, freelance basis and who have, equally incorrectly in our view, been caught in the pay-as-you-earn net.""

It also seems that the contention of the Inland Revenue is that any musician who has a regular engagement with a club (for example, a contract to appear every Saturday evening) is an employee of the club, and on the basis of the decision in Fall *v*. Hitchen, thus denying the performer's deductions for travelling and stage clothes. Some musicians in northern clubs have been recategorised accordingly by the Inland Revenue.

For national insurance purposes, members of certain well-known orchestras were found by the Courts to be self-employed (eg., Midland Sinfonia Concert Society Ltd *v*. Secretary of State for Social Services (1981) ICR 454), whereas, in the case of Warner Holidays Ltd *v*. Secretary of State for Social Services (1983) ICR 440, holiday camp entertainers were found to be employees. It is not certain to what extent the Courts would follow these national insurance decisions for income tax purposes.

Freelance workers in the film and allied industries

83 Similar action has been taken against freelance workers in the film and allied industries. In a press release of 30 March 1983, the Inland Revenue stated that they had carried out a review of the employment status of workers engaged on freelance terms within the industry. As a result of discussions with various representative bodies in the industry, the Inland Revenue consider that a number of such workers, such as studio hands and people operating cameras and lights, are engaged under contracts of service, either written or oral, and should be assessed under Sch. E. On the other hand, they have also accepted that a number of workers engaged in the industry are self-employed. These mainly comprise people exercising professional and technical skills on one production, for instance the producer or director, and people engaged for special effects.

In particular, the Inland Revenue have now stated that the following will continue to be regarded as self-employed for tax purposes in the film industry:

Animation director

Animation production co-ordinator

Animator – where providing own facilities and equipment

Animatronics model engineers

Art director

Associate producer

Camera operator – where the contract includes provision of equipment

Casting director

Chief make-up artist – if engaged for specialised skills

Choreographer

Composer

Continuity girl

Co-producer

Costume designer

Designer (other than assistant designers and repertory) – where providing own facilities and equipment

Director (other than assistant directors)

Driver – where providing own vehicles

Editor – all types (*note* – not assistants)

Executive producer

First assistant director

Lighting cameraman

Location manager

Model cameraman

Model designer – where providing own facilities and equipment

Modeller

Musical associate

Musical director

Producer

Production accountant

Production designer/head of art department

Production manager

Production supervisor

Property master

Publicist

Script supervisor

Sculptor

Senior special effects technician

Set decorators

Set dresser

Sound maintenance engineers

Sound recordist/mixer

Special effects supervisor – where contract includes provision of equipment

Specialised researcher

Stills photographer – where contract includes provision of cameras

Story editor

Supervising animation director

Transport manager – where providing own vehicles

Writer

Where the work is done in premises other than those provided by the company:

Assistant art director	Musical arranger/copyist
Background artist	Production buyer
Dressmaker	Scenic artist
Hairdresser in charge of production	Storyboard artist
Lettering artist	Tracer/painter
Lettering designer	

It is understood that a Special Commissioner has held that a freelance vision mixer in the film and television industry is assessable under Schedule D. In addition, PAYE need not be operated where the individual is employed for less than one week, ie., six consecutive days or less.

In the case of those categorised as employees, the use of service companies and partnerships to circumvent the application of PAYE on gross earnings is now widespread in the film industry. However, from 6 April 1988, the Inland Revenue have announced that such earnings will be subject to PAYE on the basis that, in general, the relationship between the production company and the individuals in such cases remains that of employer and employee even though payment is made to a company or partnership. In practice, a difference in approach has developed. For example, PAYE may not be operated in the television industry where payments are properly made to such a company.

Investigation of income of entertainers by the Inland Revenue

84 This attitude towards the operation of PAYE also illustrates the increasing attention that is being given to the affairs of actors and entertainers, particularly by West End districts, as part of their contribution to the taking up of cases for in-depth review. Districts now have the assistance of a special Entertainers' Information Unit, in London, which provides information on entertainers, particularly pop stars, and obtains s.16 TMA 1970 returns. In addition to the unit in London, there is an Entertainment Information Unit at Southend, which receives all 46P slips, retains a master index of such notifications, and distributes slips giving information on payments over a certain figure to districts. There used to be a unit at Watford, which was the first specialised unit to deal with pop stars, but its work has now been merged into the Special Office network. Bringing the entertainer within the ambit of PAYE is an easier way of combating tax evasion.

The use of standard profit ratios is generally accepted by the Inland Revenue as not applicable to entertainers, as expenses vary widely between various artistes. On the receipts side, as a check, the Inland Revenue may ask to see the agent's statements of gross fees and commission deducted, and any diary of engagements. Agents' commission can vary between 10–15% of fees; in some cases another agent or someone specialising in obtaining bookings – 'a booker' – may bring the engagement to the notice of the agent and also receive a commission. In the case of a star, the work of the agent may be done by a full-time manager and, in this situation, it is difficult to resist the contention that the manager is an employee of the star.

Loans

85 Not all 'loans' or 'advances' are taxable. Sometimes, to promote a rising star, a promoter will loan money to the entertainer to enable him to live and to meet promotion expenses. If such a loan is repayable, it is not taxable. Non-repayable advances of fees or royalties are, however, assessable when received, even if they are recouped against future royalties.

Tax returns

86 The Inland Revenue Entertainment Information Unit at Southend will send those 46P slips that show fairly substantial sums to the tax district dealing with the affairs of the payees (see **84** above). Where an entertainer's tax returns appear to show discrepancies (for instance, between outgoings or accumulated capital and known income), the inspector may attempt from time to time to reconcile the professional receipts shown in the entertainer's accounts with the amounts shown as paid to him in the 46P slips. He may have difficulties in doing so as the payers may use different accounting dates from the entertainer. He should also be aware that some of the larger payers are notoriously inefficient and may return the same payment more than once. However, if the discrepancies appear significant and continue over two or more years, the inspector may start an investigation into the entertainer's tax affairs.

Therefore, it is imperative that entertainers inform their tax advisors of all fees that are likely to be returned by the payer under s.16 TMA 1970. It is also necessary to ensure that the entertainer has also disclosed casual receipts, such as receipts for opening shops and fêtes paid by persons who, in practice, are not required to render a 46P return.

The following are items sometimes not disclosed by entertainers, that the Inland Revenue may well enquire about:

(a) rehearsal fees, which are often paid in cash;
(b) casual expenses for subsistence made by show managers;
(c) general expense reimbursement;
(d) cash payments made on tour in respect of small stage shows and local summer seasons;
(e) payments in cash by clubs;
(f) fees for articles in magazines and newspapers;
(g) 'repeat' fees, where paid through Equity. Equity often acts as a clearing house for payments to artists, for instance, where the artist has no fixed address. Also fees for the extension of a tour;
(h) TV and film repeat fees;
(i) commercial radio fees;
(j) payments in cash by advertising agencies.

Expenses

87 The distinction between self-employment and employment is important in the consideration of the expenses that can be claimed. Expenses of entertainers are often a source of contention with the Inland Revenue. The importance of being assessed under Sch. D, wherever possible, cannot be over-emphasised. Expenses allowable under Sch. E will be confined to what is wholly, exclusively and *necessarily* incurred in the performance of the duties of that employment. This at once excludes all the general expenses of promoting and preserving the person's standing in the profession and, in particular, prevents a claim for travelling expenses to and from the entertainer's home and place of work. It would also prevent a deduction for agents' fees, but for s.201A ICTA 1988 (introduced by FA 1990). This allows, from 1990/91 onwards, a deduction from Sch. E earnings for agents' fees paid to licensed agents including co-operative societies acting as such agents, up to a maximum of 17.5% of earnings for the tax year. Provisional relief may be obtained through the PAYE coding.

However, it should be noted that such agents' fees do not reduce relevant earnings for personal pension purposes although it is expected this anomaly will not last.

Generally, contributions to expenses as part of a promoter's package to a performer should be brought in as income and the actual expenses claimed whether he is assessed under Sch. D or Sch. E.

Expenses allowable under Sch. D Case II only have to satisfy the test of being 'wholly and exclusively incurred' for the purposes of the profession. A list of expenses that in most cases can be claimed against Sch. D Case II income is reproduced by kind permission of Equity, and is as follows:

(a) Agent's/Manager's fees and commission;
(b) Secretarial services for keeping books and records, answering fan mail and dealing with enquiries;
(c) Travelling and subsistence on tour if supporting a permanent home;
(d) Make-up;
(e) Hairdressing;
(f) Wardrobe and props;
(g) Laundry and cleaning of wardrobe and props;
(h) Renewal, replacement and repair of wardrobe and props;
(i) Travelling and expenses attending interview and auditions;
(j) Gratuities to dressers, call boys, doormen, make-up girls;
(k) Postage for business letters, fan mail;
(l) Business stationery;
(m) Tuition and coaching for dancing, singing, speech;
(n) Professional publications, e.g., *Radio* and *TV Times*, *The Stage*, *PCR*;
(o) Records, cassettes, scripts, sheet music;
(p) Theatre and cinema tickets;
(q) Equity subscription;
(r) Accountant's fees;

(s)   Legal charges for debt recovery, contract disputes;
(t)   Photographic sittings and reproduction;
(u)   Advertising, eg. *Spotlight* and agency books;
(v)   Maintenance of instruments and insurance.

The business proportion of the following will generally be allowed.

(a)   Telephone;
(b)   Hire of television and video together with licence payment;
(c)   Motor expenses.

In addition the following may be incurred and a case established with the Inland Revenue for an appropriate deduction.

(a)   Chiropody (mainly ballet dancers);
(b)   Physiotherapy;
(c)   Cosmetic dentistry;
(d)   Trichological treatment.

Where capital items are acquired for business purposes the Inland Revenue will consider claims for capital allowances. These are given at the rate of 25% of the cost less allowances already given on a reducing balance. A claim may be made for:

(a)   Motor Car;
(b)   Answerphone;
(c)   Office Furniture and equipment;
(d)   Video Recorder and television;
(e)   Musical equipment and instruments.

An appropriate percentage will be disallowed to cover private use.

It must be emphasised that this list has not been agreed with the Inland Revenue. It therefore has no force in any argument with the Inland Revenue except by reference to the fairness and equality of treatment promised in the Taxpayers' Charter. A similar list of expenses, appropriately modified, is available from Incorporated Society of Musicians.

Subsistence and travelling expenses abroad

88   Legislation contained in s.34 FA 1986 relaxed the rules in s.32 FA 1977 (now ss.193 and 194 ICTA 1988) relating to travel expenses incurred in employments carried on wholly or partly overseas. The changes, which are effective from 1984/85, benefit, for example, the entertainer who is resident and ordinarily resident in the UK and has set up a company to employ him solely in respect of his overseas work. He will not be taxed on any travel expenses that are reimbursed and that relate to journeys to take up or return from such an employment. The journeys can be between any place in the UK and the place of performance of the overseas duties. If he is abroad for 60 days or more, which is quite likely for, say, a theatrical tour, he will not be taxed on the travel expenses of two outward and return journeys in a tax year by his spouse and/or children to visit him during his period of overseas work.

If the entertainer does not have a separate company for overseas work but is nonetheless employed by his own company and performs only some of the duties of his employment in the UK, he will not be taxed on travel expenses in respect of all outward and return journeys between the UK and the place of performance of the overseas duties, provided the duties can only be performed overseas and the journeys are made solely for that purpose. Again he must be resident and ordinarily resident in the UK.

It should be stressed that in both cases the expenses must be reimbursed by the employer. This is presumably designed to introduce a measure of control but this is likely to be theoretical rather than real where the entertainer controls the company that employs him.

Similar reliefs are available, under s.80 ICTA 1988, for a self-employed individual who is UK-domiciled or, if a British subject or Irish citizen, who is ordinarily resident in the UK and carrying on a profession or vocation wholly outside the UK. Certain travel and accommodation expenses are allowed as Sch. D Case V deductions. These expenses would not otherwise be allowable as a deduction in arriving at income assessable under Sch. D Case V.

Travelling expenses in the UK

89 The Inland Revenue will contend that, where a person works regularly at one theatre or in one area, the work base is the theatre and not the actor's home. This may be the situation where, exceptionally, an actor is working more or less permanently on long runs in the West End, and lives in the suburbs. However, an actor performing a particular engagement in the West End that may be succeeded by work elsewhere, and certainly an actor on tour, should be regarded as operating from his own home. In the latter case, the actor has no centre of activity and travelling expenses from home may, therefore, be allowed.

Even where the actor is working regularly within a certain area, in practice the extra travelling and other expenses that are incurred over normal costs, for instance on taxis, should be allowed.

With regard to actors assessed under Sch. E, reference should be made to ICAEW guidance note TR 796 (see **82** above) for the tax treatment of travelling and subsistence expenses.

Subsistence expenses in the UK

90 Meals and accommodation expenses should be allowed without difficulty, if the travelling expenses are also allowable. The Inland Revenue will contend that lunches are not allowable, except where a person is on location or on a short tour. In this, is has the backing of the decision in Caillebotte *v.* Quinn

45

(1975) 50 TC 222, and of the decision in the case where solicitors were disallowed the cost of lunches in working hours (see Watkis *v.* Ashford, Sparkes and Harward (1985) 58 TC 468). The Inland Revenue are also particularly hard on subsistence expenses on a long engagement, where the artist has no home. Where someone has a home, subsistence is normally allowed in full.

Some inspectors may also allow claims for expenses incurred in going to the cinema or theatre for professional purposes, rather than for personal pleasure. However, no deduction will be allowed for the cost of providing business entertainment, such as the cost of a meal for other actors, agents etc. It may however be possible to establish that the meal was incidental to the main purpose of a longer meeting to research a new role, etc.

The Inland Revenue will dispute the allowance of an expense it if includes an element of personal choice, or benefit that is more than incidental to the main purpose of the expenditure. Thus, where a draftsman who played the guitar partly as a hobby and partly for payment cut his finger and had to pay for an operation, the payment was held not to be wholly and exclusively laid out for the purposes of his vocation (Prince *v.* Mapp (1969) 46 TC 169).

Clothing

91 There is usually no difficulty obtaining a tax deduction for theatrical costume and clothes. Clothes bought specifically for an audition should similarly qualify. The position here is not thought to be affected by the decision in Mallalieu *v.* Drummond (1983) 57 TC 330. The most common areas of difficulty are off-stage clothing and general expenses of keeping in the public eye, such as attendance at premieres for professional purposes. The public nature of the profession usually means that the Inland Revenue concede a deduction for limited reasonable claims. However, the cost of ordinary clothing that is also worn outside the theatre will be subject to some restriction for private use, even where it is necessary for, say, a TV personality or actor to buy particularly expensive clothing for his public image. Whenever possible expense claims should be categorised as 'costumes' rather than as 'clothes'.

Medical expenses

92 A claim for medical expenses will generally be disallowed. The cost of most treatment, even cosmetic treatment, will be resisted, as will sauna and health club fees. The 1989 VAT Tribunal case involving the actor Anthony Anholt (LON/89/487) may, however, provide some support for such claims if the health and fitness of an actor is a specific requirement of an ongoing professional role. In Mr Anholt's case this arose from his role in the TV series 'Howard's Way'.

Other expenses

93 Coaching and training costs incurred to improve performance are normally allowed.

The cost of tickets provided for publicity or advertising to others is allowable as a deduction. Such costs should be distinguished from those incurred to provide 'entertainment' for others. The inspector may also seek to disallow the cost of tickets provided for the actor himself, if duality of purpose can be proved. Thus it is easier to justify the cost of tickets if family and friends do not accompany the entertainer and where the 'research' motive can be shown to override any other reason for viewing the show or film. Similarly, the Inland Revenue will resist claims for the costs of a TV licence, or of hiring a TV set or a video, unless those assets can be shown to be of use in the exercise of the profession. Even then the deduction will probably be restricted to take account of private use.

On the other hand, it is often possible to claim part of the household expenses as relating to professional use, eg., for learning lines or music practice.

Groups' tax treatment

94 Groups pose special problems, especially if the Inland Revenue contend that they carry on business as a partnership. This can lead to complications on ownership of instruments, and copyrights – where songs have been written by one or two members of the group only. For these reasons and because of the tendency of groups to split up, it is normally advisable for each group member to have his own service company which in turn has an agreement with a central company owned by all the group members. The central company will deal with third parties on behalf of the group and distribute all its profits to the individual members' companies. The particular functions carried out by the central company will vary from group to group.

In the case of casual and less well established groups, the Inland Revenue normally accept that each member of the group is a self-employed individual for the sake of expediency, and to avoid the complications of the partnership cessation rules.

For practical accounting purposes the group is treated as a joint venture. Thus income and expenditure of the joint activity are recorded and annual joint venture statements are prepared. Profits or losses are allocated to each member. Each member maintains his/her own self-employed records (comprising a share from the joint venture plus, in some cases, other composing or performing work) which are the basis of his/her own annual accounts submitted to the Inland Revenue.

'Angels'

95 Associated with the income of entertainers is the system of theatre backers or 'angels'. If the backer is given some say in the production, he may be trading. For example, a performer who puts up money to save a show should have any profit or loss treated as arising in the course of his profession. This should apply equally to outgoings, as in the case of Lunt *v*. Wellesley (27 TC 78), where a film writer assessed under Case II guaranteed loans to a film company which was filming a novel in which he held the film rights. Payments made under that guarantee were allowed as a deduction in computing his profits. Otherwise, the performer is normally treated as recovering his investment up to the amount put in, and any excess is assessed under Sch. D Case VI. Any shortfall is treated as a Sch. D Case VI loss available to set against other Sch. D Case VI income of the same or following years. Some expenses might be allowed in arriving at the profit, including expenses such as stationery and postage, but not interest paid on borrowings incurred for the investment. There is an option to use the practice prevailing up to 1972 of being assessed on any profit under Sch. D Case III, with a loss being an allowable loss for capital gains tax purposes. However, whichever treatment is adopted, it must be applied consistently.

Pensions and retirement

96 In the case of pop singers who are employed by a company, the Pension Schemes Office will sometimes allow a pension scheme to be set up to give them a pension, at age 40, of 15/60 of their final earnings, subject to the earnings cap, etc. The Finance Act 1983 contained provisions giving the Inland Revenue power to approve similar retirement annuity contracts for individuals who, because of the exceptional nature of their work, are likely to retire early (for instance pop stars and professional sportsmen and sportswomen). This brings the law and practice for retirement annuities into line with that for equivalent occupational pension schemes.

The following is a list of agreed early retirement ages for entertainers:

Profession	Retirement age
Brass instrumentalists	55
Dancers	35
Singers	55
Trapeze artists	40
Circus animal trainers	50

However, it should be noted that the new personal pension rules in s.634(3) ICTA 1988 provide for a lower retirement age of 50, whatever the occupation. An even lower retirement age for particular occupations is still possible under the new rules.

Musicians – sale of instruments

97 Taxation on the proceeds of sale of valuable musical instruments can pose problems for musicians (see **81** above). Generally, capital gains tax roll-over relief is accepted as applying on replacement although, strictly, instruments are not within the class of assets eligible for such relief, as they are not 'fixed' plant or machinery. Also, the Inland Revenue do not usually argue that the replacement is a wasting asset, so that full roll-over relief and not just hold-over relief is available. Retirement relief should also be due, provided that the normal conditions for the relief are met.

TR 796: Taxation of theatrical performers/artists

98   Guidance note issued by the ICAEW in June 1990 regarding the taxation of theatrical performers/artists from 6 April 1990.

Introduction

1 Following the decision by the Inland Revenue that PAYE should be applied in respect of theatrical performers/artists working under standard Equity contracts, a meeting was held in March 1990 between representatives of the Inland Revenue and the Institute of Chartered Accountants in England and Wales to clarify a number of detailed points arising from the implementation of that decision.
2 This note explains the background and summarises the Revenue's replies to a number of matters raised by the Institute.
3 The main source of advice for employers is the Employer's Guide to PAYE which explains how to operate the PAYE system and gives detailed advice on a large number of particular circumstances. Inland Revenue tax offices have already received guidance on all aspects of the changes, and copies of this note will be sent to them. They will be happy to discuss any particular points with accountants, theatrical employers or individual performers/artists.
4 Advice on social security contributions is contained in the Department of Social Security's Employer's Manual on national insurance contributions (NI 269). Further detailed advice can be obtained from DSS offices.

Background

5 The background to this note is the Inland Revenue's view, which has been discussed with representative bodies from both sides of the theatrical industry, that performers/artists working under standard Equity contracts are (with the exception of guest artists engaged by opera companies) normally engaged under contracts of employment. Theatrical employers should therefore operate PAYE from 6 April 1990 against the earnings of any performer/artist engaged under such contracts (or any other which is in law a contract of employment). This will bring the income tax treatment into line with the position for national insurance contributions purposes since theatrical employers have generally already been deducting and paying Class 1 (employed) contributions.

6 For certain established performers, including stage managers, who have in the past been assessed as self-employed under Schedule D, theatrical employers will be authorised by their tax office to operate a no tax (NT) code. These performers will continue to be treated as if they were self-employed (referred to as 'reserved Schedule D status'). The notes accompanying the attached questionnaire which Equity sent in January to all its members explain how this treatment can be claimed by those qualifying.

How will the schedule D cessation be applied to those not qualifying for 'reserved Schedule D status' including those who entered the industry after 5 April 1987?

7 As there will not, in fact, be any change in the work being done, it would not be appropriate to apply the cessation provisions of TA 1988 s.63. It follows that the Schedule D assessment for 1989/90 will normally be based on the profits for the 12 month accounting period ended in 1988/89. But those who entered the industry after 5 April 1987 can elect under TA 1988 s.62 for the 'current year basis' so that their profits for each of the tax years up to 5 April 1990 will be assessed for the years in which they were earned.

8 Where there is no continuing Schedule D source after 5 April 1990, and profits have been assessed on the usual preceding year basis, no adjustment to the 1989/90 assessment will be needed. Profits from the accounting date in 1988/89 to 5 April 1990 will fall out of charge. As regards capital allowances, where qualifying expenditure is incurred in the period which will fall out of charge for Schedule D purposes, writing down allowances will be added to the capital allowances due in the 1989/90 Schedule D assessment. Similarly, where an asset on which capital allowances have been given is disposed of in the period which will fall out of charge, the appropriate balancing allowance will be given or a balancing charge made in the 1989/90 Schedule D assessment. Where, however, an election under TA 1988 s.62 covers 1989/90 all profits up to 5 April 1990 will be assessed on the current year basis. The capital allowances basis periods will follow those for income tax in these cases.

9 Where 'reserved Schedule D status' is not appropriate but there will still be income from the profession assessable under Schedule D for 1990/91 onwards, accounts and computations will be needed in the normal way. For many cases the new simplified profit statement announced in the Inland Revenue press release of 7 November 1989 will be all that is required. Where the accounts for periods up to 5 April 1990 will form the basis period for the 1990/91 Schedule D assessment – all cases except those where a claim under TA 1988 s.62 covers 1990/91 – the Schedule E income and expenses should be separately identified. These should then be excluded from the Case II computation so that the assessment for 1990/91 will include only profits properly attributable to Schedule D sources. Accounts which

form the basis period for 1991/92 and subsequent years should include only Schedule D income and expenses.

What should accountants/performers/theatrical employers do to ensure the smooth operation of PAYE where a performer has several engagements during a year?

10 Performers who think they are eligible for 'reserved Schedule D status' should, if they have not already done so, contact their tax office as soon as possible, preferably sending the details requested on the questionnaire (see para 6). The Revenue will be periodically updating the list of performers qualifying for 'reserved Schedule D status' which PAYE tax offices use to authorise the issue of code 'NT' to employers.

11 Theatrical employers should have received during January a letter from their tax office telling them to operate the normal PAYE procedures for all performers engaged under standard contracts, and any other contracts of employment.

12 It is important that forms P45 are issued promptly at the end of an engagement. When the performer hands this (or the replacement form P45(U) from the Benefit Office) to his next theatrical employer the code shown – 'NT' (no tax) if reserved schedule D status applies – can usually be operated straight away against the earnings from that engagement (as instructed in the Employer's Guide to PAYE para D42).

13 If the theatrical employer does not receive a P45 from a new employee – where for instance a performer holds two engagements at the same time eg., rehearsing for a future production whilst performing in a current show – it should send form P46 to its tax office as soon as possible. Theatrical employers may want to make arrangements with their tax office so that those employees who are entitled to 'reserved Schedule D status' can be specially identified and codes NT authorised quickly where appropriate.

14 The list of performers qualifying for 'reserved schedule D status' is updated periodically, but some time will inevitably elapse between the claim being accepted and the name appearing on the list. In such cases the theatrical employer's tax office may need to make enquiries direct to the tax office to which the claim was made before they can authorise code NT. Where such a claim has only recently been made this process will be speeded if information on where the claim was made including the tax office reference is given when the form P46 is sent in.

15 As part of the usual PAYE procedures employers issue forms P15 (coding claims) to new employees who do not produce form P45, for them to complete and send to the tax office. This will assist in establishing the correct PAYE code number if the performer is for any reason not on the Revenue's 'reserved Schedule D status' list. Where performers are confident that their names have already been included on the Revenue's

list – for instance where they have quickly received 'NT' codes for previous engagements – they may decide it is not worth completing form P15.

What travelling and subsistence expenses are allowable under Schedule E?

16 Under the Schedule E expenses rules only those expenses which are necessarily incurred 'travelling in the performance of the duties' of an employment or are otherwise incurred 'wholly, exclusively and necessarily' in its performance are allowable. Whether particular travelling and subsistence expenses are allowable depends on the facts of each case.

17 Where an actor is engaged to perform at a theatre, that theatre is usually his normal place of work and any payments for travelling between there and his permanent or temporary home, and any subsistence expenses payable while at the theatre or staying nearby are taxable. A 'temporary home' would include, for example, a hotel, guest house or rented rooms.

18 Generally, where an actor travels to a number of different theatres at each of which he performs for a few days, weeks or months – or between two theatres where he holds separate engagements at the same time – travelling and subsistence expenses are also taxable. Some particular exceptions to this rule are given in paras 19–21.

19 Some actors may occasionally hold a 'travelling' appointment where under one contract of employment they spend very short periods at a large number of different places – for instance, someone working for schools theatre giving short performances at different schools morning and afternoon. Travelling and subsistence expenses where necessarily incurred in the performance of those duties are not taxable.

Expenses whilst touring

20 Where actors work temporarily away from their normal place of work – eg., touring away from a permanent base theatre, venue or other normal place of work – the Employers Guide to PAYE para F62 details the circumstances in which the provision of transport and lodging expenses is not taxable. For example, where an actor who is normally a resident member of a theatre based in one place is required by his employer to work temporarily elsewhere, and expects to return to work in the same employment at the employer's base at the end of the tour, his normal place of work remains at the employer's base. The venues at which he performs whilst on tour do not become the normal place of work. Travel and subsistence expenses would not therefore be taxable. But an actor engaged especially for a touring production starting with a few weeks' rehearsals followed by a tour of say a week at each of four or five cities, who does not normally work for the company at a particular place, would not be regarded as being temporarily absent from his normal place of work. Each theatre at which he performs

would be the normal place of work for the period of the performance. So travelling and lodging expenses paid in respect of the rehearsals and tour would be taxable (see paras 17 and 18). Advice on particular situations should be sought from the tax office.

21 Actors may be engaged for a series of performances in one town with rehearsals, or a short trial run, taking place in another. If the theatre where the main performances are to be staged will be the normal place of work for that engagement, reimbursement of the extra expense incurred in attending rehearsals or a trail run elsewhere would not be taxable (see penultimate paragraph of F62 of the Employers Guide to PAYE). An example of this might be where, after two or three weeks of rehearsal in one place, a play is scheduled to run for the summer season somewhere else. But as the position may not always be so clearcut, it is advisable to contact the tax office for guidance based on the particular facts of the engagement.

Treatment by employer

22 Where travelling and subsistence payments are taxable, as for example in the situations outlined in paras 17 and 18, employers should include the payments in taxable pay and apply PAYE (see the Employers Guide to PAYE para F62).

23 Examples of items commonly paid under standard agreements negotiated between Equity and theatre management associations which would normally be taxable under PAYE include:

(a) The payment of fares between the performer's home address and the theatre where he is working, at the beginning and end of the engagement;

(b) Subsistence allowances – or the payment of fares to and from the theatre – paid because of the distance between the theatre and the performer's permanent address;

(c) The payment of the cost of returning home from the theatre when local public transport is unavailable.

24 If the performer has authorised the theatrical employer to pay part of his salary to his agent, PAYE should be operated on the gross salary and the commission paid out of net pay after deduction of tax.

25 Where employers reimburse expenses which are not taxable, for example in the situations in paras 19 and 20, they should not be included in taxable pay (see Employers Guide to PAYE para F81).

26 Round-sum allowances should normally be included in taxable pay. But where they are paid at a scale rate intended to do no more than reimburse actual expenditure which would be allowable, the tax office may be able to give authority for some or all of the allowance to be paid without deducting tax (see the Employers Guide to PAYE para F69).

Completion of forms P11D

27 Benefits in kind – such as travel tickets or the use of a car – are normally taxable though not within the scope of PAYE. Details should be returned to the tax office on forms P11D at the end of the tax year.

28 Employers need to show details of expenses and benefits on form P11D for each employee who earns at a rate of £8,500 or more in a year, including *all* expenses payments and benefits. This means anyone who would earn £8,500 or more if he worked at the same rate of pay for a complete year. Paragraphs C36 and E57 of the Employers Guide to PAYE explain how to work out the £8,500 limit, and what to include on the form. Most performers working under standard Equity rates are above this limit but where this is not the case there is a different form (P9D) for employees earning at a rate of less than £8,500 a year – see the Employers Guide to PAYE para C36.

29 Various benefits and expenses available in theatres need to be shown on form P11D such as all round sum allowances, and travel vouchers, including season tickets. In the case of free theatre tickets provided for employees, theatrical employers should return the cost rather than the face value. Their tax office will be able to agree what should be taken as cost for this purpose, and will give guidance if necessary on other benefits.

30 The Inspector of Taxes can also give 'dispensations' so that employers need not report certain expenses on form P11D. Dispensations can only be given for expenses which are not taxable. The Employers Guide to PAYE para F68 explains how to apply.

Does the change from April 1990 affect only performers engaged by theatrical employers under standard contracts? What is the position of other performers and non-performers?

31 The Revenue, having looked at all the circumstances surrounding the standard Equity contracts, has concluded that generally theatrical performers working under them are employees. The change from 6 April 1990 is therefore particularly directed at such performers. The employment status of performers not engaged under standard Equity contracts by theatres and other venues depends on the particular facts of the case. The Employers Guide to PAYE para. A2 tells anyone who has doubts about the status of someone working for him to ask the Tax Office for advice. Each Tax Office has a nominated inspector who is responsible for all enquiries and decisions about employment status.

32 The industry also uses standard agreements for the engagement of non-performers. The Revenue has looked at some of these and concluded that some are normally contracts for services (self-employed) and others contracts of service (employed). As a guide, non-performers engaged for specific productions under the industry's standard contracts listed below are normally regarded as self-employed (Schedule D):

Nature of engagement	Contracts negotiated between	Area of engagement
Choreographers	TMA/Equity	Subsidised repertory and commercial theatre
Designers (not assistant designers)	TMA/BETA/Equity	Theatre designers engaged for individual productions (not repertory)
	SWET/Equity	Theatre designers engaged for individual productions in West End
Directors (not assistant directors)	SWET/Equity	West End theatre (not assistants)
	TMA/Equity	Individual productions in subsidised repertory and theatre in education. Individual productions for No 1 and 2 tours and seasons and commercial repertory

33 But the following are normally contracts of employment to which PAYE applies:

Nature of engagement	Contracts negotiated between	Area of engagement
Designers including head of design	TMA/BETA/Equity	Repertory
Designer resident/ associate assistant designer	SWET/Equity	West End theatre
Directors	TMA/Equity	1 Subsidised repertory and theatre in education 2 No 1 and 2 tours or seasons and commercial repertory
Assistant directors	SWET/Equity	West End theatre
	TMA/Equity	1 Subsidised repertory and theatre in education 2 Provincial theatre engagements

34 These lists are not comprehensive. If there is doubt about the status of non-performers engaged under other contracts, the advice of the Tax Office should be sought as suggested in para. 31 above.

Figure 3.1

Taxation of Theatrical Performers/Artists

1 General Information

o Full name

o Stage name (if different)

o Address for correspondence

o National Insurance Number

o Tax Office and Reference to
your returns are sent

2 Can you answer "Yes" to all of the questions below? If you can, then you may qualify for assessment under Schedule D in respect of your income as a theatrical performer/artist.

	Yes	No
o Was your first engagement as a professional performer/artist on or before 5 April 1987?	☐	☐

Note An engagement as a teacher, examiner, model or demonstrator does not count.

	Yes	No
o Have you sent any accounts or returns of income to the Inland Revenue in respect of your income as a professional performer/artist?	☐	☐
o Did you send some or all those accounts or returns of income on or before 31 May 1989?	☐	☐
o Have you been essessed to tax under Schedule D in respect of income as a performer/artist for all of the years 1986–97, 1987–88 and 1988–89?	☐	☐
o Was at least one of those assessments based on your accounts or returns of income?	☐	☐

3 If you cannot answer "Yes" to all the questions you may still be entitled to assessment under Schedule D if

o you have been assessed as a performer/artist under Schedule D in at least 3 out of the ten years covered by the period 1979–80 to 1988–89

o you are not currently being taxed under Schedule E on your income as a performer/artist

o you have sent in accounts or returns of income for all years prior to 1986–87 on or before 31 May 1989

If you think you may qualify on this basis please use the space below to set out details of the assessment references for the relevant years. Your present tax office may need to refer to your previous tax offices and will be able to do so more quickly if you can supply this information. If you do not have this information your accountant may have it. If neither of you have details of the assessments you should tell your current tax office where you were living in each of the relevant tax years to enable him to check your claim.

Signed .... Date ....

When completed please send this form to the tax office to which you send your accounts and income tax returns

There is a special form which Theatrical Performers/Artists have been asked to complete which is reproduced in Fig. 3.1. The notes to the form open in the following fashion. 'Generally performer/artistes undertaking theatrical engagements under standard contracts are, in law, employees. (In this note, "standard contracts" mean contracts on terms agreed between Equity and theatrical employers.) Schedule E is therefore the correct schedule of charge for income tax.'

Conditions for reserved Schedule D status

(1) You will be accepted as qualifying for reserved Schedule D status where:

   (a) Schedule D assessments have been made on you in respect of income from engagements as a professional performer/artiste for at least the past three tax years, ie., 1986–87, 1987–88, and 1988–89. No account will be taken of years later than 1988–89.

   (b) If, exceptionally, you have not been assessed under Schedule D for each of the three years 1986–87, 1987–88 and 1988–89 (because, for example, you have been working abroad as a professional performer/ artiste) but nevertheless have a satisfactory history of Schedule D treatment, condition (a) will be regarded as having been satisfied if you have been assessed as a performer/artiste under Schedule D in at least three of the past ten tax years (ie., 1979–80 to 1988–89). This does not apply if you are currently being taxed under Schedule E on your income as a performer/artiste;

   (c) Assessment for at least one of the past three years of assessment in condition (a) above must be based on accounts or a return of income for that year, submitted before 31 May 1989. If the exceptional circumstances in paragraph (b) apply accounts or returns of income for all relevant years prior to 1986–87 must have been submitted before 31 May 1989.

It follows from these conditions that if you started in the profession after 5 April 1987 you will not qualify after 5 April 1990 for the continuation of Schedule D treatment for income received from engagements under standard contracts.

(2) If you qualify for Schedule D treatment under paragraph (1) you will only be assessed under Schedule D so long as you continue to meet your tax obligations satisfactorily, and continue your professional activities without a break. A break means a cessation agreed under the Schedule D rules between the Inland Revenue and the performer/artiste (which would include you retiring or abandoning your United Kingdom profession as a performer/artiste, but which would not include periods of unemployment or temporary non-theatrical engagements). Schedule E treatment will apply if at a later date you resume professional activities in the United Kingdom.

57

Entertainers

(3) These arrangements apply only to income you receive from engagements as a performer. Engagements as a teacher, examiner, model or demonstrator will be taxed under the correct Schedule (generally Schedule E).

Chapter 4
Stockbrokers and market makers

Rules of the Stock Exchange

99 There are a number of rules laid down by the Stock Exchange governing the constitution of firms and the way members can carry on business. Certain of these rules are relevant in considering the taxation treatment of stockbrokers and market makers.

100 It is now possible for a limited company to trade as a market maker or broker. Where the company is limited, a solvency margin is required. The company may carry out business like a firm as a sole corporate trader or, if it is unlimited, in partnership with individuals.

It is also possible for a partnership to use a company as a service company.

Incorporation

101 It is of course now possible, following the "Big Bang", for a stockbroker and market maker to be wholly owned by a financial institution, and most have been taken over and their functions amalgamated into one securities dealing concern. Prior to takeover, the firm will be incorporated. Depending upon the circumstances, capital gains tax relief will be claimed on the incorporation, particularly in respect of chargeable gains accruing on the goodwill of the firm. The provisions of ss.162 or 165 TCGA 1992 give the necessary relief.

S.162 gives the company a base value equal to the current market value of the assets acquired, and utilises capital gains tax indexation relief in arriving at the frozen gain realised on the sale of the shares. Section 165 may be appropriate when not all of the assets of the business are being transferred, although in this connection if the whole trade has not been transferred to the company an election under s.77 CAA 1990 (transfer of plant and machinery at tax written down value) may not be accepted. The effect of s.165 is that by first incorporating the company with a small capital subscribed for in cash by the partners, the base value of goodwill in the company will be relatively low. The base cost of shares in the company will also be negligible. There will, however, be stamp duty savings as against the other method.

Golden handcuffs

102 Arrangements for the sale of the company's shares typically involve the use of 'golden handcuffs', deferred consideration under which part of the payment was deferred and was dependent on the principal serving a minimum number of years as a director of the company. The consideration was usually given in the form of deferred loan stock redeemable at the end of the period. Provided this consideration clearly refers to it relating wholly to the individual's share of goodwill of the firm, it is not thought it could be taxed as remuneration under Schedule E or under s.775 ICTA 1988 (capital sums derived from the earning power of an individual).

However, ordinary 'golden hello' payments offered to individuals to join such financial services companies stand little chance of being taxed as anything other than Sch. E income as no asset is being given up such as the loss of a right to practice at the Bar or as a chartered accountant or the loss of amateur status (as in the cases of Vaughan Neil *v*. CIR, Pritchard *v*. Arundale and Jarrold *v*. Boustead).

Period of accounts

103 Firms sometimes draw up accounts to end on the same Stock Exchange account each year rather than on the same day. This day may vary by as much as a fortnight from one year to the next, but, in practice, the accounts are treated as the profits of one year for taxation purposes (including ranking as an accounting period for corporation tax purposes), except that, when apportioning such profits in the opening or closing years of an unincorporated business, the actual period of trading is considered.

'Bear and bull excesses'

104 Sometimes it is necessary for a market maker to 'manufacture' a dividend if he has insufficient dividends from sellers of stock to pass on to purchasers of stock who have bought cum dividend. This can happen, bearing in mind that he may find he has to buy stock which has gone ex dividend to satisfy previous purchases cum dividend. This is termed a 'bear excess'.

The rules of the Stock Exchange stipulate that he should, in those circumstances, make 'a payment in lieu of a dividend' and this is regarded as income of the recipient for tax purposes. To guard against loss of tax to the Inland Revenue because no income tax or ACT will have been accounted for in such circumstances, he is regarded as making an annual payment on which income tax would be accounted for under s.348 or s.349 ICTA 1988 and which is deductible against total income (s.737 ICTA 1988).

The reverse position, namely where he receives more dividends than he has to account for, is referred to as a 'bull excess'. It is considered that such income should form part of his trading income which has already borne tax at the basic rate.

105 The position of corporate market makers is slightly more complex in relation to these transactions because of the need to segregate franked and unfranked investment income and formerly because of the close company apportionment rules. The practice, however, is as follows:

(1) The bull or bear excess for an accounting period should be ascertained separately in respect of unfranked and franked investment income.

(2) For the purpose of Schedules 13 and 16, ICTA 1988, and of taking into account the relevant income tax, tax credit or ACT attributable to dividend excesses, a bull or bear dividend excess is deemed to arise on the last day of an accounting period and should be included only in the final return on form CT61 relating to that period.

(3) The gross amount of an unfranked bull excess is regarded as unfranked investment income in the normal way and credit for the income tax suffered allowed as a credit against the corporation tax for the accounting period (s.7(2) ICTA 1988).

(4) The gross amount of an unfranked bear excess is treated as a charge and allowed as a deduction from total profits (s.338 ICTA 1988). The amount of income tax appropriate to the excess is payable under Sch. 16 ICTA 1988.

(5) A franked bull excess plus the tax credit attributable thereto is treated as franked investment income and excluded from the CT computation and is available for deduction from franked payments in arriving at the ACT payable in respect of qualifying distributions.

(6) A franked bear excess is regarded as a qualifying distribution in respect of which no deduction is allowable for CT purposes and in respect of which ACT is payable.

(7) In the case of a close company a gross unfranked bear excess and a 'net' franked bear excess were regarded as reducing primarily estate or trading income for apportionment purposes. This is now of course no longer relevant.

(8) Bull and bear dividends consistently brought into accounting periods by reference to ex-dividend dates falling within those periods are regarded as arising in the respective periods even though some dividend payment dates may fall into a different period, ie., the bull and bear excesses shown in the accounts are accepted as the amounts to be taken into account in the CT61 relating to the return period ending on the last day of the accounting period.

106 Market makers sometimes have contracted to sell more stock than they can purchase by normal delivery date. In practice, the stock is delivered late to the buying broker but, if the sale is made before the end of their accounts and the purchase is made after, they could be taxed on a gross sum without a deduction for the liability to purchase the stock. In the circumstances, an adjustment is made to the accounts by creating a liability or reducing their stocks.

There are now often in addition complex arrangements between financial concerns, for instance for the borrowing and lending of securities (as to the tax treatment of which see below) satisfying a particular demand by one market maker for securities he does not have, and for passing dividends and interest through the market because several transactions take place in securities purchased cum dividend. It has therefore been decided to extend and clarify the provisions on manufactured dividends and interest (now in s.737 ICTA 1988) to cover such complexities. Inter alia, the provisions distinguish the position of a non-UK company market maker from a UK company market maker. They provide for a specific legal framework for the UK company marker as opposed to the practice described above in relation to such manufactured UK dividends and interest in relation to withholding tax on overseas manufactured dividends. The latter would arise in respect of overseas dividends and interest such as on a quoted Eurobond that would normally have been paid through a UK paying agent to a UK resident person (the latter provisions will be further covered in detailed regulations).

This legislation is to be found in s.736A and Sch. 23A ICTA 1988 and was introduced by s.58 FA 1991, which also provided for regulations to bring the legislation into force and to cater for the varied circumstances of particular market makers. Broadly, manufactured dividends and interest will continue to be treated in the same way as their real counterparts as far as accounting for tax on them is concerned. There have also been technical amendments to cater for the position of such manufactured payments in relation to all the various concerns, including non-residents, which are now involved in securities dealing on the Stock Exchange.

The Treasury made the necessary regulations on 9 March 1992 (SI 1992/569) for dividends and on 9 June 1992 for interest (SI 1992/134) and the new rules apply for quarterly return periods ending on or after 22 March 1992 for dividends and from 30 June 1992 for interest.

The regulations introduce some new arrangements for accounting for tax on manufactured dividends on UK equities paid or payable on or after 25 February 1992. These include:

- administrative arrangements for accounting for tax on manufactured dividends;
- arrangements to remove certain disadvantages which UK branches of non-resident companies which are Stock Exchange market makers or LIFFE members would otherwise suffer compared with UK resident companies in the same position;
- provisions ensuring that the tax treatment of manufactured dividends paid by LIFFE members in the ordinary course of their business will not be disadvantageous.

Further regulations will be needed for manufactured overseas dividends.

Returns

107 There are provisions enabling the Board to obtain information from market makers concerning transactions giving rise to such excesses of payments of interest and dividends over receipts in respect of interest and dividends, where the excesses are treated as annual payments by the market maker. The Board may serve a notice requiring the market maker to make available such books, accounts and other documents in his possession or power as are specified in the notice, for the purpose of obtaining details of the beneficial owners of the income in question (s.21(2) TMA 1970).

The Board may also serve a notice on a broker requiring similar information from him (s.21(3) TMA 1970). The broker's records may give more information than the market maker's on such dealings with market makers on behalf of their clients. Similarly where persons, acting on behalf of others, who are not brokers, have received income from or paid income to market makers, for instance, have sold cum dividend and have passed on income to a market maker, or have bought cum dividend and received the income from a market maker, they may be required to give details of the person on behalf of whom they are acting (s.21(4) TMA 1970).

The Board may not exercise their powers under s.21 TMA 1970 in relation to transactions in any year of assessment ending more than six years before the service of the notice. There are penalties for default in complying with such a notice (s.98 TMA 1970).

Dividend income and profits and losses on sales of securities

108 Where the proceeds of sale of any investments are taken into account in computing profits or gains of a trade, the income from those investments was not investment income for investment income surcharge purposes. A similar provision operated for a close company. However, in the case of stockbrokers and market makers, the Inland Revenue have resisted Case I treatment for profits and losses on sales of securities and therefore the treatment of dividend income as earned income except in the following situations:

(1) Where a market maker buys and sells in his own market, that is the shares in which the market maker specialises. Any dealings outside his own market are treated as private transactions falling under the capital gains provisions.

(2) In the case of a broker, where the dealings are directly connected with his business as a broker, for instance arbitrage transactions consisting of the purchase of shares in one market and selling them at a higher price in another market where the broker acts as a principal on his own account.

(3) Again, if a broker underwrites an issue of shares, or there is an error in carrying out clients' instructions, he may hold stock on his own account arising out of his business as a broker.

The case the Inland Revenue rely on is Bucks *v*. Bowers (46 TC 267) concerning a partner in a merchant bank who attempted to claim earned income relief on investment income arising from securities in which dealings took place by the partnership. It was decided that the income from the securities was not 'immediately derived from the carrying on of a trade' and thus not earned income (s.833(4)(c) ICTA 1988).

The point appears now only to be relevant in relation to what are net relevant earnings for retirement annuity and personal pension purposes (s.623(2) and 644(2) ICTA 1988).

Borrowing and lending securities

109 Sometimes market makers borrow from and lend securities to another market maker who is short of stock or to create an active market and the debt is repaid with securities of the same kind. Similarly, they may enter into stock lending arrangements whereby they acquire the necessary stock from institutional holders on terms which require them to return equivalent securities later. Where such borrowing and lending takes place in circumstances where the lending market maker parts with the legal interest in the securities and is subsequently repaid in other securities of the same kind, an occasion of charge strictly arises under Case I of Schedule D or under the capital gains provisions depending upon the circumstances on the criteria mentioned above.

By concession, however, such borrowing and lending was not treated as a disposal for tax purposes where it took place in conformity with standard practices designed to preserve a fluid market in securities and in satisfaction of bargains, under agreements entered into between the Inland Revenue and the Stock Exchange Council. Where, in due course, there was a normal disposal of the securities by the lender, the original cost of the security to the lender was the figure taken into account for tax purposes (ESC B15).

Such arrangements are now encompassed in detailed regulations (Income Tax SI 1989 no. 129 (Stock Lending) Regulations 1989) in exercise of powers conferred on the Treasury by s.129 ICTA 1988. Under s.129, such arrangements do not amount to a disposal in the course of any security dealing trade provided they are approved by the Inland Revenue. Similarly, where capital gains tax treatment is in point, there is also no disposal (s.271(9) TCGA 1992).

The accrued income scheme equally does not apply to loans of stock within this section (s.727(1) ICTA 1988).

Already, however, it has been necessary to extend the regulations by Extra Statutory Concession (Press Release 6 November 1990). S.129 imposes strictly two conditions: first, that the borrower undertakes to return to the lender securities of the same kind and amount as those lent. Second, that the loan is made to enable the borrower to fulfil a contract to sell securities.

The first Extra Statutory Concession allows arrangements to be approved where a loan of gilt edged securities falls due for redemption and instead of stock being retained on payment of the loan, the appropriate sum of cash is paid to the lender provided the lender accepts that, for the purposes of computing his liability to tax, he will be treated as having disposed of the securities on their redemption date.

The second Extra Statutory Concession allows, subject to certain conditions, arrangements to be approved where a stock loan is made from another lender to enable a borrower to have replaced an existing stock loan rather than to meet a sale (for instance, because the original lender may call for the return of the securities before the borrower wishes or is able to do so).

Finally, and in addition, there is a further enactment in s.57 FA 1991, with associated regulations, to accommodate a chain of arrangements between lenders and borrowers governing the lending of overseas securities. They will enable a lending chain of more than three parties without a tax charge arising on the resulting disposals.

Manufactured dividends are paid to compensate recipients for real dividends or interest they do not receive on securities which also occurs where the recipient has lent the securities. The regulations made on 9 March 1992 also cover manufactured dividends where securities are lent.

Market maker's position on purchase of own shares by company

110 There are now also special rules involving market makers where a quoted company purchases its own shares in the market. The individual shareholder, who may not be aware that the company is purchasing his shares, sells them to the market maker and qualifies for capital gains tax treatment. The market maker, when he sells them to the company, pays tax on the difference between the price he paid and what he actually receives from the company. Although the company has to pay ACT on the distribution element in the purchase price, normally the difference between the amount originally subscribed and the sale price, the market maker receives no tax credit on this element of the price paid (s.95 ICTA 1988). A market purchase by the quoted company through a market maker, as opposed to an off-market purchase, thus enables the investor to obtain capital gains tax treatment whilst leaving the market maker in a neutral position on the transaction.

Interest received

111 It is understood that the treatment of interest is more liberal in practice than that of dividend income. Interest debited or credited to a client's account is treated as part of the Case II profits and overnight interest on the investment of purely temporary surpluses of working capital is equally left in the Case II computation but interest arising in other circumstances is treated as investment income. This treatment was reinforced by the case of Northend *v.* White & Leonard & Corbin Greener (1975 STC 317; 50 TC 121) which has confirmed that interest on moneys held on client accounts by solicitors is assessable under Case III.

Interest paid

112 Any interest paid to a member of the Stock Exchange may be allowed to the borrower, if he satisifies the various rules for eligibility for tax relief for individuals (s.353 ICTA 1988).

This applies whether the interest can be regarded as annual interest, that is broadly because the loan has some degree of permanence and is capable of exceeding a year, or it is short interest.

Similarly, companies may obtain relief for such interest as a charge on income where it cannot be regarded as a trading expense, for instance, where it is paid by an investment company or is paid by a trading company on a loan used to acquire an investment (s.338(3)(b) ICTA 1988).

Unclaimed dividends

113 Unclaimed dividends sometimes arise to brokers, for instance where a buyer's broker fails to claim the amount on a purchase cum dividend. These receipts are not income of the broker as he holds them as trustee on the basis of the principle in the case of Morley *v*. Tattersall (22 TC 51).

Stock Exchange attachés and clerks

114 These are persons who are attached to a single firm and may be full members of the Stock Exchange, but are not partners in a firm or directors of a company. They introduce clients to firms and are paid a proportion of the stockbroker's commission. They used to be called 'half-commission' men because at one time brokers can pay them half of the commission. They are usually responsible for a proportion of the bad debts of any clients they introduce depending upon the proportion of the commission they receive. The same rules apply for treating their income from investments as earned income as for stockbrokers. If they are assessed under Schedule E, losses exceeding their remuneration cannot be allowed under the normal Schedule E expenses rules and where the person is an office holder, as opposed to just an employee, they are not strictly allowable under s.380 ICTA 1988 either. However, in practice, where bad debts exceeding their remuneration arise, through defaults of clients, they are allowed in all cases under s.380; but in Schedule E cases, such losses cannot be carried forward under s.385 ICTA 1988.

115 The relationship of the attaché with the particular firm will determine whether he is assessable under Sch. E or Sch. D; for instance, whether he is supplied with office accommodation and required to attend regularly at the office. If so, he will be assessable under Sch. E. Clerks are nearly always assessed under Sch. E; the few who are assessed under Sch. D are likely to be members acting as authorised clerks who carry out transactions on behalf of and in the names of their principals.

Expenses of members of the Stock Exchange

116 There are certain specific expenses which are peculiar to members of the Stock Exchange.

(1) Subscription
    A member's entrance fee is not allowable but the annual subscription is.
(2) Stock Exchange Compensation Fund
    Contributions to this fund are allowable in full. Receipts from this fund in respect of securities disposed of by a hammered broker and not accounted for, are subject to capital gains tax.
(3) Stock Exchange Benevolent Fund
    Contributions to the Benevolent Fund, which is to alleviate distress among ex-members of the Stock Exchange, are treated as donations and not allowed. Contributions to the Clerks' Benevolent Fund are allowed because they are for the benefit of employees.

Capital gains returns

117 For the purposes of obtaining particulars of chargeable gains, a stockbroker, but not a market maker, may be required to make a return giving particulars of transactions carried out by him in the course of his business during the period specified in the notice and in particular detailing the parties to the transactions, the number or amount of the shares concerned and the amount or value of the consideration (s.25 TMA 1970).

Anti-avoidance provisions

118 There are numerous anti-avoidance provisions in the Taxes Acts that relate to transactions in securities involving dealers in securities such as market makers. They are designed to take away any tax advantage arising from dealings in the securities. It is outside the scope of this book to discuss these provisions in detail, but in so far as they affect the potential tax liabilities of share dealers such as market makers, mention is made of the more important of them.

(1) The most wide ranging is s.703 et seq ICTA 1988. Circumstances A and B of s.704 are aimed at the share dealer. In particular s.704, Circumstance A, deals with the situation where, in connection with the purchase and sale of securities, a person receives an abnormal amount by way of dividend which is relieved in some way (for instance against losses).

   This covers 'dividend stripping', where a person buys shares to procure the payment of such a dividend so that he can then utilise the tax credit in one of the ways mentioned in the section to obtain a tax advantage. For instance, the effect of the company being stripped in this way may be to create a trading loss on the sale of the securities which might otherwise be set against the abnormal dividends received under s.242 ICTA 1988. Alternatively, there might be other losses which could be set against the abnormal dividend. This type of short term dealing transaction was considered in JP Harrison (Watford) Limited *v*. Griffiths (40 TC 281) and was recently reaffirmed in the Court of Appeal as creating in certain circumstances such a trading loss in Reed *v*. Nova Securities Limited (1985

STC 124) but not in Coates *v*. Arndale Properties Limited (1984 STC 637). Both of these cases concerned transactions turning a loss for capital gains purposes into a trading loss by appropriating an asset within a group to trading stock. In the former case, the trade was held to be a genuine one. There were, however, other cases decided which suggest that a loss which arises entirely from dividend stripping transactions which are carried out for fiscal motives, is simply not a trading loss at all for tax purposes. The main cases reaching this conclusion are Finsbury Securities Ltd *v*. Bishop (43 TC 591) and Lupton *v*. F A and A B Ltd (47 TC 580). It is, therefore, likely that a market maker who is engaged commercially in share dealing would be caught under the specific legislation in s.704 and any tax advantage would be nullified as he would be carrying on a genuine trade of share dealing.

Section 704, Circumstance B, also concerns *inter alia* a share dealer who seeks to relieve a loss produced by a fall in the value of securities which is caused by the payment of a dividend in respect of the securities. No relief is given whether the dividend is abnormal or not. This extends Circumstance A to cover any situation where there is such a connection between the payment of a dividend of any amount and the loss.

(2) There are provisions designed to prevent the obtaining of a tax advantage from 'bond-washing' in s.731 et seq. ICTA 1988. This occurs where there is an arrangement for the purchase of securities cum dividend and their sale ex dividend within a short period of time. The legislation refers to six months after which the legislation cannot bite or one month if it can be shown broadly there was no tax avoidance motive.

The one month rule also applies now where securities such as shares are bought or sold using options exercised within one month (s.55 FA 1991).

A tax repayment is then sought on the loss against the dividend or interest received. This trading loss would be computed in the case of a dealer in securities on the principle established in Wigmore *v*. Thomas Summerson & Sons Limited (9 TC 577) under which the cost of the securities includes any accrued interest element, thus giving rise to a trading loss to set against the interest. Such a loss is restricted in the case of ordinary dealers in securities by broadly the amount of accrued interest in the purchase price.

It should be noted that the accrued income scheme does not apply to dealers in securities if the disposal falls to be taken into account in computing their trading profits. Hence the legislation in s.731 is still potentially relevant to dealers in securities as the old case law applies to compute the trading loss in such circumstances.

However, market makers who are members of the Stock Exchange are specifically exempted from this legislation and are thus subject to no adjustment in respect of such dealings in securities, provided they are bought in the ordinary course of such business. As it is against the rules of the Stock Exchange to indulge in this sort of systematic bond washing, market makers should not in practice be affected by this legislation.

Similarly dealers in Eurobonds and managers of unit trust schemes are exempt from the legislation if they are acting in the ordinary course of their business and, following the passing of the Finance Act 1991 (s.56 FA 1991), regulations will be introduced exempting prescribed clearing houses or a member of a prescribed class or description of a prescribed recognised investment exchange if the subsequent sale is after the date to be prescribed and in the ordinary course of business. As anticipated, regulations were introduced on 9 March 1992 (SI 1992/569) extending the exemption from this legislation to principal traders as well as market makers on LIFFE, as this body will rely for its liquidity on a wider category of principal traders than just market makers. As with the stock lending reliefs, there are prescribed limitations to restrict the exemption to hedging transactions and transactions entered into as a result of the exercise of options. This will cover members of the new body set up to regulate traded options and futures contracts.

Special forms of investments

119   The tax treatment of certain types of specialised investments often dealt with by stockbrokers on their own account, has been the subject of legislation and agreement with the Inland Revenue recently. As they have been the subject of discussion between the Stock Exchange and the Inland Revenue, it is appropriate to comment on them here.

(1) Traded options

A traded option gives the right to buy or sell a particular share at a pre-established price over a given period. An option to buy a share is known as a 'call' option and one giving the right to sell a share is known as a 'put' option. A traded option can be bought and sold in the market, almost as if it were a share, so that if, for instance, an investor guesses wrong about the movement in the price of a share in which he buys a traded option, he can decide to cut his loss and sell rather than let the option lapse through time and thus lose the whole of the 'premium' or price paid for the option. The writer of the option is effectively the other side of the transaction in which an investor buys an option. The holder of some BP shares, for instance, might take the view they were more likely to fall than rise over the next seven months and would be quite happy to get 330p for them. If he 'writes' a BP 330p July call option at 11p premium, he gets an immediate 11p per share which he pockets. If he is right and the option expires worthless, that is the end of the matter. If he is wrong and the share price rises to the point where he is 'exercised', he sells the shares at 330p and thus obtains in total 341p for them.

It is possible for a person to cover his risks as an investor in traded options by reducing that risk by writing call options for premiums or fees.

The traded options market is part of the Stock Exchange and has 'market makers' much like the market in shares. These market makers are in fact normal market making firms which operate in shares as well and effectively create a market in the options by bringing together writers of options and investors.

Dealers in traded options on UK equities, whether or not they are market makers, may be faced with an obligation to deliver securities on which they have entered into options contracts. New regulations introduced on 9 March 1992 allow tax relief on stock borrowed by such dealers to hedge positions in options or to enable stock to be delivered on the exercise of an option. There are more restrictive limitations for non-market making principal traders (who can choose whether or not to deal in a particular option) than for market makers (who have to deal and who therefore require a more flexible regime). Nevertheless, the limitations in each case recognise the need to hedge, and to maintain a hedge against options positions.

Prior to the Finance Act 1980, only options to subscribe for shares were not treated as wasting assets, but following pressure from the Stock Exchange, similar treatment was afforded to traded options (s.146(1)(b) TCGA 1992). Therefore, if as is usual, the option is abandoned or sold, the full cost is allowable in computing a loss for capital gains tax purposes. If shares are acquired in pursuance of the option, the normal rules apply and the cost of the option and the shares are rolled into one and the option cost is treated as part of the larger transaction (s.144 TCGA 1992). There are, however, special rules to distinguish the cost of the option and the cost of the shares for indexation purposes so that the costs are treated for these purposes as incurred when they are payable as if they were separate assets (s.145 TCGA 1992).

The rules on the 'writing' of options, that is, selling such options to others, work in reverse to those for the acquirer of the option. The fee or premium for writing the option is simply liable to capital gains tax if the option lapses. If it is exercised and the underlying shares have to be sold at the option price, the whole operation is lumped together and the cost of the shares is compared with the sale proceeds of both the option and the shares in establishing the writer's tax position. Under the rules of the markets, a writer can extinguish the obligation with the purchaser to sell or buy the underlying security if the option is exercised, by buying back in other markets an option identical to the one he has written. If the person who has granted the traded option closes it out in this way by acquiring a traded option of the same description, the disposal involved in closing out the original option is to be disregarded for capital gains tax purposes. Any costs of acquiring the second option are added to any existing costs of the grantor for this purpose (s.148 TCGA 1992). The market maker includes his turn in his trading profits as it is a normal transaction in a specialised market so far as he is concerned.

Pension funds are exempt from capital gains tax on dealings in traded options as they are on futures contracts (s.659A(1) ICTA 1988 and s.271 TCGA 1992).

(2) The financial futures market

The London International Financial Futures Exchange (LIFFE) which opened on 30 September 1982 was set up by a group of bankers and brokers familiar with trading commodities for delivery at future dates. The London Exchange enables investors to buy and sell contracts for the future delivery of a range of currencies and fixed interest securities, such as bank deposit certificates (called Euro dollar or Sterling time deposits) or gilts or fixed interest securities, at a future date with the price agreed at the time of the deal. The market operates in a way similar to the Stock Exchange with standard contracts to buy and sell being traded. Some member firms of the Stock Exchange have shown interest in the market and acted for clients in respect of such futures transactions. The market has attracted the wealthy speculator although it has a stronger appeal for financial institutions and companies who wish to have a hedge against unexpected fluctuations in exchange and interest rates.

The traded options market and LIFFE have been merged to form one market outside the stock exchange on 23 March 1992.

Traded options and the financial futures market – CGT treatment

It is now specifically enacted that transactions in commodity or financial futures or traded options on a recognised exchange will be treated as capital in nature unless they are regarded as profits or losses of a trade (s.72 FA 1985) (now s.143 TCGA 1992). Section 81 FA (No2) 1987 extended this treatment to other transactions in futures and options. Case VI treatment, which derived from the old case law, can no longer apply to such transactions, and unless the hallmarks of trading are present as discussed in the case of Lewis Emanuel & Son Limited *v.* White (42 TC 369) capital gains tax treatment should apply. Most individuals will be taxed under the capital gains tax rules, as will the majority of companies, unless they are hedging a trading situation or have an existing financial trade or embark on the activity in a sufficiently organised way as to constitute trading. This matter is discussed in detail in a Statement of Practice SP 4/88. For capital gains tax purposes, contracts which do not run to delivery are regarded as unconditional contracts to acquire the underlying asset and are, therefore, subject to the normal rules of identification.

Where a contract runs to delivery, the tax treatment ignores the financial futures or options transactions and treats it as a method of buying or selling what is actually delivered. The LIFFE's gilt contracts enjoy exemption if the contract runs to delivery. Consequently, to ensure symmetry of tax treatment for futures and underlying cash markets, s.67 CGTA 1979 was amended by s.59 FA 1986 (now s.115 TCGA 1992) to exempt LIFFE's gilt futures and options contract from capital gains tax from 2 July 1986.

(3) The Unlisted Securities Market (USM)

The Unlisted Securities Market has become increasingly popular for companies which do not want a full quotation for their shares but require a market

71

for their shares. As it has a number of tax advantages for the investor, it is appropriate to mention them in this chapter.

The tax advantages must be weighed against the commercial disadvantage which can arise from the fact that because companies need only float off as little as 10% of their shares on the unlisted securities market, there are chronic shortages of stock which can lead to unrealistic ratings for particular shares.

Joining the USM has no impact on close company status so that investors can obtain tax relief on borrowings to purchase shares in a close company, some of whose shares are traded in the market, provided, of course, that the other conditions for such relief are satisfied.

IHT Business Property Relief is also available on the shares, whereas no relief is due on quoted shares.

An unquoted company whose shares are traded on the market can purchase its own shares and the shareholder may be able, if he fulfils the other conditions, to obtain capital gains tax treatment from such a disposal. This treatment is not possible for a quoted company except through a sale in the market to a market maker.

Income tax relief is available for losses on an investment in such a company's shares as this extends to losses on unquoted shares subscribed for in trading companies.

However, Business Expansion Scheme relief does not apply if the company has its shares traded on the USM. Unlike the rules for obtaining a full quotation, it is possible for a company with less than five years' trading to have such a listing and, therefore, it was considered it was inappropriate for Business Expansion Scheme relief to be given in the case of such companies.

Chapter 5
Lloyd's underwriters

General

120 The rules for taxing Lloyd's underwriters were substantially altered by FA 1973. The main statutory authorities concerning Lloyd's underwriters are contained in ss.450 to 457 ICTA 1988 and SIs 1974 Nos. 896 and 1330. The new rules, broadly, are effective for the 1972 and later underwriting accounts. The Finance Act 1988 amended the basis of assessment for income tax for 1986/87 (based on the results of the 1986 account) and subsequent years (see s.58 and Sch. 5 FA 1988).

Sources of income and gains

121 An underwriting member ('Name') of Lloyd's will receive income and gains from various sources. These will comprise all or some of the following:

(a) underwriting profits;
(b) syndicate investment income in respect of invested premiums;
(c) interest and dividends in respect of investments forming the Name's Lloyd's deposit, special reserve fund or any other personal reserve fund;
(d) capital appreciation in respect of investments acquired with the syndicate's premium income;
(e) capital gains arising on disposals of investments forming the Name's Lloyd's deposit, special reserve fund and other personal reserve funds;
(f) amounts to be included in the 'total income' of the Name in respect of withdrawals from the Name's special reserve fund.

The amount of a Name's share of underwriting profits, syndicate investment income and capital appreciation in respect of investments acquired with the syndicate's premium income was, in the past, all agreed with the Inland Revenue, HM Inspector of Taxes, Leeds (Underwriters Unit) and then reported to the Name's personal accountant.

The measure of profits, income and gains in (a), (b) and (d) above will be the Name's share of the underwriting account, year ended 31 December. The other sources are calculated on a normal fiscal year basis (ie., from 6 April to 5 April in the following year).

Each individual underwriter sends his personal tax returns to the inspector in Leeds, who will extract the relevant details of Lloyd's income, etc., and pass the tax return to the taxpayer's General Claims District (ie., the district that deals with his main source of income).

The auditors for each syndicate will send copies of syndicate accounts to City 35 District, who will pass on the agreed Sch. D Case I figures to the Leeds Underwriters Unit. When the profits, income and gains of a Name for an underwriting account have been agreed in respect of all the syndicates of which the Name was a member, the inspector at the Leeds Underwriting Unit reports the agreed figures to the Name's personal accountant, using Form LL9 in respect of underwriting profits and syndicate investment income, and Form LL200 in respect of syndicate capital gains (ie., capital appreciation in respect of investments acquired with the syndicate's premium income). However, the figures on Form LL9 are not always agreed: in particular, for the 1986 account, estimates of syndicate investment income were included because of the disagreements over the indexed element of certain bonds referred to in **142** below.

Underwriting account

122 The underwriting account coincides with the calendar year and includes underwriting profits or losses, syndicate investment income and capital appreciation/depreciation (both realised and unrealised). An account normally remains open for two years following the end of the year of account. If there are outstanding claims two years after the end of an account and these claims can be quantified then the account is closed by reinsurance. Hence the 1987 underwriting account was not closed until 31 December 1989 and, during the two-year 'open' period, premiums, claims, investment income and gains will have been received or paid which in fact related to 1987 account transactions. An underwriting account to 31 December is treated as co-terminus with the fiscal year ending on the following 5 April. All investment income and investment appreciation credited to an underwriting account will be assessable in the fiscal year corresponding to that account (even if received or arising in a later year). The underwriting profit will be assessed under Sch. D Case I, on an 'actual' basis, with no apportionment or application of the commencement or cessation provisions (except as mentioned below). Thus the underwriting profit, syndicate investment income and investment appreciation for the 1987 account will be assessable as income or capital gains of the fiscal year 1987/88. Syndicate investment income is normally received by the Name under deduction of basic rate income tax. From 1986/87 (the 1986 account), the underwriting profit and syndicate investment income is combined and assessed in aggregate to basic rate income tax under Sch. D Case I. The underwriting syndicate managing agent has paid the basic rate income tax on behalf of the member, leaving the latter to settle any higher rate liability. By extra-statutory concession, a managing agent could pass the basic rate tax direct to the Name, if he is notifed that there is an overall loss on the Name's syndicates. In order to save on administrative costs, the concession applied only where the total basic rate tax exceeded £1,000, and where the basic rate tax on any syndicate exceeded £200.

Most Lloyd's members are in several syndicates and since 1987 there have been large losses overall incurred by many underwriters resulting in substantial cash calls having to be made by Lloyd's. Consequently, to enable loss relief to be given at source against shares in profitable syndicates, following discussions between Lloyd's and the Inland Revenue new regulations have been introduced (the Lloyd's Underwriters (Schedule 19A to the Income and Corporation Taxes Act 1988) Regulations 1990 and the Lloyd's Underwriters (Tax) (1988–1989) Regulations 1991 and Lloyd's Underwriters (Tax) (1989–90) Regulations 1992). These transfer the obligation to account for basic rate tax from the syndicate (where the managing agent can only account for tax according to whether the syndicate has made a profit or loss regardless of the individual Name's overall position) to the individual member's agent. He is able to net off profits and losses of different syndicates and account for tax only in respect of the net amount due to the Name. The regulations supersede the Extra Statutory Concession for the tax year 1988/89 (Lloyd's 1988 underwriting year), and subsequent years. They provide in particular for managing agents to claim repayment of tax deducted from syndicate investment income and to distribute those repayments to members' agents: the members' agents then make returns to members' profits and losses and make payments of tax on the members profit on account of his liability to tax. The regulations also provide for extensions for members of Lloyd's and their spouses to make claims, elections or applications as specified in Schedule 2 Regulation 9 to the 1991 Regulations.

The amount of the Name's share of syndicate investment income is reported on the taxation advice note issued by the syndicate accountants and is supported by a Form LL185E.

The transition from a 'preceding year' basis to a 'current year' basis introduced by FA 1973 involved two years' profits being assessed for the fiscal year 1972/73. To compensate for this, a measure of relief is given when an individual who was underwriting before 1972 ceases his business in 1973 or later (Reg. 21, SI 1974 No. 896). The effect of the relief is:

(a) To reduce the assessment of the penultimate year by the amount of the 1972 account Sch. D Case I profit: it is not possible to create a loss by the claim. Thus, if the 1972 account profit exceeded the profit of the penultimate year, the assessment is reduced to nil, but no loss relief is available.

(b) In the final year, the profit arising in the period between 1 January and 5 April immediately preceding the date of termination of the business is not assessed.

Earned or unearned income

123 The profit assessable under Sch. D Case I (that is excluding capital gains) is regarded as earned income in the hands of an underwriter who is actively engaged in the business of Lloyd's and employed full-time (interpreted as being at least 75% of normal working hours) either in the room at Lloyd's or in the office of an underwriting agent or Lloyd's broker ('a working Name') and as unearned income in the hands of underwriters who do not attend Lloyd's on a regular basis ('the non-working Names'). The relevance of this distinction is for the order of set-off of losses and the ability to pay retirement annuity or personal pension premiums. Only working Names can obtain retirement annuity or personal pension relief. In computing relevant earnings for purposes of the relief, it is necessary to deduct the gross transfer to the special reserve fund from the Name's Sch. D Case I profits. If the amount of the transfer to the special reserve fund exceeds the amount of Sch. D profits, no relief can be obtained for any pension premiums paid.

It should be noted however that Schedule 19A defines a member's profits as those which are chargeable under Case I of Schedule D and s.450(2) ICTA 1988 makes it clear that the amount so chargeable shall be the aggregate of the income generated from assets forming part of the premiums trust fund. This has been the case from the 1986 accounts from which year syndicate investment income has been included as part of the Case I trading profit.

From those relevant earnings have to be deducted not only the gross amount of any special reserve transfer but also underwriting losses incurred in earlier years which have not yet been off set against relevant earnings to determine net relevant earnings of the year.

The closing year

124 Regulation 3(1) SI 1974 No 896 introduced the concept of 'the closing year' which, in relation to any year of assessment, means the year of assessment next but one following that year, ie., for 1987/88 the closing year is 1989/90. The basic rate income tax payable on an assessment of underwriting profits under Sch. D Case I is due for payment on 1 January following the end of the 'closing' year, ie., a year and a day following the date of closure of the underwriting account. Thus, basic rate income tax on a 1987/88 Sch. D assessment (based on the 1987 Account closed 31 December 1989) would be payable on 1 January 1991 by managing agents. Income tax at rates other than the basic rate would be due for payment on 1 July 1991 by Names in respect of the 1987/88 assessment.

Losses

125 Relief for an underwriting loss is available as for any other trading loss (for example, under ss. 380, 381, 385 and 388 ICTA 1988), subject to the following points:

(a) In the event of the underwriting loss causing a withdrawal from the special reserve fund, the loss must be set against the withdrawal before any other relief is claimed.

(b) Although a claim for relief under s.380(1) ICTA 1988 may be made to set an underwriting loss against other income of the year, a claim for relief under s.380(2), to set off the loss against other income of the succeeding year, is not available. Instead, relief may be claimed by setting the underwriting loss against other income of the preceding year, provided that the underwriting business was then being carried on but only if all the income of the year of loss has first been extinguished. The time limit for making the loss claim is two years from the end of the year of assessment in which the underwriting account giving rise to the loss is closed, eg., loss claim for the 1986 Account closed 31 December 1988 must be made by 5 April 1991.

(c) In the event of relief being claimed under s.385 ICTA 1988 carrying a loss forward against future underwriting profits. Lloyd's investment income on deposits and reserves is regarded as underwriting profit available for set off under s.385(4). In the case of terminal loss relief, there is a similar extension of the meaning of the term 'profits'.

Terminal loss claims may produce greater tax repayments for Lloyd's underwriters who have resigned than setting underwriting losses off against other income where tax rates in past years on underwriting profits may have been 60%. However, a large loss will be likely to give rise to the need for a withdrawal from the Name's special reserve fund, thus absorbing part or all of the loss. In addition, the Inland Revenue regard the final year in which losses arise for terminal loss relief purposes not as the final Account in which the Name participated before resignation, but as the last year for which results are shown on the form LL9 issued by Leeds (Underwriters Unit). A Name with even one 'open' syndicate at 31 December 1991, the end of the 1988 Account, will thus be precluded from treating that year as 'terminal'.

(d) As the end of the underwriting account is treated as co-terminous with 5 April following, there is no apportionment between fiscal years of a loss for an underwriting account.

(e) Any underwriting losses incurred in 1991/92 and subsequent years of assessment should be available to offset against capital gains of the underwriter (s.72 FA 1991), under the provisions introduced in FA 1991 after other income of the underwriter has been exhausted.

Because of cashflow problems caused by Lloyd's losses and cash calls, the Inland Revenue have indicated that they would be prepared to advise the Inspector dealing with an appeal against an assessment on other income that if the application to postpone payment of tax charged by the assessment is supported by the Name's Consolidated Personal Statement for the A account showing an overall loss he should accept the postponement application to the extent of 75% of the overall loss shown by the statement.

Stop-loss policies

126 If an underwriter effects a personal 'stop-loss' or re-insurance policy, the premiums on the policy will be an allowable deduction in computing his taxable underwriting profit. If insurance money is received by him as a result of a claim under the policy, the amount received will be included as a trading receipt for the year of assessment that corresponds to the underwriting account in which the loss arose (s.450(4) ICTA 1988, as amended (para. 4 Sch. 16 FA 1973, as amended)). Before the 1985 account, the insurance monies were included as a trading receipt for the tax year in which the premiums were allowed as a deduction.

Stop loss recoveries form part of Lloyd's income for calculating (or revising) a transfer to special reserve fund. A situation can arise in which the maximum transfer to special reserve is permitted and made due to a stop loss recovery in a year in which losses brought forward have wiped out Lloyd's profits. In such a case, the other Lloyd's income (on personal reserves etc) may well be less than the amount of the transfer to the special reserve. In such cases, Inland Revenue practice is informally to restrict the brought forward loss to enable the transfer to special reserve to have full effect and the balance of the restricted loss is then carried forward to the next underwriting account.

Interest paid

127 Interest paid by a Name in respect of the following loans is allowable:

(a) loans raised to fund losses;
(b) loans raised to finance his Lloyd's deposit.

Relief for interest paid in respect of loans in (b) above is limited to working Names.

Following FA 1974, which introduced restrictions on interest eligible for tax relief, Lloyd's negotiated with the Inland Revenue to establish the basis on which interest paid by Names would qualify for tax relief. The agreement reached was published in a Lloyd's Memorandum dated 27 March 1975, which should be consulted for the detailed rules.

If a Name pays interest on a debit balance with a syndicate, this is allowed against the syndicate investment income or, if the interest paid exceeds his share of the syndicate investment income, the excess is allowed against the Sch. D Case I profit, without regard to the overall position.

Capital gains – general

128 Investment appreciation arising from the premiums trust fund (syndicate investments) is based on the gains allocated to an underwriting year of account and is assessable as a capital gain for the corresponding fiscal year (ie., the 1987 account capital gain will be assessed in 1987/88). The computation of gains/losses includes both realised and unrealised gains and losses and proceeds as follows:

	£	£
Value of assets held at year-end		x
Add:		
Sales in the year (proceeds)		x
		x
Less:		
Value of assets held at start of year	(x)	
Purchases in the year (cost)	(x)	(x)
Appreciation		£ x

The resulting gain or loss is then allocated, in accordance with the normal rules and practices of Lloyd's, to the account of the year of valuation and to the two preceding accounts ('the open years'). In computing both the realised and unrealised gains or losses, the appropriate adjustment is made in respect of exempt gains or losses relating to Government securities and qualifying corporate bonds, the advantages of which have been greatly diminished by the accrued income provisions introduced by FA 1985, in respect of disposals after 27 February 1986 (see **140** below).

The tax payable on an assessment in respect of 'syndicate gains' is due for payment on 1 January in the year of assessment next following 'the closing year' (ie., tax payable on a 1987/88 assessment would be due for payment on 1 January 1991).

The underwriting agents and not the member are responsible up to 1987/88 for returning syndicate gains and losses, and tax assessed at 30% will be payable by the underwriting agents, who will have retained the tax payable from the profit distribution. From 1988/89 (the 1988 account), members' agents will under the new regulations pay tax at the basic rate (25% for 1988/89 to 1992/93) and the member will be responsible for any further liability.

The amounts assessed are apportioned among the Names and are treated like any other personal capital gain in their hands. For example, gains may be covered by an annual exemption or by losses brought forward, giving rise to a repayment of tax paid by the agents. The syndicate accountants will report the Name's share of gains or losses of that syndicate and the position for all the syndicates in which the Name participated will be reported by the inspector on Form LL200.

Capital gains arising from all Lloyd's funds other than the premium trust fund (that is, the special reserve fund, personal reserve fund, etc.) are returnable by the Name personally. Assessments are raised on the Name and he is liable for the tax charged by assessment. As a result, gains and losses are computed on the basis of realised transactions during the fiscal year, and tax is due for payment on 1 December following the end of the year of assessment, or thirty days after the date of issue of the assessment, whichever is the later.

Capital gains tax position on retirement or death

129   When a Name ceases to be an underwriting member of Lloyd's, through resignation or death, he is deemed to dispose of his interest in the investments held by the syndicates in which he participated. No special computation will be necessary in respect of a Name who retires, since he will retire at the end of an account and the gains assessed for that account will include the accrued appreciation. Under present capital gains tax rules, assets held at death do not give rise to any chargeable gain or allowable loss by reference to their deemed disposal at market value at that date. A Lloyd's underwriter is absolutely entitled to the assets in his premiums trust fund, but the application of the general capital gains tax rules would be extremely complicated and difficult to administer and are not applied. Instead, the syndicate capital gains or capital losses attributed to him for the year of assessment in which he dies were varied by an amount calculated by reference to a formula (details of which are set out in Reg. 9 SI 1974 No.896). The calculations are made by the syndicate agents or their accountants, to whom a request should be made for a note of the appropriate adjustment when dealing with the tax position of a deceased underwriter.

However, these regulations have now been withdrawn in FA 1989 as the relief required extremely complex calculations which on the whole produced very little if any relief.

Inheritance tax

130   Business Property relief of formerly 50%, now increased to 100%, is given on death on the market value of a member's underwriting interest. Such an interest comprises investments forming part of the premiums trust fund, the special reserve fund and Lloyd's deposits and profits for open years. The value of any property, including any securities deposited with a bank or insurance company, forming the collateral for a bank guarantee or letter of credit up to the maximum amount of the guarantee, qualifies for relief. Where total Lloyd's assets exceed £100,000, the amount on which relief is available may have to be negotiated with the Capital Taxes Office. This £100,000 limit has been the Capital Taxes Office's opening gambit in recent cases but where the deceased's overall premium limit was more than £400,000, the Inland Revenue could be persuaded to allow relief on 25% of the premium limit. A recent report indicates a slight relaxation in that up to 30% of the premium limit may be allowed for relief where that limit is over £400,000. Any inheritance tax payable on the death of the Name relating to his interest qualifying for Business Property Relief can be paid by ten annual instalments and, provided that each instalment is paid on time, no interest will be charged.

The other conditions for the relief have, of course, to be satisfied including in particular minimum periods of ownership. However, this relief does not apply to the extent that the Name's main residence is the collateral for the guarantee. The Capital Taxes Office is of the view that the main residence cannot be an asset used wholly or mainly for the purposes of the underwriting business to qualify for relief. If instead, the underwriter raised a loan using the residence as security and applied the borrowing to purchase Stock Exchange investments for deposit at Lloyd's, entitlement to Business Property Relief should be preserved.

The special reserve fund

131 The provision covering transfers to and withdrawals from the special reserve fund are contained in ss.452 to 456 ICTA 1988. The maximum gross transfer that can be made to the special reserve fund is 50% of the member's overall underwriting profit or £7,000, whichever is the lesser sum (s.452(5) ICTA 1988). 'Underwriting profit' in this context means the Sch. D Case I profit, adjusted for any recovery under stop-loss if applicable, and income from the special reserve fund and any other fund required or authorised by the rules of Lloyd's, including Lloyd's deposits arising in the same year of assessment. The amount transferred is regarded as a gross payment from which income tax at the basic rate has been deducted. The transfer is thus deemed to be an annual payment subject to the deduction of basic rate income tax at source, paid during the year of assessment in which the profits on which the transfer is based are assessed.

For the purposes of higher-rate income tax, the gross transfer is set only against such Lloyd's income as defined; it must be set first against Lloyd's earned income in the case of working Names. If a member wishes to make a transfer to the special reserve fund, a computation of the allowable transfer and the amount to be transferred (which may be a lesser amount) must be submitted to the Inland Revenue within 12 months after the closing of the relevant underwriting account. The transfer must them be made within 30 days after the inspector has agreed the computation, or 12 months and 30 days after the closing of the underwriting account, whichever is the later (s.452(6) ICTA 1988).

Thus, transfers to the fund for the 1988 account, which was closed on 31 December 1990, must be notified to the Inland Revenue by 31 December 1991 and the actual transfer made by 30 January 1992 or, if later, within 30 days after the notification by the inspector of his agreement to the amount transferred. These time limits are normally applied rigidly by the Inland Revenue, although extensions are sometimes allowed. For example, in the case of the 1987 account, notices of transfer had to be submitted by the end of the month following the month in which the first form LL9 was issued.

For any year in which an overall underwriting loss occurs, it is compulsory that, if a balance is held in the special reserve fund, an amount be withdrawn from the fund which, when grossed up at the basic rate of income tax applicable for the year in which the loss occurs, equals the overall underwriting loss. If the balance held in the fund is insufficient when grossed up, to equal the underwriting loss, the whole is withdrawn. The payment is regarded as an annual payment that has suffered basic rate income tax in the member's hands. Relief for the loss must be given primarily against the payment representing the gross equivalent of the withdrawal, so that the deemed basic rate income tax can be reclaimed. Any balance of the loss not covered by the withdrawal can be relieved against other income in the normal way.

If the Name ceases to be an underwriter during his lifetime, the balance in his special reserve fund is paid over to him and the payment is regarded as an annual payment in his hands from which basic rate tax has been deducted. The amount is regarded as having been paid to him on the last day of his business as an underwriter, and the payment is liable to higher rates of income tax. However, if a Name dies while carrying on his underwriting business, the amount treated as an annual payment from the fund is limited to that part of the fund which is attributable to annual gross transfers to the fund in excess of £5,000, or 35% of profits, whichever is the less. The payments are regarded as being grossed up at the relevant basic rates of income tax for the years during which each 'excess' transfer was made, and the amounts thus computed will be chargeable to higher rates of income tax, at the rates applicable for each year during which an excess transfer was made. It will, therefore, be apparent that, if a Name continues his underwriting business until death, and, during his lifetime, makes transfers to the special reserve fund of only 35% of overall underwriting profits (within the £5,000 per annum limit), there will be no further liability to tax on his executors for earlier years, in respect of the capital balance released from the special reserve fund on death.

The value of the special reserve fund, for the purposes of the above provisions, is found by adding together all the transfers into the fund and deducting them from the 'nominal' withdrawals made in respect of losses. This value is unlikely to bear any relationship to the market value of the investments comprised in the fund.

Dates of payment of income tax and capital gains tax

132 The regulations setting out the Lloyd's Underwriters tax are contained in SI 1991/851 for the 1988 account (1988/89).

Tax chargeable	Due and payable dates
(a) Income tax at basic rate assessed on member's agent for any year on underwriting profits and syndicate investment income.	1 January in year of assessment next following closing year.
e.g. 1988/89 year of assessment. (Syndicate investment income is normally received net of basic rate income tax.)	1 January 1992.
(b) Income tax charged in 'sweep up' assessment on underwriting profits and syndicate investment income.	1 July in year of assessment next following closing year.
e.g. 1988/89 year of assessment.	1 July 1992.
(c) Basic rate tax on capital gains charged on underwriting agents in respect of syndicate gains.	1 January in year of assessment next following closing year.
e.g. 1988/89 year of assessment.	1 January 1992.
(d) Capital gains charged at the higher rate on Names in respect of syndicate gains	1 January in year of assessment next following closing year
e.g. 1988/89 year of assessment.	1 January 1992.

In all cases above, if an assessment is issued after the due date, the tax will be deemed payable 30 days after the day on which the assessment is made (there is no extension to the Table Date for calculating interest under s.86 TMA 1970).

Although the securities, etc., forming a Name's Lloyd's deposit, special reserve fund and any personal reserve funds will be held in the name of the Corporation of Lloyd's or underwriting agent for the Name, the income or capital gains arising in respect of those securities, etc., will be mandated direct to the Name and will be returned by the Name on his tax return in the normal way. The 'due and payable' dates in such cases are the same as for any other non-Lloyd's sources of income and capital gains.

Run-off syndicates

133 Special rules apply where the accounts of a syndicate remain open beyond the end of the closing year. These are known as 'run-off syndicates'. The rules apply to relate back receipts and outgoings, for the purposes of Sch. D Case I, to the last underwriting year but one preceding the year in which they occur. Similar rules apply for gains and loss relief. For example, a loss arising in 1990 in respect of the 1986 'run-off' account is deemed to arise in account 1988, and is allowed for tax in the year 1988/89.

Loss claims

134 Because of the delay in computing underwriting profits, there is a two-year extension of the usual time limit for making claims to set off non-underwriting trading losses against such profits.

Wife's earned income election

135 Similarly, the wife's earned income election time limit is extended by two years if either husband or wife is an underwriting member of Lloyd's. Thus an election for 1989/90 may be made or revoked at any time up to 5 April 1993. With the introduction of independent taxation of husband and wife, no election is necessary for 1990/91 onwards.

Retirement annuity and personal pension premiums

136 The Sch. D Case I profit for a working Name qualifies as 'relevant earnings' for the purposes of retirement annuity or personal pension relief. For working Names, there is a statutory extension to the time-limit for paying retirement annuity or personal pension premiums and obtaining relief against their net relevant earnings (ie., after deducting underwriting losses brought forward and the gross amount of any transfer to his special reserve fund (see **131** above)) from Lloyd's by relating them back to the profits of the closed year (under ss.627 and 641 ICTA 1988). It is provided, in respect of premiums paid in 1982/83 and subsequent years, that, where there is an amount of unused relief attributable to those earnings for a year of assessment, the underwriter may elect that there shall be treated as paid in that year, any qualifying premium paid by him in the next year of assessment but two. Thus, if the underwriter makes an election and pays a premium in respect of the 1988 account (closed on 31 December 1990 and assessable 1988/89) by 5 April 1992, he may treat the premium as paid in 1988/89. This special carry-back provision cannot be used in conjunction with the ordinary one-year carry-back provision, nor can it be used in conjunction with the carry-forward of unused relief, although the latter did not arise until 1983/84, because 1980/81 was the first tax year in relation to which unused relief could be carried forward.

The election to relate back the premium can, by concession in the case of Retirement Annuity Premiums, be made by 5 July following the end of the year of assessment in which the premium is paid, as with other taxpayers.

Subscriptions and other expenses

137 The Sch. D Case I position on the various expenses incurred by Names is as follows:

(a) The annual subscription for membership of Lloyd's is allowable. It is normally paid by the underwriting agent and will be reflected in the underwriting profit reported. The entrance fee, currently £3,000, is not deductible.
(b) The annual percentage fee charged for a bank for providing letters of credit and bank guarantees (but not the initial arrangement fee or the cost of increasing the facility) may be deducted, even if the bank charges relate to a Name's personal reserve funds. From the 1981 account onwards, one annual percentage bank facility fee was allowable from the first year of the facility, irrespective of whether that year was also the first year of underwriting.

(c) the subscription paid to the Association of Lloyd's Members, the pressure group formed to establish relations with Lloyd's council and improve the format of accounts and information that Names receive, is allowable for tax relief in full. A claim can also be made for one-half of the published cost of the food and drink element in the cost of attending ALM meetings. The cost of travel to ALM regional meetings (but not those held in London) is allowed, in so far as this does not exceed the cost of travel from London to that regional meeting.

(d) Litigation has been commenced by affected syndicates to recover misappropriated funds, following the investigation into certain suspended underwriters and offshore companies controlled by those underwriters. Leeds (Underwriters Unit) has stated that the majority of claims for relief for reasonable legal costs will be allowed as an underwriting expense in the same way as stop-loss premiums of the year in which the costs are incurred. Similarly, any recoveries will be taxable in the year they are received. As an allied issue, the Inland Revenue consider compensation received (less legal expenses incurred) by Lloyd's Members following actions against the lead underwriters of syndicates, their syndicate managing agents or members' agents is taxable on normal principles as trading income in the year of entitlement subject to the special two year carry-back rules for running off syndicates (under Reg. 7 of Lloyd's Underwriters (Tax) Regulations 1974 SI 1974/896) (see *Market Bulletin* of Lloyds March 1992).

(e) Because of the complexities of dealing with underwriters' tax affairs, it has been the practice of the Inland Revenue at Leeds (Underwriters Unit) to allow claims for personal accountancy fees without question against the underwriting profits of Names, up to certain limits.

The Unit has stated that it will allow amounts for such fees against the underwriting profits for accounts 1987 and 1988 as follows:

	1987 and 1988		1985 and 1986
	£		£
First syndicate	400		(350)
Next five syndicates	120	(each)	(120)
Next twenty-one syndicates (nineteen for 1985 and 1986)	50	(each)	(50)
The maximum claim is, therefore,	£2,050		(£1900)

For this purpose, 'syndicate' means an individual entry on Form LL9, regardless of how many other syndicate members are given in that entry, except that, where two syndicates are combined as 'mirror syndicates', they will be treated as a single syndicate for the purposes of calculating the amount of allowable accountancy fees.

A deduction for accountancy fees, in accordance with the above table, will be given automatically via the computer, by the Underwriters' Unit without a formal claim from the Name. Formal claims are, therefore, only necessary where the Name wishes to claim a larger amount than that given

85

by the table. In practice, larger deductions will only be given in exceptional cases, eg., non-resident Names.

(f) A premium paid in respect of a stop-loss policy is an allowable deduction in the year to which the policy relates.

(g) A premium paid in respect of an Estate Protection Plan is also an allowable deduction. The premium paid is allowed as a deduction on Form LL9 for three years earlier, eg., the 1991 premium is allowed as a deduction on the Form LL9 for the 1988 account.

Foreign taxes paid and double taxation relief

138   The following should be considered.

(1) US Tax

(The following applies to UK-resident non-US Names only.)

US tax returns are submitted annually in respect of profits arising in the USA, including investment income and gains 'effectively connected' with the US business. In the past, Le Boeuf, Lamb, Leiby & MacRae have prepared consolidated US tax returns on behalf of most non-US Names. The Name's personal accountant would have supplied, through the agents, details of non-Lloyd's US income for inclusion on that return.

Under the new closing agreement with the USA, which came into effect on 1 January 1991, Le Boeuf's will in future file a US return to report the Lloyd's syndicate income and gains only. If a Name has other US source income, a separate return may need to be filed by the Name's personal accountant.

Double taxation relief in respect of US federal income tax is computed individually for each Name in respect of his Lloyd's income and gains, and the figures are agreed between Lloyd's and the Inland Revenue. The inspector then advises the Name's personal accountant of the agreed figures. A double taxation relief report is issued by Leeds (Underwriters Unit), which includes Canadian taxes paid.

Repayment of the double taxation relief due can be obtained by the Name's personal accountant on submission of a formal claim for tax credit relief.

The rules for relieving underwriting losses in the USA are different from those in the UK. Under the Tax Reform Act 1986, Lloyd's income in the USA is deemed to be 'passive' income, ie., where a taxpayer does not participate on a regular basis, and passive losses can only be set off against passive income or carried forward.

(2) Other

The reports from the syndicate accountants, and also the Form LL9 received from the inspector, will show foreign taxes paid. These will have been deducted as an expense in computing the Sch. D Case I profit or loss. If there is a profit, the foreign taxes are added to the profit and are then allowed as a credit against the tax charged. If there is a loss, there is no adjustment.

In the case of working Names, the foreign taxes paid can only be allowed as a credit against the tax due on the Sch. D Case I profit. If, however, the Sch. D Case I liability has been reduced to nil, or to an amount less than the foreign taxes paid, eg., by transfer to the special reserve fund, the foreign taxes paid are allowed as allowable Sch. D Case I expenses, and can thus create or augment a loss.

Non-resident Names

139 A non-resident Name is liable to UK tax in respect of his Lloyd's profits, as he is deemed to be carrying on a trade in the UK. His taxable profits include his Sch. D Case I profit, and income arising from investments forming his Lloyd's deposit, special reserve fund, and personal reserve funds and capital gains (s.18(1)(a)(iii) ICTA 1988 and s.10(1) TCGA 1992) on assets situated in the UK. Assets in the Lloyd's deposit and special reserve fund situated outside the UK are deemed to be part of the UK trade. Therefore, any income arising therefrom is still deemed to arise from a UK trade.

Investments held in the Lloyd's sterling trust fund are generally situated in the UK, but any non-UK securities are considered to be situated outside the UK. Investments held in the Lloyd's US trust fund or Lloyd's Canadian trust fund are regarded as situated outside the UK.

The syndicate accountant will provide details of the Name's share of gains arising in respect of investments situated outside the UK. Since all net gains arising to the syndicate in any year of assessment will have been assessed at the rate of 30% or, from 1988/89, at the basic rate of income tax, it is the responsibility of the Name's personal accountant to claim any repayment due in respect of the gains that are exempt because the Name is neither resident nor ordinarily resident in the UK.

Accrued income scheme

140 An underwriting member of Lloyd's or of an approved association of underwriters is treated (for the purposes of the bond-washing provisions) as absolutely entitled to the securities forming part of his premiums trust fund, his Lloyd's deposit, special reserve fund and any other trust fund required by the rules of Lloyd's. The accrued income scheme rules apply, therefore, in the normal way to transactions in the securities constituting his Lloyd's deposit, special reserve fund and other personal reserve funds.

However, syndicate investments that are included in a premiums trust fund are deemed to be transferred and reacquired on 31 December and 1 January respectively each year, starting with a deemed acquisition on 1 January 1986. This means that the income accrued up to 31 December each year forms part of the syndicate investment income of that year, with a corresponding deduction from the first interest receipt (or accrued interest on sale) in the following year. To achieve this result, it is provided that, where an interest period straddles

31 December in any year (starting with 31 December 1986), it is deemed to be split into two interest periods, the first ending on 31 December and the second starting on 1 January.

Liability under the accrued income scheme is assessable under Sch. D Case VI (s.714(2) ICTA 1988). The Leeds (Underwriters Unit) has confirmed that Names' non-Lloyd's Sch. D Case VI losses, including those brought forward from years before the accrued income scheme began, may be relieved, where possible, against accrued income forming part of their syndicate investment income. Future forms LL185 E should indicate the proportion of Sch. D Case VI tax paid by the agent.

Where an individual dies, there is no deemed disposal by the deceased to his personal representatives on death. As far as personal funds are concerned, the personal representatives will be liable on the basis of the deceased's acquisition details. The position regarding syndicate investments is not clear. In practice, the Name will be assessed on his share of any accrued income arising to his syndicates and credited to the accounts for years up to and including the year of his death.

Reinsurance to close

141 Following an intensive investigation, the Inland Revenue accepted that genuine reinsurance to close premiums could not be disallowed, even if very conservative or excessive. The rules have been amended for the 1985 account and later years (s.450(5) and (5A) ICTA 1988). The reinsurance to close premium is only deductible for tax purposes to the extent that it does not exceed a fair and reasonable assessment of the value of the liabilities in respect of which it is payable. This assessment is made on the basis that the person who receives the premium makes neither a profit nor a loss on the transaction. If part of the premium in respect of a member of a syndicate is disallowed for tax, that part is also ignored in calculating the tax liability of that continuing member of the syndicate that receives the premium. Where a member leaves a syndicate he will receive a full deduction for the premium payable at the close of the last account for which he is a member. In consequence, the continuing members will be taxed in full on that premium.

Index-linked US bonds

142 There was a dispute with the Inland Revenue on the treatment of certain index-linked US and Canadian bonds which affected the 1985 Account. Various Lloyd's underwriting agents stated that they had received assurances from the Inland Revenue that the indexation uplift on such bonds known as 'Sally Mae' bonds would only be liable to capital gains tax and not income tax. The low-interest capital yielding bonds have been issued in North America as an investment for premium income that had to be held for two years after the close of the underwriting year, in order to cover claims. The Inland Revenue denied giving this assurance and, in a circular in October 1988, stated that with effect from the 1985 account, they would tax the indexation uplift as income.

In a recent case seeking judicial review of the Inland Revenue's decision (R *v.* CIR and another *ex parte* DP Mann Underwriting Agency Ltd and related applications reported in [1989] STC 873), the Inland Revenue won. Following further discussions, a settlement was reached between the Lloyd's Underwriting Agency Association and the Inland Revenue whereby 23.3% of the investment return on the bonds is to be treated as capital and 76.7% as income. Full indexation relief is available on all bonds maturing up to 31 December 1988 and, from 1 January 1989, on those maturing before 14 March 1989.

Before the dispute was settled with the Inland Revenue, the taxation department of the Corporation of Lloyd's issued a bulletin on the taxation arrangements for the 1985 Account (published in *Taxation* dated 11 May 1989).

The main points from the bulletin are as follows:

"A number of syndicates have not agreed their syndicate investment income and capital gains computations for the 1985 Account because of a dispute concerning the tax treatment of the return from certain index-linked securities. In addition some syndicates have not been able to agree their Case I profit or loss. Leeds (Underwriters Unit) will shortly start to issue forms LL9 for the 1985 Account including, if appropriate, estimated figures for syndicate investment income and the Case I result. These estimates will be prefixed by the letter 'E'. The forms will fall into the following categories:

1 The Case I result and syndicate investment income are agreed;
2 The Case I result is agreed but the syndicate investment income is not;
3 Neither the Case I result nor the syndicate investment income is agreed;
4 The Case I result is not agreed but the syndicate investment income is agreed.

The tax position for each of these categories is covered in this bulletin.

Case I result and syndicate investment income agreed

The Names' tax position can be settled in the normal way.

Case I result agreed but syndicate investment income not agreed

If there is a Case I loss, relief can be claimed in the normal way. However, if any part of the loss has to be set against syndicate investment income, Leeds (Underwriters Unit) will include the syndicate investment income shown on the LL9 in their calculation but will only repay the actual tax paid by the syndicate agent.

If there is a withdrawal from the Special Reserve Fund, a computation should be submitted to Leeds (Underwriters Unit) when the claim for loss relief is made. Leeds (Underwriters Unit) will not issue the Form LL32 to certify a withdrawal until the position is finally settled but the withdrawal will be taken into account in the calculation of the repayment due for the loss and tax at 30 per cent on the estimated withdrawal refunded.

If the member wishes to make a transfer to the Special Reserve Fund, a provisional computation should be submitted by the end of the month following that in which the first LL9 is issued. The computation can be based either on the syndicate investment income computed by the syndicate agents (this will normally be shown on the taxation advices) or using the figures shown on the LL9.

Leeds (Underwriters Unit) will issue a higher rate tax assessment on the amount of syndicate investment income shown on the LL9. An appeal should be lodged against the assessment and application made to postpone the tax in dispute.

If any of the tax postponed is eventually found to be payable, interest will be charged from the earlier of 30 days after agreement is reached or 1 January 1990.

Neither Case I result nor syndicate investment income agreed

If there is a Case I loss, a provisional repayment can be claimed by setting the loss against syndicate investment income. Any repayment will be restricted though to the amount of tax paid by the syndicate agents. If 75 per cent of the loss shown on Form LL9, less ten-sevenths of the balance on the Special Reserve Fund (after taking into account any transfer or withdrawal for the 1984 Account) exceeds the syndicate investment income the excess may be set against other income for 1985–86 only.

Leeds (Underwriters Unit) will issue assessments to collect the basic rate tax the higher rate tax on the underwriting profit and the higher rate tax on the syndicate investment income. Appeals should be lodged against these assessments and an application made to postpone payment of the excessive tax charged. The postponement application should be based on the figures calculated by the syndicate agents.

If any of the tax postponed is eventually found to be payable, interest will run as follows:

1 Basic rate tax on underwriting profit – the earlier of 30 days after agreement is reached or 1 July 1989.
2 Higher rate tax on underwriting profit and syndicate investment income – the earlier of thirty days after agreement is reached or 1 January 1990.

The Case I result is not agreed but syndicate investment income is agreed

The Case I and Special Reserve Fund position should be dealt with as outlined in the preceding section. The assessment on syndicate investment income will be based on agreed figures so it will not be possible to dispute the quantum of the assessment. However, the member may not be able to agree the exact amount of tax payable until the Case I result is agreed.

Provisional transfers can be made to the Special Reserve Fund and the transfer computation must show the correct amount of syndicate investment income. It will not be possible to make a withdrawal from the fund until the final position is known.

Accrued interest

The figures shown on the LL9 for accrued interest are the amounts returned by the syndicate agents and not the figures which the Inland Revenue believe to be correct. Provisional claims for repayment by non-resident members and for relief for personal Case VI losses can be made in the normal way using these figures.

Capital gains

Forms LL200 will be issued showing the figures submitted by syndicate agents and not the amounts that the Inland Revenue believe are correct. Leeds (Underwriters Unit) are prepared, on a provisional basis, to make full repayment using these figures.

Conclusion

When a member's Case I position is finally agreed, relief for a loss can be claimed under the appropriate section. However, if a claim has already been made under the provisional arrangements applying where Case I loss is estimated, the loss relieved against syndicate investment income under the provisions of s.380 ICTA 1988 may not be set against other income. Members can if they wish defer making loss claims until the loss is agreed to avoid this restriction. Leeds (Underwriters Unit) should be advised if the member wishes to do this. No account will be taken of the loss when the estimated higher rate assessment on syndicate investment income is issued.

When the member's Case I position, syndicate investment income and capital gains are finally settled, his or her tax position can be determined. At the same time the exact amount of the Special Reserve Fund transfer and adjustments to the provisional transfer can be calculated and withdrawals from the Special Reserve Fund authorised.

Premiums trust funds: stock lending

143   The stock-lending provisions in s.129 ICTA 1988 were introduced to place Inland Revenue Extra-Statutory Concession B15 on a statutory basis. Inland Revenue Extra-Statutory Concession B15 applied to market makers in securities and enabled them to borrow from an institutional holder and return equivalent securities at a later date without treating the loan and return as disposals for tax purposes. These provisions cover disposals giving rise to a liability under Sch. D Case I, under the accrued income scheme and to capital gains tax. The provision have now been extended by s.91 FA 1989 to Lloyd's. For the purposes of the accrued income scheme and for capital gains tax, stocks lent by Lloyd's underwriters are now deemed to remain within the premiums trust fund without giving rise to disposal and reacquisition. This does not apply to the extent that the loan extends over a year-end where, as in the case of securities actually held then, they are deemed to have been sold and reacquired at the year-end for accrued income scheme and capital gains purposes (see s.207 TCGA 1992).

Independent taxation from 6 April 1990

144 It is important to remember the following in relation to independent taxation as it affects Lloyd's members:

1 If transfers of assets are made between spouses to maximise possible tax benefits, the Name must not overlook the on-going means requirement or annual solvency test required by Lloyd's.
2 Lloyd's losses will only be available against the other income of the Name and not of the spouse for 1990/91 onwards (the 1990 account results) and for 1991/92 onwards also against the Name's capital gains. They may be carried forward against future underwriting profits or related back against other income of the previous year if beneficial.
3 Syndicates are likely to produce capital losses so that the Names should retain the capacity to make personal capital gains if this is practical. The Name's capital losses are not available to set against the spouse's gains from 6 April 1990 onwards.
4 The Inland Revenue have confirmed that for Names, the time limit for making elections under s.356B ICTA 1988 (the allocation of qualifying loan interest between husband and wife) is extended to three years after the end of the year of assessment to which it relates (Lloyd's Market Bulletin 3 April 1990).
5 Any separate investment by spouses in BES assets must be considered carefully since Lloyd's results will not be agreed until more than two years after the end of the year of assessment concerned.

Chapter 6
Temporary visitors to the UK

Employees

145   The liability to UK tax of temporary visitors to the UK for employment purposes depends upon their own residence position, the place of performance of their duties, their domicile position, and by whom they are paid for their duties. The deductions for foreign emoluments described in paragraphs **150** *et seq.* apply only up to 1983–4. The position for subsequent years is described in paragraph **163** below.

Residence position

146   A person is always resident in the UK if he spends six months or more in the UK in any fiscal year (s.336 ICTA 1988). If a person maintains available accommodation in the UK, he will be regarded as resident here for any year he sets foot here (leaflet IR 20, para. 21 and Loewenstein *v.* de Salis 10 TC 424) unless all the duties of his employment are performed outside the UK except for purely incidental duties (s.335 ICTA 1988). The available accommodation rule is relaxed by concession if the temporary visitor rents accommodation, and the period of renting is less than two years for furnished accommodation and one year for unfurnished accommodation (leaflet IR 20, para. 28). A person who comes to the UK to work for a period of at least two years is treated as resident here for the whole period from the day of arrival to the day of departure whether he retains accommodation in the UK or not. He is not usually regarded as having become ordinarily resident in the UK until he has been here for at least three years, unless it is clear from the outset that he intends to be in the country for three or more years, in which event he would normally be treated as ordinarily resident from the date of arrival. The same would be true if he had available accommodation from the outset, unless it falls within the exceptions mentioned.

147   Thus, it is the Board's practice to regard someone who comes to the UK, whether to work or not, as ordinarily resident for tax purposes (a) from the date of his arrival if he has, or acquires during the year of arrival, accommodation for his use in the UK, which he occupies on a basis that implies a stay in the UK of three years or more; (b) from the beginning of the tax year in which such accommodation becomes available. In the event of an individual who has been regarded as ordinarily resident solely because he has accommodation here, disposing of the accommodation and leaving the UK within three years of his arrival, he would normally be treated as not ordinarily resident for the duration of his stay if this were to his advantage (SP 3/81).

Place of performance of duties

148 Incidental duties are ignored in deciding the place of performance of duties. What constitutes incidental duties will depend upon the facts of each case. The time taken in relation to the duties is not conclusive (Robson *v.* Dixon 48 TC 527). Reporting to one's employer or receiving fresh instructions or coming to the UK to be trained, provided it does not exceed three months in a year, will be regarded as incidental duties by the Revenue (leaflet IR 20, paras. 38 and 39). It should be noted that the Inland Revenue do not accept that any duties of a UK company director can be incidental.

Domicile

149 Domicile is a concept of general law and it is outside the scope of this book to discuss it in detail. Broadly speaking, a person is domiciled in the country in which he has his permanent home. Domicile is distinct from nationality or residence. A person may be resident in more than one country but at any given time he can be domiciled in one country only. A person acquires a domicile of origin at birth which is normally the domicile of his father. This he retains until he acquires a domicile of choice or a domicile of dependency. A domicile of choice is acquired if a person can show he has severed his ties with the country of his domicile of origin and settled in another country with the intention of remaining there permanently. A domicile of dependency occurs in the case of a minor whose domicile follows that of the person on whom he is legally dependent.

The payer of the income

150 The relevance of the payer of the income is that most visitors will be domiciled abroad and will retain their foreign domicile during any stay in the UK. If they are paid by an employer who is not resident in the UK, they will be in receipt of 'foreign emoluments'. Foreign emoluments received by a UK resident were subject to a 50% deduction in arriving at the taxable amount, reducing to a 25% deduction if the foreigner was resident in the UK in the year of assessment in which they arose and had been resident in at least nine out of the preceding ten years of assessment (s.192(4) ICTA 1988).

151 This deduction was only given where the foreign emoluments were chargeable to tax on an arising basis under Case I or Case II of Sch. E. Case I applies where an individual is resident and ordinarily resident in the UK. Case II applies where a person is resident but not ordinarily resident or not resident in the UK, in respect of duties, other than incidental duties, performed in the UK. If a separate employment of a non-domiciled person with a foreign employer is exercised wholly outside the UK, the remittance basis still applies to those foreign emoluments as the employment is specifically exempted from Case I of Sch. E. Such an employment can, therefore, only fall within Case III if the person is resident in the UK. No 50% or 25% deduction was then due on what was remitted to the UK.

152 Therefore, where a visitor holds two separate and clearly distinct employments and the duties of one are performed wholly outside the UK (except for incidental duties), if the emoluments from that employment are foreign emoluments, they will only be liable to UK tax insofar as they are remitted to the UK whilst the person is resident here and relate to work carried on whilst he is resident (s.192(2) and s.19(1) ICTA 1988). Where there are two such employments, with the same employer or with employers under common control, the emoluments referable to duties performed wholly abroad must not be unfairly weighted as compared with duties in the UK, otherwise they will be apportioned on the basis of time spent in the two employments or having regard to any other relevant factors (para. 2(2) of Sch.12 ICTA 1988).

153. This is the position whether the visitor is resident and ordinarily resident or merely resident in the UK in respect of such a separate employment. It should be noted that if the visitor is resident but not ordinarily resident, it is not necessary to have a separate employment with a foreign employer in respect of overseas duties in order to secure assessment on a remittance basis in respect of the part of the emoluments relating to such overseas duties. There is, however, then the problem of identification of remittances to the UK where there is such a single employment, the duties of which are performed both within and outside the UK, and the emoluments of which are paid wholly outside the UK. However, it was understood the Inland Revenue were prepared to apply a broad interpretation of the decision in the case of Sterling Trust Ltd *v.* CIR (12 TC 686) in the way most beneficial to the employee. In this case, it was decided that relief could be given for interest which was payable out of profits only partly liable to tax by treating it as paid primarily out of the taxable profits. Applying this principle, remittances will be deemed to come primarily out of income liable to UK tax in respect of UK duties.

For the Inland Revenue further clarified their practice in the case of such mixed employments, and announced a new concession operative from 6 April 1983, in a Statement of Practice (SP 5/84) issued on 28 March 1984. Apportionment of such emoluments is normally made on a time basis, with reference to the number of days worked abroad and in the UK, except where this would clearly be inappropriate.

For purposes of identifying what part of such emoluments has been remitted to the UK, it is now proposed to accept that Case III liability will arise only where the aggregate of emoluments paid in, benefits enjoyed in, and emoluments remitted to the UK exceeds the amount assessable under Case II on the above basis. The Case III assessment will thus be restricted to the excess of the aggregate over the Case II assessment.

154 In addition, there is the further advantage that, under most double tax agreements, including in particular the US/UK agreement, if a person is paid by an employer not resident in the UK, and the remuneration is not charged to a permanent establishment in the UK, and the employee is not present for more than 183 days in the tax year in the UK but is resident in the other country, he will be exempt from UK tax (see Article 15 of US/UK Double Tax Treaty).

155 There are, therefore, three categories of foreign visitors who come to the UK to work in the UK, including designated areas of the North Sea.

(1) The person who comes for more than six months in a fiscal year and is therefore resident here without regard to whether he has accommodation and who will not be able to rely on any double tax treaty to modify his position. In the past he should, if possible, have been paid by an overseas resident employer in order to be eligible for the 50% deduction (or 25% after a lengthy period of residence), where any duties of the employment were performed in the UK. If he was paid by a UK resident employer in those circumstances, either the whole of the emoluments were liable to UK tax under Case I, or the whole of the emoluments referable to UK duties were liable under Case II of Sch. E depending upon whether he stayed long enough to be regarded as ordinarily resident as well as resident here. Any income from a separate employment with a foreign employer, where all duties are performed overseas, will be liable on a remittance basis under Case III. The remittance basis will also apply to the overseas proportion of emoluments of a mixed employment, where some duties are carried out in the UK and some abroad, if the employee is resident here but not ordinarily resident, and thus liable under Case II of Sch. E in respect of UK duties. In this situation there would be a penalty if the person performed UK and foreign duties and was paid in the UK by a UK resident employer. The element relating to UK duties would have enjoyed no deduction in the past and that relating to foreign duties would have been fully remitted to the UK and taxed accordingly. It should be noted that such an apportionment of foreign emoluments is not possible if the employee is resident and ordinarily resident in the UK and holds one employment. In that event his emoluments will be chargeable on an arising basis wherever the duties are performed. Clearly, therefore, such an arrangement will be most unsatisfying from the visitor's point of view. The overseas investment income and capital gains from the disposal of non-UK chargeable assets of an individual resident, but not domiciled in the UK, are also taxable on remittances.

(2) The person who comes to the UK for less than six months and has temporary rented accommodation during his stay. He should be regarded

as not resident here and will only be liable to UK tax under Case II of Schedule E on money earned for duties carried out in the UK. If the emoluments are foreign emoluments, they were subject to the 50% deduction. Where the duties of the employment are carried out partly in the UK and partly outside the UK, a split of the total remuneration will be made. It should be noted that no liability to UK tax will attach to any other income arising abroad and there will be no liability to capital gains tax.

(3) As in (2) whether there is accommodation retained or not, except that the person is able to claim complete exemption from UK tax because of the provisions of a double tax treaty. Usually he must be paid by a foreign employer and the income must not be charged to any permanent establishment of that employer in the UK. The fact that a management charge may be rendered to a UK subsidiary company by its parent company in respect of services performed for it by persons who continue to be employed by the parent company should not mean that such remuneration is charged to a permanent establishment for this purpose.

Corresponding payments relief

156 It should be noted that the 50% or the 25% deduction was made from foreign emoluments after deducting from those emoluments any expenses that would satisfy normal Sch. E rules of allowability and also after deducting any payments out of the emoluments of a corresponding nature to those that would have reduced the person's liability to income tax if the income derived from a UK employer, for instance, payments to a superannuation scheme comparable to contributions to an approved UK scheme (s.192(3) ICTA 1988).

157 The Board have a discretion to allow such 'corresponding payment' claims, and in the exercise of their discretion will in practice require the claimant to show that he has insufficient overseas income on which UK tax is not chargeable to enable him to make the payments without having recourse to the foreign emoluments. Where there is some overseas income, but it is insufficient to cover the payments, relief will be given on the excess. However, in the case of corresponding superannuation contributions paid out of foreign emoluments, the foreign emoluments are treated as reduced by the contributions whether or not there is overseas income to make the payments (leaflet IR 25 (1977), page 16).

158 The availability of capital out of which the payments could have been made will be disregarded.

159 A payment is regarded as a corresponding payment only if it differs from a payment which qualifies for relief under UK tax rules not in substance but solely because it is made under a foreign obligation or in accordance with normal foreign practice. Examples are alimony paid under a foreign court order, interest on a loan to purchase a residence in the employee's home country, premiums paid to certain foreign life companies (up to 1978–79), and annual contributions to a foreign pension fund which corresponds to a UK pension fund in respect of which relief on contributions would be given. The amount of the relief is computed as far as possible by reference to the appropriate UK tax rules.

In the case of alimony, for new obligations entered into on or after 15 March 1988 the person will not be entitled to a deduction for the payments. Instead he will be entitled to the allowance for supporting his ex-wife and children of £1,720 per annum under a court order. If he had existing obligations at 15 March 1988, then he will be entitled to the continuance of the relief subject to the limits imposed under the transitional provisions in FA 1988 and the ability to elect for the new form of relief to apply.

160 The effect of the way the Inland Revenue used to apply the corresponding payment relief in the case of life insurance policies, is that they must be qualifying policies so far as the term, frequency and level of payment of premiums, etc., and only not qualify for statutory relief for instance because the company is not established within one of the countries specified in the legislation, broadly the countries which used to be known as the Dominions, the UK and the Republic of Ireland (s.266(2) ICTA 1988). Statutory life insurance relief will take precedence over the corresponding payments deduction. If the policy does not merely provide for a capital sum payable on death or earlier maturity if it is an endowment policy, for instance, if it covers other benefits such as payments received on disability, the premium will need to be apportioned. It is understood that relief is no longer given following the payment of qualifying premiums under deduction of tax in 1979–80, although it has been suggested in the professional press that it might be possible to make a claim for relief under para. 6 of Sch. 14 ICTA 1988. This allows relief to be given by the Board, where it has not been given at source, by a payment by the Board or relief by discharge or repayment of tax. In certain exceptional circumstances, the taxpayer may not receive by way of reduction of premium all the relief to which he is entitled under s.266 ICTA 1988, and in those circumstances the Board are empowered to make an adjustment. It is not known if the Board have ever accepted this line of argument.

161 Claims to relief for corresponding payments should be made on the return form 11K.

Retirement annuity premiums

162 If the recipient of foreign emoluments paid retirement annuity premiums, the net relevant earnings for retirement annuity relief purposes were calculated without reference to the 50% or 25% deduction.

Foreign emoluments: 1984–85 and later years

163 Under FA 1984, the deduction for foreign emoluments assessable under Cases I and II of Sch. E does not apply for 1984/85 onwards. However, there is transitional relief where a person has held a foreign employment giving rise to such foreign emoluments eligible for a 50% deduction in the period beginning with 6 April 1983 and ending with 13 March 1984, or, in fulfilment of an obligation incurred before 14 March 1984, has started his employment in the UK before 1 August 1984. In those situations the 50% deduction continued, dropping down to 25% for 1987–88 and 1988–89 with no deduction for 1989–90 onwards.

It appears that, where in this traditional period up to 1988–89, the visitor would only be eligible for a 25% deduction in respect of his foreign emoluments, because he has been resident for nine out of the preceding ten years, then he will not qualify for any deduction at all.

The position is not altered in relation to foreign emoluments assessable on a remittance basis.

Travel expenses

164 Where a person who is not domiciled in the UK is in receipt of emoluments for duties performed in the UK he is, subject to certain conditions, exempt from tax in respect of certain travel expenses between his home abroad and the UK which are reimbursed by his employer. He must not have been resident in the UK in either of the two years of assessment immediately preceding the year of assessment in which the employment is taken up, nor must he have been in the UK for any purpose at any time during the period of two years ending with the time of taking up the employment. The period during which the travel facilities are allowed is of 5 years' duration only.

The expenses can relate to any journey from his normal home to the UK to take up or resume his employment, and vice versa. In addition, travel expenses of a spouse and children between the home abroad and the UK will be exempt if the employee is in the UK for a continuous period of at least 60 days in order to perform the duties of the employment, and the journey is made to accompany him at the beginning of the period or to visit him during it, or is a return journey following such a journey. There is a restriction of two journeys to the UK and two return journeys per year.

It should be noted that the favourable tax treatment applies to direct payments by the employer, or to travel expenses reimbursed by the employer. It is not open to the employee to claim any personal expenditure under these heads as a deduction.

165 It is commonplace to find that employees, particularly of US concerns, receive substantial extra compensation payments to cover extra UK tax they have to pay over and above what they would have paid in the USA. All such allowances and benefits that would be assessed to UK tax have to be included in the foreign emoluments.

Under Extra Statutory Concession A5, removal and relocation expenses reimbursed to a new employee or an employee transferred within an organisation are not assessable where the employee changes his residence. This is interpreted by the Inland Revenue to mean that he must sell his former residence. Representations have been made on behalf of non-domiciled employees coming to work in the UK who have to be housed, that they should not have to sell their overseas residence in order to be within the terms of the Concession.

Normally such persons would wish to rent out their main residence, pending a return to it on the cessation of their UK employment. To date, the Inland Revenue have not accepted such representations, so that if any new employee retains his home abroad but is provided with relocation and removal assistance for the purposes of buying a house in the UK during his stay here, he will be assessed on the payments.

Where an employee is seconded to the UK from his normal piece of work abroad, it may be possible to secure exemption from UK tax in respect of reimbursed travel, accommodation and subsistence expenses. This treatment is only available where the absence is not expected to (and does not in fact) exceed 12 months, and where the employee returns to his normal place of work thereafter. The situation is covered by the rules for temporary absences from a normal place of work found in the Employers Guide 480 para 8.8. It is understood that to meet the cost of upkeep of his home country residence without the assistance of rentals, Inland Revenue practice is to allow exemption for reasonable board and lodging expenses where an individual is on detached duty in the UK for a period not expected to exceed 12 months.

Requirements of employee and employer

166 Where the employer is not resident in the UK but an employee performs duties in the UK for the benefit of a person resident here or for the benefit of a person carrying on a trade here (for example a UK branch of a non-resident concern) the person for whose benefit the duties are performed may be required to give the name and address of the employee to the Inland Revenue (s.24 FA 1974). The PAYE obligations of a non-resident employer are discussed under the section 'The North Sea' below. In addition the employee may be required to make a return of the full amount of any emoluments paid to him whether or not UK tax is chargeable on them (s.24 FA 1974 and s.8 TMA 1970). This is obviously to enable the Inland Revenue to apportion on a reasonable basis the foreign emoluments referrable to UK duties where the person is liable under Case II of Sch. E.

167 Where the emoluments are paid in the UK, the Inland Revenue seek to operate the normal PAYE regulations on them, although the gross figure of the emoluments is very often not known until all figures of UK tax liability and other benefits are worked out.

168 Where the emoluments are paid abroad, the direct collection method is normally used under which an assessment is raised on the employee based on the estimated amount of the emoluments for the current tax year and tax is paid in four instalments during the year. Appropriate adjustments are made when the final figures are known.

The new receipts basis of assessment for Sch. E has not itself altered the liability to income tax under the various cases of Sch. E. However, receipts in a year after the source has ceased are now liable, reversing the case of Bray v. Best (1989 STC 159). Equally, receipts in a year before a source commences are also liable. In the case of multi-national businesses, transferring employees to and from the UK, it may be difficult to devise packages which enable payments for UK duties to escape UK tax.

The North Sea

169 The position of persons working on North Sea oil and gas installations is that irrespective of their residence position, if they are performing their duties in a designated area (that is an area designated by Order in Council under s.1(7) of the Continental Shelf Act 1964), they will be treated as performing their duties in the UK (s.830(5) ICTA 1988).

170 Such persons will be liable to UK tax on an arising basis under Case II of Schedule E if they are not resident, or not ordinarily resident in the UK, in respect of their emoluments for the work they carry out in the North Sea; or under Case I of Schedule E if they are resident and ordinarily resident in the UK on all their emoluments. No 12½% or 100% deduction will be due as they will not be carrying out their duties abroad, although if they are foreigners paid by a non-resident employer, the 50% or 25% deduction in respect of foreign emoluments was due in the normal way, depending upon the length of their period of residence in the UK.

171 The only exemption from UK tax such employees were able to claim was if they were residents of another country with which the UK has a double tax agreement and the emoluments were paid by a foreign resident employer and not charged to any UK establishment of that employer (including a branch of the employer in the form of a North Sea installation) and the employee's tour of duty meant he was in the UK for no more than 183 days. In that event the relevant double tax agreement might confer exemption from UK tax. This had the effect of enabling the foreign employer to pay allowances that were exempt from tax in the country of origin in addition to salary which would normally be liable to UK tax under the benefits legislation for persons earning more than £8,500 per annum, for instance lodging and general expenses allowances.

However, the Inland Revenue have in any event now changed their view on the exemption article in old double tax agreements which were not amended to exclude persons working on North Sea installations. In a press release dated 3 March 1989 the Inland Revenue announced that following legal advice they would no longer be accepting as exempt from tax the residents of certain countries employed in exploration or exploitation activities on the UK Continental Shelf.

The Inland Revenue had up to this time interpreted the exception in the Dependent Services (employment) Articles of the arrangements in these old agreements for non-residents where the remuneration was not borne by a UK branch as applying both to the UK mainland and the UK Continental Shelf in preference to the taxing rights over the UK Continental Shelf including employments exercised there granted by s.38 FA 1973 (now s.830 ICTA 1988). Residents of those countries working on the UK Continental Shelf were therefore treated as exempt from UK taxation. The Inland Revenue have now decided on legal advice that the exemption granted by these old style agreements is restricted to employments performed within the territory of the UK as defined in each arrangement. Since that definition excludes the UK Continental Shelf, the UK's taxing rights granted by s.38 FA 1973 are unaffected by these arrangements. Consequently, such residents will be liable to UK tax with effect from 6 April 1989. In particular residents of the Isle of Man, Jersey and Guernsey will be affected by this change.

It follows that in all cases, UK taxing rights should take precedence over any exemption in a double tax agreement whether this is specifically stated to be the position in the agreement (as in the Philippines/UK agreement) or not.

172 It should be noted the Agreement between the USA and the UK (Articles 27A and 15) specifically denies any exemption from the UK legislation making North Sea activities liable to UK tax and states that such activities constitute a permanent establishment in the UK. Thus if a US company charges its North Sea 'branch' with such remuneration, the exemption cannot apply to the US resident individual.

173 The days spent in the UK are crucial for this purpose. Days of arrival and days of departure are normally ignored for this purpose (leaflet IR 20, para.8).

Returns by North Sea employers

174 There are special provisions requiring licence holders employing persons on activities carried on under the licence to give details to the Inland Revenue of any emoluments or other payments made in respect of services performed in the area and the names of the recipients, so that it is not possible for such an employer to escape his obligation by not having a branch in the UK or a subsidiary company resident in the UK (para. 2(b) of Sch. 15 FA 1973).

Clark *v.* Oceanic Contractors Inc

175 In addition it has been held by a narrow majority of three to two in the House of Lords in the case of Clark *v.* Oceanic Contractors Incorporated that a non-resident employer operating in the North Sea is also liable to account for tax under the PAYE procedure on any emoluments of its employees liable to UK tax (1983 STC 35).

If a non-resident company is taxed on any profits derived from activities in a designated area of the North Sea, and its employees are deemed to perform their duties in the UK when working in that area, under the special provisions in s.38 FA 1973 it follows that the employer has an obligation to apply PAYE to such emoluments.

176 There is, of course, no practical problem where an overseas employer has a branch in the UK. However, in the above case the respondent corporation, which was incorporated in Panama as a wholly owned subsidiary of a US parent, maintained only a design office and platform fabrication yard in the UK. The company's activities, which extended throughout the world, included a North Sea division with its headquarters in Brussels. This division was engaged in the installation and maintenance of platforms and the laying of pipelines, in both the UK and Norwegian sectors of the North Sea. Some 60 per cent of the employees engaged by the North Sea division were UK nationals, the remainder being principally citizens of the USA. Since 1973, some 40 per cent of the corporation's North Sea activities had been located in the UK sector of the North Sea. Employees' emoluments were paid from Brussels in US dollars by cheques made out in Brussels and drawn on a New York bank. It was common ground that, by reason of s.38, the corporation was liable to UK tax on profits arising from the activities of its North Sea division in the designated area and equally employees working in this area were assessable to income tax under Sch. E on their emoluments.

177 The Inland Revenue argued that s.203 ICTA 1988, which governs the operation of PAYE, imposed no territorial limitation, and that the PAYE regulations must also be applied wherever emoluments chargeable under Sch. E are paid. Oceanic submitted that s.203 could have no application to a foreign employer paying emoluments from some place outside the UK.

178 The House of Lords ruled that the Corporation was liable to apply PAYE. However, Lord Scarman dismissed the Inland Revenue assertion that the application of PAYE had no territorial limits. There was the practical impossibility of enforcing or monitoring the system against an uncooperative employer residing overseas. Therefore, some territorial limitation had to be applied. The existence of this limitation implied a 'tax presence' within the UK. The operations carried out by the corporation did disclose such a presence because of the application of s.38 FA 1973 and it was, therefore, liable to account for PAYE. 'For the purposes of corporation tax, Oceanic, it is agreed, carries on a trade in the UK which includes its operations in the UK section of the North Sea. For the purposes of this trade, it employs a work force in that section whose earnings are assessable to British income tax. Finally, Oceanic does have an address for service in the UK. . . . For these reasons, I conclude that Oceanic by its trading operations . . . has subjected itself to the liability to operate pay as you earn'.

Lord Wilberforce similarly considered that liability only arose where an employer had a branch or agency in the UK so as to be within the provisions of s.11 ICTA 1988.

179 This decision raises matters of some importance, particularly to those employers operating in the North Sea. It means that wherever there is some establishment employing labour in the UK or in a designated area, there will be an obligation to apply PAYE.

180 In response to representations, divers are no longer regarded as employees for tax purposes although anyone employing a diver in the UK or a designated area is required to disclose details of payments made to him (s.314 ICTA 1988). This means they will be able to claim all the normal expenses allowable to self-employed persons and if they can show that the base of their operations is their home, travelling expenses to and from the North Sea installation should be claimed on the basis of the decision in Horton *v*. Young (47 TC 69).

It should be noted that the cost of diving training courses is regarded by the Inland Revenue as capital expenditure as such courses put the diver in a position to earn income rather than being undertaken in the course of earning that income. In the case of employee divers, no relief is due. However, if the diver is treated as self-employed, it has been agreed between the Inland Revenue and the association of off-shore diving contractors that the expenditure can be treated as expenditure on 'know-how' qualifying for relief under s.530 ICTA 1988.

The expenditure qualifies for relief because the knowledge gained relates to 'techniques likely to assist in the working of a mine, oil well or other source of mineral deposits'. For the diver who also works on non-oil related activities there will be a restriction, so that the relief given in any year will be restricted with reference to the amount of s.314 profits (basically from diving in the UK Continental Shelf in the North Sea and in the UK itself on oil related activities) and the total diving earnings for the year (for instance, from dock or harbour work or work outside the UK).

Receipts may be required to substantiate the expenditure, which can amount to over £5,000 for a saturation diving course and more than £3,500 for an air diving course.

For qualifying courses undertaken prior to 1 April 1986, relief is given over a six year period. For qualifying courses undertaken after 1 April 1986, relief is given by way of a writing down allowance of 25% per annum on the reducing balance basis.

The initial costs of basic survival and fire fighting courses are regarded as capital expenditure which does not qualify for relief under the know-how provisions in s.533(7) ICTA 1988, but the costs of renewal courses are allowable as revenue expenditure.

Expenses

181 Difficulties have arisen concerning the allowability of expenses payments made to oil-rig workers and others who live at a considerable distance from their place of work and who receive travel expenses when they go on periodic leave to visit their families from the rigs. These difficulties apply to both overseas visitors and UK nationals. As there is only one fixed base from which, in most cases, they work, all expenses are arguably expenses of travelling to and from the place of work. The amounts are not so small as to be capable of being ignored as a perquisite, which appeared to be the basis of the decision in the case of the local authority teacher, Donnelly *v.* Williamson, where a mileage allowance of £13 per annum to help a teacher meet the cost of attending school functions out of hours was held to be not taxable (1981 STC 563). Neither do the payments come within the 'working rules agreements' governing the payment of travel and subsistence allowances up to certain amounts tax free to construction industry workers moving from site to site as agreed between the Trade Unions and the Inland Revenue.

The position is, therefore, that in strict law the amounts are probably assessable.

182 Consequently, Extra Statutory Concession A65 (workers on off-shore oil and gas rigs or platforms – free transfers to and from the mainland) was introduced to deal with the problem. All expenses reimbursed by the employer for transfers between the mainland and the oil and gas rigs or platforms, including the journey from home to the port of transfer will not now be taxed. Where the employees have to take overnight accommodation in the vicinity of the mainland departure point, income tax is also not charged on reasonable accommodation and subsistence costs or, in the case of employees earning £8,500 or more, on the benefit of such accommodation provided at the employer's expense.

The Norwegian sector of the North Sea

183 The Double Tax Treaty between the UK and Norway was amended by a Protocol (Protocol of 23 June 1977, now Article 31A of Double Tax Treaty) to introduce special rules applicable to certain offshore activities. One of the rules, which applies in Norway in relation to income derived on or after 1 January 1978, states, basically, that salaries and similar remuneration derived by a resident of the UK, in respect of an employment connected with the exploration of the sea bed and subsoil situated in Norwegian waters to the extent that the duties are performed in Norwegian waters, shall only be taxable in Norway. This rule is to apply only where documentary evidence is produced which satisfies the UK authorities that tax has been paid in Norway, otherwise the normal domestic laws are to apply, double taxation relief being given accordingly.

It is understood that the UK Revenue authorities do not know if the Norwegian Revenue authorities regard all the remuneration as relating to duties performed offshore where rest days are concerned, and therefore only taxable in Norway.

Visiting professors or teachers

184 In connection with visitors to the UK generally, it should be borne in mind that it may be possible to claim exemption from UK tax on earnings in the UK under a double tax agreement, if the persons concerns are visiting professors or teachers.

However, the wording of the agreement must be carefully studied as the case of CIR *v.* Vas (1990 STC 137) illustrated. In that case, the taxpayer, a Hungarian, visited the UK on three separate occasions, on each occasion to take up research appointments at the University of Newcastle. He was a resident of Hungary immediately before each visit, which did not exceed two years. He claimed exemption under the relevant article in the UK/Hungary Double Tax Treaty for each visit on the grounds that it was of less than two years' duration. The court held that no exemption was due for any period running after the expiry of two years from the date of his first visit.

Visitors for education

185   A person who comes to the UK for a period of stay and education which is expected to last for more than four years will be regarded as resident and ordinarily resident from the date of his arrival. If the period is not expected to exceed four years he may be treated as not ordinarily resident but this will depend on whether:

(1) he has available accommodation here, or
(2) he intends to remain here at the end of his period of education, or
(3) he proposes to visit the UK in future years after his educational visit is finished for average annual periods of three months of more. If, despite the person's original intention, he remains in the UK for more than four years, he will be treated as ordinarily resident in any event from the beginning of the fifth tax year of his stay (leaflet IR 20).

All visitors – investment income and capital gains

186   Any visitor may become resident and ordinarily resident in the UK depending upon the degree of presence in the UK and his intentions as indicated above. In addition, he may ultimately acquire a new domicile of choice in the UK if he decides to make his home permanently in the UK and thus ceases to be a visitor.

If he becomes resident in the UK but remains domiciled outside the UK, he will be liable on a remittance basis in respect of foreign investment income and capital gains on foreign assets. If remittances are made out of a mixed fund of capital and income, the Inland Revenue will cite Scottish Provident Institution *v.* Allen (4 TC 409 and 501) as authority for the contention that the remittances are of income up to the full amount of the income content of the fund unless the taxpayer can identify remittances as having clearly been made out of specific receipts into the fund. The same principle would apply to capital gains out of a mixed fund of pure return of capital invested and gains.

It is therefore, advisable where material amounts are involved, for resident visitors to operate three foreign bank accounts, one for income, one for capital gains and one limited to the return of the original capital invested in the chargeable asset.

187 Remittances out of a source of income which ceased before the visitor became resident are not liable to tax on the authority of the principle established in National Provident Institution *v.* Brown (8 TC 452) where it was held that income cannot be assessed for a year in which the taxpayer does not possess the source. It should be noted that a continuing source of income, assessable on a remittance basis, if income from the source has already been remitted before a period of residence, may strictly be already liable on a previous year basis under the normal rules for assessing Case V income where an individual becomes resident (Carter *v.* Sharon 20 TC 229). However, in practice, for new residents the Inland Revenue do not normally claim tax on more than the income that has arisen since the period of residence began if less than such remittances.

Capital gains

188 The process of quantification of remitted capital gains can be quite complex, bearing in mind that the gain has first to be quantified in sterling terms by reference to the sterling equivalent at the rate of exchange ruling at the date of acquisition of the foreign currency cost of the asset and a similar equivalent of the proceeds of the sale (Bently *v.* Pike 1981 STC 360). If the gain or part of it is shown to have been remitted to the UK, the foreign currency remitted will be converted at the rate of exchange at the time of remittance. If this shows a greater gain than the sterling gain on the sale of the asset, the balance will have been caused by a separate foreign currency gain which is itself liable to capital gains tax.

189 The anomaly under which all foreign currency bank accounts of a person resident here were treated as located in the UK for capital gains tax purposes was to have been corrected under the 1983 Finance Bill (clause 60). In theory, therefore, unremitted gains arising from the use of such accounts were technically liable to capital gains tax even if the holder is not domiciled here as they would arise from a UK asset. Under FA 1984 this has been put right and only such accounts held at a UK branch of a bank are treated as situated here, with effect from 6 April 1983.

It seems, however, that the practice (SP 10/84) of treating all foreign bank accounts containing a particular foreign currency as one account for capital gains purposes, thus ignoring transfers between them until all debts represented by the bank accounts have been repaid to the taxpayer, does not apply to non-domiciled persons. The text of the Statement of Practice says 'Except in relation to an account to which s.275(l) TCGA 1992 applies (accounts of non-domiciled individuals)'. On this basis, therefore, the capital gain is computed on any eventual remittance tracing through realisations by such transfers between accounts on a strict basis.

Visitors and IHT

190 Applying the principles referred to above, a visitor will normally retain his foreign domicile and will not acquire a special fiscal domicile for IHT purposes until he has been resident here for not less than 17 years of the 20 years of assessment ending with the year of assessment in which the transfer of value is made (s.267(1)(b) IHTA 1984). This is also subject in the case of a disposition on death to the provisions of any old double tax agreement made for estate duty as well as for inheritance tax which continue to operate for transfers on death and could, therefore, still mean that the person has retained his foreign domicile even after 17 years of residence in the UK (s.267(2) IHTA 1984).

191 As IHT only imposes a charge on assets situated in the UK which are transferred by a person not domiciled in the UK, it is important for any visitor to minimise his exposure to IHT by keeping his UK estate below the threshold for IHT. Thus, if it is desired to invest substantial amounts in UK assets potentially liable to IHT, this should be done through the medium of a company incorporated outside the UK so that should the person die, the asset passing on his death will be shares in a foreign company. However, it should be borne in mind that if the investments are income producing and the income is accumulated in the foreign company, the income being from a UK source, there may be a liability under s.739 ICTA 1988 in the case of visitors who have become ordinarily resident in the UK. The exclusion from the Section of non-domiciled persons will not apply to UK source income (s.743(3) ICTA 1988).

One way of avoiding a possible inheritance tax liability on the UK residence of a non-domiciled individual has been to buy it in the name of an off-shore company, so that if the individual dies while resident here, he does not own a UK situs asset. Unfortunately, the Inland Revenue are now contending that the individual in these circumstances is a director of the company for Sch. E purposes and liable to tax on the annual value of the property (under s.145 ICTA 1988) and on interest at the official rate if the property costs more than £75,000 (s.146 ICTA 1988). He would also be liable on any other outgoings met by the company, subject to the usual limits. However, in a letter from the Inland Revenue to the Institute of Taxation dated 25 January 1989, the Inland Revenue agreed to an amnesty for past closed years up to 1987/1988 if the point had not been raised. If a Sch. E assessment remains open and the question has not been raised, the Inland Revenue will not pursue the question for years up to and including 1986/87. If the point has been raised, the Inland Revenue will not seek tax for any year before the year immediately preceding that in which notification was given.

192 It should be noted that foreign currency accounts held in the UK are outside the scope of IHT on death only if the individual is both not domiciled in the UK immediately before his death and is neither resident nor ordinarily resident here at that time (s.157 IHTA 1984). Therefore, a visitor who is resident in the UK at the time of his death will still be liable to IHT on such bank balances.

Visitors – departure from the UK

193 Care needs to be taken with the UK tax position of investment income, especially bank and building society interest, when visitors cease to be

UK-resident. The Extra-Statutory Concession (No. B13) under which tax is not pursued in respect of UK deposit interest received by a non-resident, only applies for complete years of non-residence. Hence, persons ceasing to be UK resident part way through a year of assessment may be well advised to close their UK deposit accounts on departure and to open new ones in an off-shore location such as the Channel Islands or Isle of Man. Any interest received after the cessation of UK residence will then be free of UK tax.

194 If the new account is opened before departure, the Inland Revenue may treat all interest on the new account arising to the following 5 April as taxable because the source was held during a period of residence.

Chapter 7
Clergymen

General principles of taxation

195 A clergyman is usually the holder of an office (not an employment – see Davies *v*. Presbyterian Church of Wales (1986) 1 All ER 705) and is assessable under Sch. E in respect of the emoluments from that office, including any profits arising from his office not paid to him by one of his employers. He is obliged to complete a special income tax return as the sources of his income and the allowance of his expenses can be complicated.

For example, Anglican clergymen are paid by the Church Commissioners on the basis of recommendations by the Diocesan Boards of Finance. They also receive income from local sources such as wedding fees and some will receive salaries as teachers or chaplains. The Church Commissioners will 'top up' these local sources where necessary. A very few clergymen will receive nothing from the Church Commissioners because their benefice is sufficiently well-off to support them fully.

Other examples of clergymen who are paid partly locally and partly centrally include those of the Presbyterian churches of Scotland, Wales and Northern Ireland. Ministers of independent churches and of those belonging to 'looser' associations are paid predominantly if not entirely locally. However, such ministers will usually still receive income from sources other than their employers (ie., the local congregation), such as wedding, funeral or lecturing fees but in many cases they surrender such fees to their church.

In general, items received by clergymen from various sources have been held to be taxable where they arise by virtue of the office and without the fulfilment of any further condition on the part of the particular office holder. Thus in Herbert *v*. McQuade (1902) 4 TC 489, grants made by the Queen Victoria Clergy Sustentation Fund in augmentation of the income of the benefice were held to be taxable as profits accruing from the office. In contrast, in Turner *v*. Cuxson (1888) 2 TC 422, a grant paid to a particular clergyman from a religious society in recognition of past faithful service, and renewable annually on certain conditions, was held not to be taxable. The Churches Main Committee Circular 1986/10 puts it like this:

"If there is a legal right to receive, the gift is taxable. So there would normally

111

be no liability in respect of a complete windfall, such as an unrestricted gift or bonus in recognition of outstanding service; but special collections at Easter or on other occasions for the minister are liable to income tax." (see **196** below).

This circular deals generally with the taxation of ministers of religion and is available from Churches Main Committee, Fielden House, Little College Street, London SW1 3JZ, at a cost of 50p plus postage. Senior Inland Revenue officials have seen the circular and have described the notes as a reasonable guide, subject to a warning that decisions on individual claims will depend upon all the facts and circumstances.

Types of income that are taxable

196 Specific items of income that are taxable as income from the office of clergymen are:

(a)   Easter offerings. It used to be general practice for the collection in Anglican churches on Easter Sunday to go directly to the parish priest. Now it is quite common for the minister to waive this right and state that the offerings will go to some other cause. The Church Commissioners will then pay him more. However, some clergymen still receive their Easter offerings, especially those few who receive nothing from the Church Commissioners. Such offerings were held to be taxable in the case of Cooper *v.* Blakiston (1908) 5 TC 347, as a profit accruing by reason of the office in accordance with the general principles set out in **195** above. Whitsun offerings to a curate are similarly assessable (Slaney *v.* Starkey (1931) 16 TC 45). There are special arrangements for the tax treatment of Easter offerings where Easter Day falls twice in any fiscal year.

The Inland Revenue was also asked by the Church Commissioners for its opinion on the position if such collections were earmarked for a specific purpose, for instance, payment of school fees for the minister's children or wages of gardeners. As a result of this enquiry, Circular 1986/10 (see above) gives the following view:

   (i)   if offerings are solicited on behalf of a minister, he is assessable whether they are paid to him direct or into a fund to meet his expenses (eg., school fees, books), or even if they are diverted by him to a fund from which he does not personally benefit (eg., a church restoration fund);

   (ii)   if, however, the minister clearly divests himself of the right to the offerings, eg., by advance public announcement of the destination of the offerings, or by some similar notification in the church magazine, and the offerings are given in the knowledge that they are going to a fund which in no way benefits the minister, he will not be assessable.

(b)   Grants from the Church Commissioners, including dividends and interest, for instance, from the invested proceeds of the sale of glebe.

(c)   Payments-in-lieu of, or in composition for, tithes (such as corn rents).

(d) Fees for conducting marriages and burial services.

(e) Pew rents.

(f) Glebe rents.

(g) Grants from sustentation and similar funds, for instance, from the Parochial Church Council or Diocesan Board of Finance. Where the grant is a reimbursement of statutory expenses in connection with the manse or vicarage, it will be exempt (s.332(2)(a) ICTA 1988).

(h) Voluntary payments by patrons or others towards the stipend.

(i) Any part of the stipend borne by a lay impropriator.

(j) Dividends or interest from local endowments received by the incumbent either direct or from trustees.

(k) Private gifts by parishioners or church members to the minister for himself whenever given.

(l) Certain benefits-in-kind where the minister is 'higher-paid' – see **197**(4) and **200** below.

(m) Contributions towards the personal community charge of the minister and his wife. The exemption for the rates will continue to apply to payments by a Church in Scotland towards the community water charges.

Exemptions

197 There are various exemptions from income tax enjoyed by ministers of religion, as well as specific expenses that they may claim.

(1) Treatment of vicarage, manse or other church property occupied by a clergyman

A full-time minister of religion is not assessable under s.145 ICTA 1988 on the annual value of any house provided for him to perform the duties of his office. He is treated as a representative occupier (see below) and, consequently, no benefit arises on the annual value of the premises (or in respect of any rates paid on his behalf or reimbursed to him before 31 March 1990) (ss.145(4)(a) and 146(1)(b) ICTA 1988). This exemption extends, in practice, to full-time incumbents of benefices in the Church of England, occupiers of properties belonging to cathedral chapters, occupiers of properties belonging to charitable bodies such as bodies of trustees on behalf of particular denominations, or occupiers of property held by Diocesan Boards of Finance in trust for a parochial church council.

There are complications with a part-time clergyman living in Church accommodation. He has to prove that the accommodation is necessary for the proper performance of his duties, or that it is provided for the better performance of those duties. The Churches Main Committee Circular No.1986/10 indicates that the Inland Revenue do not accept automatically that there is representative occupation in all such cases.

Each case is looked at on its merits. To be exempt from liability on the annual value of any accommodation provided for him a part-time minister must demonstrate either:

(a) that it is necessary for the proper performance of his duties that he should reside in the accommodation; or
(b) that the accommodation is provided for the better performance of the duties of his employment and his is one of the kinds of employment in the case of which it is customary for employers to provide living accommodation for employees (ss.145(4)(a), (b) and 146(1)(b) ICTA 1988).

This is known as 'representative occupation'. (For these purposes an 'employment' includes an 'office' (s.145(8) ICTA 1988).)

Where the clergyman is not exempt, the measure of the benefit is the gross annual value for rating purposes of the accommodation provided (or the rent which the Church pays if this is greater), less any amount made good by the minister to the Church, plus an 'appropriate percentage' of the amount, if any, by which the cost (or in some circumstances the value) of the property exceeds £75,000. (The 'appropriate percentage' is determined by a formula laid down by statutory instrument, following s.178 FA 1989, eg., 10.75% per annum from 6 March 1992.) In addition, where the provider of the accommodation meets any pecuniary liability incurred by such a part-time clergyman, for example heating and lighting, gardener's wages or domestic or other services, the clergyman will be chargeable under basic Sch. E rules (s.19(1) ICTA 1988). This applies whether or not he is higher-paid and regardless of whether the provider meets the expenses directly or reimburses the minister. For these purposes it is irrelevant whether the accommodation is provided for the better performance of the minister's duties, unless he is higher-paid in which case the special rules referred to in (4) below apply. On the other hand, where the employer actually incurs such liabilities directly no charge will arise unless the minister is higher-paid.

(2) Statutory property expenses

Where a clergyman or minister of religion holds a full-time office, and resides in a property belonging to or leased by a charity or ecclesiastical corporation, in order to perform his duties and not as a lessee, the making good to the clergyman, or the direct payment on his behalf, of statutory amounts payable in connection with the residence, such as water rates and in Scotland community water charge, and general service charges, is not assessable on him (s.332(2)(a) and (b) ICTA 1988). This also covers repayments on behalf of or to the incumbent of loans made under the Clergy Residence Repairs Acts, or Glebe Loans by a parochial church council or diocese, or other payments made under the Ecclesiastical Dilapidations Measures (s.332(4) ICTA 1988). Where the clergyman lets part of the residence, the rent he receives will be taxable in the normal way and the exemption does not extend to statutory amounts paid that relate to such parts.

(3) Other property expenses

Where the charity itself incurs any expenses in providing living accommodation for him, these expenses will not count as part of his income provided he is not 'higher-paid'. This covers the upkeep, maintenance or insurance of the residence or provision of services such as cleaning, gardening, lighting, heating, etc. (s.332(2)(c) ICTA 1988). As the statutory position was not completely clear in the case of full-time clergymen, the Inland Revenue, in an extra-statutory concession (see Inland Revenue Extra Statutory Concession A61) published on 8 August 1986, confirmed that where the church or charity owns or leases a property for the clergyman, no tax is charged on sums paid on his behalf or reimbursed in respect of heating, lighting, cleaning and gardening expenses, although they are the contractual liability of the clergyman because he occupies the property. Similarly, where an allowance is paid to meet such costs, the Inland Revenue will not seek to tax it except to the extent that it exceeds such costs. As this concession does not apply to the higher-paid clergymen, the comments in (4) below are relevant to them.

Where a full-time minister bears any expenses in maintaining (including decorating), repairing, insuring, or managing any church premises, of the type referred to in (1) above, he may claim a deduction of one-quarter of the amounts involved (s.332(3)(c) ICTA 1988).

(4) Higher-paid clergy and directors of church charities – property expenses

Different rules apply where the clergyman is in higher-paid employment or is a director.

To determine whether a clergyman is higher-paid, it is necessary to include everything paid to or on behalf of the minister and his family, except reasonable removal expenses where the minister has to change his residence to take up a new appointment, and the cost of provision of retirement pensions for himself and his dependants. It thus includes all stipends, fees and, where applicable, Easter offerings, and expenses reimbursed or paid on his behalf including expenses which can be claimed as deductions under s.332(3) ICTA 1988, such as travelling and subsistence expenses, and the cost of his telephone or car running expenses if paid for by the Church authorities, but not anything included in (2) above.

Therefore, many church dignitaries and clergy who are reimbursed heavy travelling expenses, and those with a high service allowance to cover repairs, heating, lighting and cleaning are likely to be higher-paid, if they are not already such by virtue of their other emoluments from the same employer (see below). In determining who is higher-paid, emoluments from separate employments are not aggregated. For instance, the various emoluments of a clergyman who was a pastor of his congregation and a hospital chaplain, a schoolmaster or a university lecturer, would not be aggregated for these purposes nor would any income of his wife. However, all employments under the same employer are treated as a single employment as are those of connected companies and, therefore, the emoluments therefrom are aggregated for these purposes.

An individual is not treated as a director, for these purposes, if he is not remunerated at a rate exceeding £8,500 a year and does not have a material interest in the company (that is, broadly not more than five per cent of the ordinary share capital of the company), and either his employment is as a full-time working director, or the company is non-profit making or is established for charitable purposes only (s.167(5) ICTA 1988). These provisions should save most, if not all, clergymen from being held to be directors for tax purposes, for instance of church bookshops. In the case of companies limited by guarantee, which have been formed to act as trustees for various church purposes, the Inland Revenue have said that those companies that it has examined come within the definition of non-profit making companies. The Churches Main Committee Circular 1986/10 reports that, where in any particular case this is not so, the Inland Revenue would consider the matter sympathetically to see whether some concession could be granted.

In the case of those who are directors or higher-paid clergymen who are required to live in accommodation provided for the better performance of their duties (s.145(4)(a) or (b) ICTA 1988 – see above), the position in respect of expenses incurred by the church or charity or reimbursed to the clergyman may be summarised as follows:

(a) services not subject to tax – structural alterations and additions; repairs of a kind which would be the landlord's responsibility if the premises were let (s.155(3) ICTA 1988);

(b) services which are taxable subject to a limit (see below) – heating, lighting and cleaning; internal repairs; maintenance or decoration, which are normally the responsibility of the tenant; the provision of furniture (s.163(2) ICTA 1988);

(c) services taxable without limit – these are all services other than those listed in (a) and (b), such as the services of gardeners and domestic services other than cleaning.

The limit in the case of services included in (b) above is ten per cent of the net amount of the emoluments of the employment. The gross amount includes everything mentioned above; the net amount is the gross amount less:

(a) any capital allowances, for instance on a car; allowable expenses including expenses specifically allowable to a clergyman up to the one-quarter limit mentioned below (see (5));

(b) contributions to an approved superannuation scheme;

(c)   personal pensions and retirement annuity premiums where the clergyman is not in a pensionable office. (See s.163 ICTA 1988.)

Where part of the accommodation which is provided is used partly for living in and partly for the performance of his duties (for instance as an office or study), the costs of taxable services are allocated or apportioned so that the clergyman is liable to tax only on that which relates to the living accommodation. All the other rules of assessment of benefits for directors and higher-paid employees apply to such directors and higher-paid clergymen. Details of the application of these rules to some of the benefits more commonly enjoyed by ministers are given below at **200**.

(5) Reimbursement of property expenses

It is important for a higher-paid clergyman that, where exemption from income tax applies, property expenses should be borne directly by the charity or by specific reimbursement as, if the minister pays them out of a general grant provided to him, he will only be able to claim a quarter of the expenses under s.332(3)(c) ICTA 1988. Thus the Diocesan Boards of Finance have been advised, by agreement with the Inland Revenue, to divide payments into reimbursements and stipends.

Expenses

198   The following expenses can be claimed, where borne by the clergyman himself.

(1) Rent

If the clergyman rents a house himself, which he uses mainly or substantially for the purpose of his duties as a clergyman or minister, the inspector of taxes may allow up to one-quarter of the rent as a deduction (s.332(3)(b) ICTA 1988). However, where this situation arises it is usually advantageous for the lease to be in the name of the church authorities, so that the rent is payable by them and is not the minister's liability. In this situation no charge to income tax will arise in respect of the rent.

(2) Maintenance expenditure

A clergyman can also claim any expenses borne by him in maintaining, repairing, insuring or managing church premises that he occupies, up to one-quarter of the total amount (for instance, payments made by him under the Ecclesiastical Dilapidations Measures). This, therefore, covers the cost of decorations and property insurance. The total claim under this heading and under (3) below in respect of similar expenditure, is subject to a ceiling of one-quarter of the total of such expenditure (s.332(3)(c) ICTA 1988).

Therefore, it is important that reimbursement of such expenses should, where possible, be made to obtain complete relief.

(3) General expenses

A clergyman can claim any expenses incurred by him wholly, exclusively and necessarily in the performance of his duties (s.332(3)(a) ICTA 1988). This is regarded by the Inland Revenue as covering any duties enjoined on the minister by law or by his ecclesiastical superiors, as well as duties arising directly from his obligations to his congregation. It may often be more convenient for some of the expenses to be borne direct by the parochial church council, or by the church stewards or trustees, as then the need to claim all the allowable expenditure does not arise unless the clergyman is higher-paid. They may, for example, rent the minister's telephone even though it is his name which appears in the directory. Specifically, the following cover most of the types of claim likely to be met and are regarded as *prima facie* allowable.

(a)   the cost of stationery, postage, use of telephone, etc., incurred in connection with his duties;

(b)   travelling expenses when visiting members of the congregation, or attending meetings of official church bodies such as presbytery, where required of him by law or his superiors;

(c)   the cost of repair or replacement of robes actually used in Divine Service in accordance with church law, or by custom of the particular church. The Inland Revenue will not give an allowance other than for the basic apparel for the service. The only robes which an Anglican incumbent is by Canon Law required to wear, are the surplice and the hood. Where it is the custom or a requirement of Canon Law for a cassock to be worn such as in certain cathedrals and college chapels, the Inland Revenue also allow the cost of replacement of a cassock. The Inland Revenue also normally allow a deduction for the cost of 'dog-collars', as this is usually small. In a case before the Commissioners, a Devon vicar was successful in claiming the cost of his cloak, used mainly for funerals (see *The Times* of 22 January 1986). The Inland Revenue do not accept that this decision has general application. Nonetheless, if a priest in a similar rural parish needed a cloak to protect himself from the elements during funerals, it would probably be worth making a claim. The successful Devon vicar, however, did not win a claim for the cost of his shirt and dog collar, on the basic principle that he had to be clothed anyway (see Hillyer *v.* Leeke (1976) 51 TC 90 and Mallalieu *v.* Drummond (1983) 57 TC 330). The Inland Revenue would probably have passed the claim for the dog collar if it had not been associated with a claim for a shirt, a cloak and a computer (see (q) below);

(d)   the cost of a *locum tenens* during an illness or holiday;

(e)   the cost of reasonable entertainment on official occasions;

(f) any stipend or payment to a curate or assistant curate, whether or not licensed to officiate within the parish;

(g) secretarial assistance, including the cost of repair or replacement of typewriters, filing cabinets, etc., and payments to his wife to carry out such work, provided the wages are actually paid and are commensurate with the duties she performs. The Free Church of Scotland, in its supplement to the Churches Main Committee Circular, recommends ministers to keep a separate bank account for their wives' wages and to make regular transfers to that account from their own keeping such transfers distinguishable from housekeeping money. The sort of work for which the wife can be paid must be distinguished from work undertaken as an active member of the church, eg., as leader of a women's group, or for the organisation of Church social events;

(h) communion expenses;

(i) costs of collecting glebe income in respect of a period prior to 1 April 1978;

(j) costs of domestic help, where necessitated by the performance of his duties, for instance in cleaning, entertaining visiting dignitaries, or reasonable wages paid to his wife for cleaning that part of his house used mainly or substantially for the purposes of his duties (see (g) above);

(k) costs of heating, lighting, repairs or replacements of carpets or chairs applicable to the part of the house used mainly for the purposes of his duties. In so far as a cost is claimed under this heading, and could also be claimed under s.332(3)(c) ICTA 1988 (eg., rates or costs of repairs to the premises), the amount allowable cannot exceed one-quarter of the total costs. Otherwise, the proportion allowed is what can reasonably be regarded as incurred in the performance of the duties of the office;

(l) tenths, first fruits, duties and fees on presentation, which are usually allowed on a previous year basis;

(m) the costs of procurations and synodals are usually allowed on the basis of the average amounts paid over the previous seven years;

(n) the cost of repairs of chancels is allowed on a previous year basis;

(o) the purchase of books. The Inland Revenue now recognise that expenditure by a minister on books purchased for actual use in the conduct of church services, or in the preparation of sermons, is incurred wholly, exclusively and necessarily in the performance of his duties. Therefore, provided the church authorities do not or would not supply the books if asked, the Inland Revenue allows a deduction for this expenditure under s.332(3)(a) ICTA 1988. Books falling within this category would include the Bible, prayer books and office books such as the Book of Common Prayer. For similar reasons, the Inland Revenue allow a deduction for expenditure on books such as those given out to engaged couples or to members of confirmation, baptism, membership or Bible classes.

Where the church authorities buy the minister theological or other books that he needs to fulfil his duties, or reimburse his expenditure on such books, the Inland Revenue would not normally regard the provision of the books as giving rise to a benefit, as where the minister is 'higher-paid' he would be able to make a claim under s.332(3)(a) ICTA 1988. However, if the church authorities simply give him a cash allowance for books, without regard to his actual expenditure, the allowance would be regarded as a taxable emolument. Following the decision in Munby *v.* Furlong (1977) 50 TC 491, claims may be made for capital allowances under s.27 CAA 1990 in respect of substantial reference books that have a useful life of more than two years. Clearly this should only be tried as a 'second string' as such a claim, if accepted, would give initial relief of only 25%;

(p) car expenses. It is open to the clergyman to claim capital allowances on the proportion of the cost of his car, and running expenses relating to official duties in the normal way. The usual practice in the Church of England is for the diocese to pay a mileage allowance (to cover the whole cost of putting the car on the road including standing charges, maintenance and depreciation). Such an allowance cannot, by its very nature, be said to relate exclusively to running expenses and thus be reimbursement of allowable expenditure that is not ultimately taxable (see Perrons *v.* Spackman (1981) 55 TC 403). It is likely therefore that the inspector of taxes will seek to assess at least the depreciation element, if the amounts are material. However, it is likely a claim for capital allowances would cover any depreciation element.

It is anticipated that dioceses will in the main adopt the now statutory mileage allowances which under the Fixed Profit Car Scheme give rise to no taxable benefit (as laid out in s.197B ICTA 1988) and introduced for 1990/91 onwards. Under these a higher rate is calculated only for the first 4,000 miles as opposed to past Church practice as recommended by the Central Stipends Authority of paying a higher rate of mileages up to 7,500 miles per annum. For 1992/93 the rates are as follows:

	For the first 4000 miles	*For miles in excess of 4000*
Cars up to 1000 cc	25p	14p
Cars 1001 cc to 1500 cc	30p	17p
Cars 1501 cc to 2000 cc	38p	21p
Cars over 2000 cc	51p	27p

If the diocese chooses it could pay an undifferentiated rate for cars of all sizes which would then be restricted to 34p for the first 4,000 miles and 19p thereafter. There is special provision in the fixed car (FPC) scheme legislation for 1990/91, so that no person can obtain less relief for tax purposes than in 1989/90 provided a similar mileage is covered. This will doubtless cover any over generous allowances which continue to be paid for 1990/91 using the higher scale up to 7,500 miles per annum which is common among dioceses.

Considerable amendments have also been made to the capital allowances provisions to ensure that it is not necessary for an office holder to buy a car for his office in order to be able to claim allowances based on business use if he has not used the non-taxable mileage allowances.

Where an allowance is paid, it will be taken into account in determining whether the minister is higher-paid and, if he is, will be taxable as an emolument unless a dispensation under s.166 ICTA is in force. Where the allowance is taxed he will be able to claim a deduction for motoring expenses incurred wholly, exclusively and necessarily in the performance of his duties as a minister. For many ministers the vast majority of local visits will have at least a pastoral element and it is difficult to envisage any tax inspector seeking to argue that such visits do not meet the 'wholly and exclusively' test;

(q)   apart from expenditure on a car and certain books, as detailed above, the Inland Revenue often resist claims for capital allowances on other items of plant and machinery. This attitude is supported by the decision in White *v.* Higginbottom (1982) 57 TC 283, where a vicar lost his claim for capital allowances on the cost of a projector and other audio-visual equipment which he used in his sermons. However, relief should be given on expenditure incurred by a minister of religion on equipment necessarily provided for use in the performance of his duties (s.27 CAA 1990). Claims can only be accepted in respect of assets intended for permanent use in the ministry which have an expected life of two years or more. For example, capital allowances will be given on a computer or word processor if it enables long standing tasks such as compiling and maintaining lists of church members parish records or accounts or to issue circulars and magazines to be carried out more efficiently. (See *The Times* of 22 January 1986.)

Expenditure incurred after 31 March 1986 qualifies for a 25% writing down allowance on a reducing balance basis.

(4) Expenses of unpaid appointments

Normally any expenses incurred on such appointments are not allowable, but the Inland Revenue, in practice, allow claims under s.332(3)(a) ICTA 1988 for expenses, not reimbursed, necessarily incurred in the capacity of a rural dean, honorary canon, or other honorary ecclesiastical appointment such as a Proctor in Convocation in the Church of England.

(5) Removal expenses

Such expenses may be allowed under s.332(3)(a) ICTA 1988 against benefice income but removal expenses from one ecclesiastical office to another are not allowed when incurred by the clergyman (Friedson *v.* Glyn-Thomas (1922) 8 TC 302). However, Inland Revenue Extra Statutory Concession A5(a) would usually apply, under which removal expenses reimbursed by a new employer are not taxable, provided the expenses are reasonable in amount and their payment is properly controlled.

Second residences

199   Reliefs are available as follows for clergymen in connection with a residence owned by them in addition to the official residence provided for them:

(a)   capital gains exemption – it is provided that, where a person occupies job-related accommodation but intends to occupy his own house as his only or main residence, capital gains tax exemption will be given on the sale of that residence in respect of periods after 30 July 1978 (s.222(8) TCGA 1992);

(b)   the provisions for relief for interest paid on the purchase of a residence allow such interest where the payer occupies job-related accommodation, in respect of a house he uses as a residence or which he intends to use in due course (for instance, on retirement) as his only or main residence (s.356 ICTA 1988).

To take advantage of these provisions, it is not necessary for the clergyman to work full-time at his duties, provided that he can be regarded as a representative occupier (see **197**(1) above). There is an exclusion for directors unless they fall into the category mentioned in **197**(4) above, which should exempt most directors who hold office with companies carrying out activities connected with a church and who occupy living accommodation belonging to the church.

Benefits-in-kind

200   Consider the following:

(1) Cars

Where a car is provided for a minister on the strict understanding, confirmed in writing, that it is not in any circumstances to be used for private travel, no tax liability will arise in respect of the car, whatever the level of the minister's emoluments. However, this is normally impossible to achieve as few ministers can afford a second car for private travel. Therefore, where a car is provided, the scale charges laid down in Sch. 6 ICTA 1988 normally apply, assuming the minister is earning at a rate of £8,500 per annum or more.

(2) Car fuel

From 1984/85, any minister provided with a car by the authorities employing him may incur not only a charge in respect of the car but also in respect of fuel provided for the car (s.158 ICTA 1988). The relevant provisions are widely drawn and state that fuel is provided for a car if (s.158(3) ICTA 1988):

(a) any liability in respect of the provision of fuel for the car is discharged;
(b) a voucher or credit token is used to obtain fuel for the car or money which is spent on such fuel (this includes credit cards); or
(c) any sum is paid in respect of expenses incurred in providing fuel for the car.

The scale charges for fuel are drawn up on very similar lines to the car scale charges. The fuel scale charges may be reduced to nil if, in the relevant year (s.158(6) ICTA 1988):

(a) the minister is required to make good to the authorities providing the fuel the whole of the expense he has incurred in or in connection with the provision of fuel for his private use and he does so; or
(b) the fuel is made available only for business travel.

To substantiate a claim that this was the case, the minister would need to keep records both of his total mileage and of his business mileage. This would clearly be worthwhile if it kept his emoluments below £8,500 or, if he were higher-paid in any event, kept the level of this taxable benefits down. The requirements laid down to avoid a fuel scale charge also make it undesirable simply to pay a round-sum allowance towards fuel rather than specifically to reimburse fuel expenses incurred for recorded official travel. It would be particularly unwise to pay a general expenses allowance as, if the minister is higher-paid, he might well find himself taxed both on the allowance and in respect of a fuel scale charge.

(3) Beneficial loans

Many ministers receive loans from the church authorities that employ them. If the minister is higher-paid he may face a charge to tax in respect of the benefit from such a loan. However, if the loan is for such a purpose that if obtained at arm's length the interest on it would have qualified for tax relief, no charge to tax will arise (s.161(3) ICTA 1988). Examples of loans that do not give rise to a taxable benefit are loans to acquire assets used in the performance of the minister's duties. Another charge to tax can arise where a beneficial loan is released or written off in whole or in part.

Income of contemplative religious communities and their members

201 There is a published extra statutory concession relating to the income of religious communities from the sale of produce, pottery etc. The precise legal position as regards the title to such income which is treated by the community as belonging to a common fund is often difficult to ascertain. In practice in the case of certain orders, such as those engaged in charitable work among the poor, relief is given under the provisions relating to charities: in the case of contemplative orders and other orders which are not in law capable of being regarded as charities as they do not promote their religious beliefs among the community, a proportion of the aggregate income not exceeding a specified sum per monk or nun (as representing the amount applied for the maintenance of each individual) is regarded as his or her income for the purposes of relief from tax. For 1988–89 the figure is £2,142. Where in any year there is an excess of the total 'allowable figure' over the community's income, the excess may be set against chargeable gains of the year and, to the extent that it is not so utilised, may be carried forward and set against gains of a subsequent year.

Evangelists

202   The distinction between a personal gift and taxable income may be more difficult to define where a person does not have a parish but operates on a freelance basis.

One can think of several well-known religious figures around the world who receive sums through the post and at gatherings which are given more because of the personal magnetism of the individual and his reputation and do not attach to any office or services as in Cooper *v.* Blakiston.

It is understood that is has been accepted (in the case of one freelance evangelist at least) that personal gifts sent through the post, some from areas he has not visited recently or at all, are not assessable. They arise from a personal regard for him, an interest in his work and a desire to contribute to his personal needs.

On the other hand, where sums are received, although unsolicited, in connection with specific speaking engagements, they are regarded as arising from services rendered and are assessed. Thus where someone makes a gift to an evangelist after hearing him preach, it is accepted as assessable.

The practice is probably conceded from the following dicta of Lord Loreburn in Cooper *v.* Blakiston. (5TC 347) "In my opinion, where a sum of money is given to an incumbent substantially in respect of this services as incumbent, it accrues to him by reason of his office . . . Had it been a gift of an exceptional kind such as . . . a subscription peculiarly due to the personal qualities of this particular clergyman it might not have been a voluntary payment for services, but a mere present". It is reported in a query in *Taxation* of 21 November 1991 that the Inland Revenue are attacking the receipts of evangelists as taxable.

The general consensus of the replies is as follows:

(a)   Unsolicited receipts from family, close friends, other friends and acquaintances where no services are rendered, are not taxable;

(b)   Receipts from churches for whom the evangelist has worked are linked to services rendered and are therefore taxable;

(c) Churches with whom the evangelist has previously worked is a difficult area but the receipt is probably sufficiently closely linked to services rendered that the Inland Revenue would seek to tax it. The difficulty is that there would probably be an ongoing link with that church;

(d) Where gifts are received from Christian charitable trusts, it is likely they will have been solicited. They might also be taxable on the basis of the decision in CIR *v.* Falkirk Ice Rink (1975 STC 434) as being made to support the work of the evangelist;

(e) Unsolicited gifts from individuals of whom the evangelist has no prior knowledge should not be taxable where there are no services rendered. Unsolicited gifts from churches might pose the same difficulty as (c) as there might be the possibility of an ongoing relationship with those churches and anticipated services to be rendered.

Chapter 8
Members of the diplomatic service and other Crown servants working abroad

Place of performance of duties

203 Members of the diplomatic service are in a peculiar taxation position. Whilst their residence position follows the normal practice applicable to any individual, they are deemed to perform their duties in the UK for the purposes of liability to income tax under Sch. E on their emoluments. All persons who hold an office or employment under the Crown which is of public nature, and which is payable out of the public revenue of the UK or Northern Ireland, are deemed to perform their duties in the UK (s.132(4)(a) ICTA 1988). This includes an employee of the Crown, performing duties for the Crown abroad with a foreign government, paid by a UK government authority, even if that authority recovers the salary from the foreign government (Caldicott *v.* Varty (1976) 51 TC 403). The fact that the position held is technical or industrial does not make it any the less of a public nature (See Graham *v.* White (1971) 48 TC 163). In practice, however, UK tax is not charged in the case of locally engaged (as distinct from UK-based) unestablished staff working abroad who are not UK-resident if the maximum rate of pay for their grade is less than that of an executive officer in the UK Civil Service working in Inner London (Inland Revenue Extra-Statutory Concession A25).

The effect of deeming the place of performance of duties to be the UK is that, if the diplomat ceases to be resident (as is usual) or remains resident but not ordinarily resident, he will be liable to tax under Sch. E Case II on the full amount of his emoluments. However, if exceptionally the individual remains resident and ordinarily resident in the UK, he will be assessable under Sch. E Case I but will be ineligible for the 100% deduction under s.193(1) ICTA 1988 because his duties will be deemed to be performed in the UK.

Exempt allowances

204 Emoluments for this purpose do not include foreign service allowances, where the allowance is certified by the Treasury to represent compensation for the extra cost of having to live outside the UK to perform the duties of the employment. Such allowances are specifically exempted from UK tax (s.319 ICTA 1988). This covers allowances for boarding school education for children and any other foreign service allowance representing the increased cost of having to live abroad to do the job in question. It also covers the cost of travel to and from the overseas location by the diplomat and his family. It also seems to cover the initial cost of removal expenses to the residence abroad leaving the house in the UK to be let and thus enables the civil servant to be exempt on such relocation expenses while not having to dispose of his UK residence, unlike others who have to rely on the Extra Statutory Concession A5. Such allowances are not caught by the benefits legislation (according to a House of Commons Written Answer of 6 May 1976). Other subsistence allowances, paid to diplomatic staff whilst stationed in a foreign country, are not taxable in the same way as subsistence allowances paid in the UK to home civil servants. This is based on general Sch. E principles, as such allowances are designed to do no more than cover expenses incurred in the course of carrying out their duties away from base. The scales are set out in the Civil Service pay and conditions of service code.

Entertaining allowances paid to a diplomat would normally be taxable. However, provided he spent his allowance wholly, exclusively and necessarily in the performance of his duties, a diplomat would be able to make a claim under s.198 ICTA 1988, as s.577 ICTA 1988 only applies to business entertainment.

The value of any living accommodation occupied abroad should not be liable to income tax, on the basis that the Crown servant would be a representative occupier required to live in the premises to do his job properly. Any costs of maintaining any residence abroad, in so far as reimbursed, should not be liable under the benefits provisions as they would be part of the allowance exempt under the special provisions for allowances to cover the increased costs of living abroad.

Under most Double Tax agreements, civil servants will have no liability to foreign tax on their remuneration (including the foreign service allowance), because it falls under the provisions relating to remuneration payable out of the government funds of one of the contracting parties. Alternatively, in the case of diplomats, diplomatic privilege under international law should exempt them from local taxation and this again may also be specifically mentioned in the relevant double tax treaty.

Other income and capital gains

205 The tax position of other income and capital gains will depend upon the person's residence position. It should be noted that the provision deeming the duties of the employment to be performed in the UK applies only for the purposes of Sch. E Cases I and II. Therefore, the general rules on the residence position of persons working abroad will still apply for other sources.

If the individual is not resident in the UK, the position on liability to UK tax on UK income, other than such as is exempt in the hands of all non-residents, is governed by international law, which effectively ensures that a diplomat is not treated as a resident for fiscal purposes of the country in which the embassy is situated. Double taxation agreements usually made reference to this complete exemption from local tax on all sources of income and capital gains which corresponds with the specific exemptions the UK gives under the Diplomatic Privileges Act 1964 to foreign diplomats residing in this country. A diplomat will thus not be able to take advantage of any reduced rate of UK tax on UK dividends and taxed interest which can only be available to a person who, under the terms of agreement, is treated as a resident of the country with which the double taxation agreement has been concluded. He will, therefore, remain fully liable to UK tax on dividends, taxed interest, rents and other UK income not exempt from UK tax in the hands of a non-resident. To get over this problem, it may be possible for a member of the diplomat's family who does not enjoy this complete exemption – for instance, his wife – to hold the investments and become a resident of the other country for the purposes of the relevant double taxation agreement. However, the tax consequences in that other country should not be overlooked. Alternatively, it may be worth using an offshore investment company to avoid at least the higher rate of tax.

Husband and wife

The position with the advent of independent taxation has changed. Previously, even if the wife was technically resident in the UK, because for instance a place of abode was available there for her use, but the husband was not, there was still the possibility of transferring assets between them free of capital gains tax following the decision in Gubay *v*. Kington (1984 STC 99) if they were in fact living together. The proviso to Section 42(2) ICTA 1970 giving this relief for income tax purposes applied also for capital gains tax. This proviso has now been repealed with independent taxation so that husband and wife are separate persons for tax purposes. Therefore, following consequential amendments in the law, if they have different resident status, such tax free transfers would appear to be more difficult now unless they can clearly show they are still living together. In the circumstances, careful tax planning may need to take place before any postings abroad, taking care however not to rely on the Extra Statutory Concession to avoid tax as was hoped for in R *v*. CIR Ex Parte Fulford-Dobson (1987 STC 344).

Personal allowances

206 It should be noted that, where the diplomat is not resident in the UK, a claim to personal allowances will be possible. If, exceptionally, the person is not a British subject, he or she will still be eligible under s.278 ICTA 1988, as being employed in the service of the Crown.

UK residents

207   The following points should be considered.

(1) *Capital gains tax*

Difficulties have arisen for Crown servants serving overseas in respect of capital gains exemption on UK residences. Where the diplomat himself owns the residence, the period of absence will count as a qualifying period. If the wife owned the residence, there used to be a problem as she was not the one in employment. Inland Revenue Extra-Statutory Concession D3 now effectively covers the position by giving the owner exemption where either spouse is in full-time employment abroad.

Likewise the owner normally has to resume residence before selling so that the period of absence qualifies for exemption. This is not required under Inland Revenue Extra-Statutory Concession D4 if the owner is unable to resume residence because the terms of his employment require him to reside elsewhere, so that he sells without resuming residence in the house. In any event, it seems that it would be possible to argue in many cases that the diplomat was residing in job-related accommodation abroad so that he would not have to rely on any concession to obtain full relief for capital gains tax on a sale of his residence (s.222(8) TCGA 1992).

(2) *Mortgage interest*

Similar problems have arisen over the allowance of mortgage interest. To meet the situation of absences from a property which is not let or not let at sufficient rent to cover any interest, relaxations have been made by Inland Revenue Extra-Statutory Concession A27. Temporary absences of up to one year are in practice ignored. In addition, where a person is required by his employment to move to another place, either in the UK or abroad, for a period not expected to exceed four years, he will still qualify for mortgage interest relief on his main residence, provided that the property was used as his residence before he went abroad and he can reasonably be expected to resume residence in it on his return. If he intended to occupy it but was prevented from doing so by being posted abroad, he will be treated as having occupied it for the purposes of the concession.

Relief will not be given for more than four years unless occupation of the property is resumed for a period of at least three months, following which a new four-year period can begin. If a person purchases a property in the course of a leave period, and uses the property as his only or main residence for a minimum period of three months before his return abroad, he will be regarded as qualifying for mortgage interest relief in respect of his period of absence from the UK. If the property is let commercially but the concession is more favourable, the employee can make use of the concession.

Further, where the taxpayer holds an office or employment in respect of which he or she receives emoluments which are not chargeable to tax by virtue of a special exemption or immunity he or she will not be a 'qualifying borrower' within s.376(2) ICTA 1988. This is so even where the exemption or immunity arises from an employment with the European Commission: Tither *v*. IRC (1990) STC 416 (CJLEC). Therefore no MIRAS relief will be available in respect of interest paid in respect of a 'qualifying loan' to such a taxpayer.

(3) Job-related accommodation

Employees who live in 'job-related accommodation' are normally able to obtain mortgage interest relief and capital gains tax exemption on a private residence other than the one in which they actually have to live (s.356 ICTA 1988 and s.222(8) TCGA 1992). The Inland Revenue have confirmed that service personnel and diplomats serving overseas, who extend their overseas tour beyond four years, can be regarded as living in job-related accommodation for these purposes if they live in the following:

(a) accommodation provided by the Ministry of Defence;
(b) flats provided by the Foreign and Commonwealth Office; or
(c) officially approved hirings for which a rent allowance is payable.

Therefore, Crown servants in this position should not need to rely on any of the concessions referred to above.

Life assurance premiums

208 It should be noted that a member of the staff of a British embassy, who is not resident in the UK, is nevertheless entitled to deduct 15% from every premium paid under a qualifying policy of life assurance if that policy was taken out before 14 March 1984 (s.266 ICTA 1988). This decreased to 12½% for premiums paid after 5 April 1989.

Officials employed by the European Community in Brussels

209 It is becoming increasingly common for Crown servants to become employed by the European Community Office in Brussels. As with United Nations officials, their emoluments are subject to a special form of community tax. Emoluments (including pensions) received from the European Community are exempt from UK tax by virtue of Art. 13 of the Protocol on the Privileges and Immunities of the European Communities. Such emoluments were up to 5 April 1990, also excluded from total income for the purposes of s.278 ICTA 1988, which governs the granting of personal allowances to certain non-residents.

This exemption from UK tax extends to income received from the Council of Europe and the Western European Union.

(For the impact on MIRAS mortgage interest relief see **207**(2) above.)

However, Art. 13 deems such officials who have gone to work at the Community Office to remain resident and ordinarily resident for income tax purposes in the UK with their dependent accompanying spouses and dependent children and also domiciled in the UK for inheritance tax purposes thus protecting them from Belgian tax on their other income. However, so far as capital gains tax is concerned, this follows the normal rules of residence.

Difficulties can arise from UK officials who go to the EC office from a posting abroad with, say, the Foreign Office, so that they are not resident or ordinarily resident when they start work in Brussels. The Protocol does not appear to cope easily with this situation but it appears, as diplomats, that they can waive their right to immunity from tax including UK tax and thus come within the Protocol.

There are various other international organisations employing people where there is immunity from tax on their remuneration. Commonwealth citizens and certain other who are not UK resident are now able to set their full UK personal allowances against UK income potentially liable to UK tax such as rents, dividends, etc. (s.278 ICTA 1988). This applies to employees of a United Nations organisation (although the exemption does not extend to pensions) provided a certificate is supplied from UNO stating that during the period of employment the employee had the status of 'Official' for the purposes of Section 18 (Article 5) of the General Convention of the Privileges and Immunities of the UN dated 13 February 1946.

Other organisations where the emoluments are treated in the same way are:

Food and Agricultural Organisation (FAO)
International Civil Aviation Organisation (ICAO)
International Labour Organisation (ILO)
International Maritime Consultative Organisation (IMO)
International Telecommunications Union (ITU)
Universal Postal Union (UPU)
World Health Organisation (WHO)
World Intellectual Property Organisation (WIPO)
World Meteorological Organisation (WMO)

Exemption will depend upon completion of the appropriate certificate, the terms of which will be advised in each case by the Inland Revenue in the case of the following organisations:

Central Treaty Organisation (CTO)
Council of Europe (COE)
Customs Co-operative Council (CCC)
Inter-commission for the International Trade Organisation (ICITO)
International Atomic Energy Authority (IAEA)

North Atlantic Treaty Organisation (NATO)
Organisation for Economic Co-operation and Development (OECD)
South East Asia Treaty Organisation (SEATO)
United Nations Childrens Fund (UNICEF)
Western European Union (WEU).

Chapter 9
Doctors and dentists

Doctors

210 The tax position of doctors depends upon whether they are consultants or general practitioners, and whether they are self-employed – as in the case of the latter or in the case of many non-National Health Service consultants – or employed, as in the case of consultants, in respect of National Health Service earnings.

Consultants

211 Income received by a self-employed consultant from private practice is assessable under normal Sch. D Case II principles. On the other hand, a consultant may hold a Sch. E post in the private sector. Full-time National Health Service consultants are within Sch. E and subject to its restrictive rules for expenses claims (see s.198 ICTA 1988 and Hamerton *v*. Overy (1954) 35 TC 73). Similarly, part-time sessional payments by Regional Health Authorities are assessable under Sch. E, and s.198 ICTA 1988 again applies to expenses claims.

A clear distinction must always be drawn between Sch. D and Sch. E income. The Mitchell & Edon *v*. Ross case (1961) 40 TC 11 established that expenses incurred in relation to the office of National Health Service consultant, and disallowed under Sch. E, are not allowable as expenses of earning the profits of the profession taxable under Sch. D, because the two Schedules are mutually exclusive. However, there is a choice of Schedule for some expenses, such as professional subscriptions.

Expenses of consultants

212 Consider the following.

(1) Property expenses

The practice proportion of property expenses should be claimed by a self-employed consultant, but bearing capital gains tax in mind. A 'points' basis for the garage/s, first floor and upstairs rooms (distinguishing practice rooms, common areas and private rooms), will give a sound base for the proportion of rates, repairs, insurances, etc. A consultant holding a Sch. E post may have considerable difficulty in obtaining a deduction for such expenses against his Sch. E income, but a claim on the basis of contributions to the additional costs incurred, may be possible.

(2) Motor expenses

When claiming a deduction for motor expenses, it should be borne in mind that home to base (ie., main commitment) hospital is private mileage. The case of Pook *v.* Owen (1969) 45 TC 571 involved reimbursed travelling expenses for a part-time hospital appointment of a medical practitioner. As the appointment involved being on standby duty at certain times, the duties were treated as commencing from the time of leaving home, and the reimbursed expenses were, therefore, not assessable. Such circumstances can arise with doctors on call from outside the hospital, where advice is given before starting the journey and responsibility is taken from that time (but see **213**(4) below concerning emergency call-out expenses). Two cases involving doctors that illustrate the principles involved are Bhadra *v.* Ellam (1988) STC 239 and Parikh *v.* Sleeman (1990) STC 233.

Agreement between DSS and Inland Revenue on certain expenses

213 An agreement was reached, operative for 1978/79 onward, between the Department of Social Security and the Inland Revenue, in respect of the taxability of certain allowances paid to National Health Service staff, including consultants, under Whitley Council agreements, or by direction of the Secretary of State. This agreement (ref: HC(78)39 of November 1978) covers the taxation position on all allowances paid to National Health Service staff, including car allowances.

(1) Car allowances

The Inland Revenue have agreed a fixed, taxable amount in respect of each individual who travels a prescribed number of miles in his own car on business for the employing authority during one income tax year. However, regular car-users travelling in excess of 3,000 miles per annum on health authority business will not be subject to tax on their allowances. Subject to the rates agreed by Whitley Council, it may still be beneficial for an individual employee to opt for an FPCS (Fixed Profit Car Scheme) based arrangement. The normal scale benefits apply in respect of private use of cars allocated to doctors by health authorities, if they are in higher-paid employment.

On 13 November 1991, the Inland Revenue published a new extra-statutory concession relating to the income tax treatment of any profits on motor mileage allowances paid to volunteer drivers. The concession applies to people who drive for the hospital car service and for other volunteer organisations.

Volunteer drivers may make a taxable profit if the mileage allowances they receive exceed the costs actually incurred. Arrangements have been made to collect tax (if there is any to pay) with effect from 6 October 1991. To avoid the imposition of sudden additional tax liabilities, the tax charge is to be phased in gradually over a number of years. The text of the concession is:

'Motor mileage allowances paid to volunteer drivers may give rise to a taxable profit to the extent that they exceed the costs of running and maintaining the car for the miles travelled for the voluntary service. But, by concession, only one quarter of the profit element for the period 6 October 1991 to 5 April 1992 and for 1992–93 will be taxed; only one half of the profit will be taxed for 1993–94 and only three-quarters of the profit will be taxed for 1994–95. Tax will not be payable on the full amount of the profit element until 1995–96.'

These arrangements came into force on 6 October 1991 and the Inland Revenue do not propose to review the tax position of volunteer drivers for earlier periods. The phasing-in arrangements will not apply to taxi and mini cab drivers and similar operators who drive for the hospital car service and other volunteer organisations. Their mileage payments should always have been included in their business accounts and taxed in the normal way.

(2) Removal and associated expenses

Removal expenses, excess rent allowances where a person is moving to a higher-cost housing area, and advance of salary for house purchase, are not taxable provided they fall within Inland Revenue guidelines. Concerning the advance of salary, there is a risk this will be treated as a beneficial loan under Williams *v.* Todd (1988) STC 676.

(3) Excess travelling expenses

Reimbursement of excess travelling expenses following a change of base hospital is taxable, except where a change of residence is involved, when reimbursement of travelling expenses is exempt as part of removal expenses.

(4) Emergency call-out expenses

In spite of Pook *v.* Owen, travelling expenses for emergency call-out to the normal place of employment are regarded as taxable, except in the circumstances mentioned in **212(2)** above.

(5) Assisted travel scheme

This allowance is taxable, as it covers partial reimbursement of the costs of getting to the hospital.

(6) Journey between home and headquarters

Where a doctor, normally based at one place, uses his car to visit other places in the course of his duties, and is reimbursed mileage costs within the limit of 'base to places visited and return plus 20 miles', the allowance for actual mileage on duty will not be taxable, nor will the 'plus' element.

(7) Late night duties

Night duty allowance and meal allowances are taxable. See however Extra-Statutory Concession A66 which gives some relief to individuals in an employed capacity.

(8) Uniforms

The provision of uniforms, overalls and protective clothing, or an allowance to buy them, is not taxable. However, the Inland Revenue regard allowances to cover the cost of ordinary, everyday clothing ('mufti'), given to staff who work in psychiatric hospitals, as taxable, even if the clothing is worn only on duty. The normal rules for calculating the taxable amount apply. The use of mufti owned by the health authority and retained at the hospital for use only on duty is only taxable in the case of higher-paid employees, subject to exemption where the amounts involved are negligible.

(9) Telephone expenses

Where the employee is the subscriber, any payment by the health authority is taxable under basic Sch. E rules, as the employer is meeting the employee's pecuniary liability. Where the employing authority is the subscriber, payment of telephone rental and other charges is only taxable when the employee is higher-paid. All cost of calls in the performance of the employment will be allowable in the normal way under s.198 ICTA 1988.

(10) Fees and subscriptions to professional bodies

Recurrent annual subscriptions are allowed but initial registration fees, if required, are not allowable under normal Sch. E expenses rules.

Practice accounts

214 The accounts of partnerships of self-employed consultants should show the practice proportion of expenses and depreciation, less monies received from the Regional Health Authority for inter-hospital and domiciliary visits. Depreciation is added back and the practice proportion of capital allowances claimed in the normal way.

The other items which cause the most problems are conference expenses. In practice, the costs of attending conferences and courses are allowed where the basic requirements of any business claim are satisfied. It is helpful, however, to be able to quote Regional Health Authority approval of the course, whether or not the Regional Health Authority makes a contribution to expenses. The usual argument against allowability by the Inland Revenue is that the conference expenses are incurred in order to increase the consultant's knowledge and skills and are incurred, therefore, to enable the doctor to carry on his profession better, rather than incurred wholly and exclusively for the purposes of that profession. Not surprisingly, the Inland Revenue will take more convincing where the conference is held outside the UK (Parikh *v.* Sleeman (1990) STC 233), and even more so where the doctor's spouse also attends. Similarly, the expenses of training for some new area of medical practice, if borne by the doctor to equip him to do something quite different from his existing work, could be disallowed as the primary objective is self-improvement. The position would apply for instance to course fees of someone seeking to become a psychotherapist where the purpose is to qualify to carry out treatment in that field.

General practice

215 The move towards 'group practice' continues, as does the concentration in purpose-built premises, instead of surgeries that form part of a doctor's residential property. Where practices are carried on from a private house, the same considerations apply in relation to expenses and capital gains tax as for self-employed consultants (see **212**(1) above).

Where there is a Health Centre, at which a number of doctors or group practices are given facilities for reception and practice rooms with common access to other National Health Service disciplines, eg., district and community nursing, minor surgery facilities, maternity clinics, child psychology, etc., each doctor or group practice pays an inclusive rental figure and special arrangements are made for telephone costs.

For anyone advising general practitioners, it is essential to obtain a copy of the National Health Service 'Red Book' – *Statement of Fees and Allowances Payable to General Medical Practitioners in England and Wales*. This is in looseleaf format and is amended periodically. It gives details of the various allowances, and conditions of doctor's contracts. It is also important to read *Medeconomics* and other medical finance journals.

There may be three 'tiers' of expenses for partners in a general practice, ie.:

(a) the normal expenses of running the practice and the common surgery premises reflected in the partnership accounts;

(b) sometimes doctors meet the costs of the surgeries to which they are attached, and separate claims are made for the same basis period;

(c) almost invariably, personal expenses and capital allowances are claimed by individual doctors for motor expenses and, frequently, for subscriptions, the costs of a surgery provided at their private residence, upkeep of personal surgical equipment, etc. Again, the claims are related to the normal practice basis period.

Spouses can, therefore, be remunerated by the partnership, or by the individual doctors, provided that the remuneration is actually paid and is commensurate with the duties performed.

Individual partners often take personal loans from the Medical Finance Corporation, and interest paid is deducted in the second or third 'tier' of expenses, as appropriate. Interest so claimed in respect of the premises should not restrict capital gains tax retirement relief.

Detailed points on GP's accounts – BMA standardised practice accounts

216 The British Medical Association General Medical Services Committee has now produced standardised practice accounts. These accounts and accompanying notes are reproduced below. The following detailed points are worth noting:

(a) In the accompanying notes just mentioned, the General Medical Services Committee urges general practitioners to give their accountants a copy of the standardised practice accounts and *aide-memoire* for expenses, so that these documents can be used in drawing up the general practitioner's accounts and returns for submission to the Inland Revenue;

(b) Certain expenses are *directly* reimbursed to practitioners either in whole or in part, for example:

100% reimbursement:
  (i) rent, including ground rent;
  (ii) rates – business, water, sewage, refuse;
  (iii) employers' national insurance contributions for ancillary staff. However, where it was proved difficult to obtain exemption from national insurance contributions for round-sum travelling expenses paid to trainee doctors by partnerships, because the expense cannot be sufficiently vouched, it has also proved difficult for the employing partnership to obtain reimbursement of the national insurance contributions.

70% reimbursement:
ancillary staff salaries.

The total amount of these *direct* reimbursements is accurately known to the Department of Health from returns provided by the family practitioner committees for the appropriate year.

(c) Each year, the Inland Revenue provide a Technical Sub-committee of the Department of Health with details of the income and expenses of a statistically valid sample of general practitioners. The information is supplied by Inspectors of Taxes from the accounts submitted by general practitioners. As the only available accounts will normally be for earlier years, the Technical Sub-committee will use appropriate indices to update the figures. The Sub-committee will use the information to produce an accurate estimate of the total expenses of all general practitioners. From this figure, they will subtract those expenses that are direct reimbursment (see (b) above). The balance will be distributed by the Department by means of various fees and allowances.

This means that general practitioners must include all legitimate expenses in their accounts, if the profession as a whole is to be reimbursed adequately for these remaining practice expenses. In particular, expenses that are directly reimbursed by the Department should be shown gross, with the amount received also shown as a receipt. Where, for example, a family practitioner committee pays rent for a Health Centre directly to the Area Health Authority on a doctor's behalf, that doctor should include a figure for the notional rent both as an expense and as a receipt. Unfortunately, much of the necessary information is not communicated direct to the doctors concerned. Nonetheless, the doctor's professional advisor should take steps to obtain the information.

(d) The expenses have been divided into six main groups, which correspond with the grouping used by the Technical Sub-committee, and the use of these groups – as in the model account in **217** below – will enable a more accurate calculation to be made by the Technical Sub-committee. Items of individual expenses have been shown in some detail, and the use of the *aide memoire* in **218** below as a check list will help individual doctors and practices to minimise their personal tax liability as well as assisting the General Medical Services Committee in obtaining a full reimbursement of expenses for all general practitioners.

Model form of income and expenditure account for use by general practitioners

217   Here is a model form.

Doctors ....
Income and expenditure account for the year ended .... 199....

Expenditure	£	£	Income	£	£
Medical supplies			*Family practitioner*		
Drugs, dressings,			*committee payments*		
containers, etc.............	xx		Fees and other payments		
Sundry equipment,[1] etc	xx		for medical services		
	—	xxx	(including dispensing) ...	xxx	
			Reimbursements for:		
Premises			Premises (rented and		
Rent (where			owned including health		
appropriate)[2]	xx		centres)	xx	
Rates[2]	xx		Ancillary help	xx	
Fuel, light, power and			Trainees	xx	
water	xx		Locums	xx	xxx
				—	

continued

141

Doctors and dentists

Insurance (building and
  contents) xx

Exterior and interior
  maintenance and
  decorations xx

Cleaning, etc................... xx

Interest[3] xx

Telephone..................... xx

                   xxx

Staff costs (total salary/
  wages, national
  insurance and
  superannuation
  contributions)

Assistants xx

Trainees xx

Ancillary staff[4] xx

Staff advertising and
  agency fees xx

Locum and other
  deputising costs xx

                   xxx

Car and travel

Car rental...................... xx

Tax and insurance xx

Petrol, oil and repairs xx

Taxi and other travel
  expenses xx

                   xxx

Other expenses

Postage xx

Stationery, magazines and
  technical literature xx

Professional and other
  subscriptions xx

Refresher courses and
  professional training xx

Medical committee
  expenses[5] xx

Laundry and dry cleaning.. xx

Accountancy and legal xx

Bank interest and charges
  (not related to
  properties) xx

Hire purchase charges xx

Superannuation
  (practitioners)............. xx

Sundry xx

                   xxx

Other Sch. D income

Local authorities (and
  other government
  departments, etc.) xx

Other (including private)... xx

                   xxx

*Income assessed under
  Sch. E*

Net fees xx

PAYE deductions xx

Superannuation and other
  deductions xx

                   xxx

Depreciation

Cars............................	xx	
Equipment....................	xx	
		xxx
		xxxx

Net income for the year   £xxxx   £xxxx

Notes

1 Equipment not included under 'depreciation' eg., auriscope, stethoscope.
2 Health Centre doctors should enter the amounts supplied by family practitioner committees as rent and rates notionally charged.
3 Interest on loans relating to practice premises, including personal share of interest on group practice loans.
4 Including dispensers, receptionists and other staff. Also including salaries relating to wives.

    Health Centre doctors should enter full details of salary and national insurance contributions, not only the proportion recovered from them direct. Employers' national insurance contributions and premiums for staff pension schemes should be included.
5 This should include local medical committee levies.

The following notes used to be appended to the model form of accounts, and remain useful:

(a) All expenses should include value added tax attributable to that expense.
(b) If more than one surgery is used, it may be informative to show separately the premises expenses relating to each surgery.
(c) It may be considered appropriate to make adjustments for private use of motor cars and house expenses in the accounts themselves rather than in the tax computations, in which event it would probably be desirable to indicate this fact against the items concerned.
(d) In some cases of group practices, only the general surgery expenses are claimed in the partnership accounts and separate expense claims are made for a surgery at each doctor's own home.

Aide-memoire – expenses

218 Here is an aide-memoire.

Accounting items	Example comment
Medical expenses	
Drugs, dressings and containers	
Disposable equipment and reagents	
Sundry equipment and replacements not capitalised ie., not listed under depreciation	Auriscope, stethoscope
Repairs and servicing of equipment	ECG machine, typewriter
Premises (see Note 1 below)	
(a) *Privately rented*	
Rent	
Rates/Community charge	Business, water, sewage, refuse
Heating, lighting, power	Gas, electricity, oil, solid fuel

Doctors and dentists

Accounting items	Example comment
Water	If metered
Insurance	Building and contents
Maintenance and decoration	
Cleaning materials/services	
Security alarm system: rental and maintenance	

(b) *Premises owned by general prac-*
    titioners

Rates/community charge	Business, water, sewage, refuse
Heating, lighting, power	Gas, electricity, oil, solid fuel
Water	If metered
Insurance	Building and contents
Maintenance and decoration	
Cleaning materials/services	
Interest	
Mortgage, bank, General Practice Finance Corporation	On premises
Security alarm system: rental and maintenance	

(c) *Health centres*

Rent	Notional rent
Rates/Community charge	Business, water, sewage, refuse
Service charge	Building maintenance
Any element in (b) above not covered by service charge	Telephones

Staff costs (see Note 1 below)

For: assistants
    trainees
    nurses
    practice administrators
    dispensers
    receptionists
    secretaries
    other practice staff – specify   Physiotherapists, etc.
    practitioners' spouses
    cleaners, gardener, car park attendant

Total gross wages   Before reimbursement from family
                        practitioner committee and before
                        deduction of PAYE, employees'
                        national insurance and superannu-
                        ation contributions

Accounting items	Example comment
Employers' national insurance contri- butions	
Premiums for private pension schemes	Employer's contribution
Sickness and maternity payments	
Staff advertising: agency fees	
Uniforms	
Refreshment for ancillary staff	

Locum and other deputising costs

Locum fees	Including agency fees
Aircall (or other deputising services)	
Other locum organisations – specify	

Car and travel

Car rental/lease/hire purchase charges	
Car tax	
Car insurance	
Petrol and oil	
Repairs and maintenance	
Taxi and other travel expenses	
AA/RAC	
Parking and garaging	

Other expenses (see Note 1 below)

Telelphones	
Communication equipment	Bleep/radio telephone
Telephone answering service	
Postage	
Printing and stationery	
Magazine and technical literature	Library subscription
Professional subscriptions – specify	General Medical Council, British Medical Association
Subscription to medical defence organis- ation	
Refresher courses and professional training	
Medical committee expenses	Attending Area Health Authority, family practitioner committee, etc.
Laundry and dry cleaning	
Superannuation (practitioners)	
Accountancy, audit, tax and legal fees	
Bank interest charges	Not related to properties
Hire purchase charges	Furnishing and equipment
Clothing for doctors	White coats
Practitioners' personal sickness insurance	
Levy to Local Medical Council	See Note 4 below
Other expenses	Periodicals, flowers in waiting room

145

Accounting items	Example comment

Depreciation and amortisation

Premises
Cars
Equipment, furniture and fittings

Notes

1 Some groups of doctors have a service company to manage their staff and premises. Such groups should write in for advice to the General Medical Services Committee Secretariat at BMA House.
2 All expenses should include VAT.
3 Each surgery of a multi-surgery practice should be itemised separately.
4 The income from the family practitioner committee should be shown as a gross figure on the receipts side before deduction of the contributions to the Local Medical Council and an entry of such contributions should be shown on the expense side of the accounts.

Further matters on GPs' affairs

219 All expenses should be shown gross, ie., before reimbursement of expenses by the family practitioner committee.

(1) Superannuation

Superannuation payments will be added back in the practice tax computations and should therefore be claimed on the personal tax returns. Relief is available on an 'actual' basis as a deduction from the assessable profits.

(2) Partnership changes

Although it is the simplest method, time-apportionment of profits should not be used, unless changes take place on 1 April, which is the pay review date. An increase or decrease in the number of partners can have a marked effect on the level of profitability, due to extra/lower practice allowances. Instead, therefore, there should be a strict allocation of income to each partner, in order to arrive at his share on a change. It is unusual for goodwill to be valued by doctors, although it is by dentists.

(3) Notional rent allowance

Notional rent allowance is paid by the family practitioner committee, where the surgery is owned by one or more doctors. This allowance is part of the remuneration of the general practitioner from the National Health Service, in return for using premises that he owns in treating National Health Service patients. Under para 12(2), Sch. 6, TCGA 1992 an asset held as an investment is disqualified from the retirement relief provisions and consequently a rented property would not attract relief. However Statement of Practice D5 (issued 4 January 1973) allows a measure of relief equal to the individual partner's share of the rent. A larger fraction of the asset may qualify for relief if the rent charged is clearly less than market rent.

An alternative arrangement would be not to treat the rental payment as a credit to the individual doctor but as partnership income, which is then reflected as an appropriation of profit to the owning doctor. It is true there is no landlord/tenant relationship between the parties and the family practitioner committee and the 'cost rent' as it is called is merely a contribution by the family practitioner committee towards the financing costs of providing premises which recognise the effective subsidy which the partners are making to the health service by providing facilities for National Health Service patients. However, this treatment should avoid capital gains tax retirement relief problems and maximise relevant income for the purposes of retirement annuity premiums or personal pension payments. The same considerations apply where one doctor owns the premises and his partners pay him rent. It is in fact better for that doctor to waive the rent and receive a higher share of partnership profits.

(4) Personal awards

These are taxable and are paid through the family practitioners' committee for seniority, post-graduate training, study leave, vocational training, etc. Grants are also paid for training a trainee general practitioner. Whether these are kept personally or are to be treated as partnership income must be agreed among the partners. If the award is not included in the partnership accounts, it must be shown in the doctor's personal tax returns.

(5) Hospital appointments

Where one or more members of a partnership hold a hospital appointment, the partners should decide whether the income from the appointments is to be kept personally, or to be treated as income of the partnership. The agent should try to obtain an NT (nil tax) coding on Sch. E salaries going to the partnership, although not all inspectors of taxes will agree to this. The practice varies from one tax district to another. If an NT coding is not given, then it is necessary to deduct in the tax computations the income assessable under Sch. E on the individual partner and to make an equalising adjustment in the allocation of partnership profits. Experience shows that the Inland Revenue are becoming increasingly difficult in this matter.

(6) 'Ash Cash' and sundry fees

Some doctors receive payments, often in cash, for signing cremation certificates. Other sundry fees are often received from insurance medicals, lecturing, air-call duties and similar sources. An Inland Revenue Special Office has been examining records of such payments, particularly those kept by crematoria, and a number of investigations into the tax affairs of doctors and consultants have followed, resulting in substantial claims for tax, interest and penalties. A record of these fees should be kept and disclosed to the Inland Revenue on the annual tax return. A recent line of enquiry taken by the Inland Revenue has been into questionnaire completion fees paid to doctors and consultants by market research organisations acting for pharmaceutical companies.

(7) Salaried partners

Some partners who are genuinely self-employed are allocated 'salaries' under the partnership agreement. These are added back in arriving at the partnership Sch. D Case II profit and are then taken into account in apportioning that assessment among the partners. On the other hand, there are some partners who actually receive a salary and no more, and who, therefore, fall within the scope of Sch. E.

These latter arrangements are to be avoided, as there is a danger of such partners being treated as assistants by the family practitioner committee, with a consequent loss in partnership allowances. It is better, therefore, to let such individuals have a low share of profits, with a guaranteed minimum share.

(8) Best accounting date

For tax purposes, the best accounting date is probably 30 June, the end of the first National Health Service quarterly period. However, for practical purposes, 31 March, which is the end of the National Health Service financial year (pay is reviewed each 1 April), creates least problems concerning tax on partnership changes.

The information on general practitioners' income and expenses supplied by inspectors of taxes (**217**(c) and **216**(c) above) is from a sample of returns drawn only from those doctors whose accounting year ends between 1 January and 5 April in the year in question. In order to ensure that as representative a sample as possible is used, the BMA has urged general practitioners to use an accounting date within this period if they can.

(9) Personal expenses claim – 'third tier' expenses

The Inland Revenue's sample of practitioners' returns (see **216**(c) and **219**(8) above) takes into account 'third tier' expenses, as well as those shown in the practice accounts. Accountants are, therefore, urged by the BMA to complete these claims, 'in the same broad fashion as practice accounts', presumably meaning that they should follow the six groups referred to in **216**(d) above.

(a) Motor cars – motor car expenses should be claimed in the 'third tier' of expenses (see **215** above). It is advisable to avoid the complications of leasing of cars if the doctor is registered for dispensing because he will only be able to claim a small proportion of the value added tax on the rentals as he will be partially exempt.

(b) Wife's pension – pension provision can be made by the employing partnership or the individual partner as appropriate.

(c) Practice use of home – a supplementary practice allowance is paid by the family practitioner committee for 24-hour cover, which is a useful argument if household expenses relating to the practice area are challenged by the inspector. The claim should include a proportion of the following:

    (i) rent and water (not personal community charge);
    (ii) light and heat;
    (iii) insurance – buildings and contents;
    (iv) domestic help;
    (v) garden (maintenance of approach to the front door);
    (vi) window cleaning;
    (vii) structural repair;
    (viii) mortgage interest (on part of loan in excess of £30,000).

To ensure that the expenses are allowed, it is recommended that there be a plate outside the house, and a telephone directory entry or a private number available through the surgery.

    Capital gains tax is unlikely to be a problem, unless there is exclusive use of part of the house for the purposes of the practice. Even then, retirement relief, roll-over and/or hold-over relief should cover any potential charge. However, the comments in **219**(3) above should be noted in connection with retirement relief, where premises are owned by one individual partner. Also, it is necessary to withdraw from the practice ('withdrawal' includes 'partial withdrawal'), in order to claim relief from gains on individually owned property. A '24-hour retirement' for pension purposes is not sufficient. A reduction, as opposed to an outright disposal, in partnership share is enough, but to what extent is not clear. Each case will be judged on its facts but a restoration of the full partnership share shortly after the disposal is likely to prejudice the position.

(d) Accountancy fees relating to claims in this 'third tier'.

(e) Professional subscriptions and journals, including the subscription to the British Medical Association.

(f) Local charitable and similar donations (see Inland Revenue Extra-Statutory Concession B7).

(g) Overseas conferences – it is necessary to be ready here for an Inland Revenue challenge, on the grounds of duality of purpose.

Sometimes part of the costs of works of improvement to surgery premises can be financed by improvement grants from the family practitioner committee. A condition for obtaining a grant is often that the expenditure cannot qualify for tax allowances and a declaration to that effect has to be signed by the doctor. The claiming of such expenditure will, therefore, follow normal tax rules, namely capital expenditure on plant and machinery elements must be reduced to the extent it is met by way of grant (s.153 CAA 1990). Equally, no expenditure subject to such a subsidy can be taken into account for capital gains purposes (s.50 TCGA 1992).

It should be noted that where a doctor's surgery is at home, any mortgage interest referable to the business part of the house can be claimed for tax relief as a business expense in addition to tax relief on the first £30,000 under the MIRAS system.

(10) Retired doctors

Fully retired doctors will not be able to obtain tax relief on payments, eg., medical defence subscriptions, as they will have no professional income against which to claim a deduction. The National Health Service pension is not a source of income for this purpose.

Superannuation deductions

220 Superannuation deductions are made by all the paying authorities for fees or remuneration originating in the National Health Service.

The National Health Service takes as pensionable earnings the gross payments, other than direct reimbursements, by family practitioner committees to doctors, less an approximation of the amount that the general practitioner will typically spend by way of expenses. For dentists only, there is a maximum, adjusted annually, on this pensionable earnings figure. The general practitioner pays six per cent of his pensionable earnings by way of contributions to the National Health Service and these should be claimed by reference to the year of payment.

The availability of retirement annuity premium relief relative to private practice income and other non-pensionable earned sources is governed by Inland Revenue Extra-Statutory Concession A9 (which was updated in 1991). A practitioner who is employed in the National Health Service, and is taxed under Sch. E, merely pays his six per cent to the statutory scheme. A general practitioner is self-employed, but, most unusually, is required to be a member of a sponsored superannuation scheme. This unusual circumstance naturally calls for special arrangements, and these are set out in detail in the concession. As the rules are very specific, the general practitioner's taxation advisor should consult them, and no attempt is made to paraphrase them here. However, the

Inland Revenue have confirmed that, for the purposes of applying this concession, it is necessary to aggregate the whole of a doctor's medical earnings including any assessable in respect of a separate wholly private sector practice carried on on his own. It should be noted that where relief is claimed for contributions to the statutory scheme, this should be given strictly as a deduction on a current-year basis in the assessment although inspectors of taxes will sometimes allow the contributions to be allowed on a preceding-year basis as a business expense.

Doctors used to be able to purchase 'added years' of superannuable service, either by a single payment or by instalments over a period of five or ten years, to increase service to a maximum of 40 years at age 60 and thus increase benefits due. Tax relief is available only if the instalments do not exceed nine per cent of National Health Service earnings at the time payments commence. Where premiums towards a retirement annuity are also being paid, concessions are available to prevent an inequity, and details of the arrangement can be obtained from the Pensions Schemes Office.

These concessions will continue in relation to the personal pension rules which replaced the previous retirement annuity premium rules from 1 July 1988.

The Inland Revenue have also confirmed that under the new personal pension arrangements it is possible to choose the statutory relief for personal pension premiums calculated by reference to total Sch. D earnings, and forego concessional relief for contributions to the National Health Service scheme on a year-by-year basis. The doctor who claims the statutory relief in one year may, therefore, revert back to claiming relief on the National Health Service contributions on a non-statutory basis in a later year. It appears that such an election can also be made for the immediately preceding year of assessment where personal pension premiums are related back one year.

Dentists

221 Dentists, like doctors, have National Health Service patients and private patients. Where there are earnings from both sources, Inland Revenue Extra-Statutory Concession A9 operates to quantify what are pensionable National Health Service scheme earnings, in respect of which retirement annuity premiums cannot be paid and allowed unless relief for the National Health Service scheme contributions is disclaimed. With dentists, however, there is a limit on the amount of pensionable earnings, which is reviewed in line with average earnings of dentists under the National Health Service scheme.

This concession continues in relation to the personal pension rules which replaced the previous retirement annuity premium rules from 1 July 1988.

(1) Associates

Dental associates are accepted as self-employed by the Inland Revenue. The partnership or individual dentist that engages an associate can claim the associate's remuneration as a Sch. D Case II deduction.

Doctors and dentists

When an associate is admitted into a partnership, the cessation rules will apply to his source of income as an associate, as he changes his status completely and the source, as a matter of fact, ceases. However, the partnership may make a continuation election if it so chooses.

(2) Partnerships

Partnerships of dentists are usually either cost-sharing, where the dentists do not pool their fees but share premises and costs, or full profit-sharing where income is pooled. In either event, as with general practitioners, there will be a second tier of personal business expenses allowable against their own individual profit shares.

(3) Goodwill

Advice on the value of goodwill of a dental practice should be sought from the British Dental Association, to whom many members make requests for guidance.

General case law relating to doctors and dentists

222 Other cases of limited interest relating to doctors and dentists are:

(a) North *v.* Spencer's Executors (1956) 36 TC 668 – whether payments to executors after death are assessable.
(b) Osborn *v.* Swyer (1933) 18 TC 445 – assessability of rent and rates of a medical officer of a hospital.
(c) Duff *v.* Williamson (1973) 49 TC 1 – assessability of a research grant paid to a doctor.
(d) Sargent *v.* Barnes (1978) 52 TC 335 – travelling expenses of a dentist to and from dental laboratory, where the dental laboratory was between home and surgery, were not allowed under the 'duality of purpose' principle.
(e) Cooke *v.* Blacklaws (1984) 58 TC 255 – 'foreign emoluments' deduction due in respect of salary paid to a non-domiciled dentist by a Panamanian company to which National Health Service earnings were transferred, notwithstanding that, under NHS (General Dental Services) Regulations 1973, it was the dental practitioner who was strictly entitled to the fees (See s.192 ICTA 1988).

Chapter 10
Practising barristers, barristers' clerks and judges

Cash basis

223 Because a barrister cannot sue for fees, a barrister's accounts can be drawn up on a strict cash receipts and payments basis. Unlike members of other professions who can elect to be assessed on a 'cash' (or 'conventional') basis, it is not necessary for a barrister to prepare accounts on an 'earnings' basis for the first three years of carrying on his profession (Inland Revenue Statement of Practice A3). A barrister's earnings are assessable under Sch. D Case II.

A barrister's profession does note cease when he becomes a Queen's Counsel (Seldon *v*. Croom-Johnson 16 TC 740). A cessation occurs, however, when he takes up a full-time appointment, for instance as a judge, assessable under Sch. E, or when he retires or dies before he retires. As with doctors, income and expenses relating to part-time Sch. E appointments, such as recorderships, have to be strictly segregated in the relevant tax computations from the professional accounts in arriving at the income assessable under Sch. D Case II.

Post-cessation receipts

224 All post-cessation receipts of a barrister are now taxable (ss.103 and 104 ICTA 1988). Before the introduction of the legislation now contained in ss.103 and 104, many barristers taxed on the cash basis used to rely on the fact that their post-cessation receipts escaped tax, in order to provide for their retirement. For this reason, a deduction from the amount chargeable under s.104 ICTA 1988 is given for a person born before 6 April 1917, who was carrying on his profession on a cash basis on 18 March 1968. The net amount (after expenses and unabsorbed capital allowances) on which tax is chargeable is reduced to the following percentages (s.109 ICTA 1988):

Date of birth on or before	Percentage chargeable
5 April 1903	25
5 April 1904	30
5 April 1905	35

and so on (at 5% intervals), down to

5 April 1916	90
5 April 1917	95

'Fees earned' basis

225 It is permissible for a barrister to draw up his accounts on an 'earnings' basis, by reference to fees earned and expenses incurred in the period. The calculation of earnings by reference to fees 'booked', ie., fees that form entries in a fee book, will be an acceptable application of the earnings basis. It will not be necessary to include a figure for work-in-progress in the computations.

A barrister starting to practise may elect which basis to adopt, and it is possible to change from one basis to the other at a later stage but, once the change has been made, the new basis must be adhered to. A change from a 'cash' basis to a 'fees earned' basis will also attract a charge to tax under s.104 ICTA 1988 on the outstanding debtors, but subject to relief for the barrister's age (see **224** above). Where the basis adopted after the change takes no account of work-in-progress, a further charge under s.104 will arise on the eventual cessation of the practice, in respect of any fees received after cessation, for work-in-progress at the time of cessation (see Inland Revenue Statement of Practice A3).

Change of basis

226 Where the necessary conditions are met, relief is given under s.109 ICTA 1988 (see **224** above) from a charge to tax under s.104 ICTA 1988, whether the charge arises from a cessation, such as on retirement, or on a change from a 'conventional' (see **223** above) to an 'earnings' basis.

As the relief is given in terms of a percentage of the income charged, the higher the income the greater the relief. As barristers are not able to sue for fees, they frequently have to wait long periods for payment. This can result in a significant accumulation of debts at a particular time, and it might then be worthwhile considering a change of basis, rather than waiting for retirement in order to enjoy s.109 relief. On the other hand, because they are unable to sue for fees, barristers will rarely find it advantageous to change to an earnings basis.

Inducement receipts

227 A payment to induce a barrister to give up his status as a practising barrister, and to accept an appointment with an employer that precluded the barrister from continuing in practice in chambers, has been held not to be taxable as income (Vaughan-Neil *v.* CIR (1979) 54 TC 223).

Expenses – travel

228 A barrister's expenses of travelling between home and chambers are not allowable, following the decision in Newsom *v.* Robertson (1952) 33 TC 452, even if part of the barrister's home is used as a study. The places where the profession of a barrister is considered to be carried on are the Courts and chambers. Only travelling between the two, or between two sets of chambers, is, therefore, allowable.

The position on claiming expenses, where there is income from a Sch. E appointment, is more restrictive still. Thus, the costs of a barrister's travel between chambers in London and the place of performance of his duties as a recorder in Portsmouth were held not to be allowable for Sch. E purposes, where the barrister held a recordership as well as carrying on a practice in London (see Ricketts *v.* Colquhoun (1925) 10 TC 118). The test of allowability was what each and every holder of the office incurred. This test would exclude expenses peculiar to the circumstances of the particular holder of the office – in this instance, as recorder.

Expenses – cost of chambers

229 The appropriate costs of running and renting chambers, including a clerk's fees, are allowable. The Inland Revenue will also allow an appropriate proportion of the costs of the home that are referable to professional use. However, where a proportion of the home expenses is claimed, the capital gains implications need to be considered before a claim is made that a specific proportion of the home is used exclusively as a study, as such a claim will affect the capital gains tax private residence exemption (s.222 TCGA 1992).

Expenses – court apparel

230 Generally, the costs of replacing a barrister's special Court apparel are allowable. It is understood that a barrister's wig and gown rank as plant, following a decision before the Special Commissioners on the point, so that it will now be possible for the initial cost of such items to qualify for capital allowances. In Mallalieu *v.* Drummond (1983) 57 TC 330, however, it was held that the cost of the ordinary dark dresses and suits, with white tunics and black tights, that a lady barrister has to wear to appear in Court, is not allowable, as the reason for buying this clothing is not only to be able to appear in Court but also to provide warmth and decency.

Expenses – patent fee

231 The patent fee on becoming a Queen's Counsel is not allowable as a Sch. D Case II expense because of its capital nature.

Expenses – books

232   The replacement of books is allowable as a Sch. D Case II expense, as is the cost of servicing loose-leaf volumes. The initial cost of a barrister's library is regarded as capital and cannot be claimed as a revenue expense. However, following the decision in Munby *v*. Furlong (1977) 50 TC 491, books now rank as 'plant' for capital allowances. With the withdrawal of the 100% first-year allowance, it will probably be to the barrister's advantage to adopt the 'renewals' basis outlined above, ie., to disallow the original cost of the library and allow the cost of replacements as a Sch. D Case II expense. As an alternative, the barrister may claim writing-down allowances in respect of both his original and his replacement books. Where books have not been claimed as plant, because figures have been agreed before the decision in Munby *v*. Furlong, it will be possible, for future periods, to claim writing-down allowances on such a library on the notional written-down value.

Barristers' clerks

233   Barristers' clerks occupy a unique position as they are effectively employed by a number of principals in the chambers where they work. Because of this, special taxation arrangements are allowed to operate in respect of their earnings. They are allowed to account for PAYE quarterly themselves, by reference to the PAYE codes on their net receipts for the preceding quarter, after expenses and pension scheme payments. If they do not operate this system, the Inland Revenue have indicated that they will make quarterly 'direct collection' assessments, based on the previous year's income, excluding expenses.

The head of chambers is required to deal with both the employers' and employees' national insurance contributions in respect of barristers' clerks. However, some senior clerks have been able to negotiate self-employed status with the Department of Social Security, although this would only apply on an individual basis. Similarly, some senior clerks have succeeded in persuading the Inland Revenue that they are self-employed for tax purposes.

Self-employed status has recently been challenged unsuccessfully by the Inland Revenue in McMenamin *v*. Diggles (1991 STC 419). This case concerned the senior clerk of a leading set of barristers' chambers in Manchester. Up to 7 October 1985 he was senior clerk under a contract of employment. Thereafter, new contractual arrangements operated with each member of the chambers, under which in return for a specified percentage of the gross income of each member, he agreed at his own cost to provide a full clerking service for each member. It was open to him to act as head clerk himself or to provide some other suitably qualified person to act as such. The point at issue was whether this occupation constituted a Sch. E office. For the Inland Revenue, it was contended that as under paragraph 26 of the Code of Conduct issued by the Bar Council every barrister had 'to have the services of

156

the clerk of the chambers', each barrister must engage the services of a person holding the office of clerk of chambers.

In Edwards *v.* Clinch (1981 STC 617) it had been held that an 'office' was a continuing position, independent of the person who filled it, and occupied by successive holders. There had to be an instrument creating the office and it had to have a degree of public relevance with formality of appointment. In the McMenamin case, there was no obvious instrument creating an office, in no sense were there public duties, and the revised arrangements were the most convenient means of discharging the contractual obligations of the clerk.

Judges

234 Her Majesty's judges are assessable under Sch. E in respect of their remuneration. It is understood that the Inland Revenue have, in certain cases, allowed a deduction (currently £780 per annum) where judges have had to maintain a study at home for the proper performance of their duties. Similarly, deductions have been agreed for a judge's law books (currently £610 per annum) and for maintenance of robes, wing collars and bands (currently £200 per annum). The foregoing figures are operative for the tax year 1990/91 and future increases will be based on the annual rate of inflation to January each year. In addition to the above there is an allowance of the full cost of *The Times* and the 1990/91 agreed allowance is £110.

Chapter 11
Members of Parliament

General taxation position

235   Because of the complexity of their allowances, MPs are dealt with by a special unit of the Inland Revenue in Cardiff, which issues notes for guidance on the tax position of MPs (reissued in 1988 and subsequently updated). An MP is liable to income tax under Sch. E on his or her Parliamentary salary, as the holder of an office. An MP is also in receipt of certain allowances principally designed to cover the expenses incurred on living away from home, travel and secretarial assistance. The tax position of such allowances is set out below.

Additional costs allowance

236   The main allowance is the daily additional costs allowance for non-inner London members: inner London members have a London allowance, which is taxable. This additional costs allowance covers the additional costs of living away from home whilst engaged in Parliamentary duties either in London or in the MP's constituency, up to a maximum of £10,786 a year for 1991/92. The allowance ceased to be taxable in relation to payments received for periods from 1 April 1984 (s.200 ICTA 1988). In consequence, no claims for expenses incurred on or after 6 April 1984 in connection with staying away from the MP's home to perform Parliamentary duties, such as the cost of meals in London, rent, and the heating of a second home in London, will be admitted. In addition, under Inland Revenue Extra-Statutory Concession A54, it will be possible for the new rules to apply to earlier years for which assessments have not, before 13 March 1984, become final and conclusive. The effect of the allowance no longer being taxable is that an MP can obtain effective tax relief on interest on a mortgage to buy a second home in London, as the allowance is calculated to allow the payment of either rent or such mortgage interest in the case of an owned property.

Car allowance

237   The position is complex because the cash mileage reimbursement that the

MP receives from the Fees Office includes the cost of travel between an MP's home and Westminster, or between home and constituency, which ranks for tax purposes as private travel. In strictness, the car mileage allowance paid by the Fees Office is assessable as an emolument and an expenses claim should be made. However, it has been found that, taking one year with another, this cash allowance adequately covers both allowable running costs and depreciation. For practical purposes, therefore, the allowance is not taxed (unless the Fees Office pays an allowance on a taxable journey), nor is an expenses claim required from the member in the average case where a member claims for an annual mileage of up to 25,000.

The rates of mileage allowance for 1991/92 are as follows:

Engine size	First 20,000 miles	After 20,000 miles
up to 1,300 cc	28.8p	15.1p
1,301 to 2,300 cc	43.4p	19.9p
2,301 cc upwards	68.2p	34.1p

If an MP makes a claim for an annual mileage in excess of 25,000, the Fees Office requires detailed particulars of his journeys (*Taxation* 17 July 1987).

Other travel (by taxi, train or air)

238 Incidental travel costs in London, such as taxi fares between London rail and air terminals and Westminster, and in visiting ministers on Parliamentary business, are allowable expenses.

MPs are issued with rail and air warrants which give them free rail and air travel. Where the travel is from Westminster to the constituency, this does not rank as a benefit, because it is a facility used in the course of the performance of the duties of an office which has two places of work, Westminster and the constituency. Therefore, there should be no taxable benefit in relation to such travel. However, travel from the MP's home or main home to Westminster, or between home and the constituency (where the home is neither in Westminster nor in the constituency), will be taxable on the following basis. Where the member's home is not more than 20 miles in a direct line from the nearest point of the constituency boundary, a warrant for travel between home and Westminster, or between home and the constituency, is not taxable. Where a member's home is within 20 miles' radius of Westminster, a warrant used for travelling between home and the constituency is not taxable. Where the home is more than 20 miles from the nearest point of the constituency boundary, a warrant used for travelling between home and Westminster is taxable. Where the home is neither in the constituency nor in London, and warrants are used for travelling between Westminster and the constituency via home, provided the journey between Westminster and the constituency can be regarded as continuous, only the excess of the value of the warrant used for the round trip over the value of a warrant for a direct journey between Westminster and the constituency is taxable. 'Continuous' for this purpose means that no more than one night may be spent at the member's home before continuing the journey, unless the journey spans a weekend, when Saturday and Sunday are disregarded. The Fees Office notifies the Inland Revenue of the private proportion.

Other private air or rail travel not connected with the performance of Parliamentary duties, for instance attending political meetings, will also give rise to a benefit. The benefit will be the cost of the equivalent ticket (s.141 ICTA 1988). Special rail/air warrants are available for use by the spouses and minor children of the members for the purpose of making 15 return journeys per calendar year by rail or air between London and the constituency, and/or between London and home. Again, this is not taxable, except to the extent that the journeys are to and from the home or principal home. The basis of the exemption for other journeys is presumably the same as the concession given for directors' wives accompanying them on business trips, where the expenses are allowable if they can be regarded as helping the director in the performance of his duties.

Office costs allowance (OCA)

239   MPs receive an allowance (£28,986 for 1991/92) for office, secretarial and research expenses. This is taxable, but a deduction is made for the actual costs of any secretarial and clerical assistance, general office expenses and research assistance undertaken in the proper performance of the MP's Parliamentary duties. Such expenses include the normal costs of office accommodation such as rent, heat and light, including the use of part of the home as an office and the costs of repairs and renewals of office equipment. Telephone, stationery, and postage costs in so far as not provided free, are also allowable. An MP's secretary is paid direct by the Fees Office rather than the MP receiving the salary as part of a claim for office expenses, and PAYE is operated by the Fees Office. There are also provisions for sickness benefits and superannuation contributions. Detailed claims are generally only required where claims are made in excess of the allowance.

Other incidental expenses

240   Various other incidental expenses can be claimed, including the hiring of rooms to meet constituents, delegation expenses with all-party Parliamentary organisations such as the Inter-Parliamentary Union or the Parliamentary Group for European Unity, and payments for assistance on constituency work to a local agent or party organisation and the extra cost of meals while travelling on Parliamentary business (but not the cost of staying overnight in London – see **236** above). Amongst the items that the Inland Revenue regard as not allowable are any party political expenses (such as election expenses), extra costs of late night sittings, periodicals, books and newspaper cuttings, and overseas trips unless as part of an official all-party Parliamentary delegation.

An attempt is made to allow, in the PAYE code number of the MP, an estimate of the excess of allowable expenses over taxable allowances. To this end, a formal claim with a signed declaration is made by the MP after the end of each fiscal year. With the exemption now afforded to most allowances, such coding adjustments are rarely needed.

Pension and retirement arrangements

241 There are special pension and retirement arrangements for MPs. Compulsory contributions to the House of Commons Members' Fund and contributions to the Parliamentary Contributory Pension Fund are treated as reducing the MP's salary for tax purposes. It is also possible for an MP to purchase additional years of service reckonable for superannuation purposes, either by periodical contributions at any time during his or her service as an MP, or by lump sum payment effected within 12 months of election to the House of Commons.

Terminal grants to MPs made in pursuance of a Resolution of the House of Commons to a person ceasing to be an MP are treated as taxable under the 'golden handshake' legislation and are therefore exempt up to £30,000. Such grants include severance payments equal to three months' salary as a member.

There are special provisions (s.629 ICTA 1988) for ministers who are not participants in the Parliamentary pension scheme in respect of their extra ministerial salary over and above what is pensionable under that scheme. They can make personal pension premium payments in respect of such element of their remuneration.

Other income

242 Most MPs have other earned income in addition to their Parliamentary salaries. Where an MP has Sch. D Case II income from writing on political matters, some of the expenditure on purely political research not allowed against the salary as an MP may, in suitable cases, be claimed against such income on normal Sch. D principles.

Members of the European Parliament

243 Consider the following.

(1) Salaries

UK members of the European Parliament are entitled to a salary paid by HM Government which the Inland Revenue regard as taxable. Their tax affairs are dealt with by Public Department 1, Ty-Glas, Cardiff CF4 5XZ. In 1979 this tax district issued notes for guidance on the taxation of Euro MPs or MEPs, which were revised in March 1983 and August 1989.

(2) Travel and subsistence allowances

The Inland Revenue now accept that the substantial expense allowances paid to MEPs are not subject to UK tax. The European Parliament pays flat-rate subsistence and travel allowances to MEPs to enable them to meet their expenses in travelling to the Parliament and its various agencies. The Inland Revenue originally argued that these allowances, being flat-rate round sums rather than actual reimbursements, were emoluments taxable under Sch. E, subject to any s.198 ICTA 1988 claim.

The Special Commissioners referred a case on this point, Lord Bruce of Donington *v.* Aspden (1981) STC 761 to the European Court of Justice. The Court ruled that Community Law prohibited the imposition of national taxes on these lump sums, unless the Inland Revenue could show that they were, in part, remuneration.

Following this ruling, the Inland Revenue no longer require any MEP to enter these allowances on his tax return, unless he or she wishes to claim they were inadequate to meet the expenditure actually incurred on Parliamentary duties and that the balance was paid out of his or her Parliamentary salary. As s.198 ICTA 1988 is very restrictive, where a claim does arise, the inspector will need to examine the whole of the expenses incurred by the member under a particular heading. Tax relief will then be given on the balance by which the allowable expenditure exceeds the expense allowances received or that could have been received from the European Parliament.

(3) Deduction for expenses

The following principles are broadly followed by the Inland Revenue in determining whether an expense is allowable.

A deduction may be claimed by an MEP for travelling in the performance of official duties. This includes travelling within the constituency and from the constituency to the Parliament. When the MEP's home is outside the constituency, the cost of travelling between home and the constituency and between home and the Parliament is inadmissible in the same way as for members of the United Kingdom Parliament and for home to work travel generally. If, however, an MEP travels between the Parliament and constituency via home, the cost of the direct journey between the constituency and the Parliament is admissible, provided that the journey via home could be said to be a continuous journey (in practice, as for Westminster MPs, that any break does not exceed one night during the week or two nights at the weekend).

A deduction may be claimed by an MEP for other expenses incurred wholly, exclusively and necessarily in the performance of the duties. Examples of admissible expenses are:

(a) secretarial and clerical assistance in dealing with constituents' affairs;
(b) office accommodation (including the cost of a room at home set apart as an office);

(c) repairs to and renewals of office equipment (eg., computers);
(d) telephone and telegram charges, stationery and postage in so far as these are not provided free;
(e) hiring rooms to meet constituents (eg., surgeries in the constituency); and
(f) payments to a local agent or party association in return for which an MEP receives help in carrying out Parliamentary work, eg., clerical assistance and fixing interviews.

The following are examples of inadmissible expenses:

(a) literature issued for canvassing purposes;
(b) election expenses;
(c) newspapers, periodicals, books, news cutting services, etc.;
(d) charitable subscriptions and donations;
(e) entertaining, including the cost of entertaining constituents;
(f) expenses incurred by the wives and husbands of MEPs (eg., in deputising for or accompanying MEPs);
(g) payments to political organisations for political purposes; and
(h) generally, expenses which an MEP incurs not as a member of the European Parliament but as a member of a political party.

(4) Deduction for duties abroad

If an MEP was absent abroad on the duties of the office for a total of at least 30 days in 1984/85, he or she could claim 12½% of net income attributable to the period abroad as exempt from tax. Public Department 1 required members to keep detailed records of departures from and returns to the UK, together with a note of the purpose for which the journeys were undertaken, where such a claim was made. No deduction is available for 1985/86 or subsequent years. For years prior to 1984/85 the deduction was 25%.

(5) Terminal grants to MEPs

S.190 ICTA 1988 applies the same treatment to such payments as that given for payments to MPs referred to in **241** above. They will thus only be chargeable under s.148 ICTA 1988, subject to the £30,000 exemption in s.188.

Members of the House of Lords

244 Most members of the House of Lords receive no salary, only allowances which are not taxable. In addition they can claim the cost of travel by public transport or car at the same mileage rate as MPs from their home to the Lords.

Ministers in the House of Lords and office holders who are members of that House receive termination payments on giving up office, subject to certain conditions. Such payments are treated in the same way as the terminal grants to MPs and MEPs.

Chapter 12
Merchant navy and aircraft personnel

General principles

245 The taxation of the income of aircraft and merchant navy personnel is determined by the specific provisions relating to the place of performance of duties of such persons and their residence status. This chapter deals with the position as from 6 April 1977 when the provisions concerning the place of performance of duties and eligibility for the 100% or 12½% (formerly 25%) deduction were modified (s.132(4) and para. 5 of Sch. 12 ICTA 1988). It is easier to consider the position of seafarers first and then to comment on aircrew insofar as they differ from seafarers. The Inland Revenue have published notes on the tax position of seafarers, although these are not currently available. Reference should be made to paragraph 7 for details of the abolition of the foreign earnings deduction in the Finance Act 1984 which applies for 1985/86 onwards.

Non-resident seafarers

(1) Not resident and not ordinarily resident

246 A seafarer may claim the above status in either of two ways:

(a) If for a period which encompasses a complete income tax year he (i) serves on ships which both open and close Crew Agreements (previously known as Ships Articles) abroad and does not visit the UK at any time during the period of the Crew Agreement thus performing all his duties outside the UK; and (ii) does not visit the UK during the period of claim for more than an average of 90 days per annum or a total of 182 complete days in any one complete income tax year.

(b) If he is employed wholly abroad, that is, does not enter British ports in the course of his engagement or engagements, for a continuous period exceeding three years (36 months) he will be not resident and not ordinarily resident from the date of departure from the UK to his date of return, providing that his visits to the UK do not exceed 182 complete days in any income tax year or an average of 90 days per annum. It should be noted that the maintenance of any place of abode in the UK is ignored in deciding a person's residence in these situations (s.335(1) ICTA 1988).

(2) Not resident but ordinarily resident

247 This will normally apply if the seafarer is physically absent from the UK on voyages during the whole of an income tax year, but in the preceding and subsequent years visits the UK for periods which make the annual average over 90 days per annum. In a very old case, Rogers *v.* CIR (1 TC 225), a Master Mariner who was absent from the UK for a complete fiscal year while his wife and family continued to live in the UK in the family house, was held to be ordinarily resident in the UK for that year.

If a seafarer qualifies as not resident, he will not be liable to UK tax on his pay for the period of the successful claim as he cannot be liable under any Case of Sch. E.

Any relief where a person is not resident is normally granted by repayment on a claim being made to Cardiff Marine (Cardiff 6) District, as the master of the vessel remains responsible for deduction of tax in accordance with the seaman's code.

Foreign seamen

248 Where a foreign seaman who has his home outside the UK serves in the coasting trade or is in receipt of 'off Articles' pay (whether on ship or on shore in the UK), he is liable to tax on those earnings under Case II of Sch. E. Foreign seamen employed in the foreign going trade as opposed to the coasting trade, who can satisfy the Inland Revenue that they normally live outside the UK and do not spend six months or more in the UK in any one year of assessment, or periods of three months per annum in any one period of four consecutive years, do not become liable to UK income tax. They may claim repayment of tax deducted from their earnings in the foreign going trade by completing the appropriate form R43(M) which may be obtained from any Mercantile Marine Office or the Cardiff Marine tax office.

UK residents – 12½% (formerly 25%) or 100% deduction

249 If a seafarer is unable to qualify as not resident, he may be eligible for a deduction of either 12½% (up to 1985/86) or 100% from his pay before his liability to UK tax is calculated. The Finance Act 1977 made provision for UK resident seamen and aircrew to become eligible for deductions from their emoluments despite the fact that the duties could be treated as otherwise performed in the UK under the specific legislation in the Taxes Act (s.132(4) ICTA 1988). Before 6 April 1977, in particular, where a vessel was engaged on a voyage extending outside the UK but not involving a call at a foreign port (eg., a deep sea fishing trip), the crew's duties were treated as performed in the UK. Further, if the ship began or ended a voyage in the UK, all the duties of UK-resident crew were treated as performed in the UK. When a voyage or journey began and ended outside the UK, but part of it either began or ended in the UK, the duties of the UK-resident crew, as they related to that part, were treated as performed in the UK.

The cases where deductions may since 6 April 1977 be available for duties treated as performed outside the UK are where the voyage begins or ends outside the UK (para. 5(a) of Sch. 12 ICTA 1988) or where there is a part of a voyage which begins or ends outside the UK, although the whole voyage begins and ends in the UK (para. 5(b) of Sch.12 ICTA 1988). As before, duties will be treated as performed in the UK in respect of any part of the voyage which both begins and ends in the UK, or where the voyage extends outside the UK but there is no scheduled call at a foreign port, for instance a fishing boat going into the Norwegian sector of the North Sea on a voyage to and from a UK port. The UK side of the Continental Shelf is to be treated as part of the UK, so that voyages to North Sea installations in the UK sector will not qualify for any deduction (para. 5 of Sch.12 ICTA 1988).

250 For these purposes, the casting off from a UK berth, allied to passage for the overseas port, would be taken as the time of departure from the UK, and, of course, to count as a qualifying day the person must be absent from the UK at midnight. Duties performed on board ship *before* it actually casts off from a UK berth are not treated as performed outside the UK.

Again a ship is regarded as arriving in the UK at the time of berthing, so that if the voyage is from a foreign port to a UK port, any duties carried out after berthing, for instance cleaning the ship, and before casting off, would not be treated as performed outside the UK as at that time the vessel would not have been 'engaged on a voyage' beginning or ending outside the UK. However, if the voyage is from a foreign port back to the foreign port, then duties performed on the vessel whilst in the UK would be treated as performed outside the UK in accordance with paragraph 5 of Sch. 12 ICTA 1988. Of course, it is still necessary for the seaman to be absent from the UK at midnight when reckoning qualifying days.

12½% (formerly 25%) deduction

251 A deduction of 12½% was formerly due to a resident seafarer if:

(a) The duties of his employment were performed wholly or partly abroad on the basis outlined; and

(b) He spent at least 30 qualifying days in any income tax year outside the UK while on such overseas duties,

unless he worked for a foreign employer and all his duties were performed abroad, in which case there was no 30 qualifying day requirement.

167

For the purpose of the 12½% deduction the qualifying days need not have been continuous but could be aggregated over the whole of the income tax year. If a seafarer's service included less than 30 qualifying days in the income tax year, unless he worked full-time abroad for a foreign employer he would not be entitled to any deduction. Once he had 30 qualifying days or more he was entitled to the deduction of 12½% in respect of all his qualifying days.

While a seafarer was entitled to this 12½% deduction, his employer normally made an appropriate deduction from his earnings before the liability to UK tax was calculated. A full review was then made by Cardiff Marine Office at the end of each tax year to make any adjustments necessary. It was understood that where a seafarer qualified for the 12½% deduction, the Inland Revenue agreed that a seafarer's earnings in respect of his qualifying days included compensatory leave attributable to such earnings. Accordingly they used the following special formula for establishing the emoluments eligible for the 12½% deduction in assessing any seafarer's income tax liability for 1977/78 and subsequent years.

(a) (i) Establish the number of qualifying days.
    (ii) Add: leave attributable to those qualifying days (in the absence of evidence of any higher leave entitlement this will be taken as one-half of the qualifying days for officers and one-sixth for ratings).
    (iii) Deduct: 1/15 of the resultant total (for two days per month annual leave).
(b) Pro rata total earnings for the period of employment by the total number of days in (i) over the total number of days' employment.

EXAMPLE (1983/84)
A rating signs off at the end of a voyage of 90 days' duration. In that period he has had 70 qualifying days and 20 non-qualifying days. He has earned 15 days' paid leave. His gross wages, including leave pay, amount to £882. Calculation of taxable earnings:

(a) Qualifying days   70
    Add: 1/6 for attributable leave   12
                                   82
    Less: 1/15 for annual leave   6
                                     76
(b) Eligible emoluments = 76/105 × £882 = £638.40
(c) Emoluments chargeable to tax:
    75% × £638.40 = £478.80
    Balance   =   243.60
                       £722.40

100% deduction

252 A resident seafarer will be entitled to relief at 100% where he performs the duties of his employment abroad in the course of a qualifying period which consists of at least 365 days. Time spent in the UK during this period will not debar the claim to 100% relief provided that:

(a) It does not exceed 62 consecutive days; and
(b) The time spent in the UK does not exceed one sixth of the period, – such tests to be applied at the conclusion of each overseas visit (para.3(2) of Sch. 12 ICTA 1988) by reference to a period stretching back to the last period of absence from the UK (para.3(1) of Sch. 12 ICTA 1988) and any intervening visits to the UK which do not exceed the 62 consecutive days or one sixth test.

With effect from 1988/89, 90 was substituted for 62 consecutive days and one quarter for one sixth. With effect from 1991/92, the limits have again been raised for merchant seamen so that 183 is substituted for 90 and one half for one quarter.

The operation of the new limits needs to be carefully watched where the qualifying period overlaps the introduction of the new limits. Any seafarer who started a qualifying period during 1990/91 and expects to end that period during 1991/92 after having reached the important 365 day target must be careful not to exceed the 1990/91 limits throughout the whole of his 365 day period. If after 5 April 1991 he returns to the UK for a period which exceeds the 1990/91 limits but which is within the 1991/92 limits, he will lose his entitlement to the 100% deduction in 1990/91. A claim for relief for a qualifying period is made for a year of assessment and it is made by reference to the limits which apply in that year of assessment.

Thus, if Captain Pugwash sets sail on an overseas tour of duty on 6 December 1990, returns to the UK on 6 May 1991, leaves again 123 days later on 6 September 1991, and finally returns again on 6 December 1991, he may be alarmed to learn that the 1990/91 earnings are fully taxable. His claim for relief in 1990/91 does not succeed because his period of 365 days does not meet the conditions which apply in that year of assessment (intervening periods limited to 90 days and one quarter of total days). His claim for 1991/92 does succeed because the conditions which apply for that year of assessment are met.

253 Where a seafarer is entitled to the 100% deduction, the income tax office will allow the deduction due in a Sch. E assessment, which will be made where necessary after the end of the income tax year.

254 Formerly, it was sometimes advantageous to claim a 100% deduction against earnings whilst remaining resident in the UK. This was the case owing to the restriction in personal allowances if a person was not resident in the UK, calculated by reference to the proportion of UK income to world income. This is now no longer relevant as full personal allowances are given against income liable to UK tax in the hands of certain non-residents. However, it can avoid the withdrawal of MIRAS relief, which occurs after four years' non-residence in the case of an employment abroad. In that situation it may be preferable to retain resident status by performing some duties in the UK of an employment or spending more than three months a year here.

It is seldom the case that a seaman becomes a resident of another country as a result of lengthy absences from the UK, because the provisions of the relevant double tax treaty would normally exempt him from local tax if he was in the other country for less than 184 days and was not paid by an employer resident in the other country, that is, he remains on the payroll of the British shipping line (see for instance the US/UK Double Tax Treaty). It may be worth preserving UK residence, therefore, by reserving accommodation here and by ensuring that the employment contract requires some duties to be performed in the UK which are not merely of an incidental nature, for instance, the tour of duty ends back in the UK port.

Examples (prior to 1988/89)

255 For example:

	(A)	(B)
Days out of the UK	40	30
Days in the UK	20	10
Days out of the UK	30	30

EXAMPLE A

At the end of the total period (90 days) the days spent in the UK (20) exceed one sixth of the total (15). The period cannot, therefore, be regarded as continuous for the purposes of the 100% deduction and only the final 30 days can be augmented by later periods.

EXAMPLE B

At the end of the total period (70 days) the days spent in the UK (10) do not exceed one sixth of the total (12). The period can, therefore, be regarded as continuous for the purposes of the 100% deduction and may later, by virtue of the continuing addition of later periods, amount to 365 or more days.

Definitions

256 A qualifying day is defined as any day at the end of which the seafarer is outside the UK, ie., at midnight (24.00 hours in the UK), (para.4 of Sch. 12 ICTA 1988) whether at a port outside the UK, or on any sea passage other than between two UK ports, or in connection with North Sea oil operations within the area designated under the Continental Shelf Act (para.5 of Sch. 12 ICTA 1988), or travelling from or to the UK to join or having left a ship.

It is emphasised that the sea passage must be one to or from a port outside the UK (or to or from an oil rig outside the designated area). A voyage from a port merely to carry out operations at sea which does not touch a foreign port, will not normally count.

However, voyages by tankers which end in a lightening operation, will be treated as voyages ending at a port. If the lightening operation takes place in UK territorial waters or within the area designated under the Continental Shelf Act, the voyage will be treated as if it had terminated in a UK port: if the lightening operation takes place outside these waters, the voyage will be treated as if it were one to a port outside the UK.

257 The United Kingdom is defined for this purpose as Great Britain and Northern Ireland. Thus ports in the Republic of Ireland, Channel Islands and the Isle of Man are regarded as outside the UK. Moreover, a ship will be deemed to have left the UK at the moment at which she leaves her berth or anchorage to proceed on her voyage. Equally, a seafarer travelling by air to join a ship abroad will be deemed to have left the UK at the schedule time of his flight's departure. Arrival times will be similarly defined.

258 Thus, days of departure from the UK will count as qualifying days whilst days of arrival will not.

Administration

259 Special forms are available from Cardiff Marine District, requesting details of on-crew agreements, names of ship and employer, and the dates of voyages and ports visited to determine the appropriate amount of the deductions.

Flat rate expenses deduction

260 The flat rate expenses deduction agreed by the Unions with the Inland Revenue for tools and special clothing for seamen for 1991/92 under Extra-Statutory Concession A1 is as follows:

	£
(1) Carpenters (Seamen) Passenger liners	140
(2) Carpenters (Seamen) cargo vessels, tankers, coasters and ferries	110
(3) Other Seamen Passenger liners	NIL
(4) Other Seamen Cargo vessels, tankers, coasters and ferries	NIL

Seamen's PAYE

261 It was felt necessary to adapt the PAYE regulations because of the special nature of the conditions of employment applicable to the Merchant Navy, including engagements of a short duration with different employers and the fact that wages are not paid until the end of the voyage. They are set out in

Income Tax (Employments) Regulations 1973 Part V, regs 35–43. These Regulations were however repealed with effect from 6 April 1982 and the general PAYE Regulations apply thereafter. However, special arrangements known as the Marine Tax Deduction Scheme have been agreed between the Inland Revenue and the National Maritime Board. Their main features have been set out in the Guides issued by the Board of Inland Revenue (Master's Guide to the Marine Tax Deduction Scheme (P7 (Master) April 1977)).

262 Subject to certain exemptions for seamen engaged in normal employment, the arrangements applied to all seamen in the Merchant Navy. In particular the term 'Authorised Code' meant any normal code given by the Inspector, or if there was no such code, a code assigned to the seamen by the Mercantile Marine Office Superintendent.

263 The arrangement can apply to seamen engaged on a foreign ship who are resident in the UK. Pay includes leave pay, pay in lieu of leave, leave subsistence allowance, pay in respect of overtime, shipwreck, unemployment indemnity, and special payment while sick abroad (as defined by the National Maritime Board). Every employer paying wages to a seaman must deduct tax in accordance with the Seaman's Tables and the Seaman's Authorised Code. There are instructions for determining the code where no notification has been received of a code.

264 Normal PAYE regulations broadly apply and tax deducted from wages must be paid over not later than the 14th day of the month following the month in which the payment is made or, if the agreement with the crew terminates outside the United Kingdom, within such longer period as may be allowed by the Commissioners of Inland Revenue.

265 The administration of Seaman's tax is dealt with at Cardiff District (formerly Cardiff Marine), Pearl Assurance House, Greyfriars Road, Cardiff CF1 3QP.

Aircrew

266 Similar considerations and legislation apply to aircrew.

Residence position

267 The residence position of aircrew should be looked at in the light of the decision in Robson *v.* Dixon (48 TC 527). This case concerned a British pilot employed by KLM, his base being Schiphol Airport, Amsterdam, who maintained a home in the UK from which he commuted to Amsterdam. None of the flights commenced in the UK and of 811 take-offs and landings in the relevant year, only 38 were in the UK. He spent less than 60 days on average in the UK. He claimed to be non-resident in the UK and thus not liable to tax on his emoluments on the basis that the UK landings constituted duties incidental to the performance of the other duties outside the UK and that the employment thus was one carried on abroad, so that the maintenance of a house in the UK was irrelevant in determining his residence position (s.132(2) and s.335(2)

ICTA 1988). The Court decided that it was the nature of the duties, not the amount of time spent on them, which determined whether they were incidental, and in this case, the duties performed in the UK were the same as those performed elsewhere, and therefore the pilot was held to be resident in the UK. The Inland Revenue would normally, however, disregard on *de minimis* grounds, a single take-off and landing in the UK in a year, in considering whether any duties were performed in the UK by a pilot of British nationality, owning a house in the UK, who is otherwise resident abroad (*Hansard* written answer 28 October 1975).

268   If the employee were a foreigner landing in the UK in this way, even if, on the basis of this case, the duties were not incidental, unless he became resident here by virtue of having a place of abode here, or by virtue of the duration of his visits to the UK, he might be able to avoid a technical charge to tax under Case II of Schedule E, if he were employed by a foreign employer, by claiming the protection of a double tax treaty. Such treaties normally exempt someone working for a foreign employer where the foreigner is not present in the UK for more than 183 days on his UK duties.

12½% or 100% deduction

269   Assuming the aircrew cannot be regarded as non-resident, performing all their duties abroad, they may be able to claim the benefit of the 100% deduction (or formerly the 12½% deduction) on the same sort of basis as seamen. Again, flights must begin or end in the UK, and there must be a foreign airport involved.

The extended limits for return visits to merchant seamen do not apply to aircrew. Consequently, the conditions for a 100% deduction will seldom be achieved by aircrew unless they are primarily based abroad for lengthy periods. It has recently been decided (in Leonard *v.* Blanchard 1992 STC 20) that an airline pilot who worked almost exclusively on flights outside the UK could not for the purposes of the 100% deduction add days of absence from work spent in the UK. He claimed under what is now s.132 ICTA 1988 that emoluments for his days of leave fell within the exception to duties performed in the UK 'except insofar as it is shown that but for that absence they would have been emoluments for duties performed outside the United Kingdom'. His claim was rejected in the High Court as it was impossible to assume that if he had been working, he would have been working outside the UK. The aircraft were fully rostered and if he had reported for work it could not be shown that any available duties would have had to be performed outside the UK. This exception was designed to cover persons taken ill while working abroad and having to return home for treatment.

270   BALPA has in addition, negotiated, in connection with what constitutes qualifying days, a valuable concession with the Inland Revenue for pilots.

271   In the case of aircrew, a qualifying day runs from 'Chocks Off' to 'Chocks On' and must pass through midnight. Thus, a trip in which 'Chocks Off' is at

21.00 hours and 'Chocks on' at 24.30 hours will be counted as a qualifying day. BALPA has managed to persuade the Inland Revenue to agree to a 50% uplift in qualifying days, so that, for every two qualifying days achieved, one day will be added for the purposes of calculating entitlement to relief. Thus, if a pilot had 50 qualifying days, 25 were added to calculate relief on 50 + 25/365. Formerly, to qualify for any 12½% relief, a pilot had to have a minimum of 30 qualifying days in the year. This uplift is designed to recognise the fact that pilots have to have a considerable amount of rest time and can only fly a maximum number of hours per year.

272 A provisional coding allowance will normally be given to each pilot entitled to the relief, based on lists submitted by the relevant company to the Inland Revenue. At the end of each year the position is adjusted on the appropriate claim being made by the pilot on his income tax returns.

Expenses of aircrew

273 The two principal items of expenditure which are allowable to pilots are:

Travel expenses

Following the case of Nolder *v.* Walters (15 TC 380) which concerned an airline employee who successfully claimed the extra cost of staying in hotels and incidental travelling abroad over and above the subsistence allowance he was given, any costs of staying overnight abroad not reimbursed should be allowed. The reason is that the employment is a travelling one and therefore the duties commence at the start of the flight and do not finish until the return to the UK. Therefore, any such costs are incurred in the performance of the duties.

Uniform allowance

274 A deduction should be allowed for the cost of special clothing and uniforms insofar as incurred by the employee.

Free travel etc.

275 It should be noted that perquisites such as free or reduced price travel for the employee or his dependants were thought to be not taxable as they were not realisable in money or money's worth, and, in the case of higher paid employees, there was no identifiable cost to the employer which could be the measure of the benefit. It will be recalled that the Inland Revenue attempted, when amending the benefits legislation in 1976, to tax the value of such travel but the proposals were withdrawn during the passage of the Bill through Parliament. Employees of airlines and their dependants were similarly specifically exempted from the benefits legislation when it was extended to transport vouchers (s.141(6) ICTA 1988).

However, following the Court of Appeal decision in Pepper *v*. Hart (1990 STC 786), it appears this is not necessarily a correct view of the law. It is not identifiable marginal cost which is the criterion, but what is a fair measure of the overall costs of the airline attributable to that free or reduced price journey, including wages, overheads, etc. This would have far reaching consequences for such employees. Pending the outcome of this case in the House of Lords, it is not known how the Inland Revenue will seek to apply the decision in practice.

Chapter 13
Members of the UK armed forces

Place of performance of duties

276 The duties of the UK armed forces are deemed to be carried out in the UK wherever they are in fact performed. Thus, whether or not members of the armed forces are technically resident or ordinarily resident in the UK, their earned income, subject to certain exceptions, is fully liable to UK tax under Sch. E Case I or Case II. Members of the armed forces cannot therefore claim a 100% deduction from their emoluments, unlike other individuals working abroad for 365 days or more, although this is compensated for by the tax-free foreign service allowances that are received, and by the fact that, under international law and double taxation agreements, they are not subject to taxation in the country to which they are posted. For instance, those operating abroad under the provisions of the NATO status of forces agreement are exempt, under Art. X of the agreement, from any local taxes that result from residence or domicile in the receiving State, or on the salaries and emoluments paid to them in respect of their employment as members of the armed forces. Outside NATO, the government always seeks to ensure that similar arrangements apply (*Hansard* Vol. 135 Col. 69 Written Answers 14 June 1988).

Residence position

277 The residence and ordinary residence position of a member of the armed forces will be determined on normal principles. However, as explained in **276** this will only be of relevance to the tax treatment of income other than income from employment, such as investment income or income from property.

Extra cost of living abroad

278 If a sum is paid to a Crown servant, including a serviceman, as compensation for the extra cost of living abroad, and is so certified by the Treasury, the sum will be exempt from UK tax under s.319 ICTA 1988. This is known as the local overseas allowance. This exemption covers sums paid to assist with a child's education.

Travel facilities

279   No charge to tax under Sch. E arises in respect of travel facilities provided for members of the armed forces going on or returning from leave. This covers journeys within and outside the UK (s.197 ICTA 1988) and extends not only to travel vouchers and warrants for particular journeys, but also to cash allowances and other payments in respect of leave travel, whether or not a warrant is available and irrespective of whether the serviceman is higher-paid or not.

Exemptions in respect of allowances

280   There are various exemptions from tax applicable to members of the armed forces in respect of allowances paid to them. These exemptions are made known to service personnel by the appropriate service pay authorities acting on Ministry of Defence regulations. Thus, for example, in common with other employments, extra subsistence allowances paid to personnel whilst temporarily posted away from base are not taxable. It should be noted that service personnel are no different from any other taxpayer in respect of any allowances, unless there is a specific exemption from tax given to them, as shown by a case concerning a claim that lodging allowances paid by servicemen should be free of tax. The allowances were held to be taxable or not under normal principles (see Evans *v*. Richardson (1957) 37 TC 178).

Thus boarding school or day school allowances paid to RAF personnel are taxable pay, but the RAF pay the tax by grossing up the allowance to cover the tax liability at the basic rate. If the grossed up figure does not cover the tax liability, extra compensation is due to the servicemen to cover the actual tax liability, for instance where he is liable at the higher rate of tax. In that situation, however, this extra compensation is not in practice itself taxable.

Hotel expenses

281   In the case of Griffiths *v*. Mockler (1953) 35 TC 135 a Royal Army Pay Corps officer lost a claim under what is now s.198 ICTA 1988 for a deduction in respect of his annual mess subscription. Similarly, in Lomax *v*. Newton (1953) 34 TC 558, a Territorial Army officer failed in his claim for a deduction in respect of a share of battalion mess guests' expenditure, payments to batmen at weekend and holiday camps, the hire of camp furniture and the cost of tickets at sergeants' and other ranks' dances. The Commissioners did not accept claims in respect of mess dinners and dances. Mr. Justice Vaisey disallowed all of the above items on the basis that these items were expenses incurred from tradition and custom, accepted voluntarily by the officers of the unit, and containing elements of personal choice and benefit. However, the Commissioners accepted a claim for a deduction in respect of amounts paid for hotel accommodation at conferences and exercises in excess of official allowances. This decision was upheld in the High Court.

Annual subscriptions to a headquarters mess central fund

282 If an officer is obliged to incur such subscriptions under Queen's Regulations, they are understood to be allowable (unlike ordinary mess subscriptions, which are not wholly incurred in the performance of military duties see **281** above). However, any sums paid that the Treasury certifies to be paid in lieu of food or drink normally supplied in kind to members of the armed forces (for instance, the Navy's rum allowance) or to be payable as a contribution to the expenses of a mess, are not taxable (see s.316 ICTA 1988).

Uniform allowances

283 Officers in the armed forces may claim a deduction for expenses on uniforms, and minimum amounts have been fixed in accordance with s.199 ICTA 1988 as being, in the opinion of the Treasury, fair equivalents of the average annual amounts which full-time serving officers are obliged to expend wholly, exclusively and necessarily in the performance of their duties. In practice, such allowances are usually obtained under a 'net pay' agreement with the Inland Revenue. Details of the allowances currently available may be obtained from the Ministry of Defence, which publishes a guide to the allowances entitled 'Regulations for Army Allowances and Charges'.

Officers may claim further tax relief if a larger amount than the appropriate annual allowance has been expended. However, they will be required by the inspector to prove the necessity for such expenditure and to give details supported by receipted bills.

Gratuities

284 Gratuities paid to men in return for extending their period of service, and paid at the end of that further period of service, are not taxable (s.316(1) ICTA 1988). This exemption also applies to the Women's Royal Naval Service, the Auxiliary Territorial Service and the Women's Auxiliary Air Force (s.316(2) ICTA 1988).

Any sum paid as a bounty out of money specifically provided by Parliament for this purpose, to a serving member who voluntarily undertakes to serve for a further period, is exempt (s.316(5) ICTA 1988).

Any terminal grant, gratuity or other lump sum paid under any royal warrant, Queen's Order, or an Order in Council, relating to members of the forces, or any payment made in commutation of annual or other periodical payments authorised by any such warrant or order, are specifically exempt from the golden handshake provisions. Thus, any lump sum payment to encourage early retirement, which Parliament may enact, is exempt from tax by virtue of s.188(1)(e) ICTA 1988.

PAYE and the armed forces

285   There are special provisions within the PAYE regulations applicable to the armed forces. The paying unit will identify what are tax-free allowances and what is taxable pay. These provisions also provide in particular for a special Form P45 to be issued by the Ministry of Defence when a member of the armed forces leaves and enters other employment (Regulations 44–47).

The reserve and auxiliary forces

286   The reserve and auxiliary forces of the Crown normally receive three different types of emolument. First, they are paid a training and travelling allowance for attendance at evening drill and training sessions. This is intended as a reimbursement of out-of-pocket expenses and is exempt from tax (see s.316(4) ICTA 1988).

Second, in consideration of their undertaking the prescribed training and attaining the required standard of efficiency, such forces are entitled, subject to the approval of the commanding officer, to an annual bounty which is also tax free (see s.316(4) ICTA 1988). It should be noted that a bounty is only exempt if paid out of the public revenue and not by a local authority, as the case of Lush *v.* Coles (1967) 44 TC 169 showed.

Third, such forces receive daily pay for all training in excess of eight hours' duration. This pay is subject to tax and also to the payment of national insurance contributions, if appropriate. Normally basic rate income tax is deducted at source and a detailed pay statement is provided by the reservist's unit under special regulations for reserve and auxiliary forces (see Income Tax Reserve and Auxiliary Forces Regulations 1975: SI 1975 No. 91).

The only expenses which are likely to cause difficulty are those relating to uniforms and mess subscriptions. Officers normally receive a cash grant on initial commissioning, and an annual allowance for the upkeep of their kit, but if an individual officer spends more on the purchase of essential items (as laid down in the scale of kit prescribed for his rank and duties), then he may properly claim relief under s.198 ICTA 1988. The position with other ranks differs between the various reserves but, in general, no reservist should find he has to purchase his own kit out of his own money and, if he does, then a claim under s.198 may be made. Mess subscriptions are not allowable, as mentioned in **282** above.

Tax-free allowances are available for the upkeep of uniform items purchased from outfit allowances for Territorial Army, ACF, Combined Cadet Force (Army and Basic Sections) and Ulster Defence Regiment officers. Details may be obtained from the Ministry of Defence's publication 'Regulations for Army Allowances and Charges'.

Pensions

287 All wounds and disability pensions are exempt from tax. In the case of a disability pension, the medical unfitness giving rise to the payment must have been directly attributable to military service or have been aggravated by it. The Government has published a list of taxable and non-taxable armed forces pensions. The following pensions paid to former members of the armed forces in respect of disability are exempt (s.315 ICTA 1988):

(a) wounds pensions granted to members of the armed forces;
(b) officer's disability retired pay attributable to conditions of service;
(c) pensions in respect of disablement or disability attributable to conditions of service granted to members of the forces other than commissioned officers;
(d) disablement pensions attributable to conditions of service granted to persons who have been employed in the nursing services of the forces;
(e) war disability pensions administered by the Department of Social Security; and
(f) war pensioners' mobility supplement, which introduced more flexible provisions for war pensioners with mobility needs, by introducing a cash mobility supplement in place of the existing vehicle scheme (s.617 ICTA 1988).

The following pensions paid to former members of the armed forces in respect of long service are taxable:

(a) service career pensions; and
(b) illness or disability pensions, other than those attributable to conditions of service.

Where a member of the armed forces is invalided out of the forces on account of a disability attributable to his service, and is awarded a combined long-service and disability pension, the whole of that pension is exempted from tax because it is not possible to distinguish between the parts of the pension attributable to disability and to long service (*Hansard* 29 June 1978 cols. 654/5).

War widows' pensions

288 Any pension or allowance paid by the Department of Social Security which relates to death due to service in the armed forces, to wartime service in the Merchant Navy, or to war injuries, is completely exempt from tax (s.318 ICTA 1988). This covers war widows' pensions as well as payments for children of such widows. Similarly, any pension or allowance in respect of death due to peacetime service in the armed forces before 3 September 1939, payable by the

Ministry of Defence, is exempt from tax, along with similar pensions and allowances payable by foreign governments.

Where such war widows' pensions are reduced because of the receipt of another pension, the other pension is exempt up to the extent of the reduction (s.318(3) ICTA 1988).

Employment after leaving services

289 It should be borne in mind, in connection with retirement, that many servicemen frequently retire from the forces in their fifties and seek employment elsewhere, as an alternative to relying solely on their pensions. The normal Inland Revenue practice has been to aggregate benefits from the current employer's scheme with any pension already being received, and to restrict the total pension entitlement to two-thirds of the final remuneration from the employment held at the date of retirement. With an inflation-proof service pension, this could result in severe restrictions on the amount of pension that could be paid by the new employer. However, there is a concessionary practice by the Inland Revenue, under which former service personnel could receive a pension from their new employer, not exceeding one-sixtieth of final pay for each year of service in the particular employment, even though the resulting total pension, including the service pension, may exceed two-thirds of final salary. In other words, there are the alternative limits of two-thirds of final salary, or, if more beneficial, the service pension plus one-sixtieth of final pay for each year of service in the new employment.

Capital gains tax and residences

290 The position on residences in relation to capital gains tax exemption and relief for interest paid, is the same as for diplomats see **207** above except that job-related accommodation means, for service personnel, accommodation provided by the Ministry of Defence.

Holders of the Victoria Cross, etc.

291 Annuities and additional pensions paid to holders of the Victoria Cross, the George Cross, the Albert Medal and Edward Medal, are also exempt from tax. The exemption was extended from 6 April 1980 to pension additions paid with the awards to holders of the Military Cross, the Distinguished Flying Cross, the Distinguished Conduct Medal, the Conspicuous Gallantry Medal, the Distinguished Service Medal, the Military Medal and the Distinguished Flying Medal, and to pension additions paid to holders of the George Cross (s.317 ICTA 1988).

Life assurance premiums

292 It should be noted that a male member of HM services, or his wife, or a member of the women's services, even if not resident in the UK, is entitled to deduct 15% from any premium paid under a qualifying policy of life assurance taken out before 14 March 1984. This rate is reduced to 12.5% for premiums paid after 5 April 1989.

Death on active service

293 No inheritance tax is payable on the death of an individual from a wound or accident while on active service or from a disease contracted or aggravated in the past by such a wound or accident (s.154 IHTA 1984).

Chapter 14
Publicans holding tied houses, hoteliers and guest-house proprietors

Publicans – basis of assessment

294 Licensed victuallers who hold tied houses are assessed to tax as self-employed persons under Sch. D Case I. They are treated as carrying on a trade at the public house of which they are the tenants.

If the tenancy is granted to the husband or wife, but not to both jointly, it is questionable whether it is possible to have a husband and wife partnership that is effective for taxation purposes. Instead, it is customary in that situation for the wife to carry on a separate business relating to the selling of the food, thereby taking advantage of separate taxation of husband and wife and (before 1990/91), the wife's earnings election. A value added tax tribunal has also accepted that a licensee's wife's catering sales are a separate business from that carried on by the licensee (*Clark*, LON/82/338, February 1983(1370)). This may be helpful in keeping the licensee's sales below the VAT registration limit. Customs & Excise may challenge the view that the catering is a separate business, using its powers under para. 1A Sch. 1 VATA 1983. However, it is not clear whether para. 1A would apply in such a case.

The effect of the trade being identified with the particular public house in question is that, if the tenant leaves the public house and takes over a new tenancy, even within the same brewery, the cessation provisions will apply for income tax purposes and a new trade will be treated as set up at the new public house.

Termination payments

295 It has become the policy of certain breweries to cease using tenants and instead to appoint managers to run their public houses. The tenancies in question usually have incorporated rights to no more than very small amounts of compensation on termination. As an inducement to leave, and in recognition of the size of the business built up, it has been customary in such cases for the brewery to make substantial *ex gratia* payments. There is now an established scale of compensation payable to tenants, agreed by the Brewers'

Society, the brewers' trade body, which is based on length of service as a tenant and the rateable value of the public house.

In the case of Murray *v.* Goodhews (1977) 52 TC 86, payments were made by Watneys to a tenant of a number of public houses in these circumstances, and it was held that the payments were not liable to tax as income, as they were not in return for any services rendered, or by virtue of any right of compensation, but were entirely voluntary and unsolicited and in recognition of a long association between the tenant and Watneys. In that case, there had been no negotiation on the amount between the parties, the amount of the payment had no connection with the profits of the public houses concerned, and was not linked to any future trading relationship between the parties. The payments therefore fell within the type of payment made in the case of Simpson *v.* John Reynolds & Co. (Insurances) Ltd (1975) 49 TC 693, and were exempt from income tax.

The question of whether the above payments were liable to capital gains tax was not at issue. However, it is unlikely that they would be regarded as liable, since they cannot be said to derive from an asset.

Similarly, it was held in Davis *v.* Powell (1976) 51 TC 492 and Drummond *v.* Austin Brown (1984) 58 TC 67, that payments of statutory compensation to tenants by landlords were not liable to capital gains tax, as the payments did not derive from the leases in question. The entitlement to the compensation was a statutory right.

The Inland Revenue agreed with tenants of Watneys that they would not pursue claims to capital gains tax on the special payments, except insofar as they represented extra sums for surrendering the tenancy early (in the same way as a premium to induce an agricultural tenant to surrender his tenancy is liable to capital gains tax to the extent that it exceeds statutory compensation).

In the Watneys case, the brewery specified a basic sum which was to be supplemented by 40% if the tenant gave up his tenancy before 1 March 1974, and 20% if before 1 October 1975.

It is not known whether similar agreements were reached with the tenants of other brewers over the years but it was always open to the tenant to claim complete exemption from income tax and capital gains tax on such payments.

Expenses

296 If the licensee, etc. lives on the premises, much expenditure, the primary purpose of which is for the trade but which incidentally confers a personal benefit, will be allowable for Sch. D Case I purposes, on the basis of the decision in the case of Bentleys, Stokes and Lowless *v.* Beeson (1952) 33 TC 491. For instance, expenditure on newspapers available for customers would qualify under this heading.

The proportion of any rent, rates (prior to 1 April 1990) etc. disallowed, as relating to the private proportion of a public house, will also usually be very small. Where the trade of the hotel or public house is carried on through the medium of a company, there will be a potential charge on the annual value of the private part of the accommodation provided by the company, which fortunately is unlikely to have cost more than £75,000. Employees without a material interest in the company will be able to claim they are representative occupiers, but directors with a material interest will not be able to claim such exemption. Similarly, in the case of the costs of heating, lighting, cleaning, repairs and furniture for the private part, this will give rise to a benefit for all higher paid employees and directors, subject to a possible restriction for representative occupiers.

An adjustment to the computations may be required in respect of meals consumed by the publican and his wife. The decision in Sharkey *v.* Wernher (1955) 36 TC 275, under which stock taken for own consumption is credited at market value, is not applicable in the case of eating establishments, on the basis that meals are not trading stock. However, in the case of an unincorporated business, the cost of meals falls to be disallowed because it is 'a cost of maintenance of the parties, their families or establishments' (s.74(b) ICTA 1988). In the case of a company, the cost should be allowed and, similarly, the benefit to the director will be the cost of the meals to the company. It is understood, in this connection, that, whilst cash gratuities received by licensees are taxable, free drinks bought for them by customers, even though they are in the nature of gratuities, are accepted as not ordinarily taxable, as they are not normally convertible into cash.

In the case of ordinary employees, if they are lower paid there should be no assessable benefit on free meals and, in the case of others, it should be possible to use the exemption in s.155(5) ICTA 1988 for meals consumed in a canteen (see Extra Statutory Concession A74, which gives this exemption where part of the restaurant or dining room is designated as being for the use of staff only).

The provision of a late night taxi home for bar staff and waitresses is now common and it should be noted in this connection that there is an Extra Statutory Concession which exempts journeys made after 21.00 hours on an irregular basis from treatment as a benefit-in-kind (Extra Statutory Concession A66).

The general prohibition of any deduction for entertaining expenses in s.577 ICTA 1988 is overruled for persons such as publicans and hoteliers by s.577(10) ICTA 1988, which states that:

'Nothing in [Section 577] shall be taken as precluding the deduction of expenses incurred in, or any claim for capital allowances in respect of the use of an asset for, the provision of any person of anything which it is his trade to provide, and which is provided by him in the ordinary course of that trade for payment or, with the object of advertising to the public generally, gratuitously.'

It is presumably for this reason that entertaining airline representatives and tour operators is not normally treated as disallowable, but allowed as advertising.

Hotels – own consumption adjustments

297 Local tax offices often propose standard adjustments to the trading profits of hotel and guest house proprietors, and to the emoluments of managers of hotels, etc., in order to take account of the proprietor's private accommodation and consumption of food. These adjustments are usually revised annually in accordance with increases in the retail price index. The amounts of such adjustments vary widely between districts.

For example, the following figures were suggested by Truro District for Sch. D basis periods ending in the year to 5 April 1989 and for the Sch. E year of assessment 1988/89 (the figures for the year to 5 April 1988 and 1987/88 are shown in brackets):

	A £	B £	C £
Owner-occupied cases			
Man and wife	2,745 (2,570)	3,135 (2,935)	3,582 (3,335)
Single person	1,645 (1,540)	1,880 (1,760)	2,145 (2,010)
Children 16 and above	1,095 (1,025)	1,255 (1,175)	1,430 (1,340)
Rented property cases			
Man and wife	3,050 (2,855)	3,480 (3,260)	3,985 (3,730)
Single person	1,825 (1,710)	2,090 (1,955)	2,390 (2,240)
Children 16 and above	1,220 (1,140)	1,395 (1,305)	1,590 (1,490)

Children under 16

All categories – graded according to age as follows:

$$\frac{\text{Age}}{16} \times (40\% \times \text{approximate married couple rate})$$

A = 1–14 bedrooms
B = 15–24 bedrooms
C = 25–50 bedrooms

Hotels with 50 bedrooms or more are the subject of individual negotiations. By contrast, Poole District has agreed with the Swanage and District Hotel, Guest House and Self-Catering Association that the following flat-rate adjustments should apply to all accounts ending after 5 April 1989 (the figures for accounts ending after 5 April 1988 are shown in brackets):

	£	£
Single adult	1,275	(1,240)
Married couple	2,550	(2,480)
Children aged 0–6	420	(405)
7–10	640	(625)
11–14	860	(835)
15–17	1,060	(1,030)

The adjustments, in both districts, are for board and lodging only, and thus exclude tobacco and liquor, private use of cars, exceptional repairs and replacements, and any restriction of overdraft interest relating to the private occupation of the premises and other expenditure of a personal nature.

These proposals are intended to provide a convenient basis of adjustment in the majority of cases. They do not prejudice a taxpayer's statutory rights, nor do they preclude the Inland Revenue from investigating the facts where they consider that the standard figures are materially inadequate. Each case should be considered on its individual circumstances and these models should not be viewed as accepted Inland Revenue practice.

In the case of an employee, including a member of the family who is earning at the rate of less than £8,500 per annum, care should be taken to avoid the value of free board and lodging being taxed. Where a reduction is made from gross salary for board and accommodation, the Inland Revenue will usually contend that the full gross amount is assessable under Sch. E, on the authority of Cordy v. Gordon (1925) 9 TC 304.

Hotels – date on which trading commences

298 A hotel is usually regarded as starting to trade when bookings are first sought. However, it has been accepted that a hotel commences to trade when the proprietor undertakes staff training. In either event, expenses incurred within five years of commencing to trade which, if they had been incurred after trading commenced would have been allowable, are admissible as deductions under s.401 ICTA 1988. Where the proprietor is a company it should avoid paying yearly interest, other than to a bank, before trading commences as such interest will not count as a pre-trading expense available for relief under s.401 ICTA 1988. Instead the company should either:

(a) roll up the interest until trading commences; or
(b) negotiate a temporary loan that generates short interest.

Capital expenditure

299 Where a hotel changes hands, the allocation of a significant part of the sale proceeds to fixtures and fittings taken over from the vendors now has a two-fold benefit. From the vendor's point of view, it takes a large part of the value of the property out of capital gains tax, bearing in mind the raising of the chattels exemption to £6,000 per individual item or set of items in the Finance Act 1989. In this connection, it should be borne in mind that it is possible to claim a loss based on an indexation allowance on the sale proceeds if they are over £6,000 for each separate chattel. Any balancing charge will be taxed at the same rate as a capital gain and offers more planning opportunities to minimise the tax, for instance, by the payment of personal pension premiums. From the purchaser's point of view, capital allowances claims will be maximised in the early years of the business.

Most expenditure by a tenant, publican or hotelier will be on utensils, such as glasses and crockery for use in the trade, and will thus be allowable as a Sch. D Case I deduction. Where capital expenditure is incurred by the tenant on plant and machinery, he will be able to claim allowances on it. If it is movable plant, for instance, a television set, or tables and chairs, such allowances can be claimed in the normal way. It should be possible to categorise some of the expenditure as on short life assets which need not be pooled and on which a balancing allowance can be claimed when they are scrapped. If it consists of fixtures and fitting which become, on installation, part of the building, a claim can still be made, following an alteration in the law consequent on the decision in Stokes *v*. Costain Property Investments Ltd (1984) 57 TC 688.

Under provisions in ss.51–59 CAA 1990, the lessee who has incurred the expenditure can now claim capital allowances on it, although it has become a landlord's fixture. Similarly, an incoming lessee paying for such fixtures can claim capital allowances on his expenditure, with consequent balancing adjustments on the outgoing tenant. In either case, the lessor and the lessee must make a joint election to this effect. There are also provisions for the lessor to take over the benefit of allowances on the termination of a lease without payment by an incoming lessee.

These provisions are extremely useful for tenants of public houses. If there are loans from the brewery to carry out such improvements or for other purposes, interest on the loans will rank as a deduction against profits as an ordinary business expense, in the case of a sole trader, or as a charge on income, in the case of a company.

Plant and machinery

300   The Inland Revenue have given its view on what constitutes 'plant and machinery' on the installation of main services in new inns and hotels. A letter to the CCAB, sent in August 1977, stated that:

'. . . expenditure on the provision of main services to buildings such as electrical wiring, cold water piping and gas piping is regarded as part of the cost of the building, and therefore as not qualifying for capital allowances. We do, however, regard as eligible for capital allowances expenditure on apparatus to provide electric light or power, hot water, central heating, ventilation or air-conditioning, and expenditure on alarm and sprinkler systems. Relief is also given on the cost of all hot water pipes, and on the cost of baths, wash basins, etc. although the St John's School case [St John's School *v.* Ward (1974) 49 TC 524] suggests that the Courts might regard such expenditure as part of the cost of the building. We do not, however, propose any change of practice in this respect. Finally, to complete the picture, and since you mentioned modernisation, I should say that expenditure on alterations to *existing* buildings which is incidental to the installation of plant or machinery qualifies for relief under a separate provision (s.45 CAA 1968 [now s.66 CAA 1990]).'

The case of CIR *v.* Scottish & Newcastle Breweries Ltd (1982) 55 TC 252 broadened the scope of what can be claimed as plant and machinery in a public house or hotel. In that case, it was decided that, in various hotels and restaurants owned by the taxpayer, all additions to the walls and ceilings with a certain theme, such as murals and stags' heads, qualified as plant, on the basis that they performed a function of providing the right 'atmosphere' to promote the taxpayer's trade, and were not just a passive part of the setting. On the other hand, the two recent decisions in favour of the Inland Revenue concerning restaurant fittings in Wimpey International Ltd *v.* Warland and Associated Restaurants Ltd *v.* Warland (1989) STC 273 appear to have restricted the scope of what may be claimed as plant where an item is part of the decor of the restaurant. However, specialist lighting and display objects used for this purpose should still qualify, provided that they are not clearly part of the premises. The Inland Revenue also allow expenditure on jacuzzis, squash court wall finishings and flooring, and lifts, but not lift shafts. Also, following Cooke *v.* Beach Station Caravans Ltd (1974) 49 TC 514, the entire cost of excavating, concreting and lining a swimming pool with the surrounding terracing and fencing is treated as plant.

It may be of benefit to elect for short-life asset treatment for certain large items of equipment, where a limited life span is expected (s.37–38 CAA 1990 and Inland Revenue Statement of Practice SP1/86 which covers certain practical aspects where there are large numbers of such items).

Expenditure on fire safety equipment and precautions such as fire doors and escapes is compulsory for hotels and boarding houses under SI 1972 No. 238. Such expenditure will normally qualify for capital allowances, provided that it was specified in a notice issued under s.5(4) Fire Precautions Act 1971 or was to avoid restrictions on the use of the premises by an order under s.10 of that Act (s.69 CAA 1990).

In summary, the expenditure qualifying as plant will usually cover the following items:

Furniture, curtains, carpets and blinds;
Linen chutes;
Squash court wall coverings and floorings;
Jacuzzis;
Swimming pools (but not the building housing them);

Kitchen and laundry equipment;
Refuse compacters and waste disposal equipment;
Fire alarms and clocks;
Bathroom fittings;
Door locks and hinges;
Heating, ventilation and air conditioning equipment;
Public address systems;
Telephone equipment;
Lifts (but not lift shafts).

Sometimes it is necessary to carry out extensive repairs on acquisition of a hotel. The Inspector will often quote Law Shipping & Co Limited *v.* CIR (12 TC 621) to disallow the repairs. However, it may be possible to argue as the property is very old as many hotels are, that the nature of the work done was predetermined and unavoidable by the age and type of construction of the building concerned. It should, therefore, be allowable in full as it was in the case of Conn *v.* Robins Bros Limited (43 TC 266) and Odeon Associated Cinemas *v.* Jones (48 TC 257).

Furnished lettings – allowances for wear and tear

301   In the case of lettings which constitute furnished holiday lettings (see **306** below), the normal capital allowances rules apply, as the lettings are treated as constituting a trade for that and various other purposes. In the case of other furnished lettings, which do not amount to a trade and are assessable under Sch. D Case VI, inspectors have been instructed to apply a uniform basis of treatment for wear and tear of furniture and fittings. A claim for capital allowances is not competent by virtue of s.61(1) and (2) CAA 1990. Inspectors have therefore been advised to accept either a renewals basis or a deduction of 10% of rental income, net of water rates (and rates before 1 April 1990), and any other sums for services that would normally be borne by the tenant (see Inland Revenue Statement of Practice SP A19).

Hotel building allowances

302   In the case of new hotels or additions to existing hotels, a 4% writing down allowance along the lines of industrial buildings allowances is available (ss.7 and 19 CAA 1990). The hotel has to be open for at least four months in the season to qualify. In practice, 120 days is regarded as equivalent to four months. Hostels for workers qualify for the allowance, but not separate flats and houses provided for workers. Where the proprietor's own accommodation does not exceed 25% of the total cost, no restriction is imposed on costs attributable to that part. In common with initial allowances for industrial buildings, the hotels initial allowance is abolished for all expenditure after 31 March 1986.

Services provided for guests must normally include the provision of breakfast and of an evening meal if the allowances are to be given. Under Inland Revenue Statement of Practice SP 9/87, the Inland Revenue have now said that they will regard this condition as satisfied where the offering of breakfast and dinner is a normal event in the hotel's conduct of its business, but not where the provision of such meals is exceptional, for example, where it is only available on request.

Dilapidations

303 The tenant may be required to make good any dilapidations at the end of his tenancy. Expenditure on dilapidations of a capital nature is not allowable, but expenditure on dilapidations at the end of the lease in the nature of deferred repairs is admissible, if the repairs would have been admissible if executed during the currency of the lease. A specific provision to cover such dilapidations may also be allowable in the same way as any other specific provision for a liability estimated on reasonable grounds, provided that an accurate estimate can be made. A composition payment in lieu of making good dilapidations, made by the tenant at the end of the lease, will also be allowable to the extent to which actual payments would have been allowed.

Residences

304 Managers of public houses or hotels who are employees are normally able to obtain mortgage interest relief and capital gains tax exemption on a private residence other than the public house or hotel that they manage, in accordance with s.356 ICTA 1988. The public house or hotel is recognised as 'job-related accommodation'.

Self-employed publicans in tied houses are also able to enjoy these reliefs as s.356(3)(b) ICTA 1988 extended the provisions to traders and professionals for periods after 5 April 1983. There are anti-avoidance provisions that disallow relief where the trader has a material interest in the company providing the job-related accommodation, or is in partnership with the person providing it (s.356(5) ICTA 1988 and s.222(8) TCGA 1992).

Previously, a trader would have had to satisfy all the normal conditions for the reliefs and actually to have lived in the residence. For example, in Frost *v.* Feltham (1980) 55 TC 10, the tenant and licensee of a public house in Essex, who purchased a house in Wales, successfully claimed relief for interest on a mortgage, on the basis that the house was his main residence because he visited the house and spent some time there each month.

Now, however, it is much easier for such an individual to obtain interest relief in acquiring a retirement home, and without having to face the prospect of a capital gains tax charge if the house has to be sold before retirement.

Where a guest-house or hotel is also used as the taxpayer's main residence, it will be possible, depending on the circumstances, to obtain a measure of capital gains tax relief under ss.222 and 223 TCGA 1992. In Owen *v.* Elliott (1990)

STC 469 the taxpayer also successfully claimed additional relief under s.223(4) TCGA 1992.

The decision in Owen *v*. Elliott was that the guest house or hotel part of a property also used in part as a principal private residence constituted the letting of residential accommodation. The term residential accommodation has not to be construed narrowly as the Inland Revenue had argued, being applicable only to a flat within a house, but could cover any accommodation where people stayed and enjoyed board and lodging.

Guest-houses and roll-over relief

305 A possible problem arises where a guest-house, etc., is owned jointly by a husband and wife, but only the wife is engaged in the business. If the property is owned equally on a disposal, it seems that only 50% of the total gain may be rolled over. A similar problem arises in respect of retirement relief. In order to safeguard the reliefs, therefore, it is advisable for the husband and wife who wish to continue with joint ownership of the guest-house to carry on the business as a partnership. It is not necessary that the husband should be entitled to 50% of the profits arising under the partnership, if he has another job and it is desired to maximise the benefits of a wife's earnings election and, following the introduction of independent taxation, of the wife's income.

Income from furnished holiday lettings

306 It used to be the custom for the Inland Revenue to treat income from holiday flatlets as trading income, where some services of cleaning were provided, and to give capital gains tax roll-over relief and retirement relief where appropriate.

However, in the cases of Gittos *v*. Barclay (1982) 55 TC 633, Griffiths *v*. Jackson and Griffiths *v*. Pearman (1982) 56 TC 583, the Inland Revenue successfully contended that such income was unearned income, and that no capital gains tax relief was available. In response to parliamentary pressure, however, the Government announced that it would amend the law as interpreted in those cases so that, notwithstanding that the income derived from property, the source of the income would be treated as the carrying on of a trade. The Government's proposals were enacted in ss.503 and 504 ICTA 1988.

To qualify as earned income and for capital gains tax retirement and roll-over relief under the new statutory provisions, the accommodation must be available for holiday letting to the public for at least 140 days a year. It must also be actually let for at least 70 days and, within any 7 month period, must not be occupied by the same tenant for a continuous period exceeding 31 days. There are provisions to 'average' such conditions over several properties where some properties are over or under the relevant limits. The provisions apply to income, acquisitions and disposals arising after 5 April 1982. Under this treatment as a deemed trade, tax is payable in two instalments, losses are relieved as for trading losses, and retirement annuity premiums and personal pension premiums, can be paid in respect of such earnings.

PAYE

307   A restriction in employees' code numbers, for the estimated value of tips and gratuities that they receive and retain, can be a source of considerable irritation as, in the absence of records, amounts are estimated by the Inland Revenue. One way of avoiding the problems of recordkeeping in a large hotel is through the use of a 'tronc' system. Here the tronc-master (usually the head-waiter) has the responsibility for deducting tax from the tips and operating a special PAYE scheme with the local inspector. Income tax is deducted at the basic rate although no national insurance contributions are due, provided that the employer does not decide how the tips are to be divided among the employees (see reg. 19(1)(c) Social Security (Contributions) Regulations 1979 (SI 1979 No. 591)). However, special care is needed in order to ensure that a tronc system is properly established. In Figael Ltd *v.* Fox (1992) STC 83, the directors who operated the system were held to be acting on behalf of the company, in both organising and distributing the tips.

Chapter 15
Credit traders, pawnbrokers, moneylenders, hire purchase transactions

General

308 There are many forms of credit arrangement in connection with the sale of goods. In some cases the trader himself arranges the credit, although this is less common than it used to be. In other cases, the credit is arranged by an outside concern such as a hire purchase company. Yet again, payment may be made other than in cash using, for instance, checks bought from a check trader. These arrangements operate where goods are purchased using some form of credit. Alternatively a person may merely want a loan and may not be in a position to approach a bank for help and, instead, has to resort to a pawnbroker or moneylender.

309 This chapter deals with some of the taxation law and practice which relates to such transactions in the hands of the person carrying on the trade in question.

Credit traders

310 This is where the property in the goods passes to the customer on sale and the trader himself provides credit arrangements for paying for the goods. Often he will arrange with an agency to collect the amounts owing.

311 The difficulty in measuring the trader's profits arises from the fact that the full proceeds of sale are brought into the accounts on sale and but for any special arrangement, no allowance will be due at that stage for the collection costs, which clearly reduce the value of the sale.

Provisions

312 Under an agreement between the National Federation of Credit Traders and the Inland Revenue, such traders are entitled to set up a provision for collection costs based on the direct expenses of collection and the amount collected in the year. Any increase in the provision is then deducted from profits and any decrease ranks as an addition to profits.

313 The provision is calculated as follows:

(1) The direct expenses of collecting the book debts comprising wages, national insurance contributions and travelling expenses on the trader's own staff employed for this purpose or commissions to debt collecting agencies, must be ascertained for the period in question.

(2) The amount in (1) may need to be reduced to eliminate the expenses of selling the goods and other non-collection activities. It is normally agreed, where there is no more accurate figure, to reduce the direct costs by one fifth to take account of this.

(3) The amount as reduced in (2) is expressed as a percentage of the actual collections in the period.

(4) This percentage is applied to the good book debts outstanding at the end of the period, that is, debts after making specific provision for any bad or doubtful items and this is the provision which is carried forward at the end of the period.

314 Where a trader has not made any provision in previous years but wishes to adopt this basis, he must bring in a notional opening provision using this calculation. This is not the only basis that a trader can use and there are variations which, if consistently adhered to, are accepted.

Valuation of debts

315 There is an agreed basis of debt valuation for credit traders carrying on the business of selling goods for payment by weekly instalments. Broadly, the arrangement involves writing down the value of debts where there was no cash or goods transaction with the customer 13 weeks before stocktaking, and reducing the value of other debts more than 13 weeks old where some transactions took place. In the latter case, the value of the debt is the lower of the amount outstanding and the total amount of cash received during the twelve months ending on the date of the stocktaking.

Hire purchase business

316 There are basically two types of hire purchase agreement entered into by a retailer:

(a) The first, common in the motor trade, is where the retailer is in effect an intermediary between the customer and finance house. He sells the goods to the finance house, from which he gets the full cash price and a commission for introducing business to the finance house. The finance house will usually collect the instalments and be responsible for any bad debts, although sometimes there is a recourse clause making the retailer responsible for any amounts unrecovered after repossession and resale of the goods.

(b) The second type of arrangement is more usual for the smaller hire purchase agreement. Under this, referred to as 'block discounting', the retailer retains responsibility for collecting instalments and the burden of any bad debts remains with him. The retailer, however, each time he makes a sale on hire purchase, either sells the goods to the finance company and, acting as *del credere* agent for the hire purchase company, enters into a simultaneous sale by the finance company to the customer, or alternatively enters into the hire purchase agreement direct with the customer and then assigns his rights in the agreement to the finance house. There is a master agreement with the finance company under which it is provided that the finance company will pay a percentage (usually up to 75%) of the face value of the agreements (that is, all of the amounts due under the agreements) with the balance as and when instalments are collected. The agreements are usually dealt with in batches with the finance house which the retailer has entered into as agent for the finance company or is to assign to the finance company. There is also a provision for a discount to the finance company from the total purchase price depending upon the length of the agreements included in the batch and this is the finance house's profit on the transactions.

317 In the case of (a) above, there is an outright cash sale. Where there is a recourse clause a retailer can claim a deduction in his tax computation for any liability incurred under it as and when incurred. A provision for a possible future contingent liability under this clause would not normally be allowed as it would be in the nature of a general bad debt reserve (s.74(j) ICTA 1988).

Under (b) above the position is more complex. Strictly in law, the retailer has no hire purchase debts due to him and is thus not entitled to any deduction for the gross profit in future instalments. In some cases the agreements are not assigned but are simply held as security with the right to have them assigned in certain circumstances, so that in that situation the retailer retains title to the hire purchase debt until assignment. However, in practice, in all these situations, it is established practice to treat the hire purchase debts as due to the retailer, against which provisions are made for unearned profit and bad debts. The amount paid by the finance company is then shown as a loan and the discount given to the finance company is treated as a finance charge debited to profit and loss account. In effect, the substance of the transaction, treating it as a loan on the security of the hire purchase agreements, is followed for accounts purposes; and provided the treatment of unearned profits and discounts is consistently adhered to, the Inland Revenue accept this for taxation purposes.

Check traders

318 Check traders are far less common then they used to be. In return for a service charge, they issue checks whose face value is payable by instalments and which are used by their customers to purchase goods. The shopkeeper receives a discount from the check trader when settlement is made with him by the check trader and the check trader may employ debt collecting agents in return for a commission to collect the outstanding instalments on the checks.

Computation of profits

319 The following method of arriving at profits has been agreed with the Inland Revenue:

(1) The full amount of the service charge is included at the time the check is issued.
(2) The discount is deducted when the check is used by the customer or when the retailer renders an account to the check trader.
(3) A provision for commission which will be paid on outstanding instalments due when the instalments are collected by agents is deducted.

The provision for commission is arrived at after deducting any provision for bad and doubtful debts.

320 It is possible for a check trader to agree a different method of arriving at profits if it is consistently adhered to and does not result in profits materially different from those computed on the above basis. If he changes to a new basis, he must bring in his income and expenses in the year of change on that basis and have continuity of treatment for both opening and closing balances.

Pawnbrokers

321 Pawnbrokers advance money on a short-term basis in return for the deposit of articles of value as pledges. The pledge is redeemed when the loan is repaid with the appropriate amount of interest. If articles deposited as pledges are not claimed within twelve months and seven days, the pawnbroker may sell them. The only pledges which automatically become the absolute property of the pawnbroker on expiration of the redemption period are those given in respect of loans of under £2. All other pledges can only be sold by auction and are redeemable until that takes place. Thus, if the loan is over £2, the pawnbroker can only take the loan, interest and cost of sale out of the proceeds immediately. The balance can be claimed by the pawner within a period depending upon the amount of the loan under the Pawnbrokers Act 1872. In the case of any loan in excess of £10, the Statute of Limitations applies and the balance can be reclaimed up to 6 years and thereafter becomes the property of the pawnbroker.

322 In Jays the Jewellers *v.* CIR (29 TC 274), the profit on sale of pledged goods of a pawnbroker was credited to the profit and loss account and the reserve amounting to two-fifths of all profits on sales was debited to an account called 'Return of Profit on Sale of Pledged Goods'. Jays claimed that, as the property of the pawner never became their property, any profit on its sale was not taxable as part of its business profits or, on the authority of an earlier case,

200

Morley v. Tattersall (22 TC 51), if the profits did not belong to them at the time of sale, the expiration of the time limit for claiming the money did not convert the profits into a trading receipt. The Court held that the profits were trading receipts as they arose in the ordinary course of the business but only when they became the absolute property of the pawnbroker. The profits should therefore be placed in a suspense account and be taxed only when the pawnbroker is entitled in law to retain them.

323 In other words, it is necessary to look at the true legal position to determine if and when such receipts are trading receipts. Thus, on similar principles, deposits paid to a tailor when suits were ordered, were held to be trading receipts of the year of receipt as they belonged to the tailor at that time. If the customer did not take the garment, it was the company's policy to return the deposit to maintain goodwill but, because there was no right of recovery, Jays' case was distinguished (Elson v. Prices Taylors Ltd, 40 TC 671).

The case for taxability and the timing of when something is taxable is best summarised by the judgment of the Lord President in James Spencer & Co v. CIR (32 TC 111) at page 116, where he referred to:

". . . the broad working rule which emerges as a guide to the crediting or debiting in a tax computation subsequently maturing credits or debits is to inquire in which accounting period the right or liability was established and to carry the item into the account in that year. I use the vague word 'established' advisedly for we are now in the region of proper commercial and accounting practice rather than of systematic jurisprudence".

324 It should be noted that, as the only pledges which became the absolute property of the pawnbroker are those given in respect of loans of under £2, the Inland Revenue took the view that stock relief was only due to those items and not on other unredeemed pledges as those were not the pawnbroker's stocks. The position is similar in those cases to that of consignment stocks, although it has now been accepted by the Inland Revenue following the case of Fraser v. London Sports Car Centre Ltd (1985) STC 688, stock relief is due on consignment stocks if the 'stock' has been shown as such in the accounts.

Moneylenders

325 Interest received by a moneylender, even if annual interest, was not treated as investment income for the purposes of the investment income surcharge. Such income, in the case of a moneylending close company, was also not treated as investment income but was included in estate or trading income for apportionment purposes (para. 5(3)(b) of Sch. 19 ICTA 1988).

326 In fact, most moneylenders' interest is short interest which is treated as part of trading income because it is a receipt of the trade and not merely interest on an investment. Consequently, it will qualify as trading income for retirement annuity and personal pension contribution purposes. When the trade ceases, any outstanding interest becomes interest assessable under Case III of Schedule D (Bennett *v.* Ogston, 15 TC 374).

327 It should be noted that in the case of a moneylender or person carrying on a similar sort of business, the Inland Revenue will normally accept any reasonable basis of bringing in interest. However, it now appears possible for a moneylender to opt for a strict Case I basis, that is for tax purposes crediting interest on an arising basis as and when it is payable and not anticipating unrealised profits, even if that basis differs from that used in the accounts, which may employ an accruals basis. Thus, in Willingale *v.* International Commercial Bank Limited (1978) STC 75, the bank claimed that discounts on treasury bills, although brought into the accounts on an accrued basis, should be assessed on a strict basis excluding unrealised profits. The Court agreed with this contention. In effect, although accounting treatment may be a good guide to the treatment of an item for tax purposes following Odeon Associated Theatres Ltd *v.* Jones (48 TC 257) it must follow that where there is authority for treating income for tax purposes differently, it can always be followed by the Inland Revenue or the taxpayer. This principle of not bringing in unrealised profits has been strengthened by the House of Lords decision in Pattison *v.* Marine Midland Ltd, where notional currency profits which had not been realised were held not to be taxable (1984) STC 10.

328 As an illustration of the distinction between the capital element of any repayments and interest, even in the case of a moneylender in considering the allowance of expenses, in the case of Monthly Salaries Loan Co Ltd *v.* Furlong a moneylending company claimed to deduct, in addition to normal collection costs, an estimated reserve for expenses to be incurred in the following year in the collection of outstanding loans, the amounts being calculated on a percentage basis related to the capital element in the loans. It was held that this was not allowable (40 TC 313).

Chapter 16
Persons in receipt of foreign pensions

Remittance basis

329 Prior to the Finance Act 1974, foreign pensions, that is pensions arising abroad in respect of service in a foreign country, were taxed on a remittance basis under Case V of Sch. D. It was common practice therefore to accumulate such income abroad.

330 Under the Finance Act 1974, such pensions are taxed on an arising basis subject to a deduction of 10% of the pension, except where received by an individual who is either not domiciled in the UK or is a British subject or citizen of the Republic of Ireland and is not ordinarily resident in the UK. In the case of those persons, the remittance basis continues. If all the pension were remitted in those circumstances, the person who is domiciled in the UK would therefore be better off by reason of the 10% deduction, which is not available where the remittance basis applies (s.65(2) and (4) ICTA 1988).

Pensions paid by Crown Agents

331 Certain foreign pensions are payable in the UK by the Crown Agents, acting on behalf of the government of the territory to which they relate. Where the territory forms part of Her Majesty's dominions, is a country mentioned in s.1(3) of the British Nationality Act, or is under Her Majesty's protection, the pension is chargeable under Sch. E (s.19(1)4 ICTA 1988). However, although paid in the UK, provided it is not borne out of the public revenue of the UK and relates to service in one of those countries, it will also qualify for the 10% deduction (s.196 ICTA 1988).

332 If the liability to pay a pension has been taken over by the British Government, for instance Indian Civil Service pensions, the pension is taxed in full under Sch. E and does not qualify for the 10% deduction (s.19(1)3 ICTA 1988).

The Crown Agents will again normally act as paying agents and receive instructions on what code number to operate from HM Inspector of Taxes, Public Department 1 District in Cardiff.

333 Where the Crown Agents pay pensions other than out of the funds of Her Majesty's Government and overseas tax is deducted on instructions from the overseas tax authority concerned, by arrangement with the Inland Revenue the UK tax code number is applied to the pension amount after any such overseas tax has been deducted. This is done to reduce any overpayment of UK tax. It should be noted that, as with the former 25% deduction in respect of overseas employments, the 10% deduction does not affect the amount of tax credit relief for foreign tax paid.

Pensions paid to victims of Nazi persecution

334 Pensions paid to victims of Nazi persecution by the law of Germany or Austria are eligible for a deduction of one half, instead of one tenth, if paid to a person domiciled in the UK. Attempts to claim complete exemption from UK tax on such pensions, taking advantage of the double tax treaty with Germany on the basis that the recipients were still German nationals have failed (Nothman *v.* Cooper, 1975 STC 91; and Oppenheimer *v.* Cattermole, 50 TC 159). It should be noted, however, that there is complete exemption from income tax for annuities paid to compensate victims of Nazi persecution for any damage they suffered (s.466 ICTA 1988). The nature of the payment received therefore needs to be checked with the authorities.

Double tax agreements

335 It is important in the case of any foreign pension to check the terms of the relevant double tax agreement, as the pension may be liable to tax only in the country of residence of the recipient (the position in most cases), or, in some cases, only in the country where the pension arises. For instance, certain US government pensions paid to citizens of the USA resident in the UK are exempt from UK tax under the double tax agreement (DT Agreement, Article 19(2)).

Foreign invalidity benefits

336 There is another possible exemption from UK tax. Payments made by foreign governments which correspond to those UK government Social Security benefits for which exemption from income tax is provided in the Taxes Act (s.617(1) ICTA 1988), which exempts such items of income as invalidity benefits and non-contributory invalidity pensions are treated by Extra Statutory Concession as also exempt from UK tax (ESC A24). Thus, an invalidity pension from a foreign government might be so exempt.

Foreign war pensions

337 Any pension or allowance which is payable by a foreign government to a widow, and relates to death due to war service or war injuries, is exempt from tax in the same way as comparable war widows' pensions payable by the UK government (s.318(2)(c) ICTA 1988).

Chapter 17
Sportsmen and women

Basis of liability

338 Sportsmen like some actors and actresses, are assessed under Sch. D Case II as carrying on one profession, where their income does not derive from an employment. Provided that they are resident in the UK and carrying on at least part of their profession in the UK, they are assessable on their worldwide earnings under Sch. D Case II. If a sportsman becomes non-resident for a whole tax year, he can escape assessment to UK tax altogether in respect of his professional earnings.

Visiting sportsmen

339 Most double taxation agreements do not exempt visiting sportsmen from local tax, even if they have no fixed base in the country concerned. Thus, in the case of the US/UK double taxation agreement. Art.17 specifically excludes athletes, in the widest sense, from the exemptions afforded to self-employed visitors and visiting employees of US corporations performing duties in the UK.

The provisions introduced by s.44 and Sch. 11 FA 1986 (now in ss.555 to 558 ICTA 1988), requiring persons paying non-UK resident entertainers to deduct tax on making payments in respect of activities performed in the UK, also apply to non-resident sportsmen, in respect of activities performed in the UK (see above in connection with entertainers).

Concentration of earnings and use of cessation rules

340 If the profession is of relatively short duration, for instance that of a boxer, it is important to ensure that, as far as possible, earnings are spread and that a cessation occurs at the optimum time from a tax point of view. If it is anticipated that future earnings will be lower than those of the previous three to four years of account, it may be advantageous to arrange a cessation for tax purposes, so that one of the high years of earnings will not enter into any basis period for assessment, although care needs to be taken if an upward adjustment under s.63 ICTA 1988 is to be avoided. Equally, if there is a low initial accounting period forming the basis for the first three years of assessment and the four following years show consistently high profits, it is possible, by adopting a 30 April year end, to cause one-half of the latter years' profits to drop out of assessment, by arranging a cessation at the end of the fourth year.

A sportsperson, by the very nature of the profession, normally cannot admit his or her spouse as a partner. Although it is possible to form a partnership to deal with sponsorship and other promotional income, the only sure way to achieve a cessation is to transfer the business to a company. Under s.162 TCGA 1992, if the consideration is wholly by way of shares of the company, there will be no capital gains tax liability arising from the transfer until the shares are disposed of. However, care needs to be taken to ensure that no liability arises under s.775 ICTA 1988 (see in connection with entertainers above). The development of other trades in the company should overcome this.

The provisions of s.165 TCGA 1992 offer an alternative route. It is possible to transfer at undervalue chargeable assets used in a business, such as super-earning potential, which is presumably a form of goodwill, into a company, and to hold-over any gain under the hold-over provisions of s.165 TCGA 1992. If current assets are transferred on loan account, any goodwill will be transferred at undervalue and, should it ever be realised, which is extremely unlikely, the company will pay corporation tax on the gain arising from the ultimate proceeds.

Service company documentation

341 On any incorporation of the sportsman's activities, care has to be taken to ensure that the documentation evidencing the transfer is correctly executed, and that future contractual relationships are entered into by the company and not the individual. The individual will be contracted to the service company by a 'slavery' contract, which should give the company discretion over making the individual's services available to third parties. The contract should also define where the services are to be performed, as it may be necessary to have a separate company for overseas services. It should also indicate the rights, such as copyrights and trademarks, that the company has succeeded to.

No Inland Revenue attack on service companies under Furniss v. Dawson has so far reached the Courts. It is understood that the Inland Revenue have won a case before the Special Commissioners, but here the service company documentation was faulty.

100% deduction

342 In the case of a UK-resident sportsman, it may be advisable to form a UK company if the sportsman can obtain a 100% deduction for long absences overseas. If the sportsman is an employee of the company, and satisfies the requirements for long absences for the 100% deduction, then all the earnings of the company can be drawn out as remuneration.

Foreign companies

343 In the case of UK-resident sportsmen, it is sometimes desirable to set up foreign companies in tax havens to receive income from abroad. Similar considerations apply to those for entertainers (see Chapter 3).

Withholding taxes

344 The question of withholding taxes on payments to sportsmen by overseas countries needs to be considered. Under most double taxation agreements, independent activities carried on by a person having no permanent establishment or base in a foreign country are exempt from tax in the country of payment, except in the case of payments to sportsmen. It used to be possible to avoid such withholding taxes in the case of payments from the USA, by having the income paid to a UK-resident company. However, under the revised agreement, if the UK company is one which is created substantially for the benefit of one person, withholding tax will still apply.

If foreign tax is withheld, it is important to ensure that maximum credit is obtained for it against UK tax. Thus, if it is withheld in the case of a payment to a company, sufficient profits should be left in charge to UK tax to cover the foreign tax.

Expenses

345 Consider the following:

(1) Abroad

Again, similar considerations apply as for entertainers. However, if the sportsman is self-employed, he should, if possible, be treated as operating from his home, and the expenses claimed under normal Sch. D rules. In practice, this covers both travel and reasonable subsistence expenses, and no attempt is made to restrict for home saving.

(2) In the UK

In the case of trips within the UK, the inspector of taxes may seek to disallow those expenses that the person would have had to incur as normal living expenses, on the basis of the decision in Caillebotte *v.* Quinn (1975) 50 TC 222, although this disallowance is unlikely to be significant. In practice, a disallowance is less likely where the sportsman has a mortgage, a spouse and family.

It has been reported that the cost of alcoholic sustenance of certain professional snooker and darts players has been successfully challenged by the Inland Revenue.

General principles on liability of various receipts

346 Sports stars derive their income from many sources. In some cases, it is received in the form of prize money; in other cases, payments are made by advertisers for the use of a sportsstar's name. It should be borne in mind that professional footballers and cricketers are employees of their clubs, and any payments made to them by their clubs are subject to tax under Sch. E. Match bonuses and payments from players' pools also form part of their earnings. Consequently, under Football league rules, it is not possible to pay earnings from the club to a Service Company as the player personally is contracted to the club. Only other income from sponsorships etc. can be paid to such a company.

Payments for international matches are paid to a footballer's club by the Football Association and thus are passed on to him by the club as additional earnings subject to PAYE in the normal way. When a footballer receives part of his transfer fee, this should also be taxable in full under Sch. E, and not fall within the 'golden handshake' provisions (and thus be completely exempt from tax up to £30,000), because it would be a customary payment, even though the employee had no contractual right to it (see Corbett *v.* Duff (1941) 23 TC 763). The player's share of a transfer fee paid as a signing on fee is normally paid by instalments under Football Association rules over the length of his contract and the tax liability can, therefore, be spread forward. The question of the taxation of so-called 'loyalty bonuses' paid to footballers at the end of their contracts on transfer to another club has been under discussion between the Professional Footballers Association and the Inland Revenue. The Inland Revenue were arguing that these bonuses were payments as part of the deal with the club to which the player was moving and, therefore, were taxable as a payment for future services. The players were claiming that the bonuses were 'golden handshakes'.

It is understood that the English football authorities recently agreed with the Inland Revenue's Special Office that most termination payments made by 'custom and expectation' to footballers on a transfer to a new club by their transferring club, should be taxed as ordinary earnings.

This is now been strengthened by the House of Lords decision in Shilton *v.* Wilmshurst, (1991) STC 88 which confirmed that a payment by the old club, Nottingham Forest, to a player on a transfer was an emolument liable in full under Sch. E. The Court held that the payment represented part of the contractual arrangements for the transfer, and whether it was paid for future services or not it was part of the terms of his continuing employment with the new club and therefore taxable.

Payments from other sources that are made in the ordinary course of carrying on or exercising the profession are Sch. D Case II income of the recipient.

However, there have been exceptional payments that have been made to individuals as marks of personal esteem, or that are peculiar to those individuals, which have been held not to be liable to tax. Thus, attendance money at a cricketer's benefit match paid to the cricketer was held not to be assessable to income tax (Reed *v.* Seymour (1927) 11 TC 625). The basis of the decision was that the sum received showed the gratitude of the public and was in appreciation of the personal qualities of the cricketer. In contrast, in Davis *v.* Harrison (1927) 11 TC 707, a footballer's benefit was held to be assessable. This was principally because the benefit accrued to the person automatically under the rules of the Football League, after a specified number of years' playing service, so that it had less of the qualities of a payment to a particular individual, than a payment by virtue of the length of service performed. In Moorhouse *v.* Dooland (1954) 36 TC 1, a professional cricketer playing in the Lancashire League was assessed on the proceeds of collections from spectators that were allowed under the rules of the League where a player scored more than 50 runs. A payment for giving up amateur status was, however, held not to be assessable (Jarrold *v.* Boustead (1964) 41 TC 701). In Shilton *v.* Wilmhurst, as mentioned, it was held that, in the particular circumstances, a fee of £75,000 paid to Peter Shilton, a professional footballer, by his club, Nottingham Forest, as an inducement to him to consent to his transfer to another club, Southampton, was an emolument chargeable to Sch. E income tax under s.19(1) ICTA 1988.

In general, exotic tax avoidance schemes involving sportsmen are to be avoided, as the recent case of O'Leary *v.* McKinley (1991 STC 42) showed. O'Leary, who was domiciled in Ireland, had a contract with Arsenal. In addition to his basic wage and bonuses he was anxious to ensure that an additional annual sum of £28,985 was received in a tax efficient manner. The sum of £10 was settled on a Jersey settlement by a third party for the benefit of O'Leary for life with remainder, subject to a power of advancement, to the Catholic Church in Ireland. Arsenal lent the settlement £266,000 interest free but repayable on demand, which was invested with Jersey bank for two years at 11½% to provide an annual sum of £28,590 for O'Leary. Based on his non-domiciled status, he would only be taxed on any interest remitted to the UK. No income was remitted. It was decided that the income arising under the settlement was an emolument of the taxpayer's employment with the club, on the basis that it was income provided by Arsenal Football Club payable only for so long as O'Leary was employed by the club. If the taxpayer had had the free disposal of the £266,000 and if it had not been tied to his employment, the position might have been different. However, the case was not decided upon Furniss *v.* Dawson principles but by construing all the documents together. The position on inducement payments which this case broadly followed is discussed below.

Footballer's benefit matches

347 It is understood that the Inland Revenue have lost a case before the Commissioners concerning another footballer's benefit, and does not now argue for taxation of such benefits. However, to be safe, there must not only be no entitlement to the benefit, even in the form of verbal promises as part of the player's contract, but also neither the club nor any official of the club should be concerned in running the benefit match, which should be left to an independent committee or body of trustees. As the 'golden handshake' legislation can catch anything paid 'in connection with' the termination of an employee's contract of service, the benefit match should not take place when the player goes from one club to another or retires from the game. The receipts from the match should, if possible, be mainly on the basis of donations by spectators and only a low admission charge for the tickets should be imposed.

Operation of PAYE

There has been a crackdown on so called expenses payments made in particular to footballers in the lower divisions, non-league clubs and amateur leagues. In addition, signing on fees (see below) have been abused. Following an investigation into the affairs of Swindon Town, there was an amnesty for football clubs which enabled them to declare payments which should have been subject to PAYE, without facing interest and penalties. It is believed several clubs have now had discussions with the Inland Revenue. The enquiry by the Inland Revenue has not only covered signing on fees and expenses payments to Football League contract players. Increased sponsorship of clubs has also presented a problem, as perks provided by third party sponsors should be reported by clubs and frequently have not been. In addition, the payment of expenses to players where the contract is incomplete and only specifies certain payments has been the source of intense Inland Revenue enquiries, and the practice of so called amateurs receiving round sum payments for travelling is being attacked. If these represent genuine expenses payments, with no profit to the player, arguably the cases of Donnelly *v*. Williamson (1982) STC 88 and Pook *v*. Owen (45 TC 571) might mean there is nothing to assess, but this is frequently not the case.

Amateur sportsmen

348 In the case of athletes and rugby union players, the rules of the governing bodies preclude the payment of fees for competing, and it is understood that the generous expenses allowances that are paid are accepted by the Inland Revenue as giving rise to no taxable income. In recognition of the fact that athletes have to give much time to training, and need to support their families, special trusts for themselves and their families have now been set up by the Amateur Athletics Association, into which money from 'dedicated' meetings is paid for their benefit. It is understood that the arrangement has been approved by the Inland Revenue. Once payments for their benefit exceed £5,000, athletes have their own private trusts. As, in all cases, they are the settlors of such trusts, the income from advertising, sponsorship and prize money is treated as theirs for tax purposes in the year of receipt. Training and travelling expenses are allowed in the normal way.

Trust funds are used to regulate the flow of money to the athlete, who can claim from the trust against vouched expenses incurred in the carrying on of sporting activities. In this way, amateur status may be retained and some check maintained on the level of involvement with sponsors and commercial interests.

In theory, amateur sportsmen cannot, by definition, carry on a paid profession within Sch. D Case II. However, except in very small-scale cases, the Inland Revenue, in practice, 'looks through' amateur status and will assess sponsorship payments made under contract to amateurs, even where no advertisement for the sponsor is carried. This type of income, together with other advertising income, may conveniently be earned by a husband and wife partnership. The Inland Revenue's approach in this matter reflects its interpretation of the facts and does not have any bearing on the general principles applicable to the assessment of casual receipts.

The timing of when an activity ceases to be a hobby and becomes a profession is sometimes difficult to determine, but generally it is advisable to admit Case II status early so as to be able to claim expenses and possibly in the early days also loss relief. There may also be pre-trading expenses to claim under s.401 ICTA 1988. Usually these will be incurred before the first sponsorship is obtained and before the first appearance money or prize money is received. The athletes should be encouraged to keep detailed diaries of expenses. The most difficult areas will be the loan of cars by sponsors. Whereas the benefits legislation is very comprehensive for employees, money's worth is sometimes difficult to fit into the Sch. D Case II rules. Generally, unless someone actually receives ownership of goods in kind, so that the principle in Humphrey *v.* Gold Coast Selection (1948) 30 TC 209 will apply to tax the payment in kind for Sch. D purposes, it is difficult to tax such benefits under Sch. D.

Signing-on fees

349 The decision in Jarrold *v.* Boustead (see **346** above) does not by any means imply that all, or indeed most, signing-on fees are immune from liability under Sch. E. For example, in Riley *v.* Coglan (1967) 44 TC 481, a former amateur player signed professional forms with a rugby league club. In addition to the normal form of remuneration, the agreement between the individual and the club provided that, in consideration of the sum of £500, the player would serve the club for the remainder of his playing career. Ungoed-Thomas J. decided that the sum of £500 was paid for services to be rendered, and it became an emolument arising 'from' the employment properly chargeable to income tax under Sch. E. The decision in Jarrold *v.* Boustead was based on the conclusion that the sum paid comprised an inducement for giving up amateur status and did not reflect a reward for services rendered. This distinction does indicate the extreme caution to be exercised when drafting any document or agreement including the payment of an 'inducement' or signing-on fee.

However, in the case of rugby league players, where a player had genuinely relinquished his amateur status by signing for a league club, it was understood that no tax was payable on the signing-on fee, provided that:

(a) the total fee was clearly stated in the contract; and
(b) if the fee was payable by instalments, the dates of stage payments were clearly stated in the contract, and were not made subject to any conditions whatsoever, for example that the player should still be with the club at the time of an instalment. Such conditions would make the instalments payments for services, as with additional payments for gaining a Great Britain 'cap'.

This was the position in the past but, following a number of well-publicised signings and as a result of discussions with the Inland Revenue, it was agreed to lay down certain rules because of the areas of doubt that had arisen over the years from the wording and the conditions of some contracts involving amateur players joining rugby league clubs and concerning the true value of loss of amateur status. From 6 April 1987, a player turning professional receives tax relief on the first £6,000 of any fee paid for surrendering his amateur status, and the rest is taxable as income. The same rules apply to stage payments, as before, where the £6,000 limit is not exceeded on any outright payment on signing for a rugby league club provided no conditions are attached to the instalment. It is understood that the £6,000 exemption limit is to be reviewed in later years.

Inducement fees have now been the subject of three more recent cases, Vaughan-Neil *v.* CIR (1979) 54 TC 233, Pritchard *v.* Arundale (1971) 47 TC 680, and Glantre Engineering Limited *v.* Goodhand (1982) 56 TC 165. The principles emerging from these cases are that, to be non-taxable, it is preferable that the sum be paid other than by the prospective employer, and that the payment, whether in cash or, as in the *Arundale* case, in the form of shares, should be shown to be for giving up a valuable right, so that there is a permanent loss of a valuable asset. These decisions will, therefore, not exempt any ordinary signing-on fee paid to a player moving from one club to another.

It is understood that, in an appeal before the Special Commissioners, no tax relief was allowed to a player signing for a leading Scottish professional club in respect of his loss of amateur status on the grounds that the effects of the loss of amateur status in football are negligible these days.

Payments for winning

350 In the case of Moore *v.* Griffiths (1972) 48 TC 338, payments to the England team for winning the World Cup – paid both by outside bodies and a special bonus paid by the Football Association – were also held not to be assessable, as not being a reward for services rendered. The basis of this decision seems to be that special payments made to an individual for some unique performance or personal quality may escape assessment, particularly where the payment is unsolicited. In contrast, where it is normal for people in a sport to compete for prize money, the prizes will be assessable if it can be shown that the person is carrying on his sport as a professional rather than as a hobby. For example, it is reported that the Inland Revenue is seeking to assess prizes in angling competitions on those that they regard as professional anglers. However, 'man of the match' awards are accepted as not taxable.

Jockeys

351 Racing is not a commercial activity liable to taxation and, therefore, owners receive their winnings free of tax. However, jockeys are taxable on payments from owners that are part of their earnings under their contracts. It is understood that, until recently, extra payments for winning have not be challenged, but now both the Inland Revenue and Customs & Excise are regarding such payments as taxable, as being made for a consideration.

There is no doubt, in the Inland Revenue view, supported by the old Irish tax case of Wing *v.* O'Connell (1927) IR 84, that presents received from race horse owners by a jockey for winning are taxable receipts of a profession.

Pension schemes

352 There are special company pension schemes available for footballers, whose careers are necessarily short, so that they can receive maximum benefits at age 35. Advice should be sought on this so that every advantage is taken of the facility.

In particular, the Pension Schemes Office has provided sets of model rules for football club schemes. It should be noted that no player who is member of a club scheme may have concurrent membership of the 'Football League Limited Players Retirement and Income Scheme' or any other scheme of the club. Concurrent membership of the Football League Limited Players Benefit Scheme is, however, permitted.

Similar discretion is now given to the Inland Revenue to approve retirement annuity or personal pension contracts for individuals who, because of the nature of their work, are likely to retire early, such as other professional sportsmen and sportswomen.

The complete list is as follows:

Type of sportsman	Retirement age
Athletes (appearance and prize money)	35
Badminton player	35
Boxer	35

Sportsmen and women

Type of sportsman	Retirement age
Cricketer	40
Cyclist	35
Footballer (excluding Football League players in pensionable employment)	35
Golfer (tournament)	40
Jockey (flat racing)	45
Jockey (national hunt)	35
Motorcycle rider (motocross or road racing)	40
Motor racing driver	40
Rugby League player	35
Rugby League referee	50
Speedway rider	40
Squash player	35
Table tennis player	35
Tennis player (including real tennis)	35
Wrestler	35.

Chapter 18
Persons in receipt of gratuities

General

353 Gratuitous payments of one sort or another have probably been the subject of more case law and legislation, culminating in the introduction of Capital Transfer Tax (now Inheritance Tax), than any other forms of payment.

Tips

354 The most common form of gratuitous payment is a tip. It was held that a taxi driver's tips were assessable in Calvert *v.* Wainwright (27 TC 475). The principle behind the decision was that voluntary payments made in the ordinary way in return for services, over and above what someone is contractually bound to pay, as opposed to exceptional gifts made on personal grounds, are liable as income. The basis of the decision was essentially the same as those relating to other voluntary payments such as Easter offerings and footballers' benefits.

Retirement gratuities

355 Sometimes the gratuity is part of the terms of service and, for instance, if it is a retirement gratuity, varies with the length of service. In such cases, it will be an earned gift and taxable as such with no relief under the golden handshake provisions. Thus gratuities payable to sub-postmasters on retirement and based upon their years of service are assessable as earned income under the normal rules of Sch. E. (*Hansard* 28 February 1983, Vol. 38 Col. 18).

PAYE on tips

356 The employer's obligations in relation to the payment of tips in hotel and catering establishments need to be carefully checked. Ignorance of the PAYE regulations as contained in the Employers' Guide and the Income Tax Regulations is no defence. Where there is a sharing of 'charged tips' amongst employees, but no official tronc (that is, pooling arrangement) exists into which the tips are paid, the establishment is deemed to be responsible for accounting for tax on the amounts paid out. Any amounts paid out where deductions should have been made are treated as net payments and the employer is thus liable for tax on the grossed up value of the net amounts paid, with penalties if an incomplete declaration is made. This liability arises even if the hotel, etc, did not charge the guest in the first place or have any influence over how the amounts were shared out.

357 Charged tips means amounts added voluntarily by a customer to a bill settled with the establishment but not amounts paid in cash directly to an employee. Charged tips are normally accounted for as a 'paid out' either by the cashier or from the hotel front desk and do not become recorded as revenue of the establishment. They do not, however, include a compulsory service charge.

358 There are special PAYE regulations dealing with such tips (SI 1973 No. 334; Income Tax (Employment) Regulations 1973). Broadly, where there is an established tronc system not operated by the company or by an employee designated by the company, no liability on the company arises unless the Inspector specifically directs.

359 There are several different ways of dealing with charged tips which have different consequences for the establishment:

(1) The employees form their own tronc with a designated 'tronc-master' who registers with the Inspector of Taxes. The tronc is then responsible for operating PAYE. This also applies where a service charge is distributed through the tronc.

(2) If the employing company is involved in the distribution of tips, for instance, by designating the tronc master, but a paying point is established separate from the normal company payroll, the tronc is again responsible for PAYE.

(3) Obviously, if the company controls the distribution of tips and accounts for them through its normal payroll, PAYE must be applied by it.

These alternatives apply to charged tips, or charged tips and cash tips, or a combination of service charge and additional charged or cash tips paid to the establishment. It should be noted if PAYE is not properly operated by a tronc, the Inspector can then direct the employer to make the PAYE deductions and thus he is liable in place of the tronc master. Otherwise, in the absence of such a direction, the tronc master has personal liability for PAYE which should have been deducted.

The authority for this is the intermediate employer rules in Regulation 3 of the Income Tax (Employment) Regulations 1973, under which where there is any failure to operate PAYE the Inland Revenue may obtain the Commissioners' permission to apply the rules of Regulation 3 to collect from the actual employer any tax on amounts paid by the employer through the tronc master.

The legal problems of whether the tronc regulation applies or whether the employer is liable to PAYE were discussed in Figael Limited *v.* Fox (1990 STC 583). The facts of the case were complex. Essentially, tips were placed in a box and at the end of each day the tips were checked by the directors and placed in an envelope. The envelopes were put into the company's safe. The box and safe were under the control of the directors. At the end of the each week, the envelopes were removed and the tips divided by the directors between themselves and the waiters. There was no formal appointment by the company of any person to take responsibility for the arrangement and no record was kept of the tips distributed. The company claimed this was a tronc arrangement within Regulation 4 and the persons accountable for PAYE were the directors, not the company. It was held there was no tronc arrangement. The 1973 regulations, in particular Regulation 4, should be construed in context. In its ordinary and natural meaning, Regulation 4 did not apply where the emoluments in the form of a share of tips were paid to an employee by his principal employer. The fact that there was no organised arrangement to share the tips among two or more employees was not enough to attract Regulation 4. There had also to be a person called the tronc master who did the sharing out and under Regulation 4 that person was to be regarded as the employer. If the same person who paid the wages paid out the tips, Regulation 4 did not come into play.

360 If cash tips are received by the employee direct, that is other than via the employer's payroll or through an organised tronc, the employee must declare the tips personally and is liable personally on them.

In an Inland Revenue press release dated 28 March 1985 and entitled 'Tips and Tax', it was disclosed that certain employees of larger well known establishments had agreed, on being challenged, that they earned tips of up to £7,500 per annum and that the lowest agreed average tips per full-time employee at any one of the establishments investigated was £750 per annum. Consequently, the Inland Revenue have been in recent years increasing the restriction in waiters' code numbers to collect tax on such tips at source.

Other gifts

361 An example of an unsolicited gift not assessable was a payment to a professional man as a result of an introduction he had arranged, which produced a sale of some land which was entirely unsolicited and in no way in return for any services (Bloom *v*. Kinder, 38 TC 77). The position was well summarised in the judgment in the Court of Appeal in the case of Simpson *v*. John Reynolds & Co (Insurances) Ltd (1975) STC 271, where Russell LJ said:

"The facts as it seems to me on which that question is to be answered are these. First this was a wholly unexpected and unsolicited gift. Second, it was made after the business connection had ceased. Third, the gift was in recognition of past services rendered to the client company over a long period, though not because those past services were considered to have been inadequately remunerated. Fourthly, the gift was made as a consolation for the fact that those remunerative services were no longer to be performed by the

217

taxpayer for the donor; and, fifthly, there is no suggestion that at a future date the business connection might be renewed."

362 This case followed on the case of Carnaby, Harrower, Barham and Prykett *v*. Walker (46 TC 561), where a firm of auditors received a solatium in addition to their normal audit fee in recognition of the fact that they had been asked to resign after many years of service. The same principle was established in the case of payments to tenants of tied houses in Murray *v*. Goodhews (1978) STC 207.

There are other instances where the Inland Revenue have decided that *ex gratia* compensation is not taxable as a receipt of the trade or profession, for example, payments by building societies to their former agents. Yet in none of these cases can it be said that the loss of the agency cripples the business, although the agency is usually unique in the sense that such agents only act for one society on a full agency basis.

Prizes

363 Prizes are received by people carrying on a variety of professions and sometimes these cause arguments with the Inland Revenue. The basic principle again is that if a person is receiving the reward for work done – for instance, a writer entering a prize competition and writing a new work for it – the prize will be assessable. If, however, the prize is something that the person does not seek to win but is given in recognition of the outstanding merit of the work which is otherwise remunerated in the normal way, for instance the Nobel Prize awarded to a scientist, and is non-recurring, or the prize is given for personal qualities, it is likely to be exempt from tax. Thus a prize given by a bank to one of its employees for passing an examination was held to be not liable for income tax (Ball *v*. Johnson, 47 TC 155).

However, in an ICAEW press release (PR 786 March 1990), it is reported that the Inland Revenue consider in the case of those earning £8,500 per annum or more that examination prizes are taxable. The Ball *v*. Johnson (47 TC 155) case does not apply to the benefits legislation as the later Wicks *v*. Firth (1983 STC 25) decision recognised that cash could be a benefit so that anyone earning £8,500 or more is chargeable to tax on the award.

Long-service awards

364 As a further concession, the Inland Revenue do not seek to tax long-service awards made to directors and employees as testimonials to mark long service which take the form of tangible articles of reasonable cost when the relevant period of service is not less than 20 years, and no similar award has been made to the recipient within the previous 10 years. An article is taken to be of reasonable cost where the cost to the employer does not exceed £20 for each year of service (ESC A22).

Chapter 19
Insurance agents

Categories of agent

365 There are two categories of insurance agent: those who work exclusively for one company but are remunerated almost wholly by commission and usually work from home, and those who are agents for any company which is prepared to pay commission and are insurance brokers bringing together the insurer and the insured.

Exclusive agents

366 Certain insurance companies do not pay commission to outside brokers and thus conduct all their business through their own employees or agents. These agents are treated as employees for tax purposes where it is only the manner of their remuneration and the fact they do not have a place of work on their employer's premises which distinguishes them from other employees.

367 In order to obtain an allowance for any expenses such employees incur by virtue of use of their homes as offices, they must obtain from their employers evidence that they are required to use their homes for the purposes of the employment and that this will apply to all agents of the company. This will ensure that it is possible to show that the expenses would have to be incurred by any employee holding that position and are not peculiar to the circumstances of the individual concerned. This will then satisfy the test of allowability laid down in the case of Ricketts v. Colquhoun that the expense must be of a sort incurred by 'each and every holder of the office' (10 TC 118).

368 In order to be able to claim capital allowances, the same point applies, as the person must be able to show that the plant and machinery is 'necessarily provided for use in the performance of the duties' of the employment (s.27 CAA 1990).

369 The tax status of insurance agents working exclusively for one company has been under review by the Inland Revenue and in many cases their status has been changed from self-employed to employed. However, in the case of several well known life companies where the agent operates very much on his own account providing his own car, office equipment etc., and generally is given discretion as to the manner of carrying out his agency, it is accepted by the Inland Revenue that the agent is self-employed. Such agents have their own areas of operation within which they service their clientele and thus their operations are similar to those of a general practice doctor deriving all of his income from one source but exercising a professional skill under no supervision.

Other agents

370 The insurance broker will be assessed under Sch. D. Commission is payable as to a substantial amount when the policy is taken out and a small continuing amount every year that the premiums are paid. It is generally correct to bring in commission on a receivable rather than received basis. In most cases, agents will receive a commission statement from the insurance company with the amount of commission being received at the same time, but sometimes the commission will be due when the policy is effected and not rescinded at the option of the policyholder. There may then be a delay which could bridge a year end before the commission is received. However, normal tax principles of bringing in income on an entitlement basis will apply. Sometimes in the case of reinsurance brokers, commission may be subject to delay and difficulty of calculation, particularly where premiums are owed by the insured who may reside overseas or even be in dispute as to the amount. In such cases, it may be possible where entitlement to an amount is difficult to quantify to operate on a receipts basis. The business can carry with it the right to these commissions as well as all the normal goodwill of a business. This goodwill of an insurance agent was one of the examples quoted when the original capital gains legislation was being debated. It can, of course, be the subject of a roll-over claim if the person selling the goodwill does not cease to trade and reinvests the proceeds of sale in one of the classes of eligible assets (s.152(8) TCGA 1992). It is debatable whether goodwill arising solely out of commission on outstanding premiums is a wasting asset for capital gains purposes. If it is, it will be a depreciating asset for roll-over relief purposes and any gain rolled over into its acquisition cost can only be held over for a maximum of 10 years or until the proceeds from the sale of the assets giving rise to the claim are reinvested in a non-wasting asset (s.154 TCGA 1992).

It is interesting to note it is reported in *Taxation* of 21 November 1991 that a self-employed insurance broker has succeeded in securing capital allowances and maintenance costs for expenditure on a £150 bicycle used for business purposes. Possibly, the nature of an insurance broker's work particularly in inner city areas makes a bicycle a more sensible form of transport.

Casual insurance commission

371 It is often the case that individuals hold agencies with one or more insurance companies and receive varying amounts of commission. If the individual is otherwise employed, the commission may well be assessed under Case VI.

The above practice is reinforced by the case of Hugh *v*. Rogers (38 TC 270) where the taxpayer held a dormant agency with an insurance company. He paid reduced premiums after deduction of commission on his own policies. In addition, he introduced some pensions business from the company of which he was secretary. For that introduction, he received £750 commission. The Inland Revenue originally claimed that either the commission was taxable as an emolument of his employment, or under Case VI of Sch. D. The Inland Revenue dropped their contentions under Sch. E and it seems this conclusion still holds good under the benefits-in-kind legislation in s.154 ICTA 1988 because the commission was not received by reason of his employment but rather by reason of the agency. However, the judge said "There is no reason to doubt that the commission under an agency agreement is a subject matter for tax under Case VI, although it was a one off payment with little or no services being performed by the agent."

372 Sometimes the commission relates to premiums on policies effected by the individual in respect of his own insurance or the agent gives someone the benefit of his commission. The risks inherent in informal arrangements were underline in the case of Way *v*. Underdown (No 2) (1975) STC 425. In that case, commissions passed on under a friendly agreement by an agent of an insurance company to the person on whose behalf he had effected the policy were held to be assessable on him as he had become entitled to them. Obiter even if there had been a contractually binding obligation with the policyholder to pass on the commission, he would still have been assessable as the person receiving the commission. On the other hand, where premiums were paid net of the agent's commission, which was thus effectively waived to the insurance company by the insured, the agent was not assessable on such commission as he had never become entitled to it or received it (s.59(1) ICTA 1988).

373 Following on this case, the accountancy bodies issued a new guideline to liability on insurance commissions following discussions with the Inland Revenue (Technical Release 224) in April 1977.

374 Agents receiving commission on their own insurance will not be liable to tax on such commission as income in their hands though only the net amount of the premium after commission will be an allowable deduction where the premium ranks as a business expense in computing profits or gains for tax purposes. When it is not the agent's own insurance, if a policy holder receives commission instead of the agent and pays a premium net of such commission, the agent again will not be liable to tax. An agent who receives commission and pays it to the policy holder will be legally liable to tax, but in practice, if the Inland Revenue are satisfied that there has been a *bona fide* refund, the agent will not be taxed provided the policy holder only claims any relief due on the net premium paid after deducting the commission.

This refers to both Sch. D Case I deductions and life insurance premium relief. It also appears in the case of a single premium life policy that strictly relief can only be claimed on the net premium in arriving at the gain on a chargeable event, although doubtless the life company would use the gross figure in notifying the gains to the Inland Revenue.

375 The Board of Inland Revenue (SP 3/79) have considered this practice in the light of the provisions commencing on 6 April 1979 for premium relief by deduction in the case of life assurance policies, discontinued in the 1984 Finance Act for new policies. The position will then be that the amount of the relief given by deduction will depend upon the amount of money which passes between the individual and the life office at the time the premium is paid. Thus, if the premium is £100 and commission is £10 and only the net amount of £90 is paid to the life office, relief will only be available by deduction on £90. If, however, the gross amount of £100 is paid, the income of the individual is diminished by £100 and relief will be based on £100 even though £10 comes back by way of commission later on. In such circumstances, however, the commission, since it would be received by the individual, will be assessable to tax.

Generally, under the Statement of Practice, the practice will be to regard an individual or company who is entitled as agent of the insurance company to commission on premiums on policies effected on his own account as not liable to tax on them as income in his hands. This derives from the fact a person cannot trade and make a profit out of himself for tax purposes.

Annex D of the 1988 Inland Revenue Consultative Document on the taxation of life assurance confirms that commission on the agent's own business is not assessable except where premiums are tax deductible and the full gross premium is allowed. This is confirmed in the 1979 Statement where it reaffirms in relation to the agent's own business:

'Where the premiums are allowable deductions in computing profits or gains for tax purposes or are otherwise allowable under the Taxes Acts only the net premiums (after deducting the commission) are allowable.'

Cases also arise where the agent has agreed that all or part of his commission can be applied by the life company to enhance the policyholder's investment, perhaps by an increased allocation of units. The 1988 Consultative Document simply states that this raises a number of problems, including what premium is to be taken into account in the subsequent chargeable events computation. It appears if, from the outset, the agent foregoes all or part of his commission so that the customer receives an enhanced investment, there are no grounds for assessment of the full commission on the agent.

Although if he arranges for the reinvestment by the taxpayer of the commission he might be liable for tax on it on the authority of Way *v.* Underdown as there has been a bona fide refund of it to the policyholder, in accordance with established Inland Revenue practice the agent should not be assessed. The client should then claim only the sum invested out of his own funds as the base value for future chargeable event purposes.

With regard to ordinary employees of insurance brokers to whom commission is rebated on their own policies, the Inland Revenue apparently take the view such a rebate is emoluments and PAYE should be operated by the broker. The position will obtain irrespective of any relief due to the policyholder for the premiums he pays.

Chapter 20
Trawlermen, river and sea pilots

Introduction

376 Trawlers from such ports as Hull, Grimsby, Fleetwood and Aberdeen used to form the bulk of the UK fishing industry, and the inshore vessels operating from smaller ports were relatively insignificant. Nowadays, the picture is very different. With Icelandic waters closed to British fishermen, and many other countries imposing strict territorial limits, the distant-water trawler fleet has declined dramatically, while the inshore fleet has expanded to form the greater part of the UK fishing industry.

Employed or self-employed?

377 The following is to be considered.

(1) Trawlermen

Generally trawlers used to be owned by fishing companies or sometimes a partnership of fishing company and skipper. Where the skipper had a capital stake in the fishing vessel, he would be regarded as self-employed. Crewmen usually had the status of employees (see Boyd Line *v.* Pitts (1986) ICR 244).

(2) Share fishing

Share fishing is the pattern most commonly found in Scotland. Boats are owned by partnerships consisting typically of the skipper and one or two of the crew. The fishing companies may help to finance the purchase of the vessel and often have shares in the vessel, but this is usually a minority interest.

The modern fishing vessel operating from Scottish ports has a crew of between six and ten, all of whom are engaged as share fishermen. The proceeds of each fishing trip are first shared between the vessel and the crew so that if the net proceeds of the trip are, for example, £32,000, a crew of eight would receive £2,000 each, regardless of any other interest in the vessel they may have, with the remaining £16,000 going to the boat's account. It is presumably because of these mutual arrangements that the Inland Revenue accept that share fishermen are self-employed.

Although share fishermen are regarded as self-employed for tax purposes, they are able to claim unemployment benefit if they pay their national insurance contributions at the special rate for share fishermen. There are other aspects of a share fisherman's working arrangements which are not usually characteristic of the self-employed. For example, while at sea, a share fisherman works entirely under the direction of the skipper and/or mate and, unless he has a share in the vessel, he risks no capital. However, the level of his income depends entirely on the results of the fishing venture, and there is authority for his self-employed status in the case of CIR *v*. Francis West and Others (1950) 31 TC 402.

(3) English ports

Following the Anglo-Icelandic 'cod war', English fishing ports became severely depressed. The remaining industry consists mainly of smaller vessels suitable for inshore fishing, most of which are probably crewed by their owners.

It should be noted that it has been confirmed in a Press Release dated 29 October 1987 that UK fishing licences qualify for roll-over relief. These licences (granted to enable the UK to conform with European Community legislation) represent the right to catch a certain quantity of fish. They are treated as goodwill for capital gains tax purposes and hence qualify for roll-over relief and, in appropriate circumstances, retirement relief.

Retirement age

378 The normal retirement age for employees in company schemes and for the purposes of retirement annuity contracts is 55 for both distant water and inshore fishermen. However, the personal pension provisions in s.634(2) ICTA 1988 bring the general lower retirement age down to 50.

Special clothing

379 Employed seamen on fishing vessels are entitled, under s.198 ICTA 1988, to a deduction for the cost of special clothing. The flat rate deduction agreed with the Inland Revenue under Extra-Statutory Concession A1 for all years from 6 April 1982 to 5 April 1984 was £55 per annum. As a matter of unofficial local practice, Scottish tax districts increased this to £200 as from 1986/87 for share fishermen.

Capital allowances

380 Consider the following.

(1) Free depreciation

Free depreciation is the facility available to ship owners either to claim the full writing-down allowance due for the period in question or to postpone all or part of it to a later period. This facility used to be available only in respect of first-year allowances on new ships. However, following the abolition of first-year allowances from 1 April 1986, and the introduction of the short-life asset provisions, the option of free depreciation has been extended to writing-down allowances and to expenditure on second-hand ships (ss.31–33 CAA 1990). It is understood that the Inland Revenue accept that any vessel that can propel itself, as opposed to being towed, will be regarded as a 'ship' for the purposes of free depreciation.

Where free depreciation is claimed, the amount of the allowance to be given must be specified by the person to whom the allowance is made. Where fishermen act in partnership, the Inland Revenue regard their boat as an asset of the trade carried on by that partnership. As it is the partnership, therefore, that has an entitlement to capital allowances, the partnership must make a joint decision regarding capital allowances and free depreciation. The total allowances claimed are then allocated among the partners by reference to their individual shares in the boat. This also applies to any corporate members of a partnership.

Each time a person defers claiming any part of the allowance, he must specify in a notice to the inspector of taxes, not later than two years after the end of the chargeable period, the amount that he wishes to defer. The deferred allowance, when claimed, then ranks as an allowance for the period in which it is given, and is thus available to create a loss in that period for the purposes of set-off against other income of the same or the following year.

The amount of free depreciation claimed should be decided by reference to the trader's income for the year. It is possible to defer claiming all of it on a ship, even until after the ship has been sold and replaced with another ship, as the allowance may be claimed for any subsequent period in which the person carries on the trade. The allowances postponed have, however, to be brought in calculating the balancing adjustment. If there is little income in the period of sale, it may be better to reserve claiming any balance of the free depreciation on the ship sold until later, when income is higher.

(2) Depooling

The provisions provide for the 'depooling' of expenditure on ships as well as for the postponement (by election) of writing-down allowances on ships. This does not apply in certain leasing situations.

Each ship is assumed to be used for a separate notional trade. The effect of this is that a balancing charge on one ship cannot be offset directly against the written-down value of another ship. When a ship is sold or scrapped, a balancing allowance or charge is calculated but is not actually allowed or charged unless the actual trade ceases. Instead it is added to or deducted from the shipowner's main pool of expenditure qualifying for capital allowances.

Further options available to the ship owner are:

(i) to include his expenditure on the ship in the pool from the outset;
(ii) to transfer the ship to the pool part way through its life; or
(iii) to transfer part of his expenditure (or part of the written-down value) to the pool.

In the case of (i) above, no election to postpone allowances can be made and the normal capital allowances rules apply.

Partnerships

381 The following should be considered.

(1) Partnership changes

Where there is a change in the shares in a vessel or a change of boat but no change in partners, it is the Inland Revenue's view that there is no cessation for the purposes of s.113 ICTA 1988. In such circumstances, any payments made or received in respect of shares changing hands are ignored for capital allowances purposes, but the allocation of written-down value between the partners is revised. No balancing charge arises. This treatment also applies where there is a change in partners but an election is made under s.113(2) ICTA 1988 within the two year time limit.

Where a cessation applies on a change in partners, there is a balancing adjustment on the outgoing partner, the continuing partners will have their allowances based on written-down value, or, if there is no incoming partner, on written-down value plus the cost of additional shares. However, the Inland Revenue have stated that any cost of additional shares is not to exceed the original cost of the vessel. Any incoming partner will be granted capital allowances by reference to the cost of his share. Again the Inland Revenue have stated that the cost of the incoming partner's share should be limited to the historic cost of the vessel and any vessel improvements.

However, where a change in vessel involves a change in the method of fishing, it is sometimes possible to claim that a new trade has commenced. This may make possible a claim under s.381 ICTA 1988, which can include the capital allowances available on the new vessel. As such new vessels can cost anything from £1/2M to £2M, even writing-down allowances can create a substantial loss claim and a worthwhile repayment with supplement.

More usually, it is advantageous to claim continuation both on a change in the partnership and on a change of vessel. Where the changes coincide, there is a risk that the Inland Revenue will regard these changes as constituting a cessation and commencement, and treat any continuation elections as invalid. It is therefore advisable to ensure that changes in partnership and vessel do not occur simultaneously where continuation treatment is being sought. There should be a period of trading between the changes to establish continuity.

(2) Consent for loss claims

The use by any partner of capital allowances to create or augment a loss claim requires the written permission of the other partners. The balance of unused capital allowances is carried forward against future profits of the partnership, and is not identified specifically with the partners who are unable to use their capital allowances in the earlier period. By giving permission to some of the other partners to use excess capital allowances for loss claims, such partners are effectively surrendering some of the capital allowances to which they are entitled.

(3) Partnerships including a company

The Inland Revenue follows the guidelines listed below in dealing with a partnership that includes a company.

(a) Capital allowances due to the company are computed by reference to the accounting period of the boat partnership, and should be allocated on a strictly *pro rata* basis in accordance with the company's share in the partnership, following the case of Lewis *v.* CIR (18 TC 174) ie., the company cannot claim the capital allowances at a different rate from that of the individual partners.

(b) Capital allowances due to the individual members of the partnership are computed on a 'current year' basis, eg., if the accounting period is for the year to 31 December, the allowances due for 1990/91 would be three-quarters of the allowances for the year to 31 December 1990 plus one-quarter of the allowances due for the year ended 31 December 1991. This means, in many cases, that estimated capital allowances computations have to be provided and then changed when the next year's accounts are submitted.

(c) Changes in the individual members of the partnership will be dealt with as at **381**(1) above, without reference to the position of the company.

(d) If a company sells part of its share in the boat, the sale price will be set against the written-down value and either a balancing charge raised or a reduced allowance given.

(e) If the company leaves the partnership, there will be a balancing adjustment by reference to the sale price and the written-down value of its share.

229

Grants

382 Decommissioning grants to encourage fishermen to decommission vessels because of surplus capacity following the limits imposed by the EC on the amounts each nation could catch, ceased in 1986. Where grants have been received for the building of new vessels, the grant must be deducted from the cost for the purposes of claiming capital allowances. Grants are available from the Sea Fish Industry Authority for safety. Where approval is obtained from the EC, the Sea Fish Industry Authority will make grants for re-engining or the replacement of vessels lost at sea. This ended at 31 December 1991. The tax treatment of such grants follows normal principles.

River and sea pilots

383 Consider the following.

(1) General

Such pilots can be self-employed. However, following s.607 ICTA 1988, all contributions to a pilot's benevolent fund established under s.15(1)(i) of the Pilotage Act 1983 (or any scheme supplementing or replacing any such fund) may, if the Board gives approval to the fund, count as contributions under an approved pension scheme as if the pilot were an employee. Consequently, all contributions, from the time that approval is given by the Pension Schemes Office, will, subject (presumably) to the usual limits laid down for employees' contributions, be allowed as a trading expense for tax purposes, in the same way as the contributions of general medical practitioners and dentists. The pilots will then be treated as holding a pensionable office or employment for the purposes of the retirement annuity provisions, and thus will no longer be able to make such payments. From 1 July 1988, under ss.630 and 655 ICTA 1988, retirement annuity contracts are superseded by the new personal pension scheme rules. Existing retirement annuity contracts, however, can be continued.

(2) Compensation payments by Trinity House

Some freelance sea pilots in certain areas have had their earnings from Trinity House reduced or terminated, following the increasing use of its own boats and pilots by Trinity House, and *ex gratia* compensation payments have been made by Trinity House to such pilots. Where the Trinity House business accounted for a large proportion of the pilot's business, it is likely that the payments will be exempt from tax, following the principles outlined in Simpson *v.* John Reynolds & Co (Insurances) Ltd (1975) 49 TC 693 and Murray *v.* Goodhews (1977) 52 TC 86.

Chapter 21
Private schools, higher education institutions, teachers etc.

Definition of a charity

384 Many schools and university colleges are recognised as charities. In CIR *v.* Pemsel (3 TC 53) a charity was defined as including a body existing for the furtherance of education. In general, where the education is available to children generally and is not confined to particular categories of children or is not of a specialist kind, for instance in a narrow field of technical education, charitable status is given for tax purposes.

Public schools

385 If a school is a public school, that is in the original sense of the term open to all entrants, it will be accepted as a charity. It need not be wholly supported by charity to rank as a public school. A number of factors have been held to be indicative that a school is a public school and thus a charity. These are:

(a) Part of the income is used for providing scholarships.

(b) The foundation of the school is perpetual. Although the absence of such a foundation proved fatal in Birkenhead School Ltd *v.* Dring (11 TC 273), in the later case of Ereaut *v.* Girls Public Day School Trust Ltd (15 TC 529), it was stated that this was not decisive.

(c) The managers are a public body.

(d) No individual is financially interested in the school.

(e) The school does not aim primarily to make a profit from its activities but to provide a public school education for its pupils. Therefore, although money was paid to shareholders, as education was the primary object in Ereaut *v.* Girls Public Day Schools Trust Ltd, the trust was regarded as charitable.

(f) The objects of the school are to provide an education for a large class of Her Majesty's subjects and are not confined to a small group of individuals

(Blake *v.* London Corporation, 2 TC 209; and Trustees of the Cardinal Vaughan Memorial School *v.* Ryall, 7 TC 611).

Effect of charitable status

386 It should be noted that charitable status does not confer automatic exemption from tax on all forms of income and capital gains but, if a school is a charity, it is exempt from income tax or corporation tax (s.505 ICTA 1988) on the following specific types of income:

(a) Rents assessable under Sch. A or Sch. D.
(b) Income from which tax is deducted under Sch. C (mainly interest on British Government securities).
(c) Interest or annual payments falling within Sch. D (this would include deeds of convenant).
(d) Dividends from UK companies.
(e) Profits from a trade if either: (i) the trade is exercised in the course of the actual carrying on of the primary purpose of the charity. Thus old cases, such as Brighton College *v.* Marriott (10 TC 213), where the College, although accepted as a charity, made a profit from charging fees and was assessed on the profit although it was exempt on other sources of income, should not be relevant now; or (ii) the work in connection with the trade is mainly carried out by beneficiaries of the charity. Examples of such trades in the case of a school would be carrying on such peripheral trades as charging visitors to see historical buildings of the school or charging members of the public to see dramatic performances by members of the school.

387 Where the profits from bazaars, jumble sales, etc, in aid of a charity such as occasional fund raising by a school which is a charity, fall within the tax definition of a trade (s.832(1) ICTA 1988) and are outside the scope of these statutory exemptions for certain trading activities, there is also an Extra-Statutory Concession (ESC C5) exempting the profits from tax.

388 The following conditions have to be satisfied:

(a) The organisation is not regularly trading in this way.
(b) The trading is not in competition with other traders.
(c) The activities are supported substantially because the public are aware that any profits will be devoted to charity.
(d) The profits are applied for charitable purposes.

389 Where the school is trading and cannot claim statutory exemption from tax on its trading profits or claim the benefit of the Extra-Statutory Concession, for instance, because it is running on a regular basis a peripheral trading activity not connected with the main educational purpose of the school or run by pupils, it is allowed to make a deduction in its trading accounts of such running expenses as it might have incurred if the trade had been on a normal commercial basis. Thus a price can be put on voluntary help, rent-free premises, and any other things that would normally qualify as allowable business expenses (British Legion Peterhead *v.* CIR, 35 TC 509). Schools are allowing their premises to be used for leisure holidays, summer schools and conferences to add to their income.

390 In such a situation, it might be preferable for a separate company to be formed to carry on the above activities. Any profits can then be covenanted to the charity. It is normal practice for the payment under the covenant to be for a larger sum than the estimated profits, as it has to be paid before the end of the accounting period in question, and any refund is then made when the profits have been agreed. Even if the company is formed as a subsidiary of an existing charitable company, the covenant cannot now be paid gross under a group election (s.339(7) ICTA 1988).

391 All these exemptions are given on the basis that the income will be applied for charitable purposes, that is in defraying the general running expenses of the school.

392 Public schools are similarly exempt from capital gains tax (s.256 TCGA 1992), provided again that the chargeable gains are applied for charitable purposes.

It appears that schools which rank as charities cannot claim exemption from tax on profits chargeable as income from land under s.776 ITCA 1988 (artificial transactions in land). Therefore, if there is any risk that this section may apply, an application for clearance may be a desirable course of action.

Investment income

393 Most schools have been endowed with investments, some of which are subject to special trusts to provide scholarships, for instance, for boys from a particular prep. school. The income from such special scholarship funds falling under one of the categories of income mentioned above should normally be exempt from tax, provided that the class of potential beneficiaries is sufficiently wide to come within the ambit of a charitable purpose.

Covenants

394 Appeals for carrying out improvements to school buildings, etc, very often take the form of invitations to make payments under deeds of covenant. Provided the covenant has been capable of exceeding three years, the payment should rank as income of the school and not the settlor (s.660 ICTA 1988) and tax can be reclaimed by the school if the money is used for the purposes of the appeal. If the school needs the total amount due under the covenants at the outset, this can be loaned by the covenantor and the loan is then repaid out of the annual payments which are made over three years. This is known as a deposited covenant. Such a loan was not caught by the old interest-free loans CTT provisions as it was made to a charity (ss.115 and 116 FA 1976). These provisions were subsequently repealed. It is understood that an interest-free loan to a charity which cannot exceed three years might be construed by the Inland Revenue as a disposition for tax purposes if the income generated from money invested from the loan was clearly identifiable, so that any income would then be treated as that of the settlor. Thus, such a loan to a school to provide income for the school would not be effective for tax purposes, quite apart from the dangers of the application of other anti-avoidance provisions connected with loans (s.786 ICTA 1988).

Statement of Practice 4/90 makes it clear that in a case of a loan or deposit covenant it is the deed of covenant which creates the covenantor's obligation to make the payment to the charity so that the deed must have been completed at or before the time of the first payment.

Retrospective covenants

395 In the past, the Claims Branch of the Inland Revenue (Charity Division) has sometimes allowed payments already made to a charity to be treated as made under a subsequently executed deed of covenant. A deed takes effect from its date of execution, so that payments made earlier are made under no legal obligation. However, such a payment could gain tax relief if made both within a period of retrospection specified in the deed and within the current fiscal year. For example, a covenant to make annual payments for a 'period of four years commencing on 6 April last' would gain relief for a payment (or instalments) already made in that fiscal year. Thus an initial gift to the school could be embraced into a subsequent convenant.

This practice was withdrawn following the decision in Morley-Clarke *v.* Jones (1985) STC 660 which made it clear that the practice was not in accordance with the law. However, the Inland Revenue have stated in Statement of Practice 4/90 (Charitable Covenants) that where claims had previously been made on this basis they would continue to accept further claims made before 31 July 1990.

In the same Statement of Practice, the Inland Revenue stated that they would continue to allow existing covenants with escape clauses, although strictly these clauses invalidate the covenant for tax because the covenantor can of his own volition terminate it without the consent of the charity. Examples include ceasing to work for the same employer or to be a member of the charitable body concerned. Such covenants in existence at 20 March 1990 will continue to be accepted until they expire, but new ones with escape clauses will not be regarded as valid.

396 Generally, a deed of covenant had to be executed under seal, that is incorporate words such as 'signed, sealed and delivered . . .' or 'Given under my hand and seal . . .'. It is understood that the Special Commissioners decided that where a charity's printed deeds of covenant did not include this wording, they were ineffective. A company's deed had to have the company's seal impressed upon it in the presence of certain officials. In a Press Release dated 20 March 1990, it was pointed out that a covenant must be signed and dated. In England and Wales it is mandatory from 31 July 1990 for the covenant to be witnessed, following the coming into force of the Law of Property (Miscellaneous Provisions) Act 1989. Under the Act, the sealing requirement has disappeared with effect from the same date.

The Inland Revenue have published model deeds of covenant in the same press release.

397 It should be noted that deeds of covenant cannot be used to pay a specific child's school fees by a parent as one of the essential characteristics of an annual payment – which is what a deed of covenant is – would not be present, namely that it is pure income profit in the hands of the recipient and is not received in return for goods or services (see CIR *v.* Corporation of London (as Conservators of Epping Forest), 34 TC 293; and CIR *v.* National Book League, 37 TC 455).

A deed of covenant, therefore, can only be used for raising money for capital projects. Now it is also possible to use the Gift Aid Scheme where one-off payments to a charity of at least £400 (formerly £600) net will qualify for full tax relief. The procedure should involve only writing a letter evidencing the gift and the deduction of tax from the gift.

Payment of school fees in the case of separated parents

398 For payments falling due on or before 14 March 1988 and in respect of obligations entered into before that date, insofar as they relate to deduction of tax up to 1989/90, the only certain means of obtaining tax relief on payments of school fees was where a father made payments under a Court Order for the maintenance of his children and these payments were used to meet school fees. It was possible to make such payments direct to the school and to obtain tax relief provided the order was correctly worded.

The contents of suitable maintenance orders were outlined in a Practice Direction dated 20 November 1980 issued by the Senior Registrar of the Family Division which read as follows:

"It sometimes arises that a father is ordered to make periodical payments in respect of his children which include an element on account of school fees. Courts will wish to know that an arrangement has recently been made with the Inland Revenue whereby school fees may be paid directly to the school and tax relief will be allowed on the part of the payment made in respect of them if the order directing payment contains the following formula.

"that that part of the order which reflects the school fees shall be paid to the (headmaster) (bursar) (school secretary) as agent for the said child and the receipt of that payee shall be a sufficient discharge."

It would appear that this arrangement is not widely known, either to members of the profession or to local Tax Inspectors, and the Lord

Chancellor's Department is currently considering means of giving the matter wider publicity."

399 There were sometimes misunderstandings by schools on the form of the contract which had to be used and a reluctance to provide evidence that the contract was made between the child and the school's representative as his agent, and not between the parent and the school. Also, the original wording did not seem to be sufficiently flexible to cope with the inevitable increases in fees and the need to refer to the deduction of tax from the payments, as they had to be aggregated with other payments in seeing whether the small maintenance payments limits had been exceeded. In any event, in most cases, it was convenient for the payments to be made termly and, therefore, they could not be small maintenance payments (which have to be paid weekly or monthly).

400 In view of these difficulties, on 16 June 1983, the Senior Registrar issued a new Direction – Practice Direction (Minor: Payment of School Fees). The contents of this Direction are reproduced below:

"Maintenance orders which contain an element in respect of school fees frequently have to be varied when the school fees increase. This requirement could be avoided if the relevant part of the maintenance order were to be automatically adjusted when the school fees go up.

The Inland Revenue have agreed to this principle. A form of order which they would find acceptable is as follows:

It is ordered that the [petitioner] [respondent] do pay or cause to be paid to the child AB as from the   day of   19   until [he] [she] shall attain the age of 17 years [or for so long as [he] [she] shall continue to receive full-time education] or further order periodical payments for [himself] [herself]

(a) of an amount equivalent to such sum as after deduction of income tax at the basic rate equals the school fees [but not the extras in the school bill] [including specified extras] at the school the said child attends for each financial year [by way of three payments on   and   and   ] [payable monthly]; together with

(b) the sum of £   per annum less tax payable monthly in respect of general maintenance of the said child."

It should be noted that, even if the amount referred to in part (b) was within the limits for small maintenance payments, it still needed to be expressed as 'less tax' because the relevant figure for the maintenance order was the combined total of the two parts.

In such cases the Inland Revenue had to be satisfied that the payer under the order was under no contractual liability for payment of the school fees.

If an order expressed as payable to the child, whether made in this form, or in a form which included an element in respect of school fees for a specific amount, also provided that payment of the element representing school fees should be paid direct to the school (because, for example, it was feared that the other spouse might dissipate it) the Inland Revenue agreed, subject to the condition hereafter set out, that tax relief would be given on that element. The wording of the order was:

"And it is further ordered that that part of the order which reflects the school fees shall be paid to the [Headmaster] [Bursar] [School Secretary] as agent for the said child and the receipt of that payee shall be sufficient discharge."

The school fees needed to be paid *in full* and out of the net amount under the maintenance order after deduction of tax. Certificates for the full tax deduction were to be provided by the other spouse (or other person referred to in rule 69 of the Matrimonial Causes Rules 1977) (SI 1977 No 344) in the normal way.

It was a condition of such an order being acceptable for tax purposes that the contract for the child's education (which was preferably in writing) should be between the child (whose income was being used) and the school, and that the fees were received by the officer of the school as the appointed agent for the child.

A form of contract which was acceptable to the Inland Revenue was as follows:

"THIS AGREEMENT is made between THE GOVERNORS OF ....
....
by their duly authorized officer .... (hereinafter
called "the School") of the first part; ....
and the [Headmaster] [Bursar] [School Secretary] of the second part, and
.... (hereinafter called "the child") of the third part.
WHEREAS [it is proposed to ask the .... Court to
make an order] [the .... Court has made
an order] in cause number .... that the Father of the
Child do make periodical payments to the child at the rate of £ .... per annum
less tax until the Child completes full time education (or as the case may be) and
that that part of the order which reflects the school fees shall be paid to the
[Headmaster] [Bursar] [School Secretary] as agent for the Child and the receipt of
that agent shall be a sufficient discharge.

1. The Child hereby constitutes the [Headmaster] [Bursar] [School Secretary] to
   be his agent for the purpose of receiving the said fees and the Child agrees to pay
   the said fees to the said School in consideration of being educated there.
2. In consideration of the said covenant the [Headmaster] [Bursar] [School
   Secretary] agrees to accept the said payments by the Father as payments on
   behalf of the Child and the School agrees to educate the Child during such times
   as the said school fees are paid.

Dated the   day of   19

This direction supersedes the registrar's direction of 10 November 1980, which is hereby cancelled; see *Practice Direction (Minor: School fees)* (1980) 1 WLR 1441. Issued with the concurrence of the Lord Chancellor.

B.P. TICKLE
Senior Registrar"

401　It can be seen from this Practice Direction that, where an Order required an annual payment by reference to a fixed formula rather than a specific sum of money, it could attract tax relief, a fact which the Inland Revenue have confirmed. It was also necessary for the payments to be 'annual payments'. If the Court merely ordered a parent to pay a child's school fees, relief would be refused on the grounds that the order did not require an annual payment (that is a transfer of taxable income) but only a continuation of the parent's normal responsibility to provide his child with a proper education.

402　The alternative, not involving the school, was for the Court order to provide for increased payments to be made direct to the child, including Magistrates Court Orders as was possible since the Magistrates Courts Matrimonial Proceedings Act 1978. There could, however, be a risk of the increased maintenance being utilised by, say, the custodian mother for some other purpose, as the maintenance had to be paid into a bank account, at the very best, in the joint names of the child and his/her custodial parent or the parent having care and control of him/her where there was joint custody. The only safeguard against this was to open the account in the name of the child and another relation, or perhaps a solicitor or other professional adviser.

The position has changed with the revisions in the Finance Act 1988 to the tax position of maintenance payments generally. Existing obligations at 14 March 1988 will continue to enjoy tax relief, subjects to the "freezing" of limits by reference to the amounts paid in 1988/89. In addition, payments are made gross from 1989/90 so that in the case of school fees, the gross equivalent of what was paid in 1988/89 may be paid to the school in future years.

In the case of new obligations entered into after 14 March 1988, the maintaining parent will simply be entitled to the special allowance or the amount of the maintenance whichever is the lesser, the former being the same as the married couples allowance for all maintenance payments to or for the benefit of all his children(s.347B ICTA 1988).

Capital allowances

403　Should it be necessary for a school to prepare tax computations, for instance, because it is not a charitable body, the accounts and computations will proceed on the normal basis for an unincorporated business or a limited company as appropriate. In this connection, the importance of keeping records sufficient to enable claims to be made for capital allowances on items ranking as plant and machinery was illustrated in the case of St John's School (Mountford and Knibbs) *v*. Ward (1975) STC 7. In that case, a claim that a prefabricated school gymnasium and its contents was plant in its entirety was rejected and it appears from the facts of the case that the school put forward this claim partly because it had not been able to segregate satisfactorily costs relating to items which were admitted as plant such as gymnasium equipment.

Academics, teachers, etc.

404 Employees of non-trading bodies, including charities, are potentially brought within the scope of the benefits provisions for directors and employees earning at a rate of £8,500 per annum or more (hereafter called higher-paid employees) (see especially ss.153–168 ICTA 1988). Equally, *all* employees are potentially liable to tax on the value of living accommodation provided for them by reason of their employment, and directors and higher-paid employees are also potentially liable on any expenses of upkeep of such accommodation borne by the employer (ss.145, 146, 155(2) and 163 ICTA 1988).

(a) Taxation of bursaries, scholarships, etc.

Income in the form of a 'scholarship or bursary' is specifically exempt from tax, although no guidance is given as to what is meant by those terms in the Act (s.331 ICTA 1988).

In some cases, this includes income from fellowships, etc., which have been agreed by the Inland Revenue to be tax-free where, broadly, the income is designed to enable the recipient to do research towards a higher degree rather than to teach. In most cases, the college will have agreed the position with the Inland Revenue.

Generally, research grants will be taxable where a person is engaged in other professional work for which he is or has been paid as the research grant will usually be to enable him to do the research without undue loss of income (see Duff *v*. Williamson (1973) STC 434).

Exemption or relief from tax may also be available under a Statement of Practice and two Extra-Statutory Concessions published on 8 August 1986.

Under the Statement of Practice, where certain qualifying conditions are met, payments for attendance on a full-time educational course (including a sandwich course) at a university, technical college or similar educational establishment open to the public at large are exempt from tax. The period of enrolment must be at least one academic year and actual full-time attendance during that period must average at least 20 weeks a year. The rate of payment including lodging, subsistence and travelling allowances, but excluding any university etc. fees, must not exceed the higher of £5,500 a year (or the equivalent monthly or weekly rates) or the grant which would have been payable in similar circumstances by a public awarding body. Where payments exceed the above limits, they are taxable in full (Inland Revenue Statement of Practice 4/86, dated 8 August 1986 and Inland Revenue Press Release dated 12 April 1989).

Similarly, exemption from tax for course fees paid or reimbursed by an employer and a deduction for the cost of essential books may be available under two Inland Revenue Extra-Statutory Concessions (A63 and A64), published on the same date.

The first concession grants an employee exemption from tax in respect of certain expenses borne by the employer in respect of course fees and the cost of essential books. The course in question must be a general education course of a type commonly undertaken at school and the employee must be under 21 when the course starts. Alternatively, the training must lead to the acquisition of knowledge or skills that are necessary for the duties of the employment or directly related to increasing the employee's effectiveness in the performance of present or prospective duties.

The second concession allows a deduction to an employee in respect of the cost of essential books and course fees that he has personally incurred, provided that the employee continues to receive his full salary and that he is allowed time off to attend the course during normal working hours. The course must be one which the employee is required or encouraged to attend by his employer to increase his effectiveness in the performance of present or prospective duties in the employment. The course must be full time and require attendance on every, or virtually every, working day for four consecutive weeks or more. Where a course consists of a number of blocks, only those blocks which last for four weeks or more will qualify for relief. Re-sit courses are excluded, as are courses outside the UK.

Both Extra-Statutory Concessions are extended to cover fees, additional travelling expenses and reasonable subsistence payments if the employee is temporarily absent from his normal place of work while attending the course. The requirement for the absence to be temporary will not be satisfied unless the period of absence will not exceed 12 months and the employee will return to his normal place of work at the end of that period. Neither concession depends on the course leading to the employee gaining a qualification.

This second concession was to avoid the problem that occurred in Humbles *v*. Brooks (1962) 40 TC 500, where a history teacher had paid to attend a course of history lectures. His claim was denied as the course was not attended in the performance of his duties. It made no difference that he was a better teacher for having attended the lectures. Formerly, the employer received tax relief on payments for technical education related to his trade and made to a university, school or technical college. Since FA 1991, this has been repealed and replaced by a section allowing relief for gifts of articles to educational establishments manufactured by him or used in his trade. This encourages gifts of computers and technical equipment. It means, however, that tax relief for whatever is not taxed on the employee under the Concession and Statement of Practice will follow general principles, ie., it will be part of his remuneration package and, therefore, deductible by the employer on general principles.

(b) Meals and entertaining

The provision of meals in any canteen in which meals are provided for the staff generally, is not taxable (s.155(5) ICTA 1988) and this includes refectories. It is also understood that expenditure on festive occasions when members of the school, etc. entertain guests of the school and parents, will not, in practice, give rise to a charge to tax on higher-paid employees, provided the expenditure is modest and the occasion is open to the staff generally. The Inland Revenue Press Release of 26 October 1984, which clarified the position, defined 'modest' as £30–35 a year for each member of staff. An Inland Revenue Extra-Statutory Concession, announced in an Inland Revenue Press Release dated 20 October 1988, increased this limit to £50 per head per year, and expenditure up to this amount need not be reported on form P11D. If the £50 limit is exceeded, tax is payable on the *full* amount.

Where a university teacher is reimbursed for entertaining expenses directly connected with the employment, such as those arising from tutorial duties or on the occasion of official visits, he or she generally will not be assessed to tax, even if 'higher-paid'. It is also likely that modest round-sum allowances will not be taxed, provided that the inspector can be satisfied that the allowance does not exceed the actual expenditure so incurred. According to the Association of University Teachers, expenses incurred out of a teacher's own remuneration on such entertaining will be allowed, although not strictly within s.198 ICTA 1988. However, the safest course is probably to seek to have the expenses reimbursed. The Inland Revenue are likely to look more kindly on expenditure that has first satisfied an employer's scrutiny.

(c) Remission of school fees

The whole issue of the tax impact of the remission of school fees has been squarely raised in Pepper *v*. Hart (1990) STC 786.

In that case the taxpayers were the bursar and assistant master at Malvern College, who were entitled under a concessionary fees scheme to educate their children at the college on payment on one-fifth of the ordinary fees. The Inland Revenue took the view that since the employees were higher-paid, the concessionary education was a benefit which fell within the provisions of s.154 ICTA 1988. Further, the measure of the charge (the 'cash equivalent' of the benefit) was a proportionate part of the total cost of running the school less the sums made good by the taxpayers in question. This view was rejected by the Special Commissioner but accepted by Vinelott J in the High Court. Under s.156 ICTA 1988 the cost of providing the benefit of a cheap education for the sons of employees of Malvern College was, insofar as the facilities used were those used by other boys in the school, a rateable proportion of the expenses incurred by the school in providing those facilities less the sums made good by the parent. Vinelott J described this as 'the inescapable effect of the legislation'. The interpretation of the legislation taken by the taxpayers and agreed by the Special Commissioner, that the value of the benefit was equivalent only to the direct additional costs referable to educating those pupils in addition to others, is the view which has historically been adopted. The decision has been upheld in the Court of Appeal but at the time of writing the House of Lords decision is awaited. In the meantime, revision to assessments should be resisted including the reopening of past years where the Inland Revenue have accepted the marginal cost method or any agreed scale benefit.

If the teacher's salary is adjusted downwards in return for the free education of the child, this reduction will constitute a taxable benefit on the principle decided in Heaton *v*. Bell (1969) 46 TC 211, whether the employee is higher paid or not.

(d) Research costs

Sometimes, a school teacher will undertake research projects as part of his duties. Where research costs are reimbursed in whole or in part by the school, the reimbursement is not taxed in the hands of a higher-paid employee, as the assessable income could be covered by an expense claim under s.198 ICTA 1988. Where it is not reimbursed, the inspector may, in practice, consider an expense claim where it is reasonable in nature and not unduly large (see also (h) below).

Similar considerations apply to university teachers. The AUT advises that deductions may be claimed for research expenses that are directly related to the teacher's subject and that are moderate in amount, if reimbursement is not available.

A claim is less likely to be successful to the extent that the research is voluntary on the teacher's part. Expenses incurred in preparing a thesis to secure advanced qualifications are not allowable for income tax purposes.

(e) Conference and course expenses

Reimbursed conference expenses are not taxed. However, a claim for allowance of unreimbursed conference expenses is likely to be challenged as not having been incurred wholly, exclusively and necessarily in the performance of the duties of the employment because there may be duality of purpose involved (see Bowden *v*. Russell and Russell (1965) 42 TC 301 and Edwards *v*. Warmsley, Henshall & Co. (1967) 44 TC 431).

A teacher seconded on full salary to attend a full-time course of training lasting at least four weeks may claim concessional relief on expenses necessarily incurred in attending the course, including the costs of accommodation, course fees, essential books and travelling (notes circulated by the Association of Teachers in Further and Higher Education and the Association of Polytechnic Teachers).

(f) Travel expenses

Most travelling expenses of academics on official business are reimbursed and, where the academic is higher-paid and taxed on the reimbursed expenses, an equivalent s.198 ICTA 1988 claim should be allowed or not on normal principles (Ricketts *v*. Colquhoun (1925) 10 TC 118 and Pook *v*. Owen (1969)

242

45 TC 571). However, it is reported that, where teachers or lecturers have to incur expenses of travelling between different places of work in the same town, the Inland Revenue have been reluctant to allow the expenses if they are not reimbursed by the school, college, etc., on the basis that they cannot have been necessarily incurred in the performance of the duties if the school does not reimburse them.

It is now reported that the Inland Revenue are prepared to give some measure of relief to college lecturers in respect of the cost of travelling between different parts of a college. Sessional lecturers employed at colleges of further education under typical County Council contracts are not entitled to claim travel expenses for distances under 10 miles. Full-time lecturers normally receive reimbursement. The Inland Revenue had argued against allowance on the basis that a college, albeit on two sites, was one place of employment, so that a person was not temporarily away from his normal place of employment. It is reported that the Inland Revenue have granted relief where the campuses in question are in different towns that were only 2.8 miles apart. It appears that in this situation, expenses of travelling can be claimed by teachers, lecturers and other part-time employees who work on the same day at different sites for the same employer.

The reimbursement of expenses incurred in going to the school from home will be taxable or not on normal principles. However, where no 'profit' has been made from the reimbursement, it appears that a lower-paid employee will not be taxable on the reimbursement, following the case of Donnelly *v.* Williamson (1982) STC 88, which concerned a lower-paid teacher who was reimbursed in respect of her expenses of voluntarily attending parents' evenings. In view of the small amount involved, the payment could not have been a contribution towards the overhead expenses of putting her car on the road. Thus the Court followed the principle in Pook *v.* Owen (1969) 45 TC 571 that no taxable profit can arise from a pure reimbursement of an actual outlay. In practice, Donnelly *v.* Williamson has only a limited application to small amounts of reimbursed expenditure. Reimbursed expenses of higher-paid teachers are treated as emoluments, subject to any claim for deductions under s.198 ICTA 1988 (s.153 ICTA 1988).

(g) Books, subscriptions and special clothing

Where there is an obligation for the teacher to provide his own text books for use in class or in the preparation of lectures, a deduction may be claimed for their cost. This would normally only be relevant in higher education.

The inspector may ask for a list of titles. Where substantial reference books are purchased, a claim for capital allowances may be accepted, unless the books are available in university or departmental libraries.

A deduction may be claimed for annual subscriptions to learned societies, so far as they are paid to secure professional literature for use in lectures or for research. No deduction is available for payments for life membership. The annual subscriptions to the National Association of Teachers in Further and Higher Education and to the Association of Polytechnic Teachers are allowable in full as subscriptions to professional bodies. The Inland Revenue normally allow a deduction of two-thirds of any annual subscription paid to the National Union of Teachers and to the central office of the Association of University Teachers, provided that it is defrayed out of the member's emoluments as a university teacher.

Academic dress, protective clothing (such as is used in laboratories) and gymnastic dress are examples of special clothing for which a deduction may be claimed on a 'renewals' basis.

(h) Study allowances

The position is different from university lecturers and those dealing with degree courses on the one hand, and ordinary teachers on the other.

The National Association of Teachers in Further and Higher Education, and the Association of Polytechnic Teachers, have circulated to all their members notes for guidance on deductible expenses. In connection with the use of accommodation at home, the Inland Revenue are prepared to grant a concessional allowance to those teachers involved in higher education (ie., degree level work) who can show that a study is required by the nature of their duties and is not used merely as a matter of convenience. It is unlikely that this concessional allowance will be granted to any teacher who is not obliged to engage in research.

Factors that such a teacher might bring to the attention of the inspector of taxes when seeking an allowance are the need to consult journals and reference books for the preparation of lectures as well as for research (where such material cannot reasonably be kept in a polytechnic or college room), and the overcrowding of staff accommodation at the polytechnic or college. The amount of any allowance will depend upon all relevant facts and, because of the exceptional nature of the concessional treatment, there can be no question of a flat-rate allowance. Where a room is set aside at home for exclusive use as a study, a broad guideline is to compare the floor space covered by the study with total floor space, excluding common areas such as entrance halls and bathrooms, and then apply this ratio to expenses such as heat and light, and cleaning and rent (but not water rates).

It has further been agreed that, where a study allowance is given under Sch. E, no liability to capital gains tax will be incurred on the sale of the dwelling, as regards the proportion of the sale price attributable to the study, provided that the dwelling is the teacher's only or main residence under the normal rules (s.222 TCGA 1992).

This nationally negotiated concession is not normally available to teachers at the primary or secondary level, who, therefore, have to rely on proving that the terms of their employment require them to work at home, not merely on research, but directly on school work. Otherwise, even if the availability of private study facilities at home improves the teacher's academic knowledge, the expenses of providing it are likely to be disallowed by the Inland Revenue on the basis of the case of Humbles *v.* Brooks (1962) 40 TC 500, where, as stated above, the Court refused to allow a school teacher's expenses of attending weekend lectures to improve his knowledge of the subjects he taught.

(i) Living accommodation

In most cases, employees such as wardens of halls of residence, headmasters, housemasters, chaplains and caretakers will escape a charge in respect of the provision of accommodation, by virtue of the exemptions for representative occupiers. If the employer paid the rates as well, this was included in the exemption (s.145(4) ICTA 1988). Furthermore, the additional charge under s.146 ICTA 1988 cannot apply where the master, etc. is exempt from any charge on the annual value of the property as a representative occupier (s.146(1)(b) ICTA 1988).

If there is a liability to the community charge on the part of a resident teacher, the Inland Revenue take the view that payment of the charge by the employer is a taxable benefit, as the employer is meeting a liability of the employee. Consequently, many schools and other educational establishments in such cases are paying additional salaries equal to the grossed-up equivalent of the charge, to prevent their residential staff becoming out of pocket.

If, in addition, a director or higher-paid employee is provided, by reason of his employment, with other services, including heating, lighting, cleaning and repairs, the provision of furniture and other effects normal for domestic occupation, he will be liable to income tax on the cost of those services (less any amount made good by the employee). However, if he is exempt from income tax on the value of the accommodation, because he is in representative occupation, his liability will be limited to ten per cent of his net emoluments after deducting expenses, capital allowances and payments to any superannuation scheme (s.163 ICTA 1988). The amount of the benefit will exclude any proportion of the cost of the services that is referable to professional use of the accommodation as a study, or for meetings connected with school matters.

(j) Other services

In addition, the cost of other services such as gardeners and domestic services other than cleaning, are treated as emoluments of directors or higher-paid employees and are taxable (without limit), under Sch. E (s.154(2) ICTA 1988), to the extent that they have not been made good by the director or employee. Lower-paid employees escape being charged, provided that the costs incurred are not their own liability that has been met by the employer. It is understood, in regard to gardeners, that, if the garden is not completely private but is open to the public or staff and pupils, the cost of upkeep will not be regarded as a benefit (for instance an Oxford college garden).

(k) Residences

It is now possible for someone who lives in job-related accommodation to obtain tax relief on a mortgage to buy another residence, and to obtain capital gains tax exemption on the sale of that residence (s.356 ICTA 1988 and s.222(8) TCGA 1992).

(l) Other income of teachers

As part of an attempt to reclassify certain earnings as falling within Sch. E rather than Sch. D, and thus to apply PAYE to them, one of the Inland Revenue Special Offices has issued instructions that all fees paid by local examination boards to GCSE and other examiners should be subject to PAYE. Most examiners have, in the past, been assessed to tax on such fees under Case II or sometimes Case VI of Sch. D. It is possible for the examiner still to receive the fees gross, where he can prove that he is not liable to tax by virtue of available personal allowances, and he completes a signed statement obtainable from the examining board in question, enabling that board to pay the fees gross.

The Inland Revenue have also required that, from 6 April 1983, basic rate income tax be deducted from payments to university teachers for setting, marking and invigilating examinations. An exception is again made for those who can demonstrate that no tax liability will arise on the income. There is also an exception for payments for occasional examining for an individual higher degree. Where expenses of travelling to examiners' meetings are reimbursed, the reimbursement may be made without deduction of income tax. Fees received for extra-mural lecturing, etc., should also be paid under deduction of tax. Payments for travel expenses in connection with such lecturing are likely to be in respect of travel from home and should be made under deduction of tax. Generally reference should be made to the recent cases of Walls *v.* Sinnett (1987) STC 236 and Sidey *v.* Phillips (1987) STC 87, in which part-time lecture fees paid by local authorities were held to be within Sch. E.

There is no special treatment for royalties received by academics. Some universities give a 'loan in aid' to a member of staff publishing a book and stipulate that the first charge on any royalties be the repayment of the loan. This can lead to the author being liable to income tax on income that he does not actually receive. Careful attention must be given to the wording of the contract with the publisher.

(m) Director of non-profit-making company

It should be noted that a director of a non-profit-making company, or a company established for charitable purposes only, who does not hold a material interest in the company (that is, who does not own with his associates more than five per cent of the ordinary share capital of the company), will not be treated as taxable on benefits within Chapter II, Part V ICTA 1988, unless he is also higher-paid (see s.167(5) ICTA 1988). This could cover a headmaster who is also a director of the company running the school, if his emoluments (including benefits and assessable expenses) do not exceed £8,500 in any tax year.

(n) Study leave overseas

Where a teacher continues to be paid while on study leave overseas, it might be argued that his remuneration arose from duties performed in the UK. However, by concession, it has been agreed between the teachers' associations and the Inland Revenue that an individual on such study leave will be treated as performing his duties wholly overseas for the purpose of the 100% deduction.

Chapter 22
Inventors and persons holding patent rights

Expenses – general

405 Unless an inventor is carrying on a wider trade of which devising a particular invention is the natural development or extension, the costs incurred in carrying out this work will not be allowable as a deduction from any income unless he obtains a patent in respect of the invention. If he is carrying on such a trade, then the allowance of the costs will be given on the basis of the normal test of whether they are incurred wholly and exclusively for the purposes of the trade.

The law of patents

406 To appreciate the means by which allowances are given to inventors, it is necessary to know something of the law governing patents in the UK. To ensure that no one pirates an invention, the inventor applies to the Patent Office for Letters Patent. Certain fees are payable to do this and usually the services of an experienced patent agent are used. A brief specification of the invention is lodged first in case anyone subsequently applies for a patent for a similar invention. Subsequently a complete specification is filed, and, if it is found acceptable, formal acceptance is notified by the Patent Office and details of the invention are published by the Patent Office. The date of acceptance for filing is the date on which the patent rights commence, although the actual Letters Patent are not issued until some time afterwards. The acceptance of the specification gives the inventor the exclusive right for 20 years from the date the rights commence to make or exploit in any way the invention in the UK under the Patents Act 1977. Formerly, before the introduction of that Act, the period was 16 years.

407 The rights lapse after four years unless annual renewal fees are paid and only exceptionally are the rights extended beyond 20 years. The rights so granted protect the invention only within the UK; other countries have similar provisions controlling the exploitation of inventions within their boundaries.

Inventors and persons holding patent rights

Unless otherwise stated, the tax provisions relating to patents cover patent rights acquired under the laws of any country.

408 Patent rights are thus defined (s.533(1) ICTA 1988) as 'the right to do or authorise the doing of anything which would but for that right be an infringement of a patent'.

The legal position has been further modified in the Copyrights, Designs and Patents Act 1988, but not so as to affect the tax treatment described below.

Income tax position on expenses

409 The income tax position is as follows on expenses of devising an invention:

(a) Where an individual or individuals have devised an invention and the expenditure incurred on it cannot be deducted in computing Case I profits, that is, there is no existing trade out of which the work flows naturally, an allowance is given for the amount of the expenditure by discharge or repayment against patent income of the year of assessment in which the expenditure was incurred (s.526(2) ICTA 1988) and any balance unrelieved can be carried forward and set against patent income of subsequent years. It cannot be allowed against other income in any year (s.528(2) ICTA 1988). It should also be noted that this allowance is only available to individuals. Where the individual carries on a trade, and the patent rights are to be used for the purposes of the trade, the allowance is given for the year in which the expenditure was incurred.

(b) Where any person incurs expenses on applying for or maintaining a patent, they are deductible in arriving at the Case I profit if the application is to obtain a patent for the purposes of a trade (s.83 ICTA 1988), otherwise they are allowed by discharge or repayment against patent income, any balance unabsorbed being carried forward against future patent income only (s.526(1) and 528(2) ICTA 1988). These fees and expenses are allowed whether or not patent rights are granted in respect of the invention concerned. A similar allowance is given for expenses incurred in maintaining or obtaining an extension of the term of a patent.

Treatment of receipts

Capital sums

410 Where patent rights are sold for a capital sum, that is where the person selling them is not carrying on a trade of dealing in patent rights and the sum can be classed as capital on the tests mentioned below, that sum is still charged to tax as income. The sale of patent rights includes, for this purpose, the sale of part of patent rights, the sale of a right to purchase patent rights, and the grant of a licence in respect of the patent in question (s.533(2) and (3) ICTA 1988).

Where the person selling the rights himself acquired them for a capital sum, only the profit is assessable.

411 The sum received is assessed under Case VI of Sch. D in six equal instalments spread over the six years commencing with the year in which the sum is received, with the option to have the whole sum assessed in one year (s.524(1) and (2) ICTA 1988). This will rank as earned income where the invention in respect of which the rights are sold was devised by the recipient of the capital sum (s.529 ICTA 1988).

Death

412 If the seller dies before the beginning of the sixth year of assessment, the unassessed balance of the capital sum will be assessed in the year of death unless the personal representatives claim that the extra tax payable in the year of death should be reduced to the tax that would have been payable if the unassessed balance had been taxed by equal instalments in each of the years to the year of death. The time limit for making such a claim is 30 days after receiving the notice of assessment relating to the year of death (s.525(1) and (2) ICTA 1988).

Non-residents

413 A person resident in the UK is liable on the sale of any patent right. A non-resident is liable in respect of the sale of UK patents, and, in that event, the payer is liable to deduct tax at the basic rate on the sum paid on account of the liability of the recipient unless exemption from UK tax is conferred by the terms of a double tax treaty (s.524(3) and (4) ICTA 1988) and the payer has been authorised by the Inland Revenue to make the payment gross.

Incorporation of business

414 Difficulties could arise in relation to patent rights on the incorporation of a business, as a capital sum for the sale of patent rights could include shares issued by the new company in exchange for the patent rights. Depending on the value of the shares, which in turn would depend on the value of the rights, a substantial income tax liability could arise to the inventor although the purchasing company could claim capital allowances as described below. The facility to elect for tax written down value on the rights because the purchaser could claim capital allowances under the old system for pre-1 April 1986 expenditure, can apply on transfers between persons under common control instead of the actual price paid, but this would only be relevant if the original rights had been purchased and thus had attracted capital allowances, not if the invention had been devised by the person assigning it to a company so that no original expenditure qualifying for capital allowances would have arisen (ss.157 and 158 CAA 1990). A similar problem arises if the rights are sold on loan account to a new company controlled by the vendor for a capital sum rather than in exchange for shares. In both cases, the rights would normally be treated as sold at open market value to fix the consideration paid by the purchaser for his capital allowances because the sale would have taken place between persons under common control. To get over this difficulty, an Extra-Statutory Concession was introduced under which, if an inventor sells the patent rights in this invention to a company which he controls for less than their open market value, whether on loan account or in exchange for shares of a low nominal value, the assessment on him is restricted to the actual sale price provided the purchasing company undertakes to restrict its capital allowances claim to that amount (ESC B17). The Inland Revenue apply the concession even where the company shows the patent in its account at its full market value, creating a share premium account in respect of the excess of the market value over the nominal value of the shares issued. It is arguable that Companies Act 1985 s.130 would apply to the transfer of a patent in exchange for shares, particularly following the case of Shearer *v*. Bercain Ltd (1980 STC 359), so that it is necessary for the company to reflect the patent in its accounts at its full market value. Provided, however, this is done by share premium account, it seems the concession is still applied by reference to the nominal value of the shares. The Inland Revenue do not take the point that the difference between the open market value and the amount taxed as income in those circumstances could also technically be liable to capital gains tax under the 'connected persons' rules as deemed consideration which has not suffered tax on it as income, provided the company only claims the actual cost should it dispose of the patents in arriving at its liability to corporation tax on any capital sum received.

This concession does not apply to patents sold on or after 1 April 1986 between persons who are under common control. The right to transfer at tax written down value between persons under common control patents which will qualify for capital allowances, was repealed in respect of expenditure on such rights incurred after 1 April 1986 (s.532(2) ICTA 1988). Instead, it is laid down that for capital allowances purposes, broadly, the sale price sticks provided it does not exceed the original capital expenditure. In addition, if there is no original expenditure on purchase, as is frequently the case with an inventor, but the seller receives a capital sum on which he is charged to income tax, the amount of that sum is brought into charge to tax (s.521(6)(b) ICTA 1988). Therefore, if a nominal amount is paid by the company for the patents, that will be effective for income tax purposes. The shares could be issued to the individual and subsequently the nominal amount paid by the company for the invention. If nothing is paid, the sum brought in for capital allowances purposes is the smallest of:

(a) The market value of the rights;
(b) The capital expenditure incurred by the seller; or
(c) Where capital expenditure was incurred by any person connected with the seller, that amount.

Therefore, it can be seen that if there was no capital expenditure, there will be no disposal value for capital allowances purposes and the vendor is free to minimise the capital amount in order to avoid an income tax liability.

So far as capital gains tax is concerned, the difference between the price paid and the market value can be held over if the transaction represents the disposal of an asset used in a trade to the company (s.165 TCGA 1992). However, if there is no use in the trade by a professional inventor, it is still thought the Inland Revenue would not argue for capital gains treatment on the basis that ultimately all the capital proceeds received by the company would be taxed as income.

It is interesting that although the facility to transfer assets at tax written down value between persons under the same control does not apply to patents, the provisions concerning assets qualifying for capital allowances and successions to trades between connected persons do apparently apply. Therefore, if the inventor carries on a trade, an election to transfer the patents at tax written down value should be possible, whatever the price paid, but only if they qualify on the basis of having been purchased in the first place. If the inventor has paid nothing for the patents, as is usually the case, the election (under s.77 CAA 1990) cannot be made.

Capital allowances

Old system for expenditure prior to 1 April 1986

415 Capital allowances could be claimed where a person paid a capital sum for the purchase of patent rights or a part of patent rights or for the grant of a licence. If the claimant was carrying on a trade and the rights were used for the trade, the allowance was given against trading profits. Otherwise, it was given by discharge or repayment against patent income only (s.520(1) and (2) ICTA 1988). The allowance was conditional upon either:

(a) the allowance being given against trading profits because the patent rights were to be used for the purposes of the trade; or
(b) the income from these rights being chargeable to UK income tax. For instance, under a double tax agreement, it is possible that patent royalties payable to a non-resident will not be liable to UK income tax. In that event, the purchase of the rights by such a non-resident could not attract allowances.

416 The amount of the allowance was a fraction of the expenditure of which the numerator was always one and the denominator varied as follows:

(a) If the rights were purchased for a specified period, the denominator was the number of years in that period up to a maximum of 17 – for this purpose a part year was counted as a year.
(b) If the rights were purchased outright before one complete year had elapsed since commencement of the patent, the denominator was 17. If after 16

complete years had elapsed the rights were purchased, the allowance was the amount of the expenditure. Otherwise the denominator was 17 less the number of complete years which had expired (s.520(3) ICTA 1988).

417 The allowances continued as long as the person remained eligible, that is, by carrying on a trade in which the rights were used, or by deriving income from the rights or until an event occurred to alter or stop the allowance. This could happen as follows:

(a) The rights coming to an end without being revived, in which case there was a balancing allowance for the expenditure unallowed.
(b) All the rights being sold for a capital sum. The person would then be given a balancing allowance or suffer a balancing charge, although the latter could not exceed the allowances already given.
(c) Part of the rights being sold or a licence being granted and any capital sum received equalling or exceeding the unallowed expenditure. In that case, there was a balancing charge on any excess over expenditure unallowed subject to the limit of the allowances already given. Any excess over cost was, of course, taxed under Case VI as income (s.523 ICTA 1988).

418 The allowances were given to a trader against trading profits, otherwise by discharge or repayment against patent income whilst a balancing charge was made by assessment under Case VI (ss.520, 521 and 523 ICTA 1988).

419 The allowances might alter if there had been sale of part of the rights or the grant of a licence where the capital sum received was less than the capital expenditure unallowed. In that event the capital expenditure unallowed was reduced by the capital sum received and the allowance became a fraction of that figure based on the number of remaining complete years for which the original allowances would have been due (s.524(7) (8) and (9) ICTA 1988).

Expenditure post-31 March 1986

For post-31 March 1986 capital expenditure the position is that allowances are given broadly on the same basis as for plant and machinery, ie., 25% of the balance in the pool of expenditure after allowing for sales.

An allowance will be made only in respect of expenditure where the person is carrying on a trade, or income receivable in respect of the rights would be liable to tax. Any pre-trading expenditure is treated for this purpose as incurred on the commencement of trading.

The allowance is based on 25% of the excess of any expenditure over any disposal value to be taken into account. There is a proportionately reduced percentage if the period does not cover a complete year. If the trade ceases, there is a balancing allowance equal to all the excess. Alternatively, if the last of the relevant patent rights lapses in the period without being renewed, there is a balancing allowance equal to the excess.

Where the whole or any part of the rights are sold, and on earlier purchase the vendor incurred capital expenditure qualifying for capital allowances, the disposal value is brought into account in calculating the writing down allowance or balancing adjustment. The disposal value will usually be the sale proceeds, subject to it not being in excess of cost, with the modifications mentioned above for special circumstances.

As with the previous system, allowances and charges are made in taxing the trade or given against patent income only in the case of a non-trader.

Royalties

420 The distinction between income and capital sums from the exploitation of patents has to some extent lost its significance with the taxation of capital sums as income in the manner described. However, there may in certain cases be situations where payer and payee are materially affected by the fact that they are paying and receiving a royalty; for instance, the incidence of tax may be higher in the case of a royalty in a particular year. A royalty covers payment in respect of past or future limited user restricted as to amount or quantity where there is no acquisition of a defined portion of the property in the patent. Other payments in respect of patents, for example, for outright acquisition, for exclusive use during the whole of the unexpired life, or for future unlimited user within a defined area or for a term of years, are generally treated as capital. If the Crown pays a lump sum to a patentee for the acquisition of a defined portion of the property in a patent, the transaction is treated as a capital sum (s.533(1) and (4) ICTA 1988).

421 A patent royalty is thus a sum paid for the user of a patent which ranks as income rather than capital. For this purpose, sums paid for rights incidental to the user of such a patent are to be regarded as sums paid in respect of the user of a patent.

422 Whether a sum derived from patents is income rather than capital has been before the courts several times. In Constantinesco v. Rex (11 TC 730), Mr Constantinesco and another person patented a mechanism used in many fighter planes. A Royal Commission appointed to consider claims for use of inventions by the Crown in war awarded them £70,000, from which tax was deducted. It was held that the £70,000 was not a capital sum but a payment for successive users of the patent in the past. Rowlatt J. remarked: "What ground is there for saying that this is not the total sum for the actual use as opposed to a lump sum to abolish the payment for the actual use and capitalise it?" In CIR v. British Salmson Engines Ltd (22 TC 29), the company obtained a licence for exclusive use for ten years in the UK and certain other areas of an invention and in return paid for the licence a lump sum payable in instalments, and, in addition, a royalty of so much per annum. It was held that the lump sum was capital.

423 In other words the sum paid must have the character of income to be treated as a royalty. The consequence is that, if the patent is a UK patent, the payer should deduct tax from the payment and account for it (s.348(2)(a) and s.349(1)(b) ICTA 1988) and no deduction is to be allowed for Case I purposes in respect of such a payment (s.74(p) ICTA 1988). A company will of course be able to claim the payment as a charge on income deductible from total profits (s.338(3)(a) ICTA 1988).

Deduction of tax

424   It should be noted that deduction of tax can only take place where the patent is protected by a UK patent, as there can be no machinery for deducting UK tax from an agreement made outside the UK. However, under some double tax agreements, patent royalties paid by a UK resident to a resident of the other country which would otherwise be subject to deduction of UK tax are exempt from UK tax if the Inland Revenue are satisfied that the provisions of the treaty apply.

Foreign patents

425   Royalties received from foreign patents by a UK resident are taxed under Case V of Sch. D. Royalties received under deduction of income tax are income of the year for which the deduction of income tax is made (s.835(6) ICTA 1988), for the purposes of any liability to higher rates. Royalties from foreign patents follow the normal Case V rules of assessment.

Earned income

426   All royalties will rank as earned income if received by the inventor of the patented device (s.529 ICTA 1988) and should thus qualify as relevant earnings for retirement annuity and personal pension purposes.

Spreading provisions

427   To prevent the bunching of income in one year in respect of a royalty, there are provisions for spreading patent royalties over several years (s.527 ICTA 1988). If the use extends to six years or more, and tax is deducted, then the recipient may claim to have his liability computed as if he had received one-sixth of the sum annually for the six years ending with the year in which the payment is made. Where the period of use is two complete years or more but less than six, the payment may be spread over the years of use.

Know-how

428   An inventor is unlikely in most cases to be the possessor of know-how in the taxation sense. This is defined as 'any industrial information and techniques likely to assist in the manufacture or processing of goods or materials' (s.533(7) ICTA 1988).

429   Specific legislation was introduced in 1968 relating to dealings in such known-how as a result of a series of cases involving the sale of know-how for what were claimed to be capital sums. In some cases this was upheld by the court on the basis usually that the sale also involved effectively the sale of part of the vendor's business and the capital assets of the business were permanently reduced (see Evans Medical Supplies Ltd *v.* Moriarty, 37 TC 540; Jeffrey *v.* Rolls-Royce Ltd, 40 TC 443; Wolf Electric Tools Ltd *v.* Wilson, 45 TC 326; and Thomsons (Carron) Ltd *v.* CIR, 1976 STC 317). Where shares were issued as consideration for the know-how, and the shares were issued in instalments, the know-how was taxed in the year of receipt of the shares (John & E Sturge *v.* Hessel, 1975 STC 573).

430 Where exceptionally an inventor does generate such know-how, if he is able to exploit it by selling it without selling a trade or part of a trade, and it would otherwise still be treated as capital, he will now be charged on any profit he makes (after deducting any expenses on the acquisition or disposal of the know-how) under Case VI which will then be treated as earned income if he devised the know-how in question (s.531(4)(5) and (6) ICTA 1988). This provision does not apply if the sale is to a person under his control, for instance his own company, in which event the sale would be treated as the sale of goodwill chargeable to capital gains tax.

431 It is important to avoid this charge to income tax on a sale of know-how as there are no spreading provisions. It might be sensible, if practicable, to arrange a prior sale to a company controlled by the inventor and for that company to sell on at no profit so that the sale to the company is liable only to capital gains tax depending on base values of course of the know-how for capital gains tax purposes.

432 The other provisions on know-how are unlikely to be relevant in the case of an individual inventor and therefore are not dealt with in this book.

In the case of capital allowances where capital sums are paid for the acquisition of know-how, the rules similarly have been changed depending upon whether the acquisition is after 31 March 1986. Before then, broadly, the expenditure qualified for allowances of 1/6th of the expenditure every year. Thereafter the rules follow closely those for patents. Similarly, there is no longer the facility to elect for tax written down value in the case of controlled sales (Section 532(5) ICTA 1988).

Trade marks and designs

433 A design 'right' is an original non-common place design of shape or configuration of articles which is now covered by ss.213–216 Copyright, Designs and Patents Act 1988. Protection for a design right is an exclusive right of marketing for 5 years with extensions to 10 to 15 years, but allowing others to have licences in this period.

The inventor may wish to register a trade mark or design. The registration of trade marks or designs protects the goods and also offers opportunities for exploitation of the mark or design as with a patent by licensing or straight-forward assignment of the rights.

The Registered Designs Act 1949 (as amended by s.265 Copyright, Designs and Patents Act 1988) defines designs (s.3) as 'features of shape, configuration, pattern or ornament applied to an article by any industrial process or means being features which, in the finished article, appeal to and are judged solely by the eye'. Trade marks, defined under the Trade Marks Act 1938 as marks 'distinctive of' or 'capable of distinguishing' the product, acquire permanent protection.

434 Unlike patents and copyrights there is practically no mention of trade marks or registered designs in the Taxes Acts. Licensing to manufacture a product will involve patent licences, copyright drawings and licensed use of trade marks and designs of the inventor. Royalties for the use of a design or trade mark are not normally subject to deduction of tax by the payer and will be taxable when receivable as trading income in the hands of the inventor. The inventor will want relatively more attached by way of royalty to trade marks than designs or patents which have limited lives but the Inland Revenue can challenge the allocation if it is totally artificial (see Paterson Engineering Co Ltd *v.* Duff 25 TC 43).

However, following the enactment of the Copyright, Designs and Patents Act, with effect from 1 August 1989 under s.537A and B ICTA 1988, the designer who assigns or grants a licence for that design which has taken more than 12 months to create, may claim to have the lump sum or periodic payments taxed over a period of two years, in two equal instalments, one instalment being assessed on the date of receipt and the second being assessed 12 months previously (s.537A(1) and (2) ICTA 1988).

If the creation of the design has taken more than two years then an election can be made to have the receipts assessed in three equal amounts on the date of receipt, 12 months prior to that date and the third assessed 24 months prior to the date of receipt (s.537A(1) and (3) ICTA 1988).

If the owner of the design in respect of which royalties are paid lives abroad, then tax must be deducted under s.349 ICTA 1988 and accounted for to the Inland Revenue after taking into account agents' commissions in respect of royalties.

Case III and trade marks

435 If the registered trade marks and designs were hived off from the inventor's trade, for instance into a company, they would be held as an investment so that the income would probably be assessable under Case III with formerly all the problems of apportionment in the case of a close company and deduction of tax at source. In this situation, it appears that, as the royalties will be pure income profit in the hands of the recipient, they would be regarded as an annual payment of the payer and subject to deduction of tax under s.349 and 350 ICTA 1988 in the same way as patent royalties.

Capital or income

436 If the inventor sold his invention and with it the trade mark or design for a lump sum and nothing was left of his business as a result, the parts of the proceeds attributable to the trade mark or design should be capital as being for the total loss of the sub-stratum of the business (see Handley Page Ltd *v.* Butterworth 19 TC 328). It also seems from that case that an outright sale of one of several designs or trade marks by an inventor would be a capital receipt if the capital asset concerned ceased to be owned. However, if the lump sum was paid for a licence, it would normally be treated as income on general principles on the basis that the asset had been retained.

437 Any capital receipt will, of course, be liable as a chargeable gain under s.21 TCGA 1992. The same principles would apply if the inventor was unable to register the design.

Fees and expenses

438 It is specifically provided that the fees or expenses incurred in the registration of a design or trade mark, or in an extension of the period of copyright in a design or a renewal of the registration of a trade mark, can be treated by virtue of s.83 ICTA 1988 as a trading expense, even if they may give rise to a capital asset and would otherwise be disallowed under s.74(f) ICTA 1988.

Chapter 23
Subcontractors

Tax deduction scheme

439 A tax deduction scheme for subcontractors in the construction and building industry was introduced in 1971. Under the scheme in its original form, a contractor making a payment to a self-employed subcontractor had to deduct tax at the current standard rate and pay it over to the Inland Revenue, unless the subcontractor had an exemption certificate or was a limited company. The system led to abuses in the falsification of certificates or the proliferation of small companies and has been completely revised by FA (No 2) 1975 with effect from 6 April 1977 (s.559 *et seq* ICTA 1988). The Government announced in 1979 that it was reviewing the present system and invited views from the construction industry on how it could be modified in certain areas where there were abuses or where a strict application of the law involved hardship. The results of this review gave rise to a number of relaxations incorporated in the Finance Acts 1980 and 1982.

440 The present scheme is designed to ensure that payments are only made without deduction of tax to persons who have a record of settling their tax liabilities in a satisfactory manner and it incorporates a number of checks to monitor the correctness of the returns such people make to the Inland Revenue. It now also accommodates the position of those whose history of continuous employment is too short, such as school leavers.

Main features of the scheme

441 The main features of the scheme are described in the following paragraphs.

442 The scheme operates in relation to payments made by a contractor to a subcontractor under a contract relating to construction operations. Contractor for this purpose includes a local authority, any development corporation or new town commission or housing corporation, and large concerns which maintain their own building departments which, broadly, spend on average more than £250,000 a year on construction operations as well as ordinary builders and contractors and a gang leader where the members of the gang work for him and are self-employed (s.560(2) ICTA 1988). A subcontractor means anyone carrying out construction operations for a contractor and therefore includes a person working for another subcontractor such as someone doing contract work for a local authority (s.560(1) ICTA 1988). The term covers a company as well as an individual or partnership.

Exemption certificates

443 Subcontractors who meet the qualifying conditions will receive from the Inland Revenue an exemption certificate so that they can be paid for their services without deduction of tax. There are four sorts of certificate:
(a) The I certificate (Form 714I) issued to an individual in business on his own account.
(b) The P certificate (Form 714P) issued to an individual who is a partner in a firm and to certain companies.
(c) The C certificate (Form 714C) issued to certain other companies.
(d) The S (or Special) certificate (Form 714S) issued, subject to certain conditions, to an individual in business on his own who cannot qualify for an I certificate. Unlike the I, P and C certificates there is a limit to the payments an S certificate holder can receive without deduction of tax, currently £150 per week.

In the case of a company, the Inland Revenue have the power to require the directors and shareholders to satisfy individually all the conditions that sole traders have to satisfy. The Inland Revenue can make a direction that the relevant individual requirements can apply to all or any of the directors where the company has not carried on construction business for three years preceding the application or does not hold a certificate. The Inland Revenue will exercise this power except in the case of the largest companies. Once it has made a direction, it will request a written agreement of the directors and/or share-holders specified in the direction that their individual affairs can be looked at in connection with the company's application. The Inland Revenue can also make the direction where there has been a change in control of a company (which must be notified to the Inspector within 30 days).

A company may be issued with certificates 714P bearing the name and photograph of the director empowered to present it. Where it would now be appropriate, the Inspector may issue a 714C which does not bear the name or photograph of any individual, does not necessarily need to be presented personally and does not require the use of vouchers. A 714C is usually issued only to large companies.

New style certificates (forms 714I, 714P, 714S and 714C) and vouchers (forms 715/715S) were introduced on 6 November 1986. The statutory authority for these changes is contained in s.561 and 566 ICTA 1988 and the Income Tax (Subcontractors in the Construction Industry) Regulations 1986. Specimens of the new style certificates and vouchers are illustrated on a revised contractors Checking Guide (IR 14/15) (Chart)(1986) to replace that shown at

Appendix H of the booklet IR 14/15 (1982). New style certificates can only be used with new style vouchers once old style vouchers have been exhausted.

444 Information about the certificates is given on the chart reproduced from IR 14/15 (1982):

Type of Certificate	I (Form 714I) (issued for most individuals)	P (Form 714P) (issued for a partnership)	P (Form 714P) (issued for a company)	C (Form 714C) (for a company not required to use vouchers)	S (Form 714S) (Special certificate for certain individuals)
Colour	Yellow	Red	Red	Pink/Beige	Green diagonal
Name of individual holder	√	√	√		√
Name of partnership to which holder belongs		√			
Name of company holder			√	√	
Business name (optional) (3)	√	√	√	√	√
National Insurance Number of individual holder	√	√			√
Company Registration Number of company holder			√	√	
Signature	√	√	√	√ (4)	√
Photograph of individual holder	√	√	√		√
Date of expiry (1)	√	√	√	√	√
Certificate number	√	√	√	√	√
Whether "Original" or "Official Copy" (and, if an "Official Copy", its number) (2)				√	

Note (1) The certificates show only the months and year for the date of expiry. They do not show the date of commencement. The actual date of expiry is the last day of the month of the year shown.
(2) A company holding a C certificate is issued with one C certificate marked 'Original' and sometimes a reistricted number of others marked 'Official Copy'. These official copies have their own additional serial numbers.
(3) Only one business name may be shown on a certificate.
(4) The signature is that of the secretary of the company at the date of issue.

445 The appropriate certificates must be applied for and exemption will only be given if the conditions laid down in FA (No 2) 1975 (as amended by the 1980 and 1982 Acts) and associated Regulations are met (ss.562–565 ICTA 1988). In the case of an application by an individual, the business must to a substantial extent be carried on by means of a bank account with proper records to enable accurate returns to be made and from proper premises with proper equipment, stock and other facilities. If the person was setting up such a business, he had, for the period of three years up to the date of application, to have been employed in the UK or carried on a trade, profession or vocation. He had also to have complied with his obligations to render accounts and returns under the Taxes Acts within the previous three years and to have paid any contributions due under the National Insurance and Social Security Acts. Thus, temporary absence overseas during the three-year period prevented compliance, as was illustrated by the case of Cooper *v.* Sercombe (1980 STC 76). The General Commissioners and the Courts have no power to exercise discretion in this sort of matter. Similar conditions, *mutatis mutandis*, have applied for partnerships and companies. Where a company has not been trading for a period of three years, the conditions mentioned may be required to be fulfilled by the directors of the company or the shareholders as appropriate, and in that case, a P Certificate will be issued to the company and not a C Certificate. Relaxations were introduced in FA 1980 allowing for periods of unemployment and absence abroad provided, in the case of the latter, that the applicant has complied with any comparable obligations in the country where he was living as those mentioned above applying in the UK. Similarly, FA 1982 (s.559 et seq ICTA 1988) has allowed persons who have been receiving full-time education or full-time training to qualify. From 1 December 1982 all these subcontractors have been able to get the special S certificate (Form 714S). In the case of those who have been unemployed or abroad, they can apply for a 714S certificate provided they can provide a bank guarantee, the form of which is prescribed by the regulations, for tax liabilities of up to £2,500 for each year in which the certificate is valid.

446 There are rights of appeal against refusal of a certificate to the General Commissioners or the Special Commissioners (s.561(9) ICTA 1988). The Inland Revenue's powers of discretion in issuing certificates were the subject of a judicial decision in the case of Kirvell *v.* Guy (1979 STC 312). If the Inland Revenue had looked at Mr Guy's case and decided against the application for a certificate, he would have had a right of appeal. However, instead, it refused even to consider his case. There was a history of not keeping proper records and undisclosed income of his wife. When this had been put right, he applied for a certificate but this was not considered because of his previous record. The case was heard by the General Commissioners who proceeded to issue a certificate, but it was held that they had no power to do so if the Inland Revenue had exercised their discretion in this way. Under an amendment in FA 1980 the exercise of the Inland Revenue's discretion and the full facts on which any refusal is based can be reviewed by the Commissioners on appeal to them by the subcontractor.

447 The Inland Revenue have issued a statement about their policy on the issue, renewal and withdrawal of subcontractors' tax certificates which is reproduced in full:

'(1) This statement explains how the Board of Inland Revenue intend to use the power, given to them under FA (No 2) 1975, to refuse tax certificates to businesses which have failed to comply with their taxation obligations.

(2) In the first place the Board wish to dispel any fear that the threat to withhold or withdraw a certificate may be used to encourage agreement with the Revenue's views in matters unrelated to the deduction scheme. This will not happen; the question of entitlement to a certificate does not affect the taxpayer's own liability to tax and will not be brought into negotiations relating to his assessment – for example where there may be a difference of opinion between the taxpayer and the Revenue on a point of law or accountancy – or to the amount to be postponed pending the determination of an appeal. In such circumstances, the Revenue will rely on the same legal and administrative processes in relation to the construction industry as those that apply to taxpayers generally, and will not use the threat of the refusal or withdrawal of the certificate to bypass or reinforce those procedures.

(3) On the other hand, at the time when they are considering the entitlement of a business to the issue or renewal of a certificate, the Revenue are bound by FA (No 2) 1975 to have regard to the extent to which there has been failure to comply with tax obligations. They intend that the powers shall be used with discretion and commonsense; and minor delays in submitting accounts or returns, or other instances of non-compliance which throw no suspicion on the general tax reliability of a business, will not in themselves jeopardise entitlement to a certificate.

(4) The circumstances in which the issue or renewal of a certificate will be jeopardised are where the non-compliance has been so substantial, or of such seriousness, that it gives rise to reasonable doubt about the reliability of the business in relation to the way it handles its tax affairs, and therefore to the way in which it is likely to operate the subcontractor's deduction scheme. Apart from irregularities in connection with the deduction scheme itself, examples of non-compliance of this order include failure to account for PAYE tax deducted, continued failure to pay the business's own tax once the amount payable has been agreed, deliberate or reckless failure to meet normal obligations (including the submitting of accounts) or to answer enquiries; or the evasion of his own tax liability by a person holding a key position in the business, such that it gives rise to reasonable expectations that any business in which he holds such a position is unlikely to comply with its tax obligations. Before reaching a decision on the issue or renewal of a certificate in these cases, the Revenue will, of course, take into account all the relevant factors, including the degree of involvement of the directors or proprietors as a whole and any extenuating circumstances.

(5) Once issued, a certificate will be withdrawn during its period of validity only if there has been serious irregularity in the operation of the subcontractor's deduction scheme, or in the case of some significant occurrence (such as a change in the persons controlling the business) which gives reason to doubt whether there will continue to be compliance with the scheme. In such cases, it would be usual for the certificate holder to receive some form of preliminary warning. There may, however, be exceptional cases where immediate action, without warning, to withdraw the certificate will be the only way in which the Revenue can be protected.'

A right of appeal against cancellation of a subcontractors certificate was introduced with effect from 23 July 1987 (see s.561(9) ICTA 1988). If an Inspector does cancel a certificate, he will at the same time advise the subcontractor what to do if he does not accept the decision.

448 The certificates run for periods laid down on the certificate which may vary and must therefore be renewed when required. About six months before the expiry date, the Inland Revenue normally remind the holder that the certificate will soon run out. The detailed provisions about the operation of the scheme are contained in Regulations made by the Board in accordance with their powers (s.566(2) ICTA 1988).

Vouchers

449 In the case of an I or P Certificate the contractor has to check it carefully before making a payment, and the subcontractor must give him a voucher from a book of vouchers obtained from the Inland Revenue within seven days of payment as a receipt for the payment which has to be sent to the Inland Revenue within 14 days of receipt from the subcontractor. He should send them to the Inland Revenue Construction Industry Processing Centre, Freepost, Liverpool L69 4AB. A similar procedure applies when payment is made to a subcontractor holding an S certificate, except that the voucher obtained from the Inland Revenue (Form 715S) must be signed and given to the contractor *before* payment without deduction is made. Also in the case of S Certificates, the holder may not use the vouchers to obtain more than £150 in any week (Sunday to Saturday) without deduction on account of tax. In the case of a C Certificate holder, the procedure can be more complicated as there is a modified procedure for companies involved in a substantial amount of subcontract work. No vouchers are issued by the holder of C Certificates. Returns have to be made to the Inland Revenue by contractors at the end of the year in the case of all payments made to those holding I, P and S Certificates and in respect of 'labour only' contracts, in the case of C Certificate holders.

Deduction of tax

450 A contractor making a payment to any subcontractor who is not the authorised holder of a valid exemption certificate or where the payment exceeds the S Certificate weekly limit, must deduct tax currently at 25% from the payment or the excess payment and pay over the amount deducted to the Inland Revenue under the same monthly procedure as for PAYE. The deduction must be from the full amount of the payment less the direct cost to the subcontractor of any materials to be used in the contract and supplied by the subcontractor. Materials for this purpose would include such items as consumable stores, fuel and plant hire. The contractor must give the subcontractor a deduction certificate on Form SC.60 and keep a deduction card (Form SC.11 New) for submission to the Collector of Taxes at the end of the year. In calculating the amounts on which the tax is to be deducted, VAT is excluded whether charged by the subcontractor if he is a registered person or suffered by him on the cost of materials.

451 It will be seen, therefore, that in preparing accounts for submission to the Inland Revenue in the case of an individual subcontractor, if a person claims to be receiving payments gross, he should be able to produce a valid up-to-date exemption certificate together with a record of the payments received which should match the vouchers (Form 715) which will be in possession of the Inspector of Taxes. The used voucher book will be evidence of these payments. Where someone has no exemption certificate, he should have all payments covered by Forms SC.60 so that, if necessary, he can reclaim any tax overdeducted. However, only if the total of the deductions shown by the Forms SC.60 is greater than the total amount of tax *and* Class 4 National Insurance Contributions payable for the year of deduction (whether or not yet due) plus any sums outstanding for other years, will the difference be repaid to the subcontractor.

Payer's position

452 It should be noted that tax liabilities and penalties can fall on the payer if he fails to carry out the necessary checks required of him. The case of Ladkarn Ltd *v.* McIntosh (1983) STC 113 provides an illustration of the care which needs to be taken by the contractor in complying with the regulations in establishing the identity of the subcontractor. The company made cash payments to persons purportedly representing B Ltd. A search had been made by the company's accountant which confirmed B Ltd existed but no steps were subsequently taken to determine the connection, if any, between that company and the persons to whom cash payments were made. Assessments were raised by the Inland Revenue to recover the tax which should have been deducted. Whilst admitting that B Ltd was a sham, the company maintained reasonable steps had been taken to determine its existence. Although accepting the directors had not knowingly attempted to defraud the Inland Revenue, the Commissioners were not satisfied reasonable steps had been taken to check on the bona-fides of the company nor did they conclude any valid contract existed between the company and B Ltd. Mr Justice Vinelott, in deciding in favour of the Inland Revenue, did not consider the Commissioners' findings were inconsistent. Whilst reasonable steps may have been taken to establish the bona-fides of B Ltd, the Commissioners could properly determine whether a valid contract did exist with that company. No such contracts did exist and, therefore, payments were made to persons who did not retain the necessary exemption certificates. Although this appeal related to the legislation and regulations which existed before 1977, it illustrates the need for the contractor to exercise great care before making payment without deduction of tax to the subcontractor.

The only exception from the requirement to see a subcontractors certificate is where a company holding a 714C presents a certifying document. In order to do this, the company has to notify the Inspector of the bank account that it will use for payments from a contractor. The company can produce on its own paper a document giving full details of its certificate and bank account which is given to the contractor for his retention. This method is used by larger companies which would find it inconvenient to show their certificate to every contractor.

Under a revised procedure, certificates are no longer issued to the accountant. The accountant does not know when the certificate has been issued and is thus unable to make enquiries where there is delay in issuing it. From April 1990, applicants for first certificates have been required to attend a tax office when making the application and the identity check is made at that stage. Renewal applications do not require this check and postal applications continue. All certificates are issued by post and an accountant is notified when a certificate is authorised.

The Inland Revenue undertake to supply certificates within 21 days of the notification of authorisation.

453 The advantages of being a self-employed subcontractor are thus seriously diminished if the cash flow advantage of not suffering deduction of tax at source is not available.

Expenses

454 If the subcontractor is treated as self-employed, operating from his home, and can be said to move around frequently from contract to contract so that the only fixed place from which he works is his home, he can claim to deduct an allowance of part of the costs of running his house, the payment of a secretarial wage to his wife, if she acts in this capacity, and travelling expenses to and from the sites. The allowability of such expenses was confirmed in the test case of Horton v. Young (47 TC 60). However, it is known that the Inland Revenue do seek to distinguish this situation from that of subcontractors working for long stretches on particular contracts for one contractor where they seek to allow only the notional cost of travelling from the contractor's paying office to the sites. There seems to be no justification for this attitude.

455 The cost of lunch on the site and other living rather than working expenses are not allowable (Caillebotte v. Quinn, 1975 STC 265). To this extent, therefore, the self-employed subcontractor is worse-off than employ-ees in the construction and allied industries who are not taxed on allowances towards travelling, subsistence and lodging made by their employers if they fall within the working rule agreements (1981) STI p.64.

The Inland Revenue published in 1991 a Consultative Document on the subcontractors scheme proposing that unless income was below certain limits, subcontractors would suffer tax by deduction, probably at the basic rate for the year. Various alternative limits have been proposed for comment. The Inland Revenue argue that subcontractors often work like employees and therefore it would be much more economical to collect tax at source. It was not envisaged that the scheme for certification would cover so many subcontractors when it was introduced. It remains to be seen whether these proposals are adopted.

Chapter 24
Local councillors and members of Government boards

Reimbursed expenses

456   It should be noted that the holder of an unpaid office is not liable to tax on any amount reimbursed to him as expenses. This position has been accepted by the Inland Revenue for many years and includes members of the House of Lords, local authority councillors, Justices of the Peace, etc., in receipt of expenses allowances only, and members of government committees in the same position.

Attendance allowances

457   Under the Income Tax (Councillors' Attendance Allowances) Regulations 1974 (SI 1974 No. 340, as amended by SI 1981 No.44), attendance allowances, paid to local councillors under the various UK Local Government Acts, may, at the taxpayer's option, be paid under deduction of basic rate income tax where the taxpayer is unhappy with the manner in which his coding is determined. In such a case, however, part of any attendance allowance may be paid gross, to the extent that the councillor can show that he has to incur expenses allowable under normal Sch. E rules.

Office or profession

458   Practitioners in a particular professional field undertake special assignments for Government departments and other similar bodies for a fee. Is such an appointment part of the exercise of the profession, taxable under Sch. D, or is it an office taxable under Sch. E? This was the point at issue in Edwards *v.* Clinch (1981) 56 TC 367.

The question that the Court had to decide was whether certain fees of a professional man were emoluments of an 'office' in the sense of s.19 ICTA 1988. The taxpayer was a chartered civil engineer, who had for some years been one of a panel of persons invited by the Department of the Environment to conduct independent public inquiries and to make reports thereon. The Crown

271

maintained that each appointment was a separate 'office'. However, in the Court of Appeal, Buckley LJ did not accept that the statutory, public character of the appointed inspector's duties was sufficient to make the appointment an office. An office had to have a sufficient degree of continuance to admit of its being held by successive incumbents, an existence not necessarily prolonged or indefinite, but not an existence limited to the tenure of one man. This requirement for continuance was supported by authority. On this basis, it was decided that the taxpayer was exercising his profession and not holding an office when being remunerated for each appointment. This decision was upheld by the House of Lords.

Chapter 25
Farmers (including market gardeners) and owners of commercial woodlands

One trade

459 All farming is treated as the carrying on of a trade and all farming carried on in the UK by the same person or partnership is treated as one trade (s.53(1) and (2) ICTA 1988). This is particularly useful in relation to the carry-forward of losses as it is possible, for instance, for the same person to give up farming in one area and recommence elsewhere, and carry forward any unabsorbed losses against future profits from the new farm. In practice, the Inland Revenue also allow a gap between the sale of one farm and the purchase of another, and do not insist on the cessation provisions being applied in those circumstances, provided that the gap (generally) is not more than 12 months and that there is a genuine intention to continue to carry on farming.

Where there is a change in the persons carrying on a business, extra care is needed, in order to ensure that maximum loss relief is obtained as early as possible. For example, where a business is transferred from a sole trader to a partnership, any trading losses of the sole trader are only available to carry forward against his share of the partnership's subsequent profits. If, therefore, such a sole trader has very substantial trading losses brought forward, it will be wise to draft the partnership agreement carefully so that initially, if possible, the former sole trader will receive the greater part of any profits arising.

The position regarding unused capital allowances will depend upon whether or not the business is deemed to be continuing.

If the business continues, unused capital allowances are carried forward and deducted from future profits of the business. If there is a cessation, all unused capital allowances lapse, except for those applicable to the continuing partners and attributable to the part of the year before the change.

It should be noted that, where there is a succession between connected persons, s.92 FA 1988 has amended para.13 Sch. 8 FA 1971 (see now s.77(3)–(5) CAA 1990). Previously, an election (with a six-year time limit) could be made to treat the trade as continuing for capital allowances purposes.

Now the election, with a two-year time limit, is restricted to persons chargeable to UK tax on the profits of the trade. The trade is not deemed to be continuing, but the successors can take over the plant and machinery at tax written-down value. However, there is an extended definition of 'connected persons' to include partnerships.

The ability to carry forward losses from one farm to another was the subject of the decision in Bispham *v.* Eardiston Farming Co (1919) Ltd ((1962) 40 TC 322). In that case, unrelieved losses of one farm sold were allowed against another farm's subsequent profits. The point is particularly relevant in a company situation where there is a change in ownership, as s.768 ICTA 1988 might otherwise restrict the carry-forward of losses. Such a challenge is less easy for the Inland Revenue in the case of a farming company, as all farming is specifically deemed to be one trade.

Losses

460 The following provisions are relevant to farming losses:

(a) *Section 397 ICTA 1988*, known as the 'hobby farming' provisions. S.397 prevents the set-off of losses against general income or total profits, under ss.380 (individuals) or 393A(1) (companies) ICTA 1988, including related capital allowances given in taxing the trade, where there have been five years of continuous losses by the same person. Any revenue loss is computed on normal Sch. D Case I principles, without regard to capital allowances. In giving income tax relief for losses, it is *normally* possible to use the loss incurred in the accounting period ending in the year of assessment to establish whether there has been a loss or a profit. For hobby farming purposes, however, the Inland Revenue generally insist on apportioning profits and losses on a fiscal year basis. The farmer must, therefore, make a profit in one of the five years of assessment preceding that for which a loss relief claim is made.

There are anti-avoidance provisions (s.397(10) ICTA 1988), to prevent husband-and-wife partnerships being formed or dissolved in order to recommence another cycle of five years' losses. Generally, where at least one person is involved in carrying on a trade both before and after a deemed discontinuance under s.113(1) ICTA 1988, the discontinuance is ignored in reckoning whether there have been five years' losses.

There is a 'let-out' from these provisions if the farmer can prove that no competent farmer could have made a profit in the sixth year if he had undertaken the farming at the beginning of the five years concerned. The Inland Revenue also make a concession concerning the rearing of certain forms of livestock, for instance, deer farming or other long-term breeding projects.

As the losses are based on the ordinary adjusted loss before capital allowances, it is advisable to minimise revenue expenditure, such as repairs, where possible, in the fifth year. Equally, where there is a choice of structuring interest as an expense, or as a deduction from total income, the latter course should be taken as this will not then enter into the calculation of the loss. Thus, if a partnership wishes to buy more land, the partners should borrow and inject their personal borrowings into the partnership as capital or interest-free loans, in order to purchase the land as *partnership* property. The interest will then be a charge against their total incomes. The Inland Revenue do not operate any concession where the high cost of borrowing is the cause of the loss.

(b) *Sections 384 (individuals) and 393A(3) (companies) ICTA 1988*. These sections have the effect of denying relief under ss.380 and 393A(1) ICTA 1988 where a trade is not carried on on a commercial basis and with a view to the realisation of profits.

(c) Where a loss has been incurred, insofar as it cannot be relieved against income, it will be available against capital gains of the same or following year (s.72 FA 1991). This applies to losses sustained in 1991/92 and subsequent years of assessment. It appears that there is no objection to claiming losses by reference to the accounting year ending in the year of assessment where that would apply under normal practice for trading losses against income.

Where the owner of a farm makes a loss, but is debarred from making a claim under ss.380 or 393A(1) ICTA 1988 by virtue of one of the above sections, Inland Revenue Extra-Statutory Concession B5 allows him to claim the same relief, against general income, for the cost of maintenance, insurance and repairs of agricultural land (including a third of the relevant expenditure on a farmhouse), that an agricultural landlord could claim under s.33 ICTA 1988 against rents.

Where the Inland Revenue contend that a trade is not carried on on a commercial basis, this will also pose a threat to any relief claimed by an individual under s.381 ICTA 1988. Where an individual carries on a trade and sustains a loss in the first year of assessment or in any of the next three years, he may make a claim to carry back the losses to the period before he commenced that trade. However, s.381(4) ICTA 1988 denies this relief where the trade is not conducted on a commercial basis and:

"in such a way that profits . . . could reasonably be expected to be realised in [the period in which the loss arose] or within a reasonable time thereafter".

An inspector may mount a challenge both under s.381(4) ICTA 1988 and under s.384 ICTA 1988, where relief has been claimed under both s.381 ICTA 1988 and ss.380 and 383 ICTA 1988.

Cases have been known where an inspector appears to have been convinced, in part, that a farm is run on a commercial basis because some of the improvements, the costs of which gave rise to the losses, have received approval from the Ministry of Agriculture.

Stocks

461 All animals for farming are treated as trading stock for tax purposes (para.1(1) Sch. 5 ICTA 1988) unless the 'herd basis' applies (see **462** below). This means that the animals should each theoretically be valued at the lower of cost or net realisable value. However, the National Farmers' Union has negotiated with the Inland Revenue that the cost of home bred cattle can be estimated at 60% of their market value (for sheep and pigs the percentage is 75%). These arrangements will not apply in the case of pedigree stock, or in any other case where 60% or 75% of the market value would not give a reasonable result. In such cases, it is necessary to negotiate a figure with the inspector of taxes. Similarly, where stock is bought in, the lower of cost or market value *must* apply and not the method agreed between the Inland Revenue and the National Farmers' Union.

Growing crops may be valued at the cost of seeds, labour, fertilisers, etc. Where the normal value of tillages, unexhausted manures and growing crops does not currently exceed £7,000, a certificate that the value at the beginning of the year did not differ materially from that at the end of the year will usually be accepted.

For dead stock, ie., corn and hay in stock or barn, seeds, roots, straw, etc., it is possible to have a full valuation at historic cost, or to elect for 85% of market value as being the equivalent cost. The Inland Revenue will insist upon consistency, whichever method is chosen.

The Inland Revenue are investigating livestock markets with a view to creating a record of purchases and sales made through these markets. Therefore, farmers should be careful to keep records of all their own purchases and sales of livestock, as they could be challenged in material cases by reference to market records.

Herd basis

462 It is possible to elect for the 'herd basis' to apply, as an alternative to the usual trading stock basis (see **461** above), in respect of production herds, such as a dairy herd or a ewe flock, kept only for the sale of milk, wool, eggs, young animals or other produce. The herd basis cannot apply to animals kept for only a short time, such as steers for fattening or a 'flying flock' of ewes. (See Sch. 5 ICTA 1988.)

A herd basis election is useful in times of high inflation and where numbers in the herd or flock are stable. By contrast, such an election is unlikely to be of use where the numbers in the initial herd are likely to be increased. Where numbers are likely to fluctuate, averaging may be a more appropriate strategy to adopt.

An election has to be made to adopt the herd basis, and normally it should be made within two years of the end of the chargeable period in which the farmer first keeps the production herd of the class in question. The election, once made by the farmer, is irrevocable. As the election has to be made by the farmer, a fresh election has to be made on a change of partners or on an incorporation of the farming business. If an election has not been made previously, such a change would provide a fresh opportunity to make one.

Farmers who did not make a herd basis election because of the benefits of claiming stock relief were given a fresh opportunity by s.48(6) FA 1984. It was possible to elect, not later that two years after the end of the first period of account commencing on or after 13 March 1984, for the herd basis to apply. The election made within that time could first have effect, if the claim so specified, in relation to the period of account straddling 12 March 1984 or in relation to the first period of account commencing on or after 13 March 1984. The reason for the choice was that stock relief could not be claimed for any period of account commencing after 12 March 1984. It was thus possible for a farmer to make an election in the period in which he ceased to keep a production herd, and to receive the proceeds of sale of the herd tax free.

It is also possible to make an election if a farmer's production herd, or a substantial part of it (normally 20% or more), has had to be slaughtered compulsorily on account of disease, in which case the election should be made within two years of the end of the year of assessment that is based on the accounts for the year in which the compensation is receivable. Similarly, if the farmer ceases to keep a production herd of the class in question for a period of at least five years, he may make an election in respect of such herds after the end of that period, if he acquires such a herd again.

Generally, the effect of making an election is that, if the whole herd is sold without being replaced, or if a substantial part of it is sold (normally 20% or more), any profit on the sale is free of all tax, as profits from the animals are also exempt from capital gains tax because the animals are wasting assets. If the numbers in the herd increase within five years of such a substantial reduction, a proportion of the previously 'tax-free' profit is brought back into account. Any profit on a lesser reduction of the herd is brought into account as income, whilst replacements, provided that they are not home-bred, are written off to the profit and loss account as the cost of rearing new home-bred animals will already have been deducted as part of the expense of labour, foodstuffs, etc. Any extra cost due to any improvement element in the replacement animal will not be deducted. Immature animals are generally not treated as part of the herd, with a few exceptions, such as hill sheep. From the above, it will be clear that, where an election is made and numbers in the herd are likely to fluctuate, accurate records of herd transactions must be kept.

It should be noted that making an election for the herd basis to apply, other than on first keeping a herd, does not mean that the animals are appropriated from stock at market value. If that were the case, the benefit of the election would be lost. Rather, the animals are treated as never having been part of the stock in the period in question, and are thus removed at their book value from stock for tax purposes, with no income or corporation tax charge resulting from this change.

Generally, the legislation is unclear as to whether, where there are sales and replacements spanning the end of an accounting period, the sale proceeds have to be brought in and taxed when received and relief only given for the replacement when incurred, or whether some other basis be adopted. In practice, provided that the replacement occurs within 12 months, the Inland Revenue have allowed the sale proceeds to be carried forward to be credited against the cost of replacement. There seems to be no particular time limit for replacement, provided that there is a clear intention to replace the animal. An attempt to ignore this practice by one inspector has been rejected by the Commissioners. In some cases, farmers have not replaced animals for several years. This is especially likely to occur with pedigree herds, where replacements are found from home-bred stock. However, the position is far from clear and a cautious approach should be adopted.

It should be noted that in a share farming arrangement, each part-owner has to elect for the herd basis to apply for the election to be valid.

Strictly the law does not provide for the use of the herd basis where a farmer only has a share in a herd or an animal. An Extra Statutory Concession was published on 12 November 1990 which treats the provisions as applying in these circumstances and also covers the long standing practice under which the Inland Revenue treat a share of a single animal (such as a bull) whose ownership is spread among a group of farmers as being part of a herd for herd basis purposes.

Averaging

463 It is possible for unincorporated farmers to average profits for income tax purposes, in order to remove themselves from the effect of high marginal rates of income tax, caused by severe fluctuations in their farming income. An individual or partnership may thus claim to average the profits of the business for any two consecutive years of assessment. The profits are the profits as adjusted for Sch. D Case I purposes, before any deduction for losses or adjustments for capital allowances, balancing charges or stock relief. The relief does not apply to profits subject to corporation tax (eg., profits of UK-resident companies). (See s.96 ICTA 1988.)

Averaging can be claimed if the profits for either of the two years do not exceed 70% of the profits of the other year or are nil. A loss is treated as a nil profit for this purpose. There is a marginal relief where the profits of one year exceed 70% of the other but are less than 75%. If the profits have been revised under an averaging claim, it is the revised figure that is then used in any averaging claim for the second year and the next year.

A claim must be made within two years of the end of the second year to which the claim relates, and is irrevocable.

No claim is possible in respect of the year in which a trade commences or is discontinued. This includes a year where a partnership change is treated as a discontinuance. A claim does not affect relief for losses, and is ignored in deciding whether the profits of the two years prior to a cessation are to be increased. If such profits are increased, the original claim becomes invalid, but a fresh claim can then be made using the revised profits, thus spreading back profits outside the two years.

It should be noted that averaging can create profits against which losses can be set and time limits for loss claims are, therefore, extended to the end of the period during which the averaging claim must be made.

Averaging relates to a partnership assessment as a whole, and not to individual profit shares.

It should be noted that, once an averaging claim has been made for two consecutive years, it cannot be made for any years preceding those years, and the effect on retirement annuity premium and personal pension payment relief needs to be considered in all cases.

Under Inland Revenue Extra-Statutory Concession A29, farming for averaging purposes also includes the intensive rearing of livestock or fish on a commercial basis for the production of food for human consumption.

Capital allowances

464 There may be difficulty in determining whether an item of farm capital expenditure is 'plant' or is a building qualifying only for agricultural buildings allowances. Where a Ministry of Agriculture grant has been claimed, the problem is usually readily resolved in practice, as machinery and plant attracts a lower rate of grant than building work. If expenditure could qualify under either category, strictly, agricultural buildings allowances took precedence under the pre-FA 1986 provisions (by virtue of s.148(5) CAA 1990) but, in practice, this provision was seldom invoked. The new scheme of agricultural buildings allowances refers only to the fact that it is not possible to have double allowances under both systems. For chargeable periods, or basis periods, ending on or after 27 July 1989, a person may elect for one allowance or the other, if expenditure can qualify for different types of allowances (s.147 CAA 1990).

Some of the main problems in this area concern purpose-built structures for intensive rearing of livestock or dairy houses, where the equipment element is so integrated with the rest of the structure that the building works can be regarded almost as no more than cladding for the plant and machinery, and thus the whole structure should qualify as plant. The Inland Revenue resist this approach except in the case of mobile poultry houses, pig units or similar items.

Also, whilst Land Rovers qualify for writing-down allowances without restriction, it should be noted that a Range Rover is regarded as a private car, subject to the £12,000 limit. The Inland Revenue have been known to argue that personal choice may restrict capital allowances on a car in the case of a farmer (following the case of GH Chambers (Northiam Farms) Ltd *v.*

Watmough (1956) 36 TC 711), although the earlier £8,000 limit for writing-down allowance has, in general, meant that this point is not often raised.

Agricultural buildings allowances

465 The whole scheme of agricultural buildings allowances has been recast for expenditure incurred on or after 1 April 1986. For expenditure incurred before that date, broadly, allowances were given to the person incurring the expenditure, provided that he had an interest in the land. The allowances were given primarily against agricultural or forestry income of the year following the year to 31 March, or the end of the accounting period in which the expenditure was incurred. The balance of the expenditure was available against other income of that year and of the next following year. Thereafter, any remaining balance was only available against agricultural or forestry income. There was no system of balancing adjustments, and the successor took over any balance of allowances due.

With the abolition of the initial allowance and the reduction of the writing-down allowances to four per cent per annum, the allowances would not have taken account of the short life of some agricultural buildings. The new system, therefore, has introduced a system of balancing adjustments, at the option of the taxpayer, on the disposal of buildings, including where they are pulled down or otherwise destroyed. The scheme (ss.123–133 CAA 1990) is now broadly similar to that for industrial buildings. In particular, allowances are given on the cost of any buildings, cottages, fences, or other works incurred for the purposes of agriculture, including one-third of the expenditure on a farmhouse or, if the farmhouse is relatively large in relation to the farm, such lesser fraction as is reasonable. What is a 'farmhouse' for this purpose was discussed in Lindsay *v.* CIR (1953) 34 TC 289. Generally, it is the house from which the farming operations are controlled and managed, even if it is occupied by an employee.

The terms 'works' includes such things as demolition, drainage and sewerage works, water and electricity installations, walls, shelter belts of trees, glasshouses on market garden land, and the reclamation of former agricultural land.

The allowances belong to the person having the 'relevant interest' at the time the expenditure was incurred (ie., the freehold or leasehold interest). When that interest is transferred, the allowances pass to the transferee, with a division of the allowance where the transfer occurs part-way through a year.

If an agricultural building is purchased unused, no allowance is given to the vendor, but the purchaser obtains allowances only based on the lower of the costs of construction or the price paid by him.

If no election is made for a balancing adjustment to apply on a sale of the relevant interest, the purchaser takes over the vendor's entitlement to the allowances for the remainder of the 25 years. Otherwise, on either a disposal of the relevant interest, or if a building is demolished, destroyed or otherwise ceases to exist, a balancing adjustment is made. Where appropriate on a sale, future writing-down allowances are calculated in the same way as for industrial buildings allowances for the remainder of the 25 years. For example, the demolition of a short-life building will probably give rise to a balancing allowance in the year in which it is demolished, equal to the balance of any allowances due.

It appears that, as with industrial buildings allowances, if an inferior interest is granted out of the relevant interest on sale (for instance, a long lease out of a freehold), the vendor will retain the allowances, although he would not now do so on a sale and lease-back.

Unlike allowances under the old pre-FA 1986 scheme, the new agricultural land and buildings allowances will be given in taxing the farming trade. This means that allowances can now, in certain circumstances, figure in loss claims under s.383 ICTA 1988. In the case of landlords, as before, such allowances will be given primarily against agricultural income such as rents.

It used to be the position that the Inland Revenue were not particularly concerned as to whether a farmer had an interest in the relevant land, provided that he had incurred the qualifying expenditure. There were fears that this might no longer be true under the new system, where the concept of a 'relevant interest' has been introduced. It was thought that it might be necessary, for instance, for a partnership to own a lease of property granted by the partner owning the freehold in order for the partnership to qualify for allowances in respect of any expenditure that it incurred on agricultural buildings on that land. However, the Inland Revenue have now confirmed that they will not interpret the new legislation more restrictively than the old. Therefore, a lease could include a licence for this purpose.

It is important to obtain the landlord's consent for any improvements made to tenanted farm land. If approval is not obtained, no compensation can subsequently be claimed. Furthermore, under the Law of Property Act 1925, unless approval has been granted, any benefit of the improvement reverts to the landlord upon cessation of the lease.

Revenue receipts and payments

466 There are a number of special points concerning revenue receipts and payments. Where compensation is paid for compulsorily slaughtered stock for which a 'herd basis' election cannot be made, the profits arising, being the excess of the compensation over the book value of the animal (or over cost in the case of animals bred or purchased during the current year) can, under Inland Revenue Extra-Statutory Concession B11, be taken out of the accounts for the current year and spread over the next three years in equal amounts. As mentioned in **462** above, there is a right of election for the herd basis where a substantial part (normally 20% or more) of a production herd is compulsorily slaughtered. In such a case, this spreading relief cannot be claimed for the mature animals in the herd, even if the farmer chooses not to elect for the herd basis thereafter. The relief will normally, therefore, only apply to young stock and followers, flying flocks and animals kept for fattening, and to mature animals where less than one-fifth of the herd is slaughtered.

Grants and subsidies have to be analysed to determine whether they are capital or revenue receipts. The new land set-aside payments will be treated as trading income under the normal principles of taxation for such receipts, to the extent that the payments are made for keeping land out of production for a period of five years on a 'care and maintenance' basis, and thus compensate for lost trading income.

The Regulations (Statutory Instruments 1988 No. 1352; 1989 No. 1042; 1990 No. 1716) made under the European Communities Act 1972 provide the land must be set aside for a period of five years for one of the following purposes:

(a) Permanent fallow where the same parcels of land are set aside for the full five years.
(b) Rotational fallow whereby different parcels of land are set aside each year as part of a rotation with land which was in arable cropping during the year to 30 June 1988.
(c) Grazed fallow whereby livestock can be grazed on the fallow at (a) and (b) above provided the livestock units do not exceed the numbers held in the year ended 30 June 1988.
(d) Non-agricultural use allows for example tourist or recreational activities but no form of agricultural production, mineral extraction or permanent buildings unless for approved farm diversification activities.
(e) Woodlands for which payments available depend on whether or not the set aside is integrated with the farm woodland scheme.

Payments under (d) although of an income nature on the principles outlined in White *v.* G & M Davies (1979) STC 415 and CIR *v.* Biggar (1982) STC 677 may not be agricultural income if the existing farming trade does not continue on other land. It is submitted they are not Schedule A income as they do not derive from an interest in land. As the payments are arguably pure income profit, a charge under Case III of Schedule D might be appropriate or failing that Case VI.

Payments under (e) as they are integrated into the Regulations with the farm woodland scheme will arise from the commercial occupation of woodland and following the FA 1988, will be tax free.

Where the land is treated as continuing to be farmed, retirement, roll over and hold over reliefs will continue without restriction. If the set aside period represents an interruption in the trade which then resumes, there will be a restriction to retirement, roll over and hold over relief by reference to the period of non-trading use.

If the trade does not resume, retirement relief will be lost but as confirmed in the Court of Appeal decision in Richart *v.* J Lyons and Co Ltd (1989) STC 665 this will not apply to roll over and hold over reliefs where proportionate relief will continue.

In some cases, receipts can be of a mixed nature, as in the case of the Farm and Horticulture Development Scheme. Price-guarantee payments, subsidies and grants of a non-capital nature, such as cereals deficiency payments, constitute income. Certain deficiency payments in respect of home-grown cereals could, under Inland Revenue Extra-Statutory Concession B6, be brought in on a notified basis, rather than by reference to the date of harvesting, except in the opening and closing years. Any grant of a capital nature towards buildings or equipment, unlike certain regional development grants for industry, has to be deducted from the cost of the assets, in order to establish the expenditure qualifying for capital allowances.

It should be noted in this connection, however, that it is specifically provided that grants for relinquishing occupation of uncommercial agricultural units, by virtue of a scheme under s.27 Agriculture Act 1967, are not to be taken into account for capital gains tax purposes (s.249 TCGA 1992).

On the expenses side, usually only up to one-third of the cost of the repairs to a farmhouse will be allowed as an expense. However, it is understood that some inspectors are currently seeking to challenge this long-established practice, and representations are being made on the point.

Under Inland Revenue Statement of Practice SP 5/81 necessary net expenditure incurred, after crediting any grants receivable, in order to restore efficient draining or on redraining (the land having become waterlogged), will be admitted as revenue expenditure, provided that it excludes:

(a) any substantial element of improvement; and
(b) the capital element, where the current owner is known to have acquired the land at a depressed price because of its swampy condition.

Generally, 'wages' paid to minors will not be allowed, but will be regarded as no more than pocket money, as the case of Dollar and Dollar v. Lyon (1981) 54 TC 459 illustrated. The operation of PAYE also has to be watched, and details of exceptions for casual workers such as harvest workers, and workers genuinely engaged for no more than a day, are contained in the special 'Farmers Guide to PAYE', available free of charge from local tax offices.

In particular, however, it should be noted there has been a change of practice for casual harvest workers announced in a Press Release dated 29 May 1991. Under the 1984 agreement between the NFU and the Inland Revenue, PAYE need not be applied to wages paid to a daily casual worker. These workers are defined as employed for a period not exceeding a day whose employment ends on that day with no agreement for further employment and who are paid cash at the end of the day. Until now, the Inland Revenue regarded the words 'agreement for further employment' as including both contractual arrangements and cases where the farmer and employee expected there to be further employment. In future, the expectation will be ignored and it is only where there is an agreement that the concession will not be applied. This interpretation will apply to existing cases which have not been settled. The farmer must still inform the Inland Revenue of details if the amount exceeds £100 in total for the year per worker.

The 1984 agreement also says that PAYE need not be applied to harvest workers who are not daily casuals but are taken on for two weeks or less (this concession can only be applied once a year for any particular worker by any one employer).

In addition, there are now special arrangements exempting from PAYE foreign students coming to work in the vacation on UK farms.

The Inland Revenue have a special unit to deal with tax compliance by agricultural gangmasters (middlemen who supply casual labour for farmers at peak times). Its functions are to ensure that gangmasters deduct, and account for, PAYE and NIC from the earnings of their workers, and that they make proper returns of their profits. The unit is based in Sheffield, and is initially concentrating on East Anglia, where the gangmaster system is most common. In a recent development, the Inland Revenue is insisting that the farmer, being the principal employer, should be responsible for PAYE in respect of payments to his casual workers, notwithstanding the presence of a gangmaster.

This area of the law has been the subject of a recent decision in Andrews *v*. King (1991) STC 481. The taxpayer was engaged by a firm of potato merchants in connection with potato picking and grading. The potato merchant would inform him how many men were required and he would select the men, although they were not obliged to accept the work he offered them. The Inland Revenue argued that he was self-employed and also that he should be responsible for PAYE on the workers selected as a gang-master and made Regulation 29 determinations on him. The court held he was not self-employed as apart from selecting the workers, he took no financial risk and was not in business on his own account.

Applying the regulations, the taxpayer and other workers worked under the general control and management of the merchant who was, therefore, the principal employer and as such was the employer for the purposes of the regulations. The taxpayer did not employ the workers or pay them wages. Accordingly, the determination under Regulation 29 was invalid.

In an extra-statutory concession dated 8 August 1986 (now listed as Inland Revenue Extra-Statutory Concession A60), the Inland Revenue confirmed that they will follow past practice and will not seek to tax the provision of free board and lodging for lower-paid agricultural employees, even if off the farm, provided that, in the latter case, the employer has a contract with third party for its provision, and that payments under the contract are made direct to the third party. Strictly because under the Agricultural Wages Acts workers are entitled to take a higher wage on which they would be taxed and to pay their own board and lodging, they are taxable on the value of the board and lodging supplied (under the principles laid down in Heaton *v*. Bell (1969) 46 TC 211). However, provided that the worker is not a director or higher paid, and that his contract of employment provides for a net cash wage with free board and lodging, he is not taxed on such free board and lodging. Where the agricultural worker is entitled to a gross cash wage, he is assessable on the gross amount, even if his contract of employment provides for his employer to deduct a sum to pay for the worker's board and lodging.

The whole (formerly seven-eights) of the membership subscription to the National Farmers' Union is allowed under an agreement with the Inland Revenue.

Interest on business loans will be allowed in the normal way. If a partner borrows to buy farmland, which is then used by the partnership, the interest that he pays can effectively be treated as a partnership expense, provided that the partnership pays him an amount equal to the interest that he has to pay. Under Inland Revenue Statement of Practice, SP 4/85, he is treated as being paid a rent by the partnership equal to the amount of the interest that he has to pay. However, the effect of receiving rent on capital gains tax retirement relief should not be overlooked (see **468(4)** below). Furthermore, he may deny himself the higher rate of agricultural property relief, now 100%, for inheritance tax purposes. It will usually be more tax-efficient for the farmer to transfer the land to the partnership. A special capital account could then be set up for the partner to which any surpluses on disposal or revaluation could be credited. The farmer would then be entitled to claim a deduction for loan interest, he would not deny himself capital gains tax retirement relief, and he would be entitled to the higher rate of agricultural property relief.

Partnerships and joint ventures

467   If it is desired to set up a partnership from a certain time, it is necessary to ensure that the facts support the existence of the partnership from that time, irrespective of what any partnership agreement says. This point was emphasised in the farming case of Dickenson *v.* Gross (1927) 11 TC 614, and in the cases of Waddington *v.* O'Callaghan (1931) 16 TC 187 and Saywell and Others *v.* Pope (1979) 53 TC 40. It is thus not possible to make a partnership retrospective. Similarly, a partnership agreement of itself is not conclusive evidence of a partnership if it conflicts with the realities of the situation eg., where the children are not really acting as partners but are employees.

There are numerous forms of joint ventures in farming. Usually one party supplies the land as his capital, and the other supplies the rest of the fixed and working capital and manages the farming operations on the land. Such arrangements are usually entered into in order to ensure that the landowner continues to trade for tax purposes, particularly where there are unabsorbed losses, and also to avoid the grant of a tenancy. However, the letting of land on a 364-day grazing licence for grass keep might not be regarded as trading. Also, any arrangement under which the profit share of the landowner is guaranteed, whatever the outcome of the venture, might also not be treated as a trading activity. The share of the landowner should, therefore, fluctuate, so that a claim to loss relief can be sustained.

It is understood that the Inland Revenue started recently to contend that many share farming agreements did not give trading income to the owner. They were maintaining that only the operator is farming, the owner merely receiving a form of income derived from the land and assessable under Schedule A. The Inland Revenue were apparently arguing that where persons do not have qualitatively the same occupation rights, only one can be treated as occupier of the land in receipt of farming income for tax purposes.

The person in receipt of farming income on this basis was deemed to be the one with the greater presence and control over the land and occupation rights, and on this analysis only the operator would be in receipt of farming income.

The Inland Revenue contentions were based on decisions in certain old cases relating to the occupation of land for Schedule D purposes. As farming was brought within Section D only in FA 1948, it was argued that these cases are irrelevant and that the question of occupation may be disregarded in determining who is carrying on the trade. At stake are:

Averaging of profits;
Set off of trading losses;
Roll over and retirement relief;
Agricultural property relief for IHT at formerly 50%, now 100%.

This view was, therefore, vigorously contested by the CLA and similar bodies.

As a result of such opposition, it has now been reported (*Tolley's Practical Tax* 22 January 1992) that the CLA's president has announced a change of heart by the Inland Revenue. They now accept that both parties to a share farming agreement may be considered to be carrying on farming. The landowner in an agreement based upon the CLA model may be regarded as trading provided he takes an active part in the share farming venture, at least to the extent of concerning himself with details of farming policy and exercising his right to enter onto his land for some material purpose even if only for the purposes of inspection and policy making. Where a new share-farming agreement does not amount to a partnership, the landowner should, for tax purposes, continue to carry on any existing farming trade, so that any unabsorbed losses are available to set off against his share of any profits. From his agreed proportion of the outputs of the venture there is deducted his agreed inputs, in order to arrive at the profit assessable on him only. Stocks sometimes cause complications in share-farming arrangements. If they are transferred from one party to the other when mature, 60% or 75% of their market value will be accepted as cost in the normal way for home-bred animals. However, if there are joint interests in the animals, each party must account for a proportionate share of 'cost' in his profit and loss account. Such joint ownership, if the joint venturers also share in the ultimate results for the year, can be construed as a partnership, with consequential 'one assessment' implications. Instead, therefore, shares of inputs and outputs should be different, so that one joint venturer can make a loss and the other a profit.

Companies sometimes enter into joint-farming ventures with individuals or other companies. A company, even if it is a partner, is assessed separately on its share of profits, capital allowances, etc., as if it were carrying on the trade on its own (under the special rules for partnerships involving companies in ss.114 and 115 ICTA 1988). It appears, therefore, that, where it has sustained losses in the past in its farming trade, these can be set against future profits from the joint venture.

Institutions, in particular pension funds, have been involved in investing in agricultural land. Typically, the pension fund will own the land and the farmer will be the fund's own subsidiary or a third party in partnership with such a subsidiary. The pension fund can then receive its share of profits in the form of rents which can be geared partly to profits. These rents will be exempt from tax in its own hands, unlike trading income. Provided that the rents paid do not exceed the highest possible tender rent, they should be deductible by the subsidiary or the third party, on the authority of the case of Union Cold Storage Co Ltd *v*. Adamson (1931) 16 TC 293. Because the pension fund will not want normally to grant an agricultural tenancy to a third party, its own trading subsidiary will usually share occupation of the land in partnership with the outside operator. Consequently, any expenditure generating tax allowances should be incurred in the trading company rather than in the pension fund, which will only receive exempt income.

Capital gains tax

468 The following should be considered.

(1) Hold-over relief

It should be noted that all land which qualifies for agricultural relief for inheritance tax purposes whether at the 100% or 30% (previously 50% or 30%) rate will continue to qualify for hold-over relief where, for instance, it is given by a father to his son, or where a trust comes to an end and a person becomes absolutely entitled to trust assets (see Sch. 7 TCGA 1992). In addition, it has been confirmed by the Inland Revenue that even if the land has development value which does not qualify for agricultural relief for inheritance tax purposes, hold-over relief will still apply.

(2) Roll-over relief

Roll-over relief is likely to be especially useful for farmers. In this connection, improvements to land and buildings are accepted by the Inland Revenue as 'new assets'. Such improvements can include, for example, drainage channels and other building work that cannot rank as 'fixed plant', eg., sprinkler systems. In addition, if a tenant farmer purchases the freehold reversion, that will also be accepted as a new asset. However, if he has to sell part of the land to which the freehold relates, for example, in order to meet the cost of the freehold, he cannot roll over the sale proceeds of that part against the cost of the freehold. In that situation, the proceeds would derive from the same asset as the 'replacement' asset, and thus there would be no new asset. The farmer can only roll over the sale proceeds of other land already owned against such an acquisition (see Inland Revenue Extra-Statutory Concession D22).

As there is no territorial limitation to roll-over relief (subject to restrictions in connection with dual resident companies), it is possible for a farmer, who remains UK-resident, to sell a farm in the UK and roll over the gain into the acquisition of a farm, say in the USA, provided that, where the UK trading operations cease, the new trade is carried on successively by him. This means, in practice, not more than three years from the cessation of the old trade – the same period as that normally allowed for purchasing new assets.

Agricultural cottages should qualify as eligible assets, provided that they can be said to be used in the farm business. This means that they must be in the representative occupation of a farm worker. Following the case of Anderton *v.* Lamb (1980) 55 TC 1, it is not clear whether a house occupied by a partner, other than the farmhouse, would qualify. However, if such a house were partnership property and restricted as to occupation to someone engaged in agriculture, it might rank as a business asset for roll-over relief.

Land that is in joint ownership often has to be partitioned to enable, say, two brothers to farm separately. A partition is also accepted as qualifying for roll-over relief. Provided that there is equality of exchange, full relief is given for the gain, with restriction on relief where there is a partial gift or where the land includes or becomes a dwelling house (see Inland Revenue Extra-Statutory Concession D26). This concession is now extended to include exchanges of joint interests in milk and potato quota, where these accompany exchanging joint interests in land to which the quota is attached.

The proceeds on small part-disposals can be deducted from the cost rather than be assessed. This can help farmers who have to sell land to repay borrowings. However, for the relief to apply, the value of the land being disposed of cannot now exceed one-fifth of the whole. There is also a monetary limit of £20,000. If the transferor makes any other disposals of land in the same year of assessment, the relief will not apply if the total value of the consideration for all disposals by him exceeds £20,000 (s.242 TCGA 1992).

Where land has been held for a long time and has a relatively low base cost compared with its market value, it may be to the owner's benefit to use the part-disposal, or a 'just and reasonable' formula, to compute the gain (see below).

In general, it is not necessary to apply the strict part-disposal formula where part of an estate is disposed of. Instead, the Inland Revenue will accept that the part disposed of can be treated as a separate asset and any just or reasonable method of apportioning part of the total cost of it will be accepted, for instance, by reference to the value of that part at acquisition. Similar treatment can apply where an election is made for market value as at 6 April 1965 to be treated as cost. The cost identified will then be deducted from the total cost for future part disposals. Consistency should, in general, be followed and, once the taxpayer has opted for this basis, he should adhere to it. This basis means that it is possible to choose whether to elect for 6 April 1965 value on each disposal, unlike the situation where the normal part-disposal formula is used.

Presumably, in the absence of an election under s.120(5) TCGA 1992 for all relevant disposals to be based on the value of the asset at 31 March 1982, this practice will have to be adapted to allow either original cost or the market value at 31 March 1982 to apply on each disposal, whichever is the more favourable.

(3) Tenancies

It was held in Henderson *v.* Karmel's Executors (1984) 58 TC 201 that, even where land is let to a company controlled by the owner of the land, the freehold should still be valued for capital gains tax purposes having regard to the tenancy, ie., without vacant possession. In that case, the existence of the tenancy depressed the value at 6 April 1965.

However, unlike a tenancy in favour of an individual, a tenancy granted to a company can effectively be assigned by the transfer of shares in the company. Hence, both for capital gains tax and inheritance tax purposes, the Inland Revenue may argue that a company tenancy has a value in assessing the value of the company's shares.

The Capital Taxes office have successfully argued in a recent case before the Scottish Lands Tribunal (The Executors of George A Baird *v.* CIR – see *Country Landowner* September 1990) that a share in a tenancy formed by a Scottish partnership had a very substantial value for capital transfer tax purposes on death because it was transferred on death to the wife and son of the deceased.

A similar decision was given by the Lands Tribunal on 31 July 1991 in the case of the Executors of the Honourable Myra Alice Lady Fox (Deceased) where a share in a partnership tenancy was held to have a significant value for capital transfer tax purposes (45% of vacant possession premium), although it had to be valued separately from the reversion and not as a single unit of property with the reversion as the Inland Revenue contended.

It is understood the CLA is sponsoring the English case of John Headley Walton deceased, where the CTO are similarly contending that a share in a tenancy in favour of a partnership has value on death.

The final outcome of these cases will probably affect the capital gains position on tenancies particularly where they are granted to partnerships and succeeding partners can take over a share of the tenancy.

It is understood a meeting has been held between representatives of the Law Societies and the Inland Revenue at which the Inland Revenue agreed they would be prepared to look at differing circumstances and factors in each case, such as whether the landlord was more or less likely to offer to buy out the tenant, and not rely in all cases on a percentage of vacant possession value or premium.

A sum paid to a tenant to give up his tenancy, insofar as it is statutory compensation for disturbance (usually measured by reference to five times the annual rent under s.60 Agricultural Holdings Act 1986, which replaced the

Agricultural Holdings Act 1948 and the Agriculture (Miscellaneous Provisions) Act 1968) is free of capital gains tax, following the case of Davis *v*. Powell (1976) 51 TC 492. It had been accepted by the Inland Revenue, before that case, that payments under the 1968 Act were free of capital gains tax, but the case established that a payment under the 1948 Act was not derived from an asset and was thus free of capital gains tax.

Where there is no notice to quit, or where there is a negotiated payment to induce the tenant to surrender the lease, the Inland Revenue argue that no part of the compensation is free of tax, on the basis that the payment is derived from the lease.

All such payments should be deductible by the landlord as enhancement expenditure in computing capital gains tax liability.

It should be noted that all surrenders of leases are now standard rated for VAT purposes, provided the person does so in the course of business (Note 1 to Group 1 of Sch. 6 VATA 1983). However, the surrender of a leasehold interest in a residential property by the person who actually lives in the property is outside the scope of VAT. Therefore, the surrender consideration attributable to a farmhouse is outside the scope of VAT.

(4) Retirement relief

Retirement relief for farmers follows the normal rules. However, if a farm is run by a partnership, one of the partners owns the farmland, and the partnership pays him rent, para. 10 Sch. 6 TCGA 1992 will operate to restrict the amount of the relief available. The land will be treated as an investment, except to the extent of the owner's own share of the rent paid. If the rent is below a market rent, a larger proportion of the gain may qualify.

Thus, if an individual is entitled to a 50% profit share and the rent paid is one-half of a market rent throughout the period of ownership, the restriction will be $50\% \times \frac{1}{2}$ or 25% of the gain qualifying for relief. As has been mentioned, interest paid by a partnership for this purpose is treated as rent. It is also a matter of argument as to whether a prior profit share would be considered to be rent in these circumstances. Probably it will depend upon the extent to which the prior profit share is in return for the partner's extra efforts or seniority, rather than consideration for the use of the land (see **466** above for a more tax-efficient way to approach this in order not to lose capital tax reliefs.)

The availability of the relief depends, except in the case of a cessation of the business followed by a sale of the assets formerly used in the business, on the disposal not just of a business asset but also of the whole or a part of the business or, in the case of a sale of an asset held outside the business, withdrawal from the business. What constitutes part of a business was considered in McGregor *v*. Adcock (1977) 51 TC 692, where it was held that a farmer merely selling farmland was not entitled to the relief. There was no evidence, in that case, that the nature and extent of the farming after the disposal of the land was any different from what it had been before, as there had been a disposal of only 4.8 acres out of a total holding of 35 acres, with no diminution in the scale of the farming activities following the sale. Similar decisions in favour of the Inland Revenue were given in the two recent cases of Mannion *v.* Johnston and Atkinson *v.* Dancer (1988) STC 758.

It is understood that the Inland Revenue will normally accept that there has been a disposal of part of a business where more than one-half of an area of farmland is disposed of, provided that there is reasonable evidence of a diminution in the scale, or of a change in the nature of the farming carried on on the remainder of the farm.

(5) Time apportionment

Where, say, a cottage has a low original cost but substantial subsequent improvements, the attribution of proportionately more of the gain to the original cost, on the basis of the value of the cottage immediately before the improvements, is likely to be very beneficial as it will increase the time-apportioned part of the gain (para. 16(5) Sch. 2 TCGA 1992). However, rebasing at 31 March 1982 is likely to make this relief largely otiose.

'One estate' election

469   A special relief for the owners of estates managed as one unit at the end of the tax year 1962/63 operates where the estate-owner made the relevant election within the stipulated time limit, but not later than 5 April 1965. A new owner can renew the election, provided that the original election was validly made and successive owners have all made the election. Once made, the election cannot be revoked (s.26 ICTA 1988).

The effect of the election is that, in return for bringing in the annual value of property occupied by the landowner, repairs and maintenance costs of that property can be set off against that annual value and against other rents from tenanted farms on the estate. In the case of property let at less than a full rent, an amount must be added to increase the actual rent to the full annual value. This is not required, however, for an estate office or tied cottages occupied rent-free.

By pooling rents and such notional rents in this way and offsetting all repairs and maintenance expenditure, surplus relief is transferred from one property to the other. If the result of the computation is a loss, that loss can be set against other Sch. A income, except where it arises from tenant's full repairing leases.

The properties in the election can be augmented by additional properties, provided that they are managed as part of the estate, although certain conditions have to be fulfilled where they are not let at a full rent.

To the extent there is no agricultural income against which any such excess expenditure can be set, it can be set against other income of the same and the following year of assessment as if it comprised excess capital allowances (under s.141 CAA 1990).

Quotas

470 Consider the following.

(1) Milk

Under the original EC outgoers' scheme for giving up dairy production (a grant was available under the Dairy Herd (Alternative Enterprise) Scheme), the compensation was held to be taxable as income on normal principles because it was designed to compensate the farmer for loss of income (see White *v*. G & M Davies (1979) 52 TC 597 and CIR *v*. Biggar (W. Andrew) (1982) 56 TC 254).

The 1984 scheme resulted in a reduction of 2½% of the quota for Great Britain and 5% for Northern Ireland. Under that scheme, in consideration of a farmer agreeing to cease production of milk for resale entirely and not to restart again while the quota system or any similar system is in existence, he can choose to receive compensation of either:

(a) 2.6p per annum per litre of milk production given up for each of the five years immediately after the date on which he ceases milk production; or

(b) a lump sum of 13p per litre, with payment being made in five equal annual instalments.

The Inland Revenue have agreed that compensation under (i) above will be taxable as income for the year of receipt, and that compensation under (ii) will be wholly liable to capital gains tax for the year in which notice of acceptance of inclusion in the outgoer's scheme is issued. If the capital gains tax charged, after allowing for all normal reliefs, is more than one-half of the amount received by the due date for payment, payment of the excess can be deferred, without interest, until a further instalment is received, under the normal capital gains tax 'hardship' provisions for payments by instalments. From 30 October 1987, roll-over relief is available where there is a disposal or an acquisition of a milk quota (Inland Revenue Press Release, 29 October 1987 and s.155 TCGA 1992). In a press release dated 11 July 1988 (1988) STI 578, the Inland Revenue confirmed that roll-over relief would be available if either:

(a) the milk quota was disposed of before 30 October 1987, and the replacement asset was acquired on or after that date; or

(b) the milk quota was acquired before 30 October 1987 and another asset was sold on or after that date, but within one year after the acquisition of the milk quota.

As the proceeds from the sale of the cows is a separate matter from the compensation, it was possible for a farmer to elect for the herd basis under s.48(6) FA 1984, make a tax-free profit on the sale of the herd, and then to receive the compensation under one of the options available.

As the compensation arises from a quota allocation operative from 2 April 1984, there is no time-apportionment, or March 1982 value for indexation. Depending upon the individual farmer's situation, it may be beneficial, therefore, to opt for income tax treatment (ie., (i) above) rather than capital gains tax treatment (ie; (ii) above).

It is thought that the quota should qualify for retirement relief as a chargeable business asset if the other conditions for the relief are met, for instance, if the compensation is received as an element in the disposal of part of the farmer's business.

It is understood that retirement relief has been given in a hearing before the General Commissioners where a farmer took a capital sum under the outgoers scheme in 1984. The dairy herd was sold and after a short period of livestock rearing the farming activities were reduced to the selling of keep.

In spite of the decision, it appears that the Inland Revenue are still of the view that retirement relief is only due where the sale of quota is accompanied by the sale of both the dairy herd and the land.

Reductions in milk quotas have resulted in the selling of existing quotas on the sale of the herds with which they are associated. This is usually done by the seller granting to the buyer temporary grazing rights over the land to which the quota attaches. A lump sum is paid for the benefit of the quota. Under a separate agreement, the seller agrees to co-operate with the buyer in securing the identification of the quota with land belonging to the buyer, following the transfer of the cattle to his land. In some cases, the quota is 'leased' to a neighbour. It seems that a sale of the quota is a chargeable occasion for capital gains tax purposes, whilst leasing the quota would generate receipts assessable under Sch. D Case VI or, alternatively, under Sch. D Case III. There are provisions in the regulations for a straightforward transfer of the quota on a change of occupation of the farm. If no part of the sale price of the farm is allocated to the quota, it is arguable that the Inland Revenue cannot apportion a notional value for tax purposes to the quota. It is also possible for a direct sales quota to be exchanged for a wholesale quota, on terms agreed with the Ministry. Roll-over relief would now be due on such an exchange.

There are now provisions in the Agriculture Act 1986 enabling tenants who have built up a milk production unit to receive statutory compensation from the freeholder for giving up their interest in the production unit on quitting the land. It is not clear whether such compensation would be liable to capital gains tax or exempt under the principles set out in **468(2)** above. The Inland Revenue argue it is liable, subject to a claim for roll-over relief or in appropriate circumstances retirement relief.

(2) Potatoes

In the case of potato quotas, it is possible for there to be a transfer of the basic area for 1985 between registered producers. Where the basic quota is permanently transferred, it is considered by the Inland Revenue to be a capital transaction that is liable to capital gains tax in the hands of the vendor, with no relief to the purchaser. The only cost that can be set against the sale proceeds will be the acquisition of any basic quota purchased in the past. It is considered that a March 1982 value is probably minimal. A quota is considered to be an asset separate from the land itself. From 30 October 1987, roll-over relief is available on a disposal or acquisition of a potato quota (Inland Revenue Press Release, 29 October 1987 and s.155 TCGA 1992). See the comments in **470**(1) above, on milk quotas, for disposals and acquisitions available for relief. Retirement relief may be due in appropriate circumstances.

(3) Hops

A basic hop quota no longer has a value whereas, when the right to grow hops was acquired, whether alone or on a purchase of the land, it presumably had one. It has been agreed with the Inland Revenue that it is possible to claim an allowable capital loss on the basis that the quota is now an asset that is of negligible value. The basic quota was not transferable before 1 April 1956, the date on which the Hops Marketing Board was established. Thereafter, it could be transferred at a price and, where a farm is sold with a quota, it will be necessary to apportion the part of the price applicable to the quota. It has been agreed with the Inland Revenue that, where the cost is not known, such as where a quota was not purchased on its own, that the records of the Hops Marketing Board can be used by taking the average price of the basic quota for the year in question to find the cost. The Board has records of the quantities of basic quota belonging to each member and, by using this average, it should be possible to arrive at the cost.

A claim can be made on the basis that the quota was of negligible value in respect of any date after 5 April 1981. The usual two year time-limit applies in respect of a claim.

Commercial woodlands

471 Consider the following.

(1) Abolition of charge under Schedules B and D

The provisions of s.65 and Schs. 6 and 14 FA 1988 abolished the charge to tax under Sch. B in respect of the occupation of commercial woodlands with effect from 6 April 1988, and also the right to elect to be assessed under Sch. D instead (s.54 ICTA 1988), with effect from 15 March 1988, subject to transitional provisions.

(2) Income tax charges under Schedules B and D

Prior to their abolition, the alternatives of charges to tax under Schs. B or D gave considerable scope for tax planning. Provided that the woodlands were managed on a commercial basis with a view to profit, an election for taxation under Sch. D in the planting and growing phases permitted relief for the initial expenses, including interest, and the resulting losses against other income. The irrevocable election for Sch. D had to be made within two years after the end of the chargeable period, and applied to all future periods so long as the woodlands were occupied by the same person. Consequently, it was necessary for there to be a change in that person for the election to cease to have effect. In practice, this was contrived by bringing in a partner or some other party. This enabled the proceeds of sales of cut timber to escape tax under Sch. D, and the tax charge was then only one-third of the annual value of the land, under Sch. B.

Agricultural buildings allowances were also given, under Sch. D, for capital expenditure on roads, new fencing, etc.

(3) Transitional income tax provisions

These will cease to apply in any event on 5 April 1993. It is still possible for a person to elect for Sch. D if he was in occupation on 15 March 1988; or if, prior to that date, he had entered into an agreement, in writing, for his occupation; or if, prior to that date, he had applied for a relevant grant. Under these circumstances, he will continue to obtain relief for interest paid until 5 April 1993.

(4) Capital gains tax

The profits from the sales of timer are exempt from capital gains tax on both the Sch. B and D bases. However, gains from the sale of the land remain liable to capital gains tax, so expenses and income from trees are excluded from any computations. Roll-over relief is available on disposal, as well as gifts relief.

In this connection, there is no territorial limitation on roll-over relief for UK residents (subject to limitations in respect of dual resident companies), and the entire cost, therefore, of foreign woodlands, including that relating to the timber which is not exempt from UK capital gains tax, is qualifying expenditure for this purpose.

Table of Tax Statutes

References are to paragraphs, not pages

	Paragraph		*Paragraph*
Taxes Management Act 1970		S.48(6)	462,470
S.8	166	Finance Act 1986	
S.12	11	S.34	88
S.16	84,86	Finance (No.2) Act 1987	
S.21(2)	107	S.81	119
S.21(3)	107	Income and Corporation Taxes Act	
S.21(4)	107	1988	
S.25	117	S.5(2)	30
S.78	11	S.5(3)	30
S.98	107	S.6(4)(b)	35
Finance Act 1973		S.7(2)	105
S.38	171,175,176,178	S.11	178
Schedule 15		S.13A	50
paragraph 2(b)	174	S.18(1)(a)(ii)	1
Schedule 16		S.18(1)(a)(iii)	1,52,139
paragraph 4	126	S.18(3)	49
Finance Act 1976		S.19	458
S.115	394	S.19(1)	152,197,346
S.116	394	S.19(1)3	332
Value Added Tax Act 1983		S.19(1)4	331
Schedule 1		S.26	469
paragraph 1A	294	S.33	460
Schedule 6		S.42(2)	205
Note 1 to Group 1	468	S.53(1)	459
Inheritance Tax Act 1984		S.53(2)	459
S.30	67	S.54	471
S.154	293	S.59(1)	372
S.157	192	S.60(4)	26
S.267(1)(b)	190	S.61(4)	15
S.267(2)	190	S.62	98
Finance Act 1984		S.63	78,98,340
S.24	166	S.65(2)	330

	Paragraph		*Paragraph*
Income and Corporation Taxes Act		S.155(5)	296,404
1988		S.156	404
S.65(3)	31	S.158	200
S.65(4)	330	S.158(3)	200
S.72(2)	15	S.158(6)	200
S.74(a)	31	S.161(3)	200
S.74(b)	296	S.163	197,404
S.74(f)	438	S.163(2)	197
S.74(j)	317	S.166	198
S.74(p)	423	S.167(5)	197,404
S.80	88	S.188	243
S.83	409, 438	S.188(1)(e)	284
S.95	110	S.190	243
S.96	463	S.192	222
S.103	53, 224	S.192(2)	152
S.103(3)(b)	53	S.192(3)	156
S.104	3,53,224,225,226	S.192(4)	150
S.104(1)	53	S.193	88
S.104(4)	23,24	S.193(1)	72,203
S.104(5)	23	S.194	88
S.109	63,224,226	S.196	331
S.112	5	S.197	279
S.113	381	S.197B	198
S.113(1)	460	S.198	204,211,213,243
S.113(2)	381		281,286,379,404
S.129	109,143	S.198(1)	32
S.132	269	S.199	283
S.132(2)	267	S.200	236
S.132(4)	245,249	S.201A	87
S.132(4)(a)	203	S.203	177
S.141	238	S.231(3A)	50
S.141(6)	275	S.242	118
S.145	191,197,404	S.266	208
S.145(4)	404	S.266(2)	160
S.145(4)(a)(b)	197	S.278	8,206,209
S.145(8)	197	S.313	80
S.146	191,404	S.314	180
S.146(1)(b)	197,404	S.315	287
S.148	243	S.316	282
S.153 et seq	404	S.316(1)	284
S.154	371,404	S.316(2)	284
S.154(2)	404	S.316(4)	286
S.155(2)	404	S.316(5)	284
S.155(3)	197	S.317	291

	Paragraph		Paragraph
S.318	288	S.388	125
S.318(2)(c)	337	S.393A(1)	460
S.318(3)	288	S.393A(3)	460
S.319	204,278	S.397	460
S.331	404	S.397(10)	460
S.332(2)(a)	196,197	S.401	348
S.332(2)(b)	197	S.450	120
S.332(2)(c)	197	S.450(2)	123
S.332(3)	197	S.450(4)	126
S.332(3)(a)	198	S.450(5)	141
S.332(3)(b)	198	S.450(5A)	141
S.332(3)(c)	197,198	S.452	131
S.332	197	S.456(6)	131
S.335	146	S.466	334
S.335(1)	246	S.503	306
S.335(2)	267	S.504	306
S.336	146	S.505	386
S.337	12	S.520	418
S.338	105	S.520(1)(2)	415
S.338(3)(a)	423	S.520(3)	416
S.338(3)(b)	112	S.521	418
S.339(7)	390	S.521(6)(b)	414
S.347B	402	S.523	417,418
S.348	49,104	S.524(1)	411
S.348(2)(a)	423	S.524(2)	411
S.349	49,104,434,435	S.524(3)	413
S.349(1)(b)	423	S.524(4)	413
S.350	435	S.524(7)	419
S.353	112	S.524(8)	419
S.356	199,207,304,404	S.524(9)	419
S.356(3)(b)	304	S.525(1)	412
S.356(5)	304	S.525(2)	412
S.356B	144	S.526(1)	409
S.376(2)	207	S.526(2)	409
S.380	54,71,114,125	S.527	427
	142,460	S.528(2)	409
S.380(1)	125	S.529	411,426
S.380(2)	125	S.530	180
S.381	54,125,381,460	S.531(4)	430
S.381(4)	460	S.531(5)	430
S.383	460,465	S.531(6)	430
S.384	71,460	S.532(2)	414
S.385	71,114,125	S.533(1)	408,420
S.385(4)	125	S.533(2)	410

	Paragraph		Paragraph
Income and Corporation Taxes Act 1988		S.660	394
		S.663	38
S.533(3)	410	S.703	118
S.533(4)	420	S.704 Circ A	118
S.533(7)	180,428	S.704 Circ B	118
S.534	52,60,66	S.714(2)	140
S.534(4)(b)	61	S.727(1)	109
S.534(7)	62	S.731	118
S.535	63	S.736A	106
S.535(4)–(7)	64	S.737	104,106
S.535(8)	63	S.739	42,72,191
S.536	57	S.740	72
S.537A	434	S.743(3)	191
S.537B	434	S.768	459
S.538	66	S.775	41,78,79,80
S.539	75		102,340
S.555	74,339	S.776	392
S.556	74,339	S.786	394
S.557	10,339	S.830	171,175,176,178
S.558	74,339	S.830(5)	169
S.559	439,445	S.832(1)	387
S.560(1)	442	S.833(4)	43
S.560(2)	442	S.833(4)(c)	108
S.561	443	S.835(6)	425
S.561(9)	446,447	Schedule 5	462
S.562	445	paragraph 1(1)	461
S.565	445	Schedule 12	
S.566	443	paragraph 2(2)	8,152
S.566(2)	448	paragraph 3(1)	252
S.577	204,296	paragraph 3(2)	252
S.577(10)	296	paragraph 4	256
S.607	383	paragraph 5	245,249,250,256
S.617	287	paragraph 5(a)	249
S.617(1)	336	paragraph 5(b)	249
S.623(2)	108	Schedule 13	105
S.627	136	Schedule 14	
S.629	241	paragraph 16	160
S.630 et seq	383	Schedule 16	105
S.634(2)	378	Schedule 19	
S.634(3)	96	paragraph 5(3)(b)	325
S.641	136	Schedule 19A	123
S.644(2)	108	Schedule 23A	106
S.655	383	Finance Act 1988	
S.659A(1)	119	S.58	120

	Paragraph		Paragraph
S.65	471	S.21	437
Schedule 5	120	S.22(1)(c)	80
Schedule 6	471	S.25	13
Schedule 14	471	S.50	219
Finance Act 1989		S.115	119
S.91	143	S.120(5)	468
S.178	197	S.143	119
Capital Allowances Act 1990		S.144	119
S.7	302	S.145	119
S.19	302	S.146(1)(b)	119
S.27	198,368	S.148	119
S.31–33	380	S.152(8)	370
S.37–38	300	S.154	370
S.51–59	299	S.155	470
S.61(1)	301	S.162	35,101,340
S.61(2)	301	S.165	13,35,49,101
S.66	300		340,414
S.69	300	S.207	143
S.77	101,414	S.222	229,304,404
S.77(3)–(5)	459	S.222(8)	199,207,304,404
S.123–133	465	S.223	304
S.141	469	S.223(4)	304
S.147	464	S.242	468
S.148(5)	464	S.249	466
S.153	219	S.256	392
S.157	414	S.258	67
S.158	414	S.262	67
Finance Act 1991		S.271	119
S.55	118	S.271(9)	109
S.56	118	S.275(1)	189
S.57	109	Schedule 2	
S.58	106	paragraph 16(5)	468
S.72	54,125,460	Schedule 6	
Taxation of Capital Gains Act 1992		paragraph 10	468
S.10	13	paragraph 12(2)	219
S.10(1)	139	Schedule 7	468
S.10(5)	3		

Table of Statutory Instruments

		Paragraph
SI 1973/334	Income Tax (Employments) Regulations	358,359,466
SI 1974/340	Income Tax (Councillors' Attendance Allowances) Regulations 1974	457
SI 1974/896	Lloyd's Underwriters (Tax) Regulations 1974	120,122,124,129
SI 1974/1330	Lloyd's Underwriters (Tax) (No 2) Regulations 1974	120
SI 1975/91	Income Tax (Reserve and Auxiliary Forces) Regulations 1975	286
SI 1986/1240	Income Tax (Sub-Contractors in the Construction Industry) Regulations 1986	443
SI 1987/530	Income Tax (Entertainers and Sportsmen) Regulations 1987	10,74
SI 1989/1299	Income Tax (Stock Lending) Regulations 1989	109
SI 1991/851	Lloyd's Underwriters (Tax) (1988–89) Regulations 1991	122,132
SI 1992/511	Lloyd's Underwriters (Tax) (1989–90) Regulations 1992	122
SI 1992/569	Income Tax (Dividend Manufacturing) Regulations 1992	106,118
SI 1992/1346	Finance Act, Section 58 (Commencement No 2) Regulations 1992	106

Table of Cases

Case	Ref	Paragraphs
A		
Ahmedabad New Cotton Mills Co Ltd *v*. IT Comr (Bombay)	8 ATC 575	20,23
Alloway *v*. Phillips	1979 STC 452	52
Anderton *v*. Lamb	1981 STC 43	468
Andrews *v*. King	1991 STC 481	466
Anthony Anholt	LON/89/487	92
Aplin *v*. White	1973 STC 322	43
Associated Restaurants Ltd *v*. Warland	1989 STC 273	300
Atkinson *v*. Dancer	1988 STC 758	468
B		
Ball *v*. Johnson	47 TC 155	363
Baxendale *v*. Murphy	9 TC 76	29
Beare *v*. Carter	23 TC 353	47,52
Bennett *v*. Ogston	15 TC 374	326
Bentley *v*. Pike	1981 STC 360	188
Bentleys, Stokes & Lowless *v*. Beeson	33 TC 491	33,296
Bhadra *v*. Ellam	1988 STC 239	212
Billam *v*. Griffith	23 TC 757	46
Birkenhead School Ltd *v*. Dring	11 TC 273	385
Bispham *v*. Eardiston Farming Co (1919) Ltd	40 TC 322	459
Black Nominees *v*. Nicol	1975 STC 372	79
Blake *v*. London Corporation	2 TC 209	
Bloom *v*. Kinder	38 TC 77	361
Bolton *v*. Halpern & Woolf	1981 STC 14	34
Bowden *v*. Russell & Russell	42 TC 301	40ᴬ

Case	Ref	Paragraphs
Boyd Line *v*. Pitts	1986 ICR 244	377
Bray *v*. Best	1989 STC 159	168
Brighton College *v*. Marriott	10 TC 213	386
British Legion Peterhead *v*. CIR	35 TC 509	389
Bucks *v*. Bowers	46 TC 267	108

C

Caillebotte *v*. Quinn	1975 STC 265	90,345,455
Caldicott *v*. Varty	1976 STC 418	203
Calvert *v*. Wainwright	27 TC 475	354
Carnaby, Harrower, Barham & Prykett *v*. Walker	46 TC 561	362
Carson *v*. Cheyney's Executor	38 TC 240	52,57
Carter *v*. Sharon	20 TC 229	187
CIR *v*. Aken	1990 STC 497	1
CIR *v*. Biggar	1982 STC 677	466,470
CIR *v*. British Salmson Aero Engines Ltd	22 TC 29	422
CIR *v*. Corporation of London (as conservators of Epping Forest)	34 TC 293	397
CIR *v*. Falkirk Ice Rink	1975 STC 434	202
CIR *v*. Francis West & Others	31 TC 402	377
CIR *v*. Hang Seng Bank Ltd	1990 STC 733 PC	9
CIR *v*. Longmans Green	17 TC 272	47
CIR *v*. Maxse	12 TC 41	1
CIR *v*. Morrison	17 TC 325	22
CIR *v*. National Book League	37 TC 455	397
CIR *v*. Pemsel	3 TC 53	384
CIR *v*. Peter McIntyre Ltd	12 TC 1006	35
CIR *v*. Scottish & Newcastle Breweries Ltd	1982 STC 296	300
CIR *v*. Vas	1990 STC 137	184
Clark	LON/82/338	294
Clark *v*. Oceanic Contractors Inc	1983 STC 35	175
Coates *v*. Arndale Properties Ltd	1984 STC 637	118
Colquhoun *v*. Brooks	2 TC 490	4
Conn *v*. Robins Bros Ltd	43 TC 266	300
Constantinesco *v*. Rex	11 TC 730	422
Cooke *v*. Beach Station Caravans Ltd	1974 STC 402	300
Cooke *v*. Blacklaws	1985 STC 1	222
Cooper *v*. Blakiston	5 TC 347	196,202
Cooper *v*. Sercombe	1980 STC 76	445

Case	Ref	Paragraphs
Copeman *v*. William Flood & Sons Ltd	24 TC 53	36
Corbett *v*. Duff	23 TC 763	346
Cordy *v*. Gordon	9 TC 304	297
Crossland *v*. Hawkins	39 TC 493	79

D

Davis *v*. Braithwaite	18 TC 198	55,71,82
Davies *v*. Presbyterian Church of Wales	1986 1 AER/705	195
Davis *v*. Harrison	11 TC 707	346
Davis *v*. Powell	1977 STC 32	295,468
Dickenson *v*. Gross	11 TC 614	467
Dollar & Dollar *v*. Lyon	1981 STC 333	466
Donnelly *v*. Williamson	1982 STC 88	181,347,404
Down *v*. Compston	21 TC 60	2
Drummond *v*. Austin Brown	1984 STC 321	295
Duff *v*. Williamson	1973 STC 434	222,304

E

Edwards *v*. Clinch	1981 STC 617	233
Edwards *v*. Warmsley Henshall & Co	44 TC 431	404
Elson *v*. Prices Tailors Ltd	40 TC 671	323
Ereaut *v*. Girls Public Day School Trust Ltd	15 TC 529	385
Evans *v*. Richardson	37 TC 178	280
Evans Medical Supplies Ltd *v*. Moriatry	37 TC 540	429
Exors of George A Baird *v*. CIR	Lands Tribunal 14.6.90	468
Exors of the Honourable Myra Alice Lady Fox deceased	Lands Tribunal 31.7.91	468

F

Fall *v*. Hitchen	1973 STC 66	82
Figael Ltd *v*. Fox	1992 STC 83	307
Finsbury Securities Ltd *v*. Bishop	43 TC 591	118
Fraser *v*. London Sports Car Centre Ltd	1985 STC 688	324
Friedson *v*. Glyn Thomas	8 TC 302	198
Frost *v*. Feltham	1981 STC 115	304
Fry *v*. Burma Corporation Ltd	15 TC 113	12,55
Furniss *v*. Dawson	1984 STC 153	78,341,346

Case	Ref	Paragraphs
G		
G. H. Chambers (Northiam Farms) Ltd *v.* Watmough	36 TC 711	464
Gittos *v.* Barclay	1982 STC 390	306
Glantre Engineering Ltd *v.* Goodhand	1983 STC 1	349
Glasson *v.* Rougier	26 TC 86	46
Graham *v.* Green	9 TC 309	2
Graham *v.* White	48 TC 163	203
Grainger & Son *v.* Gough	3 TC 462	9
Griffiths *v.* Jackson	1983 STC 184	306
Griffiths *v.* Mockler	35 TC 135	281
Griffiths *v.* Pearman	1983 STC 184	306
Gubay *v.* Kington	1984 STC 99	205
H		
Hamerton *v.* Overy	35 TC 73	211
Handley Page Ltd *v.* Butterworth	19 TC 328	436
Heaton *v.* Bell	46 TC 211	404,466
Henderson *v.* Karmel's Executors	1984 STC 572	468
Herbert *v.* McQuade	4 TC 489	195
Higgs *v.* Olivier	33 TC 136	80
Hillyer *v.* Leake	1976 STC 490	198
Hobbs *v.* Hussey	24 TC 153	52
Horton *v.* Young	47 TC 6	180,454
Housden *v.* Marshall	38 TC 233	52
Household *v.* Grimshaw	34 TC 366	52
Howson *v.* Monsell	31 TC 529	52
Hoye *v.* Forsdyke	1981 STC 711	8
Hugh *v.* Rogers	38 TC 270	371
Humbles *v.* Brooks	40 TC 500	33,404
Hume *v.* Asquith	45 TC 251	49
Humphrey *v.* Gold Coast Selection	30 TC 209	348
J		
James Spencer & Co *v.* CIR	32 TC 111	323
Jarrold *v.* Boustead	41 TC 701	102,346,349
Jarvis *v.* Curtis Brown Ltd	14 TC 744	57
Jays The Jewellers *v.* CIR	29 TC 274	322
Jeffrey *v.* Rolls Royce Ltd	40 TC 443	429
John & E Sturge *v.* Hessel	1975 STC 573	429
Jones *v.* Wright	13 TC 221	29
J. P. Harrison (Watford) Ltd *v.* Griffiths	40 TC 281	118

Case	Ref	Paragraphs
	K	
Kirvell *v.* Guy	1979 STC 312	446
Kneen *v.* Martin	19 TC 33	12
	L	
Ladkarn Ltd *v.* McIntosh	1983 STC 113	452
Law Shipping Co Ltd *v.* CIR	12 TC 621	300
Lawrence & Others *v.* CIR	23 TC 333	50
Leonard *v.* Blanchard	1992 STC 20	269
Lewis *v.* CIR	18 TC 174	381
Lewis Emanuel Ltd *v.* White	42 TC 369	119
Lindsay *v.* CIR	34 TC 289	465
Lomax *v.* Newton	34 TC 558	281
Lord Bruce of Donington *v.* Aspden	1981 STC 761	243
Lunt *v.* Wellesley	27 TC 78	95
Lupton *v.* FA & AB Ltd	47 TC 580	118
Lush *v.* Coles	44 TC 169	286
	M	
MacKenzie *v.* Arnold	33 TC 363	52
MacKinlay *v.* Arthur Young McClelland Moores & Co	1989 STC 898	31
Mallalieu *v.* Drummond	1983 STC 665	91,198,230
Mannion *v.* Johnson	1988 STC 758	468
Mason *v.* Innes	44 TC 326	48,67,78
McCash & Hunter *v.* CIR	36 TC 170	34
McGregor *v.* Adcock	1977 STC 206	468
McMenamin *v.* Diggles	1991 STC	233
Midland Sinfonia Concert Society Ltd *v.* Secretary of State for Social Services	1981 ICR 454	82
Mills *v.* CIR	1974 STC 130	79
Mitchell & Edon *v.* Ross	40 TC 11	28,211
Monthly Salaries Loan Co Ltd *v.* Furlong	40 TC 313	328
Moore *v.* Griffiths	48 TC 338	350
Moorhouse *v.* Dooland	36 TC 1	346
Morley *v.* Tattersall	22 TC 51	113,322
Morley-Clarke *v.* Jones	1985 STC 660	395
Munby *v.* Furlong	1977 STC 232	198,232
Murray *v.* Goodhews	1978 STC 207	295,362,383

Case	Ref	Paragraphs

N

National Provident Institution *v.* Brown	8 TC 57	187
Newsom *v.* Robertson	33 TC 452	228
Newstead *v.* Frost	1980 STC 123	72
Nolder *v.* Walters	15 TC 380	273
North *v.* Spencer's Executors	36 TC 668	222
Northend *v.* White & Leonard & Corbin Greener	1975 STC 317	43,111
Nothman *v.* Cooper	1975 STC 91	334

O

Odeon Associated Theatres Ltd *v.* Jones	48 TC 257	300,327
Ogilvie *v.* Kitton	5 TC 338	4
O'Leary *v.* McKinley	1991 STC 42	346
Oppenheimer *v.* Cattermole	1975 STC 91	334
Osborn *v.* Swyer	18 TC 445	222
Owen *v.* Elliott	1990 STC 469	304

P

Parikh *v.* Sleeman	1990 STC 233	212,214
Partridge *v.* Mallandaine	2 TC 179	2
Paterson Engineering Co Ltd *v.* Duff	25 TC 43	434
Pattison *v.* Marine Midland Ltd	1984 STC 10	327
Pearce *v.* Woodall Duckham Ltd	1978 STC 372	20
Pepper *v.* Hart	1990 STC 786	275,404
Perrons *v.* Spackman	1981 STC 739	198
Pook *v.* Owen	45 TC 571	212,213,347,404
Prince *v.* Mapp	46 TC 169	90
Pritchard *v.* Arundale	47 TC 680	102,349
Purchase *v.* Stainer's Executors	33 TC 367	52

R

R *v.* CIR ex parte Fulford-Dobson	1987 STC 344	205
R *v.* CIR & Another ex parte DP Mann Underwriting Agency Ltd	1989 STC 873	142
Reed *v.* Clark	1985 STC 323	55,71
Reed *v.* Nova Securities Ltd	1985 STC 124	118
Reed *v.* Seymour	11 TC 625	346
Richart *v.* J. Lyons & Co	1989 STC 665	466
Ricketts *v.* Colquhoun	10 TC 118	228,404

Case	Ref	Paragraphs
Riley *v.* Coglan	44 TC 481	349
Robins *v.* Durkin	1988 STC 588	8
Robson *v.* Dixon	48 TC 527	148,267
Rogers *v.* CIR	1 TC 225	247

S

Case	Ref	Paragraphs
Sargent *v.* Barnes	1978 STC 322	222
Saywell & Others *v.* Pope	1979 STC 824	467
Scottish Provident Institution *v.* Allen	4 TC 591	186
Seldon *v.* Croom-Johnson	16 TC 740	1,223
Sharkey *v.* Wernher	36 TC 275	48,296
Shearer *v.* Bercain	1980 STC 359	414
Shilton *v.* Wilmshurst	1991 STC 88	346
Shiner *v.* Lindblom	39 TC 367	80
Simpson *v.* John Reynolds & Co (Insurances) Ltd	1975 STC 271	295,361,383
Slaney *v.* Starkey	16 TC 45	196
Smart *v.* Lincolnshire Sugar Co Ltd	20 TC 643	69
Smith *v.* Abbott	1991 STC 661	33
St John's School (Mountford & Knibbs) *v.* Ward	1975 STC 7	300,403
Stephenson *v.* Payne Stone Fraser & Co	44 TC 507	39
Sterling Trust Ltd *v.* CIR	12 TC 686	153
Stokes *v.* Costain Property Investments Ltd	1984 STC 204	299
Sun Insurance Office *v.* Clark	6 TC 59	19
Symons *v.* Weeks	1983 STC 195	19

T

Case	Ref	Paragraphs
Taylor *v.* Dawson	22 TC 189	52
Thomsons (Carron) Ltd *v.* CIR	1976 STC 317	429
Tither *v.* CIR	1990 STC 416 (CJEC)	207
Trustees of the Cardinal Vaughan Memorial School *v.* Ryall	7 TC 611	385
Trustees of Earl Haig *v.* CIR	22 TC 725	52
Turner *v.* Cuxson	2 TC 422	195

U

Case	Ref	Paragraphs
Union Cold Storage Co Ltd *v.* Adamson	16 TC 293	467

Case	Ref	Paragraphs
V		
Vaughan-Neil *v*. CIR	1979 STC 644	102,227,349
Vestey *v*. CIR	1980 STC 10	72
W		
Waddington *v*. O'Callaghan	16 TC 187	467
Walls *v*. Sinnett	1987 STC 236	404
Warner Holidays Ltd *v*. Secretary of State for Social Services	1983 ICR 440	82
Watkis *v*. Ashford Sparkes & Harward	1985 STC 451	31,90
Way & Underdown (No 2)	1975 STC 425	372,375
White *v*. G & M Davies	1979 STC 415	80,466,470
White *v*. Higginbottom	1983 STC 143	198
Wicks & Johnson *v*. Firth	1983 STC 25	363
Wigmore *v*. Thomas Summerson & Sons Ltd	9 TC 577	118
Williams *v*. Todd	1988 STC 676	213
Willingale *v*. International Commercial Bank Ltd	1978 STC 75	327
Wimpy International Ltd *v*. Warland	1989 STC 273	300
Wing *v*. O'Connell	1927 IR 84	351
Withers *v*. Nethersole	28 TC 501	47
Wolf Electric Tools Ltd *v*. Wilson	45 TC 326	429

List of Revenue publications

Title	Reference
Residents and non-residents liability to tax in the United Kingdom	IR 20 (1986)
Income Tax assessments on business profits-changes of accounting date	IR 26 (1982)
Notes issued for MPs	1988 (with updates)
Notes issued for Euro-MPs	1979 (with revisions 1983 and 1989)
Patients and income tax	IR 490
Payers guide – foreign entertainers	FEU 50 (1987)
Return of payments to entertainers etc	IR 46Q
Construction industry tax deduction scheme	IR 14/15 (1982 with 1992 supplement: chart 1990)

Index

References are to paragraphs, not pages

Actors
  capital sums, 80
  change of residence, 12
  double tax relief, 73
  exercising a profession, 71, 82
  overseas work, 72
  reserved schedule D status, 98
Aircrew, 245
  deduction for duties overseas, 249
  duties in UK, 267
  expenses, 273
  free travel, 275
  residence position, 267
  uniforms, 274
'Angel', 95
Architects
  work in progress, 19
Armed forces
  allowances, 280
  awards for gallantry, 291
  gratuities, 284
  life assurance premiums, 292
  pensions, 287, 288
  place of performance of duties, 276
  principal private residence, 290
  reserve forces, 286
  residence position, 277
  subscriptions to mess, 282
  travel facilities, 279
  uniform allowances, 283
Arts Council Awards, 69(2)
Athletes
  double tax agreement with USA, 10, 339
Authors
  awards, 69
  categories of for tax purposes, 52
  change of residence, 55
  copyright, 44
  death, 64
  discontinuance of profession, 64
  income spreading provisions, 58
  losses, 54
  post cessation receipts, 53
  public lending right, 65
  royalties paid abroad, 57

Back pay, 25
Barristers
  apparel, 230
  books, 232
  cash basis, 223
  change of basis, 226
  clerks, 233
  expenses, 228–32
  fees earned basis, 225
  inducement payment, 227
  part-time recordership, 228
  post cessation receipts, 224
  Queen's Counsel, 223, 231

Capital allowances, 81, 198, 300, 380, 403, 415, 464
Capital Gains Tax
  armed forces, 290
  clergymen, 199
  diplomats, 205, 207
  doctors, 219
  farmers, 468
  insurance agents, 370
  school staff, 404
  underwriters, 128

visitors to UK, 186
works of art, manuscripts, etc., 67
Check traders, 318
    changes in basis of computations, 320
    computation of profits, 319
Clergymen
    books, 198
    Easter offerings, 196
    exempt items of income, 197
    expenses incurred by church, 197
    expenses incurred by clergymen, 198
    higher paid, 197
    rent, 198
    residence owned by, 199
    taxable items of income, 196
Commercial woodlands, 471
Company
    carrying on profession, 35
    for overseas work, 40
    pension schemes, 38
    service companies, 39
    trust holding shares in, 37
Conventional basis
    barristers, 17
    bills rendered basis, 21
    cash basis, 21
    change to, 22
    meaning of, 21
    post-cessation receipts, 23
Copyright, 45
    authors, 48
    non-residents, held by, 57
    royalties, 47, 50
    spreading of royalties, 63
Credit traders, 310
    hire purchase business, 316
    provisions, 312, 317
    valuation of debts, 315
Cricketers
    benefit match, 346
    collections from spectators, 346

Diplomats
    allowances, 204
    Diplomatic Privileges Act, 205
    entertainment expenses, 204
    European Community, 209
    life assurance premiums, 208
    living accommodation abroad, 204

mortgage interest, 207
    other income, 205
    personal allowances, 206
    place of performance of duties, 203
    principal private residences, 207
    residence position, 203, 205
Doctors and dentists
    accounts, 216
    capital gains, 219
    conference expenses, 214
    consultants, 211
    executors, receipts paid to, 222
    expenses of consultants, 212
    expenses of general practitioners,
        213, 218, 219
    general practice, 215
    loans to, 215
    red book, 215
    rent and rates reimbursement, 216
    research grant, 222
    roll-over relief, 219
    superannuation deductions, 220
    travelling expenses, 213, 222
Double tax treaties
    aircrew, 268
    diplomats, 205
    foreign pensions, 335
    patents, lump sums, 413
    patents, royalties, 424
    sportsmen, 339
    USA/UK, 10, 73, 154, 339
    visitors, 154, 155

Employments
    basis of assessment, 28
    casual, 82
    directors' fees assessed, schedule D,
        28
    expenses, 31
    with Crown, abroad, 203
Entertainers
    club musicians, 82
    double tax agreement with USA, 73
    employment or profession, 82, 98
    expenses, 87–93, 98
    foreign entertainers, 74
    investigation by Inland Revenue, 84
    overseas partnerships, 72
    pension schemes, 96

reserved schedule D status, 98
returns of payments to, 84, 86
slave contracts, 72, 78
tax avoidance schemes, 79
European MPs, 243
allowances, 243
duties performed abroad, 243
expenses, 243
terminal grants, 243
Evangelists, 202
Expenses
car expenses, 237
clergymen, 197–198
clothing, 91
conferences, 214, 404
consultants, 212
debt collection, 313
diplomats, 204
doctors, 213
entertainers, 87–93
entertainment, 198, 204, 404
European MPs, 243
general principles, 31
household, 93, 212, 215, 229, 367
Members of Parliament, 236
moneylenders, 328
patents, 409
publicans, 296
removal expenses, 198
sportsmen, 345
stockbrokers, 116
subcontractors, 454
subsistence, 88, 236, 455
travelling, 87, 89, 164, 181, 198, 213,
222, 228, 273, 345
uniforms, 274, 283
unpaid offices, 456

Farmers
agricultural buildings allowances, 465
averaging, 463
capital allowances, 464
capital gains tax, 468
casual labour, 466
grants, 466
herd basis, 462
joint ventures, 467
losses, 460
one trade, 459

quotas, 470
stocks, 461
Film technicians, 83
Financial futures, 119
Footballers
amateur status, receipt for loss of,
346, 349
benefit matches, 347
payments for winning, 350
pension schemes, 352
signing-on fees, 349
transfer fees, 346

Gratuities
auditors in receipt of, 362
awards for long service, 364
gifts, 361
PAYE on tips, 356
prizes, 363
tips, 354

Holiday lettings, 306
Hoteliers, 297, 302
House of Lords, 244

Insurance Agents
capital allowances, 368
commission, 371
employees, 366
goodwill, 370
household expenses, 367
self-employed agents, 369
Interest paid
armed forces, 290
clergymen, 199
diplomats, 207
Members of Parliament, 236
school staff, 404
Interest received, 43, 111
moneylenders, 326
Inventors
see Patents
Itinerant Workers
expenses, 181

Judges, 234

Local councillors, 457
Loss

authors, 54
Case VI, 16
farmers, 460
underwriters, 125, 133

Market gardeners
see Farmers
Market makers
borrowing and lending securities, 109
bull and bear excess, 104
expenses, 116
incorporation, 101
interest, 111
manufactured dividends and interest,
106
profits on sales of securities, 108
returns, 107
solvency rules, 100
Members of Parliament
additional cost of living away from
home, 236
car expenses, 237
Euro-MPs, 243
mortgage interest, 236
office expenses, 239
pensions, 241
secretarial allowances, 239
terminal grants, 241
travel expenses (other than by car),
238
Merchant Navy personnel, 246
administration, 259
deductions – 12½%, 251
deductions – 100%, 252
duties performed in UK, 246
non-residents, 246
qualifying day outside UK, 256
UK residents, 249
Moneylenders, 325
expenses, 328
interest received, 326
Musicians
double tax agreement with USA, 10
groups, 94

North Sea employments, 175
Norwegian sector of North Sea, 183

Office

councillors, 456
expenses of unpaid, 456
Member of House of Lords, 244, 456
what constitutes for tax purposes, 458

Painters, 66
Partnership
accounts, 214, 216
capital allowances, 381
overseas, 4, 72
Patents
capital allowances, 415
capital sums, 410
deduction of tax, 424
double tax agreements, 415, 424
earned income, 411, 426
expenses, 409
foreign patents, 425
know-how, 428
law of patents, 406
non-residents, 413
royalties, 420
spreading of royalties, 427
transfer to company, 414
Pawnbrokers, 321
Pensions
armed forces, 287, 288
Crown agents paid by, 331
double tax agreements, 335
foreign pensions, 330
invalidity benefit, 336
Nazi victims, 334
Pilots
pension arrangements, 383
Profession
barrister, 1, 223
basis of assessment, 15
carried on wholly abroad, 4, 5
change of accounting date, 26
companies, 35
deduction for overseas work, 6, 7, 8
definition, 1
effect of change of residence, 12, 55
entertainers, 82
expenses, 31
non-residents carrying on in the UK,
10
payment of tax, 30
Public lending right, 65

Publicans of tied houses
  basis of assessment, 294
  dilapidations, 303
  expenses, 296
  fixtures and fittings, 299, 300
  own consumption, 296
  principal private residences, 304
  termination payments, 295
  utensils, 299

Religious orders, 201
Residence
  change of, 12, 13, 55, 56

Schools
  benefits, 404
  capital allowances, 403
  charitable status, 385
  conferences, 404
  covenants, 394–97
  entertaining, 404
  exempt income, 386
  investment income, 393
  living accommodation for staff, 404
  principal private residences, 404
  scholarships, 404
  trading income, 387
Sculptors, 66
Seamen, 245
  PAYE, 261
Sportsmen and women
  amateurs, 348
  basis of liability, 338
  change of residence, 338
  deductions for activities abroad, 342
  double tax agreements, 339
  incorporation, 341
  residence position, 338
  travel expenses, 345
  visiting, 339
  withholding taxes, 344
Stock relief
  pawnbrokers, 324
Stockbrokers
  attachés, 114
  clerks, 114
  expenses, 116
  incorporation, 101
  interest, 111

manufactured dividends and interest, 106
  period of accounts, 103
  profits on sales of securities, 108
  returns, 107
  solvency rules, 100
  unclaimed dividends, 113
Subcontractors
  contractor, definition of, 442
  deduction of tax, 450
  exemption certificates, 443
  expenses, 454
  returns by contractors, 449
  subsistence, 455

Teachers, 404
Trade marks and designs, 433
Traded options, 119
Trawlermen
  capital allowances, 380
  decommissioning grants, 382
  partnership arrangements, 381
Trinity House payments, 383

Underwriters
  account, 122
  capital gains, 128
  closing year, 124
  death, 129, 131
  earned income, 123
  expenses, 137
  inheritance tax, 130
  interest paid, 127
  losses, 125, 134
  payment of tax, 132
  procedure, 120
  reinsurance to close, 141
  retirement annuity and personal
    pension premiums, 136
  run-off syndicates, 133
  special reserve fund, 131
  stocklending, 143
  stop loss policies, 126
  termination of membership, 131
Unlisted Securities Market, 119

Visitors to the UK
  accommodation in UK, 146
  benefits, 165

categories of visitors, 155
Continental Shelf, 169
corresponding payments, 156
domicile, 149
double tax agreement, 154, 155, 172
entertainers, 74
foreign emoluments, 150, 155
incidental duties, 148
North Sea employments, 169
overseas income and capital gains,
  186

professors, 184
residence, 146, 147
returns, 162, 174
separate employments, 153
sportsmen, 339
teachers, 184
travelling expenses, 164
Vocation, 2

Work in Progress
  valuation, 18

Business Briefings

Specialist accounting and auditing advice

A new looseleaf service, which will ensure that you understand your clients' industries, gives you the confidence to talk to prospective clients with a real understanding of their needs and keeps you up-to-date.

The main work consists of 20 briefings and a binder, covering Solicitors Accounts to Chartered Surveyors, Doctors Accounts to Insurance Brokers.

The briefings include:

- detailed industry background, including statutory and professional regulations
- accounting procedures - problems and requirements
- all the industry audit procedures - from statutory requirements to a review of special reports
- specimen working programmes; disclosure, completion and review checklists; audit reports.

The mainwork costs £120. Your annual subscription in 1993 of £80 will cover the updating of at least 10 briefings plus any new briefings which may be published.

Main Work c680pp £120

Annual Subscription for 1993 £80

To order

Please contact Customer Services, Accountancy Books, PO Box 620, Central Milton Keynes, MK9 2JX **or** phone 0908-668833.

Tax Digests

To keep you fully informed on all tax matters.

Tax Digests tackle the latest legislation and its implications, technical developments and topical concerns. They will save you valuable research time and improve your understanding of the latest issues. Prepared by acknowledged experts, each digest covers one subject in depth.

An annual subscription of £165 saves £99 on the single issue price. It also gives you a free binder. As a subscriber you can also buy back issues at 36% discount.

A Subscription to Tax Digests gives you:

- clear and practical information
- worked examples
- checklists
- tax planning tables
- 12 Digests every year
- a twice yearly index

Subscription to Tax Digest series £165.00

To order

Please contact Customer Services, Accountancy Books, PO Box 620, Central Milton Keynes, MK9 2JX **or** phone 0908 668833.